INTRODUCTION TO GLOBAL STUDIES

INTRODUCTION TO
GLOBAL STUDIES

John McCormick

First published 2018 by
RED GLOBE PRESS

Red Globe Press in the UK is an imprint of Springer Nature Limited, registered in England, company number 785998, of 4 Crinan Street, London, N1 9XW.

Red Globe Press® is a registered trademark in the United States, the United Kingdom, Europe and other countries.

ISBN 978–1–352–00399–4 paperback

This book is printed on paper suitable for recycling and made from fully managed and sustained forest sources. Logging, pulping and manufacturing processes are expected to conform to the environmental regulations of the country of origin.

A catalogue record for this book is available from the British Library.

A catalog record for this book is available from the Library of Congress.

BRIEF CONTENTS

LONG CONTENTS

ILLUSTRATIONS AND FEATURES

TABLES

MAPS

ABOUT THE AUTHOR

John McCormick is Professor of Political Science at the Indianapolis campus of Indiana University in the United States. His academic interests focus on global studies, comparative politics, the state of the environment, and the work of the European Union. He is the author of more than a dozen books, including *Comparative Government and Politics*, *Environmental Politics and Policy*, and *Understanding the European Union* (all from Palgrave). He has taught courses at several universities in North America and Europe, has visited more than 40 countries in Africa, Asia, the Americas, and Europe, and has lived for extended periods in five of them: the United States, Britain, Kenya, South Africa, and Zimbabwe.

TOUR OF THE BOOK

CHAPTER PREVIEWS AND HIGHLIGHTS

Each chapter begins with a brief preview, a set of six key highlights, and a list of the contents.

COMPARING NORTH AND SOUTH

Each chapter contains a box that takes a focused topic and compares experiences and attitudes in countries of the North and the South.

GLOBAL AND LOCAL

Each chapter also contains a box that compares global and local approaches to a focused problem or topic, showing the links and contrasts between the two levels.

TABLES AND FIGURES

The text is dotted with tables and figures that present key numbers or express complex ideas in visual form. Most are based on the latest data available from the websites of key national and international organizations.

Figure 2.1: Global population growth
Source: UN Population Division (2017).
Note: Shaded area shows projected figures.

MAPS

Maps of the world, or of particular states and regions, have been placed strategically throughout the book to offer a global view of topics within each chapter, comparing countries on a variety of topics. The Asia projection has been chosen because of its relatively clear and balanced representation.

More than half the world's population lives in these countries

Map 2.1: The population dominance of Asia

DISCUSSION QUESTIONS

Each chapter ends with a set of six open-ended and occasionally provocative questions designed to help students think critically about some of the issues raised in the chapter, and to suggest topics for further research.

DISCUSSION QUESTIONS

1. Should we be worried about the global rate of population growth?
2. Is the demographic transition model a useful way of thinking about population trends in the South?
3. What can we do to reduce food waste?
4. What are the likely political, economic and social effects of urbanization?
5. What would it take to move us off our global dependence on fossil fuels?
6. Does the North have an obligation – whether strategic, economic, environmental, or moral – to help tropical countries better protect and manage their forests?

KEY CONCEPTS

Each chapter ends with a list of the key terms introduced in the chapter, all of which are highlighted in boldface and accompanied by marginal definitions. They are all reproduced (with page references) in the **Glossary** to the book.

KEY CONCEPTS

- Common pool resources
- Demographic transition
- Demography
- Food security
- Fossil fuels
- Global city
- Green revolution
- Malnutrition
- Megacity
- Natural resources
- Renewable energy
- Tragedy of the commons
- Zero population growth

USEFUL WEBSITES

Most chapters end with a short selection of websites, most of them for institutions that are discussed within the chapter.

USEFUL WEBSITES

Food and Agriculture Organization of the UN at http://www.fao.org
International Energy Agency at https://www.iea.org
UN Convention on the Law of the Sea at http://www.un.org/depts/los
United Nations Population Fund at https://www.unfpa.org

FURTHER READING

Each chapter ends with a short list of books chosen to provide detailed and current information and to act as resources for research assignments. The emphasis is on survey texts that provide a good introduction to the topic.

FURTHER READING

Balliett, James Fargo (2010) *Forests and Oceans* (Routledge). Two brief survey books by the same author in a five-part series on separate environments, each providing scientific background, offering cases from around the world, and discussing human impact.
Gardner, Brian (2013) *Global Food Futures: Feeding the World in 2050* (Bloomsbury). An assessment of current food production patterns, speculating on how matters will evolve over the next few decades.
Glaeser, Edward (2012) *Triumph of the City: How Urban Spaces Make us Human* (Pan). A compelling and readable analysis of the past and the possible future of cities.
Harper, Sarah (2016) *How Population Change will Transform Our World* (Oxford University Press). An assessment of the likely changes in global population, taking into account fertility, mortality and migration.

SUMMARY OF THE BOOK

1 HISTORY

This chapter provides the historical context within which to understand the origins and the evolution of the global system. It begins with a review of the emergence of the modern world, looking particularly at its European roots in discovery, colonization, industrialization and imperialism. It then looks at the causes and effects of the two world wars, the end of Europe's empires, and the Cold War. It reviews the economic, political and social changes that have come since the end of the Cold War, and their effects on the global system. The chapter ends with a discussion about the meaning and effects of globalization.

2 POPULATION AND RESOURCES

This chapter looks at the links between population and natural resources, as well as some of the key demographic trends shaping (and being shaped by) the global system. It begins with an assessment of key population changes before focusing on the causes and effects of urbanization. It then looks at the challenges of feeding a growing population, noting that the problem is more one of quality than of quantity. The chapter finishes up with a review of how natural resources are used (and misused), focusing on the cases of energy, forests and oceans.

3 IDENTITY AND CULTURE

The keyword for this chapter is *identity*, meaning the qualities that determine who we are and what makes us distinctive. The chapter begins with a discussion of the meaning of identity generally, and of the particular place of national identity in global studies. It then looks in turn at culture, race, ethnicity, and religion, beginning with a discussion of the difficulties in defining most of these terms before moving on to a discussion of the different contexts within which they are used. In each case, it reviews the impact of these concepts on global consciousness and global issues.

4 SCIENCE AND TECHNOLOGY

The focus of this chapter is on the intersection between science and technology. It begins with a discussion of the way in which both have impacted our understanding of the global system, before looking at the state of global health, backed up by a case study of the globalization of infectious diseases such as influenza, HIV/AIDS, and malaria. The chapter then turns to technology, with a review of the digital revolution, and a discussion of the global implications of changes in information and communication systems, ending with an assessment of the role of technology in helping foster international travel and tourism.

5 STATES AND GOVERNMENT

We cannot fully understand the global system without appreciating the qualities and the changing nature of states. The chapter begins with a survey of the meaning and features of the state (including authority, legitimacy, and sovereignty), looks at the meaning of citizenship, compares and contrasts states and nations, and then looks at the evolution of states (emphasizing their proliferation since 1945). It then discusses the nature and role of government, compares democratic and authoritarian states, and reviews the current condition of the state system, contrasting arguments that it is declining, strengthening, or simply changing form.

6 LAW AND INTERNATIONAL ORGANIZATIONS

The chapter looks first at the nature of international law, and at how international treaties are developed and implemented. It then looks at the work of international organizations, reviewing the structure and goals of intergovernmental organizations such as the United Nations (UN), and then at the work of non-state actors such as international non-governmental organizations (NGOs), multinational corporations, religious organizations, and those working outside the law. The chapter ends with a study of regional integration and its particular role in the global system.

7 HUMAN RIGHTS

The focus of this chapter is human rights. It begins with an outline of the Universal Declaration of Human Rights, and examples of rights violations. It then discusses the evolution and expansion of human rights, tracing the story from the issue of slavery to emerging views about LGBT and intergenerational rights. The chapter goes on to outline the dimensions of the global human rights regime, based mainly on a series of focused treaties, UN bodies, international courts, and international NGOs. The chapter ends by discussing the difficulties of measuring and comparing human rights records, using the case of women's rights and the insights it provides.

8 ECONOMY

This chapter offers a survey of the global economy. It begins with a review of the way in which economies are measured, compared, and understood. It then looks at the changing global economic landscape, assessing the changing balance of the North and the South, the debate over development, the European Union, the emergence of the BRICs (Brazil, Russia, India and China), and the effects of the 2008 global financial crisis. The chapter goes on to discuss the global financial regime before contrasting the effects of wealth and poverty, and reviewing some of the ways in which global poverty and inequality are being addressed or overlooked.

9 TRADE

This chapter builds on Chapter 8 by looking at the specific subject of trade. It begins with a review of the global trading picture, and of the recent and rapid rise in trade volume. It then looks at the changes that have come to the global trading system since 1945, before reviewing the qualities of the global trading regime, including the role of the World Trade Organization, the implications of changes in technology, and the rise of multinational corporations and global cities. The chapter ends with a discussion about free trade, comparing different levels of trade cooperation and the pros and cons of free trade.

10 MIGRATION

This chapter looks at one of the most controversial issues in global matters. It begins with a review of the dimensions of migration and how they have changed over the last century, then looks at migration patterns, at the major sources and destinations of migration, and at recent trends such as increased mobility and the contrasting effects of more migration and greater efforts to control the movement of people. It assesses the global migration regime, and ends with a discussion about the effects of migration, the pros and cons of migration, and a comparison of approaches and attitudes in Europe and the United States.

11 ENVIRONMENT

This chapter looks at the environment as a global issue, beginning with an overview of environmental problems, of our changing understanding about their causes and effects, and of the meaning of ideas such as sustainable development. It goes on to look at the global environmental regime, and at the focus and effects of key pieces of international environmental law. The chapter finishes with two cases: the threats faced by biodiversity, followed by the ultimate global threat of climate change. It reviews the causes and effects of both problems, and discusses the political, economic and social arguments that have shaped the response.

12 WAR AND PEACE

This chapter looks at the meaning of war and peace. It begins with a discussion of the different kinds and causes of war, noting the increased rarity of interstate wars. It then discusses the qualities of peace, noting the differences between the absence of war (negative peace) and efforts made to sustain a positive peace. It then looks at the structure and the personality of the global security regime, focusing on the kind of peacekeeping operations in which the United Nations participates. The chapter ends with a discussion of terrorism: its meaning and causes, and responses to the threats it poses.

ONLINE RESOURCES

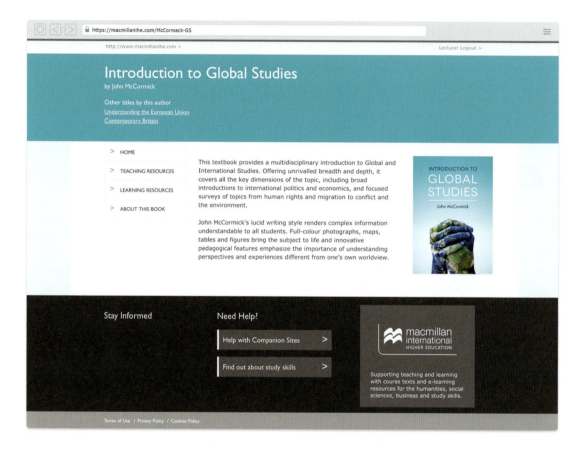

www.macmillanihe.com/McCormick-GS is a freely accessible website containing comprehensive resources for both students and lecturers.

For students

▸ A media library of videos, primary sources and relevant news articles, which have been carefully selected to illustrate the themes in each chapter.

▸ Interactive flashcards of key terms in global studies.

For lecturers

Lecturers who adopt the book gain access to a password-protected selection of resources to help plan and deliver their courses.

▸ Lecturer slides: PowerPoint® presentations to accompany every chapter, richly illustrated with photographs, figures and tables from the textbook.

▸ Testbank of multiple choice and true/false questions for every chapter.

LIST OF ABBREVIATIONS

BRIC	Brazil, Russia, India and China (or BRICS if South Africa is added)
EU	European Union
FAO	Food and Agricultural Organization of the United Nations
FTA	free trade agreement
G7	Group of 7
G20	Group of 20
G77	Group of 77
GATT	General Agreement on Tariffs and Trade
GDP	gross domestic product
GHG	greenhouse gases
ICC	International Criminal Court
IGO	intergovernmental organization
IMF	International Monetary Fund
INGO	international non-governmental organization
IO	international organization
IPPC	Intergovernmental Panel on Climate Change
IR	international relations
LGBT	lesbian, gay, bisexual, and transgender
MNC	multinational corporation
NATO	North Atlantic Treaty Organization
NGO	non-governmental organization
OECD	Organization for Economic Cooperation and Development
UDHR	Universal Declaration of Human Rights
UN	United Nations
UNEP	United Nations Environment Programme
UNESCO	United Nations Educational, Scientific and Cultural Organisation
USSR	Union of Soviet Socialist Republics
WHO	World Health Organization
WTO	World Trade Organization

ACKNOWLEDGEMENTS

Every book of this kind is a team effort, combining the creativity and hard work of many people, some of whom I have met in person, others of whom I know only through email exchanges, and yet others of whom (the reviewers) were anonymous. I thank them all of their contributions and for making the writing and production of this book such a pleasure.

The story begins with Stephen Wenham, who is no longer at Palgrave but with whom I had the first conversations about writing this book. Stephen was consistently efficient and helpful, and the broad structure of the finished book – as well as a number of its more detailed features – owe much to his initial ideas.

When it came to shaping the proposal and working through the finished manuscript, Lloyd Langman and Lauren Zimmerman took charge, and both helped me develop the ideas in the book, read every chapter carefully and thoroughly, and provided a wealth of detailed and helpful feedback that has greatly improved the finished result. Working with Palgrave is always a pleasure, and I much appreciate the support, encouragement, and rapid responses that Lloyd and Lauren provided.

I would also like to thank the eight anonymous reviewers of the original book proposal and the six anonymous reviewers of the initial draft manuscript. Among them, they came from Australia, Canada, Egypt, Singapore, South Africa, the United States, and several European countries, and offered helpful reflections and ideas from a variety of institutions and environments. My thanks also to Ann Edmondson for her excellent copy-editing, and to Aine Flaherty and the production staff at Palgrave for their patient efforts to convert Word files into the finished book.

Last but not least, my love and appreciation to Leanne, Ian and Stuart for their support and for providing happy distractions.

The author and publishers are grateful for permission to reproduce the following copyright materials:

The Fund for Peace for Map 12.1: Fragile States Index.

The World Economic Forum for Map 7.1: The Global Gender Gap Index.

Yale Centre for Environmental Law and Policy for Map 11.1: Environmental Performance Index.

INTRODUCTION

Isolation, it is often said, is the hallmark of the life of a writer. This is certainly true in my case, because – except when I am travelling – I spend much of my working life sitting before a computer, either at home or in my campus office. Except for my fellow scholars and the students in my classes, I see few people during regular working hours. And yet while I may not see them in person, I am actually connected in ways that are far deeper, wider, and more complex than even a few years ago, or that past generations could have imagined.

▶ I can call up vast amounts of information through the internet, and my social media feeds send me a stream of news stories from around the world.

▶ I send and receive emails and text messages, or make (free) calls on Skype or WhatsApp, some connecting me to people just down the road, others to people on the other side of the world.

▶ I can stream many more movies, TV shows, and music than a human could hope to watch or listen to in a lifetime.

▶ I am surrounded by products made all over the world: a smartphone assembled in China, a German car assembled in South Africa, an American computer made in Mexico, and clothes that bear American brand names but were made in Malaysia or Sri Lanka.

▶ I can refresh myself periodically with coffee from Colombia or tea from Kenya, and dinner this evening might include pasta from Italy, rice from India, fish from Indonesia, vegetables from Canada, or fruit from Brazil. Or, if the family decides to eat out, we can choose among restaurants nearby serving anything from Chinese to Ethiopian, Greek, Indian, Mexican, Moroccan, or Vietnamese cuisine.

This is all immediate and real evidence of the globalized world in which we live. True, not everyone has access to this variety of options; millions still live in abject poverty, in societies shattered by war, under governments that deny their basic rights, and in urban slums or isolated villages that lack even a reliable supply of clean water. Many are also denied access to modern technology; barely one in five own a road vehicle, and only half of the people in the world have access to the internet at home. In spite of such limitations and inequalities, however, we are all still connected, directly or indirectly, through the political, economic, social, technological and environmental links that have made the world a smaller place. It is these connections that are at the heart of global studies. As we look into its different facets in the chapters that follow, we will be asking many questions. How did these connections evolve? How are they shaped and influenced? Are they good, or bad, or a mix of both? Do they unite us or divide us? How have they changed our lives? How should we prepare for the future? And what exactly *is* globalization and the global system?

In this book, we will be exploring what such connections mean for our identities, our jobs, our societies, our governments, and our markets. We will look at how populations are changing, how we feed ourselves, how technology is changing, how medical science is evolving, how we govern ourselves, why people migrate, how trade works, how our rights are defined and limited, what is happening to our environment, why we go to war, what is needed to keep us at peace, and whether or not the changes that have come to the global system have made us safer, happier, and healthier.

Before we do that, though, we need to be clear on the meaning of a few key concepts.

WHAT IS GLOBAL STUDIES?

The Chinese philosopher Confucius is reputed to have once said that the beginning of wisdom is to call things by their right name. Whether or not he did, it is certainly hard to understand the world around us unless we agree on the meanings of the terms we use to describe it. Natural scientists have made more progress on this than most, because the terms they use mainly have consistent definitions. In the social sciences and the humanities, though, there is a lot more fluidity, with terms and ideas often open to interpretation, and definitions often contested according to the different perspectives of those doing the defining – we will see plenty of examples of this in the chapters that follow. The problem brings to mind the claim made by Humpty Dumpty in *Through the Looking Glass*: 'When I use a word … it means just what I choose it to mean – neither more nor less'.

As a subject, global studies suffers its share of uncertainty, fluidity, and imprecision. Its intellectual roots may be long and deep, but as a distinct field of study it dates back only to the turn of the new millennium, which means that our understanding of its content and outlines is still evolving. To complicate matters, it is made up of many different subjects and ideas, our understanding of which changes with time and with the viewpoints of those who assess them. And to complicate matters even further, global studies is easily confused with four other concepts, each of which we need to tie down.

First, there is **international studies**, focused on the interactions between two or more countries and on what these countries share or have in common. (To be pedantic, it should really be *interstate studies*, since the term *international* is usually used in the context of states, not nations. There will be more on this problem in Chapter 5.) Although international studies looks beyond state borders, it remains founded on states, the prefix *inter-* originating from the Latin word for 'between' or 'among'. If we study something happening within a single state, then our interest is national or domestic, but as soon as we start looking at states in relation to one another, we move into the realms of the international. Our interest might be in how states interact with one another, or we might be interested in making comparisons among them. Either way, the *international* part of this stops short of the holistic approach that characterizes global studies.

For its part, the word *studies* implies that our interests are broad, and might range from the historical to the political, economic, legal, social, cultural, religious, scientific, technological, linguistic, and environmental. Jan Nederveen Pieterse (2013) jokingly notes the suggestion that we should avoid investigating subjects whose title includes the word *studies*, because it suggests a lack of the kind of structure and depth we find in a formal discipline, such as history, political science, or economics. He also points out that the use of the word – as in *global studies, gender studies, media studies*, and so on – has been a relatively recent development, but this should not imply that any of these fields of research is any less interesting or important than the disciplines that preceded them. He rightly warns that newness can mean greater unevenness and a looser understanding of the focus of a field, but he fails to point out that newness also implies possibilities: global studies has made great strides in its short life, and is wide open in terms of its potential.

The second concept to tie down is **international relations**. As usually applied and understood, it is more limited than international studies because it focuses on the political and economic interactions between states. In some countries, international relations (or IR, as it is known) is considered a sub-field of political science, where it is both related to (but contrasted with) the sub-field of comparative politics. In other countries, it is a free-standing discipline. Either way, it is interested in topics such as diplomacy, war, peace, security, international organization, and foreign policy. In contrast to the broader idea of *studies*, the narrower idea of *relations* implies a specific interest in how states relate to one another. Some, though (such as Barnett and Sikkink, 2011), see evidence that IR has moved in recent decades towards a new interest in the global as opposed to merely the international.

Figure 0.1: Key concepts in global studies

TERM	MEANING
INTERNATIONAL STUDIES	The study of interactions, comparisons and commonalities involving two or more states.
INTERNATIONAL RELATIONS	The study of (mainly) political and economic interactions between or among states, with a focus on diplomacy and policy.
GLOBALIZATION	The process by which the political, economic, social, and cultural links between people, corporations, and governments in different states become integrated through cooperation, trade, travel, communications, media, investment, market forces, and technology.
GLOBALISM	A philosophy, ideology or policy based on taking a global view of politics, economics, society, security and the environment.

The third concept is **globalization**, which is distinct from international studies or relations in the sense that it describes a process: one in which the links between people, institutions, and governments in different parts of the world have evolved and deepened. This has resulted – as Robertson (1992) puts it – in 'both the compression of the world and the intensification of the consciousness of the world as a whole'. Globalization is both a cause and an effect, and – as with all terms that have the suffix –*ization* (such as *democratization*, *Europeanization*, and *polarization*) – it describes a phenomenon that is always moving and evolving, and is neither static nor final. It is important to note that while globalization is usually associated with political and economic change, it actually applies to almost every facet of human endeavour, including culture, religion, science, and health. It is even more important to note that while the term comes up frequently in the chapters that follow, this is not a book about globalization.

The fourth and final concept is **globalism**, which is an ideology, a set of beliefs, or an attitude that favours a global view on politics, economics and society, and supports the kinds of trends we find in globalization. In contrast to nationalists, who see the world from the perspective of their home countries, and place the interests of those countries first, globalists see the world as a whole, arguing that national interests add up to global interests, and that global interests help shape national interests. In spite of the criticism directed by many nationalist movements against globalism in recent years (spearheaded by leaders such as Donald Trump in the United States, Vladimir Putin in Russia, and Narendra Modi in India), the two ideas are not mutually exclusive, and nationalist criticisms of globalism as elitist and anti-democratic threats to national sovereignty miss much of the story. It is possible to simultaneously pursue local, national and global views (see Rosenboim, 2017).

All of this brings us back finally to the meaning of global studies. Where *international* literally means *between* nations (or states), the word *global* implies a more holistic and transnational view of the world. In other words, it is concerned with the world as a whole. If all other perspectives are partial, separated or contained, global perspectives are aggregated, combined, and connected. State borders cannot be ignored, to be sure, but global studies is concerned with matters that are of common interest to us all, regardless of those borders. Human rights, for example, are the rights that all of us have by virtue of being human, and they rise above citizenship of a particular country or community. Migration is not something that is limited to a particular time or place; it has happened throughout human history, and continues to happen today, for different reasons and with different results. And when air pollution causes changes in the earth's climate, we are all affected, regardless of any identity we might have other than simply being human.

If you are using this book, you are probably enrolled in a course or a module whose title includes some combination of the words *international*, *global*, and/or *globalization*, and that may be offered by a department, a programme or a school of either international studies, global studies, or both. These possibilities tell you something about the unsettled nature of the field. You would see even more possibilities with just a quick scan of the titles of other textbooks in this field, which include not just *global studies* and/or *international studies*, but sometimes spill over into *global issues*. And the list expands still further if you look at the contents of these books, which reveal an overlap between international, regional and global studies, and a wide range of possible topics. In preparing to write this book, I looked carefully at all the others on the subject, and found that no two covered the same ground. The most common topics were economics, population, culture, war, and health, followed by history, government, human rights, and the environment. Meanwhile, several books were each unique in addressing geography, foreign policy, technology, crime, and terrorism.

Unconcerned and undeterred by such mixed signals, this book defines **global studies** as follows:

> The systematic study of the global system and of its related features, qualities, trends, institutions, processes, and problems.

The **global system**, meanwhile, which is a term that appears often in the chapters that follow, can be defined as follows:

> The collected elements and components – including people, institutions, principles, procedures, norms and habits – whose interactions make up the global whole.

In the world of global studies, we are ultimately interested in understanding how the global system is constructed and how it works. We are focusing on the logical final point in a progression that begins with the individual and moves through the familial to the communal, the local, the national, the regional, and the international. In its efforts to understand global connections and phenomena, global studies has four important qualities:

▸ It is *transnational*, meaning that it is concerned with events, ideas, activities, and phenomena that are not limited by state boundaries. To be sure, global studies is grounded in the local, the national, and the international, which is why Map 0.1 shows the world, but also indicates the states with which most of us most readily identify, and at which level most of the decisions that most immediately impact us are made. Global studies takes the discussion about these decisions to the transnational level.

Map 0.1: The world

▶ It is *integral*, meaning that it is concerned more with what unites us than with what divides us, and with the manner in which decisions are shaped and implemented at the global level. We will see that all states are influenced by the actions of other states, that economies are impacted by cross-border investment and trade, and that cultures borrow from one another, promoting a sense of global consciousness. But it is our interconnectedness and interdependence that interests us when we take the global view.

▶ It is *inclusive*, meaning that it does not see the world from the perspective of any one group of people, but works to engage with the multiple perspectives of the entire human race. As we will see in Chapter 3, the term *ethnocentrism* is usually used to describe the phenomenon of looking at other cultures according to the values and standards of one's own, and even perhaps believing in their relative inferiority. But it also includes the more general idea of taking a narrow and exclusive view of everything we see. In contrast to the ethnocentric (or the nationalist), global studies is interested in taking an inclusive view, in fostering a sense of global literacy, awareness and belonging, and in helping us all better understand our place within a diverse global community.

▶ It is *interdisciplinary*, meaning that it looks at the world from the perspective of multiple disciplines, including history, geography, sociology, anthropology, demography, science, technology, politics, law, and economics. Although this book has 12 apparently separate chapters, none of the topics with which they deal are isolated, and they constantly overlap. There is a chapter on human rights, for example, but those rights – and the persistent problems of inequality – are threads that can be found woven throughout the book, and within each of its individual chapters. And there is a chapter on the environment, but environmental problems are intimately related to science, politics, law and economics.

The world is so big and diverse that we can never fully grasp how people of different nationalities, religions, cultures, educational backgrounds, and economic situations see it, but global studies can help us find our way through the maze. Consider the Indian parable of the blind men and the elephant: in order to learn what it looks like, they assign themselves to different parts of the animal, which they touch with their hands before comparing notes. They disagree about what the part they have touched tells them about the whole, but if they ask the help of others, they gather more information, their perspectives widen, and they build a more accurate picture of what the elephant looks like. Global studies works in a similar way by combining multiple perspectives on the world, helping us more accurately describe the qualities and dimensions of the global whole.

THE WORLD AS A COMMUNITY OF 100 PEOPLE

The focus of our interest is nothing less than the entire world. However, it is a big and complex place, and grasping its dimensions and diversity is not easy. It contains about 7.5 billion people living in almost 200 independent states, identifying with numerous nationalities and ethnicities, speaking thousands of languages and dialects, following dozens of different religions, and interacting both directly and indirectly through constantly changing webs of interests, needs, and opportunities. It would be impossible for any of us – even if we travelled widely and spoke multiple languages –

to come fully to grips with all this diversity. One way of working around this problem is to reduce the world to more digestible proportions by thinking of the world as a community of 100 people. This is what it reveals:

There is an even split between men and women. This should come as no surprise, because nature will make sure that there is a balance between the two. But within those numbers there are important trends: higher male mortality, for example, means that as populations age, the number of women increases relative to men. Men and women also differ in terms of their social roles, their economic status, and their political power.

Asians dominate. There are about 60 Asians in the community, living alongside 15 Africans, 14 people from the Americas, and 11 from Europe. Despite the preponderance of Chinese, Indians, Indonesians, Japanese, and Koreans (among others), the community is still very much defined and influenced by its Western minority, and the focus of political and economic power has long rested with Europeans and North Americans. This is changing, though, as the number, wealth and global influence of Asia grows.

Many languages are spoken. Although English is the language that most people in the community use to communicate, particularly those who are better educated, only 5 people are native speakers. About 12 speak different forms of Chinese, and 5 speak Spanish, but the remaining 78 speak a multitude of languages, and most are unable to communicate with anyone else other than indirectly, or through a basic version of English. Those who speak English find they can mingle more widely and build stronger ties with the community, while those who cannot find themselves at a disadvantage.

The community is aging. Thanks to better health care and nutrition, people are living longer, although there are many internal differences. Of the 100, 26 are aged 14 or younger, and 9 are 65 or older, leaving nearly two-thirds of the community within the optimum age range to work and to have and raise children. The median age of the community is 28, although the North Americans, the Chinese, and the Europeans are older on average (35 and above), while the Africans and Middle Easterners are the youngest on average (20 and below).

Democracy for the minority. Only about 40 people in the community live under democratic systems of decision-making, while the remaining 60 still languish under authoritarian rule. Most of those living under democracy are European, North and South American, and Indian, while the Chinese and Russian members of the community – along with most of its Middle Eastern and African members – struggle to make themselves freely heard, and find their rights routinely limited. Those who live under democracy worry increasingly about the quality of their influence, and throughout the community there is speculation about inequality, elitism, and a lack of accountability and transparency.

A small minority controls most of the wealth. Although the community has more than doubled the value of its economic output since 2000, just 17 members account for more than 60 per cent of that output, and 20 of them consume almost 90 per cent of its resources; these are almost all Europeans, North Americans, East Asians, and Australasians. The 18 Chinese members of the community are catching up fast, though, and exerting influence more widely. About 80 members of the community live on less than $10 per day, while 10 live in extreme poverty, barely scraping by on less than $1.90 per day.

Gender

50 men

50 women

Ethnicity

60 Asians

15 Africans

14 Americans

11 Europeans

Language

12 speak Chinese

5 speak English

5 speak Spanish

78 speak other languages

Age

26 are under the age of 14

26 is the median age of the community

9 are 65 or older

Literacy

84 can read and write

14 cannot

Education

7 have a college degree

12 have no more than a primary education

10 have no formal education

Shelter

77 have shelter

23 do not

Clean Water and Sanitation

90 have access

10 do not

Figure 0.2: The world as a community of 100 people

Compiled from sources used in the chapters that follow.

Urban areas dominate. Until recently, most of the people in the community lived in its rural areas, but there has been a steady drift over the decades to its urban areas, where 54 people now live. Many of those 54 remain poor and marginalized, while a central elite has accumulated most of the wealth and the power and consumes most of its resources. Meanwhile, many of those in the rural areas must rely on subsidies in order to grow the food on which the community relies.

Unequal access to education. Only 7 people in the community have a university degree, while – at the other end of the scale – 12 are unable to read or write. The community is better

educated than at any time in its history, and education is helping level the economic and social differences within the community, but higher education is still the privilege of a small minority, and remains tied to higher levels of wealth and better opportunities.

A large minority lacks shelter. While 77 of the members of the community have shelter (some of it sophisticated and well supported by utilities and services), the remaining 23 have none. Even for many of those with shelter, it is less than ideal, often consisting of slum dwellings and shanties with high crime rates and poor connections to basic services. Most people in the community have access to clean water and sanitation, but about 10 people do not, leaving them more susceptible to the resulting health problems.

Few members of the community eat well. About 30 of the members of the community have enough to eat, 13 of them so much so that they have become obese. Meanwhile, about 50 are malnourished and 20 are undernourished, many among the latter suffering from starvation. The problem is less one of supply than of distribution; the community has more than enough resources to feed itself, but its poorer parts have less access to supplies, which are often interrupted by conflict.

Access to health care is unequal. Although the health of the community overall has improved, not everyone has benefitted. In its wealthier parts, members can expect to live into their seventies and even their early eighties, and to have access to fine health care. In its poorer parts, life expectancy may be in the forties or the fifties.

Unequal internet connection. The wealthier and better served members of the community mainly have ready access to the internet, on which they rely for an increasing number of services and for almost all their information. But half of the members of the community remain unconnected, and are thereby denied the knowledge, information, convenience and access that come with being part of this critical network.

Many religions are followed. The community is far from united in its religious beliefs. Thanks to the influence of its Christian members, and their missionary achievements, Christianity has had an important role in the history of the community. But while nearly one-third of its members formally think of themselves as Christian, many of them are drifting away from organized religion. Meanwhile, the number of those who are Muslim is growing fast, about one-third of the members of the community subscribe to other religions, and 16 have no religion at all.

Of course, there is only so far that we can take the analogy with a community of 100 people, because in the real world the population continues to grow (it has doubled in size just since 1970) and most of its internal ratios are constantly changing. Even so, these numbers give us an idea of the diversity of the global system, and of the considerable inequalities that continue to persist within that system in spite of the enormous strides that have been made over recent decades in economic productivity, education, the provision of basis services, and technology.

SOME NOTES ON THIS BOOK'S APPROACH

Before moving on, four points will be helpful in understanding the approach taken by this book.

First, it is – above all – an introductory textbook designed for students coming to the topic of global studies with little background, in a variety of different settings and countries, and most of whom will be taking their first module or course on the topic. It grew out of the needs and preferences of my own students, who were valuable if unwitting guinea pigs for the approaches taken in the chapters that follow. Everything was tested on them before it appeared in this book, and they helped me determine what should be included and excluded. Because it is introductory, it sets out to cover the entire field of global studies, which means an emphasis on breadth over depth. Think of it as a sampler dish, offering a taste of the variety of topics within global studies, each of which can be covered in more depth using more specialized sources and bodies of literature. Also, because it is introductory, it sets out to include as many perspectives as possible, although focused positions are taken throughout the book.

Second, I have titled each chapter with selected key words, carefully chosen to encapsulate a variety of connected topics contained within each chapter. Chapter 4, for example, is titled 'Science and technology', but it is about a variety of topics found at the intersection of science and technology; hence it looks at health care, infectious disease, the digital revolution, and at changes in communication and transportation. At the same time, other chapters in the book cover topics that also relate to science – consider population growth, trade, and the environment, for example – so Chapter 4 is not the end of the discussion. This is where we see the kinds of connections that are at the heart of global studies.

Third, in a book that takes the broad and introductory view, generalizations are often necessary. They have the disadvantage of sacrificing precision, but they have the advantage of providing the shortcuts that are sometimes needed to make larger points. The most potentially troublesome generalization made in the chapters that follow is the division of the world into two communities based on a mix of political, economic and social features: the North (more democratic, wealthier and post-industrial states) and the South (less democratic, poorer and/or industrializing states). Most states fit squarely within one of these groups, but others do not, and this point is always worth remembering. Not everyone will like the use of these labels, which critics dismiss as outmoded, but they can be useful as a guide through a complex global community. More nuanced political categories are discussed in Chapter 5, and more nuanced economic categories in Chapter 8.

Finally, because this is a book about global studies, it is obviously important that it should take a global view. In some ways, the book itself stands as a microcosm of the global at work: it is written in English by an American-based author who is British-born, Kenyan-raised, and has citizenship of the US and the UK. It is published by a German-owned company headquartered in the UK (with offices in many countries), the production overseen by an American development editor, an Irish production editor and a copy editor in New Zealand, with the finished book printed on paper sourced in the Netherlands. As a repeat-migrant, and someone who sees himself as a global citizen, I have made a particular effort not to see everything from a Western perspective. However, as a Westerner who draws heavily off research and data generated mainly by other Westerners and made available through Western publishers, I find this sometimes easier said than done. The book also combines international and comparative perspectives: global studies is just as much interested in how communities relate to one another as with how they compare with one another.

KEY CONCEPTS

▸ Global studies
▸ Global system

▸ Globalism
▸ Globalization

▸ International relations
▸ International studies

USEFUL WEBSITES

Global Studies Association at https://globalstudiesassoc.wordpress.com

Global Studies Consortium at http://globalstudiesconsortium.org

World Bank Development Indicators at https://data.worldbank.org/indicator

(Note: The Victorian British Prime Minister Benjamin Disraeli is credited with having once railed against 'three kinds of lies: lies, damned lies, and statistics'. Sources of data will always be contested, but I have long chosen – wisely or unwisely – to have faith in the World Bank, which maintains a website that includes data on a wide variety of topics, much of it credited to other UN agencies. They, in turn, usually rely heavily on national governments. Unless otherwise specified, most of the data in this book come from that source.)

FURTHER READING

Anheier, Helmut K., and Mark Juergensmeyer (eds) (2012) *Encyclopaedia of Global Studies* (Sage). A four-volume edited encyclopaedia with numerous entries dealing in detail with many aspects of global studies.

Smith, Dan (2012) *The Penguin State of the World Atlas*, 9th edn (Penguin). Although not an example of global studies as such, this is nonetheless a useful and provocative visual summary of current events and global trends.

Juergensmeyer, Mark (ed.) (2014) *Thinking Globally: A Global Studies Reader* (University of California Press) and Manfred B. Steger (ed.) (2015) *The Global Studies Reader* (Oxford University Press). Two collections of useful readings from multiple authors, offering different perspectives on global studies.

Steger, Manfred B., and Amentahru Wahlrab (2017) *What is Global Studies? Theory and Practice* (Routledge). A survey of the field, showing its links with globalization, and outlining its key principles.

A single issue of the journal *Globalizations* from 2013 contains a forum involving scholars discussing the meaning and the purpose of global studies. Particularly interesting is the lead paper in the set – Jan Nederveen Pieterse (2013) 'What is Global Studies?' in *Globalizations* 10:4, pp. 499–514 – and a later issue of the same journal – Mark Juergensmeyer (2013) 'What is Global Studies?' in *Globalizations* 10:6, pp. 765–9.

ACADEMIC JOURNALS

The following are some of the major academic journals dealing with global studies and globalization.

Asia Journal of Global Studies   http://www.aags.org

Global Affairs   http://www.tandfonline.com

Global Challenges	http://onlinelibrary.wiley.com
Global Environmental Politics	http://www.mitpressjournals.org
Global Governance	https://www.rienner.com
Global Media and Communication	http://journals.sagepub.com
Global Networks	http://onlinelibrary.wiley.com
Global Policy	http://www.globalpolicyjournal.com
Global Social Policy	http://journals.sagepub.com
Global Society	http://www.tandfonline.com
Global Studies Journal	http://onglobalization.com/journal
Global Studies Law Review	http://openscholarship.wustl.edu/law_globalstudies
Globalization and Health	https://globalizationandhealth.biomedcentral.com
Globalizations	http://www.tandfonline.com
Identities: Global Studies in Culture and Power	http://www.tandfonline.com
Indiana Journal of Global Legal Studies	http://ijgls.indiana.edu
Journal of Global Analysis	http://cesran.org/globalanalysis
Journal of Global Ethics	http://www.tandfonline.com
Journal of Global Health	https://globalizationandhealth.biomedcentral.com
Journal of Global History	https://www.cambridge.org
Journal of Globalization and Development	https://www.degruyter.com
New Global Studies	https://www.degruyter.com
Transcience	http://www.transcience-journal.org

HISTORY

1

PREVIEW

This chapter provides the historical context within which to understand the origins and the evolution of the global system. It begins with a review of the emergence of the modern world, looking particularly at its European roots in discovery, colonization, industrialization and imperialism. It then looks at the causes and effects of the two world wars, the end of Europe's empires, and the Cold War. It reviews the economic, political and social changes that have come since the end of the Cold War, and their effects on the global system. The chapter ends with a discussion about the meaning and effects of globalization.

CONTENTS

▸ **The emergence of the modern world**

▸ **World war and the end of empire**

▸ **The Cold War**

▸ **The new global system**

▸ **Globalization**

HIGHLIGHTS

▸ The origins of the global system can be traced back over several centuries, but its construction has accelerated over the last 150 years.

▸ Europe led the way through expanding its global interests and connections, such that much of what today defines 'global' is also Western (although this is changing).

▸ The two world wars dramatically changed the structure of the global system and the balance of power, reducing the previously dominating role of Europe.

▸ The Cold War saw tensions between two new super-powers (the US and the USSR) as well as a period of decolonization and the emergence of the 'Third World'.

▸ The end of the Cold War ushered in a new era marked by rapid economic and technological change, and by new non-Western influences.

▸ In terms of understanding the global system, globalization is the dominant theme, although it is not as new as it seems, and opinion is divided on its implications.

Source: tonefotografia

THE EMERGENCE OF THE MODERN WORLD

Fort Jesus stands guard over the entrance to the harbour of Mombasa, Kenya's second-largest city and major port. Built by the Portuguese in the 1590s, it was captured and recaptured at least nine times, falling to Omani Arabs in 1698 after a two-year siege, before finally being taken over by the British in 1895. The fort no longer serves a defensive purpose, but it has stood as a witness to the emergence of what we now think of as the modern world. Its construction followed in the wake of Portuguese success in navigating their way around Africa, its ownership changed hands as political influence in the region moved from one power to another, and – more recently – the fort has witnessed the arrival of naval vessels from major military powers, of tankers from major oil producers, of containers carrying goods through the global trading system, of tourists seeking the palm trees and white sands of the Kenyan coast, and of terrorists seeking to make a political point.

This single building symbolizes and captures many (but by no means all) of the changing qualities of what we now define as the global: the ideas and forces that encouraged people to build connections with one another and to redefine boundaries and opportunities. They have migrated, invaded and gone to war with one another, built trade connections, built cooperative institutions, and agreed complex rules for governing their interactions. The effect has been to change the way they see themselves and each other, and to reshape cultures, economies, governments, and the physical environment. How and why did this happen?

For the majority of human history (in what we might call the pre-modern era), most people were local in their experiences, their outlook, and their consciousness. Some societies were (and remain) nomadic, others participated in migrations and invasions that took them to new locations, and yet others traded with one another. But most people had neither the capacity nor the desire to travel, and their interests and knowledge rarely extended far beyond their immediate farm, village or town. Unless they were wealthy or powerful, most lived and died not far from where they were born, and knew little of the wider world. Political and economic relationships were geographically limited in scope, and even the few who left home as soldiers, explorers, or entrepreneurs had little idea what they would find over the horizon, and no certainties that they would see home again.

Today's circumstances are quite different: the modern world is distinctive for the reach and interconnectedness of human interests and contacts. True, most people still have neither the time nor the resources to travel far from home, and continue to live in or near the communities in which they were born, but global connections have grown, and more people have been directly impacted by those connections: people travel and migrate in greater numbers, they can follow the news and collect information from around the world with relative ease, and they are routinely subject to the effects of decisions made hundreds or even thousands of kilometres away. At the same time, the world has been influenced by common ideas, languages and cultures promoted by the global reach of corporations, media, and technologies.

Although we think of globalization as a relatively new phenomenon (see later in this chapter), the process of building global connections began centuries ago. This process was long dominated by changes emanating from Europe, because it was Europeans who led the way in exploring, colonizing, and industrializing. As a result, the building of the global system was founded on values and ideas emanating from the **West**, which in turn came to sit at the heart of what we define as the **modern** world. It would be wrong, though, to think of either modernity or the global system as Western, or to think that Western is European. True, the West has deeply influenced most other parts of the world, and it remains powerful in political, economic and cultural terms, but this is not the end of the story.

It is important, for example, that we recognize that the West was shaped and influenced to a large degree by external ideas and pressures. Consider, for example, the influence of the Arabs on Europe, still seen today in much of the architecture of Spain, and felt more widely in Arabic numerals, the decimal system, algebra, geometry, the concept of zero (borrowed by the Arabs from India), and many Arabic words used in Western science, such as *nadir, zenith, alkali,* and *alcohol.* It is also important to recognize that many people in the world have lives and values that are distinctly non-Western, and some make a point of struggling against the historical dominance of the West. Finally, it is important to notice that while much of the history told in this book is centred on Europe, our future promises to be influenced deeply by Asia.

Strictly speaking, 'modern' means the present, but historians date the modern era to the early 16th century and the European Renaissance. It was during the early modern era (lasting from approximately 1450 to the French Revolution in 1789 (Wiesner-Hanks, 2013)) that transformative changes came to science, technology, politics, and the arts in Europe, forming the basis for its expansion. Change had also come to China, India, West Africa, the Middle East, and the Americas, and Europe was not unaffected; it was impacted by the spread of the Arab Empire, peaking in the 10th century, and later by the expansion of the Ottoman Empire, but the threats posed to Christian Europe by the latter ended with the Battle of Vienna in 1683.

Under different circumstances, it might not have been the Europeans who prevailed, and the history of the world might have turned out very differently. Between 1404 and 1433, for example, seven massive and expensive naval expeditions were dispatched by Ming China, reaching southeast Asia, then India, then the Persian Gulf, and finally the east coast of Africa. The first voyage alone included more than 300 ships. Had the expeditions gone further, and had it been China that colonized and settled other parts of the world, the story of globalization would have taken quite different directions. As it was, a combination of political divisions, overspending and natural disasters brought the voyages to an end, and China's horizons contracted. Later, the Mughal Empire of India – the world's largest economy at its peak in the 18th century – might have achieved wider influence had it not also decayed from within.

Although there were many landmark events during the early modern era, one in particular stands out. It was between May and October of 1648 that delegates met at a series of conferences in the cities of Osnabruck and Munster, within what was then the Duchy of Westphalia (now part of Germany), and made a number of decisions that were to have important repercussions for Europe, and ultimately for the world. Their goal was to bring an end to two wars: the Thirty Years' War in the Holy Roman Empire and the Eighty Years' War between Spain and the Dutch Republic. They succeeded, agreeing three treaties that are known collectively as the Peace of Westphalia.

West: A political, economic and cultural concept associated with Europe and with communities that grew out of European settlement and invasion. Distinguished from Eastern ideas associated with Asia, notably China, Japan and India.

Modern: Literally the present or contemporary times, and a term most often used in connection with history, technology, social norms, culture, and the arts.

Figure 1.1: Five stages in the growth of the global system

STAGE	DATES	FEATURES
PRE-MODERN	Prior to the early 16th century	Few connections, no sense of a global system.
EMERGENCE	Early 16th–early 20th century	Emergence of Europe as global actor via exploration, colonialism, industrialization, imperialism.
WORLD WAR	1914–45	Global conflict centred on Europe.
COLD WAR	Late 1940s-late 1980s	Bipolarity; ideological conflict between superpowers.
GLOBALIZATION	Since 1990	Multipolarity; strengthening of global connections; rise of Asia.

These treaties brought a new political order to central Europe: they made several adjustments to European state borders, helped make national secular authority superior to religious edicts from Rome, and established the principles of respect for the boundaries of states and of non-interference in the internal affairs of states. Several European states were already in existence in 1648, including England, Ireland, France, Spain and Portugal, but the terms of the peace gave clearer definition to the powers of those states. The modern state system – also known as the **Westphalian system** – now took hold in Europe, was later exported to other parts of the world through the global reach of Europe, and is today at the core of the global community of states within which we all live. As we will see in Chapter 5, many have since questioned the wisdom and the reality of the Westphalian system, and the future of states is debated, but for better or for worse it is the point of reference from which we understand today's global system.

The Westphalian system was ultimately exported on the back of four key developments that would establish and draw the outlines of the modern world: discovery, colonization, industrialization, and imperialism.

Discovery. The era of discovery and exploration, which ran from the late 15th to the late 16th century, saw Europeans set out to visit, understand and connect with other parts of the world, in what has since been described as the first age of globalization (Black, 2002). The Chinese and the Persians had been active explorers, but it was a confluence of three developments that gave Europeans the upper hand: they sought to trade with more distant parts of the world, they had invented long-distance sailing ships that made this possible, and they had the support of governments and benefactors.

The Portuguese and the Spanish led the way, Prince Henry the Navigator (1394–1460) of Portugal launching an interest in exploration that would outlast him by decades. The roster of European explorers grew with the exploits of Christopher Columbus (an Italian sailor supported by Spain, who reached the Americas in 1492), Vasco

> **Westphalian system**: The modern state system that emerged out of the 1648 Peace of Westphalia, based on the sovereignty of states and political self-determination.

da Gama (who reached what is now India in 1498), Pedro Álvares Cabral (who reached what is now Brazil in 1500), and Ferdinand Magellan (who completed the first known circumnavigation of the earth in 1519–22).

Source: Stockbyte/PunchStock

The monument celebrating the achievements of Prince Henry the Navigator, which stands by the mouth of the estuary leading to the Portuguese capital of Lisbon.

Colonization. The discoveries of the era of exploration not only changed Europe, leading to competition among its leaders and peoples for the new opportunities so revealed, but also brought change to other parts of the world, created new connections, and expanded the opportunities and desire to trade. In 1600, the East India Company was founded in London to oversee British interests in India (Robins, 2012), to be followed two years later by the Dutch East India Company, with its sights set on Southeast Asia. Trade interests combined with competition for political influence to launch the era of European **colonialism**, in which control of foreign territories was established by the governments or citizens of mother countries in Europe, underpinned by four key motives:

▸ Settlement, as in the case of England's North American colonies.

▸ Extraction, as in the case of efforts to set up trade ties in pursuit of commodities such as spices, sugar, minerals, or slaves. (It is revealing that stretches of the West African coastline were originally named by Europeans as the Grain Coast, the

Colonialism: Efforts by the governments or citizens of one region to occupy and control foreign territories with a view to settlement, economic exploitation, or strategic advantage.

Slave Coast, the Ivory Coast and the Gold Coast.) Slavery was to become one of the most contentious and tragic aspects of European trade policy, its long-term impacts continuing to be felt even today – see Chapter 7.

▶ Strategic advantage, as in the case of the establishment of military bases to protect economic and political interests.

▶ A desire to 'civilize', expressed in the efforts of missionaries to spread Christianity, and of colonizers to 'improve' peoples and cultures that were considered inferior.

The Spanish and the Portuguese established claims to large swathes of the Americas between 1492 and the early 19th century, while the British and the French established claims in eastern North America. When Britain was defeated in the American War of Independence, it shifted its interests to other parts of the world (mainly Asia and Africa), where it competed with the French and other Europeans. Perhaps the ultimate act of colonial conquest was the agreement reached among European powers at the 1884–85 Berlin conference. Aimed at resolving brewing tensions over the control of Africa, it also launched the 'scramble for Africa' that would result in the continent's division between Britain, France, Belgium, Portugal, Germany, Italy, and Spain. Only Ethiopia, Liberia, and present-day Somalia remained unclaimed.

Industrialization. Just as European powers were busy expanding their interests in other parts of the world, so their domestic economies were undergoing dramatic change as a result of the invention of new technologies that allowed them to shift from limited production using animal and human power to mass production using machines

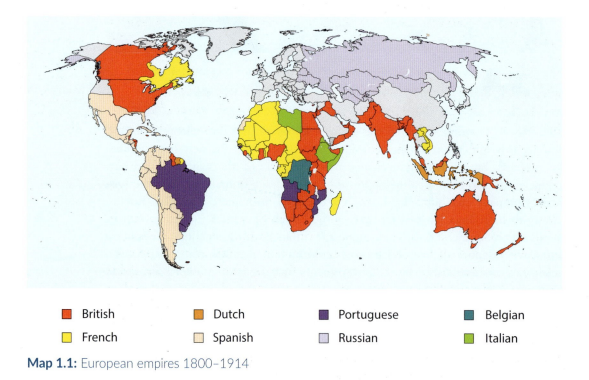

	British		Dutch		Portuguese		Belgian
	French		Spanish		Russian		Italian

Map 1.1: European empires 1800–1914

driven by steam and coal. The industrial revolution (approximately mid-18th to mid-19th century) allowed Europeans to produce more, encouraging them to seek new sources of raw materials and new markets in which to sell their commodities, thereby building on the pressures to colonize and expand trade links., and in turn creating more global connections The rise of industry also fundamentally changed domestic economies and societies: factories were created, people moved to cities, populations grew, education improved, and workers made new demands for political rights. Industrialization also resulted in the accumulation of wealth and capital in the urban centres of Europe and North America, changing the balance of power in ways whose effects are still felt to this day. It also – as we will see in later chapters – led to the mismanagement of resources, and widespread environmental damage.

Imperialism. While colonialism saw tangible change in the sense that direct control was assumed by colonizing powers over foreign territories, **imperialism** describes both a philosophy and a set of effects, expressed both in colonialism and in efforts to build spheres of influence. One of the most prominent European imperialists was Cecil John Rhodes (1853–1902), a British entrepreneur whose immediate goal was British rule from one end of Africa to the other, but whose longer-term hope was for British rule over the entire world; he once suggested that to have been born an Englishman was to have 'won the lottery of life'. His name lived on with the creation of the southern African colonies of Northern and Southern Rhodesia (now Zambia and Zimbabwe), and the provision in his will for Rhodes scholarships that support study at the University of Oxford by students from the English-speaking world. This was all well and good for the privileged elites of imperial powers, perhaps, but the working classes who made up the bulk of soldiers and labourers upon whom imperialism was able to grow would have taken a different view. So would many of the residents of European colonies, who were treated at best with condescension, and at worst with brutality.

> **Imperialism**: A policy – usually by a government or a state – to extend power and influence through diplomacy or military conquest.

The end of Europe's empires in the 20th century did not mean the end of imperialism, and charges continue to be made to this day of **neo-imperialism**. This is usually used to suggest that different actors – which may be states, institutions, or even corporations – are using economic, social or even cultural means to exert influence. That many international banks, or organizations such as the World Bank and the International Monetary Fund, are dominated by the rich countries, and that they often demand concessions from poorer countries in return for loans or investments, is often criticized as a form of neo-imperialism.

> **Neo-imperialism**: Efforts by powerful actors to extend their influence by demanding changes or concessions from less powerful actors.

WORLD WAR AND THE END OF EMPIRE

Even if the world had changed a great deal as a result of discovery, colonialism, industrialization and imperialism, it was to witness deeper and broader changes during the first half of the 20th century. New developments would reconfigure the balance of political and economic power, and continue the construction of the global system we find around us today. Few events played a bigger role in this process than two **world wars** that took the world in dramatic new directions. Both World War I (1914–18) and World War II (1939–45) were in many ways European civil wars that pulled in others, and can be seen as one war with a 21-year break; the disputes that led to the first outbreak of violence were not resolved with the peace treaty that ended World War I, paving the way for World War II.

> **World war**: Military conflict involving many states in different parts of the world.

The tensions that led to the outbreak of the first war in 1914 were not immediately obvious. There had been few major conflicts involving the major powers since the end of the Napoleonic wars in 1815, trade was expanding, medicine and sanitation were improving, and new technology – headlined by the invention of the steamship, the public railway, the telegraph, the telephone, and the automobile – had brought new levels of economic productivity and had tightened global connections among states, making peace a more preferable state of affairs than war. Before 1914, Britain and Germany – the two major protagonists in what was at first known as the Great War – had become each other's biggest trading partners.

But the global system had also come to be dominated by the so-called **great powers** – Britain, France, Germany, and Russia – which, for Levy (1983: 16–18), had four shared qualities:

> **Great power**: A state with a large military and continental or global interests.

▸ They had a high level of military capability and self-sufficiency in security issues, with the ability to project power beyond their borders and to conduct offensive as well as defensive operations.

▸ They had interests that were continental or global in scope rather than local or regional.

▸ They pursued a distinctive pattern of behaviour, including a willingness to defend their interests aggressively and with a broad set of tools.

▸ Their status was acknowledged by other powers.

The great powers had the largest economies, the most powerful militaries, the strongest positions in international trade, and the deepest investments in the global system. Meanwhile, most other parts of the world were either part of the empires controlled by the great powers, or else (like the United States) they avoided becoming involved in great power rivalry, or else (like China and Japan) they remained on the margins of the emerging global system.

While the great powers emphasized peace and prosperity in their relations with one another, they also made large investments in weapons and armies, and had built a network of alliances and diplomatic ties that were overlaid by nationalist aspirations, economic competition, and colonial rivalries (Macmillan, 2014: Introduction). Tensions grew such that it took only the assassination in June 1914 of Archduke Franz Ferdinand, the heir to the Austro-Hungarian throne, by a Bosnian Serb nationalist to set off a chain of events that would lead to the outbreak in August 1914 of a war that was not only avoidable but was also improbable (Clark, 2012). Although the Great War was fought mainly in Belgium and France, it reached as far as the Middle East and parts of Africa, and involved combatants from European colonies and dominions (notably Australia, Canada, India and New Zealand), and eventually the United States.

The effects were tumultuous:

▸ There were as many as 40 million casualties, including an estimated 18 million deaths.

▸ The new technology of war meant much greater numbers of civilian deaths than in any previous war.

▸ The economies of the major combatant states were severely shaken.

Source: Universal Images Group/Getty Images

The stresses of the Great War are reflected in the faces of these soldiers from the Royal Irish Rifles, during a brief respite on the first day of the Battle of the Somme in July 1916.

- ▶ Divisions were imposed on the Middle East that would cause many problems later.

- ▶ The war sparked the collapse of the Russian regime and the creation of the Soviet Union.

- ▶ The way was paved for the rise of Hitler.

Another effect of the war was to broaden support for international cooperation, leading to the creation in 1920 of the League of Nations, headquartered in Geneva, Switzerland. Its goal (according to the Treaty of Versailles that ended the Great War) was to 'promote international co-operation and to achieve international peace and security' based on 'open, just and honourable relations between nations'. But the League had many structural weaknesses, not least being that it required unanimity in order to take action, not all sovereign states were automatically allowed to join, and several either declined to join (as in the case of the United States), or joined but then left (as in the case of Germany), or joined but were then expelled (as in the case of the USSR). While it was able to help resolve a number of minor disputes involving smaller states, it was unable to stop the Japanese invasion of Manchuria in 1931, or Italy's invasion of Ethiopia in 1935. At the same time, argues Pedersen (2015), the League offered a channel through which the efforts of the great powers to maintain their authority could be challenged for the first time, setting the scene for changes that would come after 1945.

The most obvious failure of the League was its inability to address the tensions that would lead eventually to World War II. These were many, but included ongoing great power competition, the reparations demanded of Germany after 1918, limitations on its military, the instability of the German political system, the militarization of

Timeline: Key events in the evolution of the global system

1492–1500	Second wave of European exploration of Americas and India
1648	Peace of Westphalia
1683	Battle of Vienna ends expansion of Ottoman Empire
Mid-18th century	Start of the industrial revolution
1804	Global population reaches one billion
1884–85	Berlin Conference
1914–18	World War I (the Great War)
1920	Creation of League of Nations
1930s	Great Depression
1939–45	World War II
1944	Creation of Bretton Woods system
1945	Creation of United Nations
1947	Independence of India and Pakistan
Late 1940s	Start of Cold War
Late 1940s–late 1960s	Era of decolonization
1958	Creation of what is now the European Union
1973	International energy crisis
1980s	Personal computing takes hold
Late 1980s	End of Cold War
1991	Break-up of Soviet Union
Early 1990s	The internet begins to go global
1990s	Early signs of emergence of China as global actor
2001	Terrorist attacks in the United States
2007	Breaking of global financial crisis
2012	Global population reaches seven billion

Japan, and the desire of Germany and Japan to have empires of their own (see Overy, 2017). The problems built in stages to the outbreak in September 1939 of a war that was more truly global in its reach than World War I, involving most of Europe and its empires, the Middle East, the United States, China, and Japan.

The effects were even more tumultuous than with World War I:

▶ It cost an estimated 50–80 million lives, including about 20 million military personnel, about 30 million civilians, and about 23 million deaths from famine or disease.

▶ Further developments in the technology of war meant even deeper and broader destruction than had been the case in the Great War.

▶ European powers lost the capacity and the will to sustain large militaries or empires, sparking an intensive process of decolonization that led to the most intensive phase of new state creation in history: between 1946 and 1970, nearly 60 states became independent – see Chapter 5.

▶ The atomic bombs dropped on Hiroshima and Nagasaki ushered in the nuclear age.

▶ Europe celebrated peace in 1945 but soon found itself divided into two spheres, one dominated by the Americans and one by the Soviets.

▶ Globally, power shifted away from Europe, and by the late 1940s the world found itself caught up in the Cold War, an entirely new kind of conflict.

▶ International cooperation moved into a higher gear, beginning with the creation in 1945 of the United Nations.

The combined effects of the two world wars were to reshape the global system in fundamental ways. Prior to 1945, the centres of political, economic and military gravity had all lain in Europe, and they were now to start moving in new and unexpected directions as the definition of the global system changed, global connections grew, and global consciousness entered a new and dynamic phase of growth and expansion.

THE COLD WAR

By 1945, the four great powers had begun to be replaced by a new kind of **superpower** capable of operating at a global level (for the origins of the term, see Fox, 1944). There were only two of these – the United States and the Soviet Union – and their powers were given new significance by their possession of nuclear weapons. Other countries soon developed a nuclear capability (notably Britain, France and China), but the post-war era was dominated by tensions between the US and its allies, on the one side, and the Soviets and their allies, on the other. This era was known as the **Cold War**, because there was no direct military conflict between the two sides, but instead a competition for influence driven by mutual suspicion, hostility, and distrust. Meanwhile, a **Third World** of mainly developing countries nervously watched the new rivalry, some being encouraged to take sides with the Americans or the Soviets while others tried to keep their distance.

Cold War tensions deepened during the 1950s and 1960s as the Americans and the Soviets vied for influence, promoting their competing capitalist and communist views of politics, economics and society. While they never fought directly with one another, in part because of the deterrence offered by the devastation that would inevitably follow in the wake of nuclear war, their competition was reflected in numerous local and regional conflicts and tensions, including the Berlin blockade (1948–49), the Korean War (1950–53), the Cuban missile crisis (1962), the Vietnam war (mid-1950s to 1975), the Arab–Israeli conflict, wars of independence in Africa, and the 1979 Soviet invasion of Afghanistan.

The global economic system was also changing: its features had been mapped out at a landmark meeting in July 1944, when economists and government leaders from 44 countries gathered at the resort of Bretton Woods, New Hampshire, and agreed the principles of what became known as the **Bretton Woods system**. These included the convertibility of currencies, free trade, non-discrimination, and stable rates of exchange (see Conway, 2014). The system would be underpinned by the new global strength of the US dollar, and by the creation of two new international

Superpower: A state with the capacity and willingness to be active globally, particularly in a military sense.

Cold War: The war of words and ideas that took place between the late 1940s and the late 1980s involving the United States, the Soviet Union, and their respective allies or client states.

Third World: An informal grouping of developing Asian, African, Middle Eastern and Latin American states that were not immediately part of the US-led capitalist bloc or the Soviet-led communist bloc.

Bretton Woods system: The international economic system designed to encourage post-war peace and prosperity through free trade and exchange rate stability.

COMPARING NORTH AND SOUTH 1

UNDERSTANDING NORTH AND SOUTH

Generalizations can be problematic, because they often overlook exceptions, variations, and nuances. At the same time, they are often necessary in order to offer short-hand points of reference through what might otherwise be lengthy and complex debates and analyses. As noted in the Introduction, the prime generalization used in this book involves placing the countries of the world into one of two groups: the **North** and the **South**. Every chapter includes a boxed feature such as this one, designed to assess a problem or a phenomenon from the contrasting perspectives of the citizens and governments of the North and the South. Before going any further, then, it is worth explaining in more depth the meaning of the terms, and briefly reviewing their advantages and disadvantages.

The terms trace their origins back to the use of the label *Third World* to describe a 'third force' of emerging countries that were marginalized in the Cold War confrontation between capitalist democracy (the First World) and communist authoritarianism (the Second World) (see Tomlinson, 2003). With the end of the Cold War, these three labels ceased to have much value, and they had also been criticized for their implied ranking. There have also been doubts about the value or accuracy of alternative terms – such as *advanced, developed, developing, less developed, underdeveloped, newly industrializing,* and *emerging* – that are based on a mix of political, economic and social factors whose balance has never been clearly outlined or universally agreed.

Beginning in the 1980s (see Independent Commission on International Development Issues, 1980) it became more usual to describe the Third World as the South, and everywhere else as the North, leading to the following division:

▶ The terms *North* and *Global North* are most often associated with Europe, North America, Japan, South Korea, Australia and New Zealand. They include poorer eastern European states, as well as Russia, even if it is an outlier. At least two states in the group – Australia and New Zealand – are actually in the geographical south.

▶ The terms *South* and *Global South* are most often associated with Asia, Africa, the Middle East, and Latin America. They include some of the most dynamic and fastest-growing economies in the world (such as Argentina, Brazil, China, and Singapore), raising the question of how long such countries will continue to be considered part of the South.

In spite of the controversies the two labels raise, they continue to be used widely and frequently, appearing in book and journal titles (see, for example, Williams et al., 2014), conference themes, and the names of research centres. Four key points are worth making, though: the distinction between the two is not as clear as Map 1.2 implies, the labels should be considered conceptual as well as geographical, the South is becoming increasingly important and influential, and we should not ignore South–South interactions.

organizations: the International Monetary Fund (IMF) would encourage exchange rate stability in the interests of promoting international trade, and the World Bank would help European countries recover from the war. At the same time, the General Agreement on Tariffs and Trade (GATT) was set up to oversee negotiations aimed at the progressive reduction of barriers to trade.

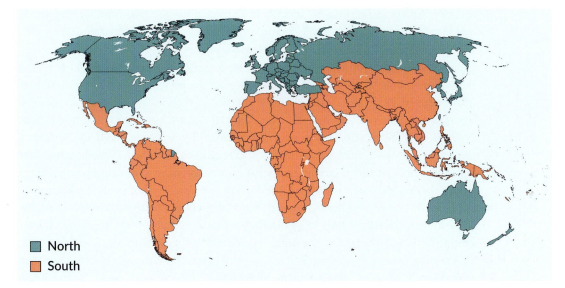

■ North
■ South

Map 1.2: The North and the South

The IMF and the World Bank were specialized agencies of the United Nations, created in 1945 as a new effort to promote international peace and cooperation, learning off the mistakes of the League of Nations. As we will see in Chapter 6, the decades after World War II saw a dramatic increase in the number of international organizations and the agreement of international treaties, all designed to build on the connections among states by working together on shared interests. In few parts of the world was there more interest in cooperation than in Europe, where many had become determined to put an end to the recurring wars and conflicts that had for centuries brought so many problems to the region, and now explored ways of encouraging cooperation. This led them during the 1950s to take the first steps towards what would eventually become the European Union (EU), whose core original aim was to build a single, integrated European market. Only six countries originally joined, but membership eventually expanded to cover most of Europe. The model of the EU was later to inspire many similar regional organizations in other parts of the world.

The Bretton Woods system collapsed in 1971 when the United States – struggling to control inflation and to meet the costs of the war in Vietnam – unilaterally ended the convertibility of gold and the US dollar. This launched an era of international monetary turbulence, made worse by an international energy crisis set off by the October 1973 war between Israel and the Arabs, which resulted in mainly Arab oil producers quadrupling the price of oil. The decade ended with the Soviet invasion of Afghanistan, a disastrous decision that committed the USSR to an unwinnable war, and revealed many of the internal weaknesses in the Soviet political and economic system.

The Cold War era also saw the rising influence of non-state actors (see Chapter 6 for more detailed discussion) such as international organizations, international non-governmental organizations, and multinational corporations. Even against the background of Cold War tensions, international cooperation was deepening and widening, and a host of new organizations were created to shape and reach new agreements on subjects as diverse as human rights, migration, the environment, and

North and **South**: Short-hand terms for 'advanced' and 'developing' economies, most of which are found – respectively – in the northern and southern halves of the world. Often prefaced by the adjective *global*.

security. At the same time, multinational corporations grew in number and reach, making decisions on jobs, trade, marketing, and the exploitation of resources that brought them to the heart of the global system.

Meanwhile, developing or newly independent states began to assert themselves as new actors on the world stage. They were behind the formation of the Non-Aligned Movement in 1955, an effort to send a not-always-convincing message about their desire not to take sides in the Cold War. Many also came together within the United Nations in 1964 as the Group of 77, whose goal was to promote the collective interests of its members (see Chapter 6). Despite their disadvantaged status, they could not be ignored: many had large or rapidly growing populations, often large labour forces, and often valuable stocks of raw materials. Others played a key role in the Cold War, and yet others had negative influence in the form of internal instability that often spilled over into neighbouring states, for example by sparking refugee crises. China and India were the biggest potential new global actors, but neither was yet exerting themselves in more than a regional capacity, although both had nuclear weapons (China from 1964 and India from 1974).

A change of leadership in the Soviet Union in 1985 – when conservative hardliners were replaced by the administration of the more progressive Mikhail Gorbachev – brought new openness to the country and a desire for economic change, soon inspiring democracy movements in those parts of Eastern Europe that had been under Soviet control. These pressures led to the reunification of Germany in October 1990, the break-up of the USSR in December 1991, the break-up of Yugoslavia in the 1990s, and the end of the Cold War. With the end of the Soviet Union, the United States was the only remaining superpower, and the bipolar world of the Cold War era was at least briefly replaced by a new unipolar era of American dominance. But numerous changes were already under way that led to questions about American dominance, and speculation instead about a new era of multipolarity. If the 19th century had been the British century, and the 20th century had been the American century, then perhaps – as we will see in the chapters that follow – the 21st century will likely be the Chinese century (see Nye, 2015).

THE NEW GLOBAL SYSTEM

In 1989, the American political economist Francis Fukuyama was inspired by the speed of the democratic transition in Eastern Europe to declare the final triumph of democracy as the **end of history**. 'What we may be witnessing,' he wrote, 'is not just the end of the Cold War, or the passing of a particular period of post-war history, but the end of history. … That is, the end point of mankind's ideological evolution and the universalization of Western liberal democracy as the final form of human government' (Fukuyama, 1989).

But Fukuyama spoke too soon. The Cold War might have been an era of enormous danger, but there was an element of predictability and stability brought about by the threat of nuclear war, and by the dominating global power of the Americans and the Soviets. The end of that troubled balance now ushered in a new era of change, and it was not long before the political commentator Robert Kagan (2008) was writing of the 'return of history'. The world had 'become normal again', he argued, because states and nationalist ambitions were as strong as ever, and struggles for status and influence were back, along with the old competition

End of history: The idea that a political economic or social system will evolve to the point where it would reach its conclusive end-state.

between liberalism and autocracy, to which was added the struggle between radical Islam and modern secular cultures and powers. Many analysts began to write about the emergence of a 'new world disorder'.

Eight particular trends are noteworthy for the extent to which they are helping define the new global system. First, the economic balance of power is changing. From a time when first the Europeans dominated, and then they were joined by the Americans, the relative influence and power of the West has declined. The change inspired the invention in 2001 of the acronym **BRIC** (O'Neill, 2001) to reflect the new global roles of Brazil, Russia, India and China. South Africa was later nominated as an addition to the group (changing the acronym to BRICS), and something of a game began to add clever new acronyms, such as the MIST group (for Mexico, Indonesia, South Korea, and Turkey). Equally quickly though, Brazil and Russia ceased to be thought of in the same terms as China and India, because the economies of the last two were developing so much more quickly. Meanwhile, the ties among economies have been altered with the development of free trade agreements and regional association agreements, designed to open markets and break down barriers to trade – see Chapter 9 for more details.

BRIC: A collective acronym for Brazil, Russia, India, and China, reflecting their newly influential global roles.

Figure 1.2: Current global trends

ECONOMICS	Relative decline of the North, and emergence of the South, against a background of growing free trade.
POLITICS	Changes in the balance of power, and questions about the future of democracy.
SECURITY	New insecurities in the face of terrorism, cyber threats, and economic uncertainties.
MOBILITY	Mass tourism has grown, and patterns of migration are becoming more complex.
TECHNOLOGY	Rapid change in the wake of the digital revolution.
CULTURE	The globalization of culture, which may be leading to homogenization or hybridization.
ENVIRONMENT	New awareness of the effects of human actions on the natural world.
GLOBALIZATION	Integration of politics, economics, society, and culture.

Second, the political balance of power is changing. Most notably, we have seen the rise of China and the Islamic world as critical new actors on the world stage. The United States may still be the dominating military and economic power, but it has lost much of its credibility in the wake of controversial foreign policy decisions (such as the invasions of Afghanistan in 2001 and Iraq in 2003), of domestic economic problems, and of deep internal divisions. For a time, it seemed as though the European Union might translate its economic power into political influence, but there has been a backlash against European integration, and the breaking of the European sovereign debt crisis in 2009 created damaging political shockwaves, as did the decision by British voters in a 2016 referendum to have their country leave the EU. Further afield, the trend towards greater democratization appears to have stalled in recent years, as authoritarianism grows in countries such as Hungary, the Philippines, Russia and Turkey.

Third, many new insecurities are emerging. The manner in which economies have become interlinked was emphasized by the manner in which the effects of the global financial crisis of 2007–9 and the European debt crisis spread so quickly and widely. While interstate war may have become a rarity (see Chapter 12), international terrorism has become all too common, impacting not just the major powers – exemplified by the attacks of September 2001 in the United States – but bringing death and destruction to Afghanistan, Britain, Egypt, France, Indonesia, Iraq, Kenya, Nigeria, Russia, Syria, Turkey and Yemen, among others. Meanwhile, cyber threats have brought new and not yet fully understood challenges. Recent analyses have pointed to signs of global disorder (see Fink. 2017, and Haass, 2017), with Guillen (2016) suggesting that the world has become more prone to crisis; the complexity and the coupling of the components of the new global system have – he argues – created an 'architecture of collapse', or situations in which stability is undermined and we have made ourselves more prone to periodic disruptions, such as the global financial crisis and the European debt crisis.

Fourth, personal mobility is growing. The era of mass tourism that began after World War II saw more people with more disposable income exploiting expanded transport networks to travel further from home for leisure and personal fulfilment (see Chapter 4). Tourism was once the preserve of the wealthy, and mainly of Europeans and Americans, but it is now well within reach of the middle classes, and the Chinese are becoming prominent by their addition to the throngs who now find their way to the world's tourist destinations. Meanwhile, new patterns of legal and irregular emigration have emerged, driven by a combination of economic need and personal choice, and becoming increasingly complex. Where migrants once moved to a few key destinations for similar economic reasons, they now target a greater variety of destinations, seeking new opportunities, education, respite from war, and even simply a new style of life.

Fifth, technological change is accelerating and the reach of that change is becoming global. Twentieth-century inventions such as radio, television, penicillin, air conditioning, jet engines, and credit cards all eventually became global, but it usually took most of them some time to do that. The digital revolution – bringing us the personal computer, the internet, e-mail, mobile phones, digital television, and social media – has brought dramatic and rapid changes in the way we do business and communicate with each other, at least for those who have access.

Sixth, culture is feeling the effects of globalization. The continued dominance of the West is reflected in the rise of English as a global language, the popularity of films and television programmes made originally in English, the global reach of businesses with their roots in Europe or North America (including banks, fast-food outlets, fashion stores, and technology companies), and the worldwide following of sports invented in the West (notably football, basketball, cricket, tennis, rugby, and golf). But the patterns of cultural interchange are complex: Mandarin Chinese has more native speakers than any other language, and the Indian movie industry – headed by Bollywood – sells more tickets than Hollywood. Opinion is divided about the effects of the globalization of culture, with Samuel Huntington (1996) once famously warning of the 'clash of civilizations' (particularly between Islam and the West) (see Chapter 3), while other commentators worry about the effects of a homogenization of culture. Nederveen Pieterse (2015) suggests that we are seeing the formation of a 'global mélange culture' as a result of cultural mixing or hybridization, where local identities continue to be preserved, even if they are being transformed.

Seventh, while warnings of global and regional environmental change are far from new, they are becoming more strident as many problems are worsening. Many environmental problems were once treated as local in their causes and solutions, but then transboundary air pollution became a troubling new issue in the 1970s. It was mainly addressed in the old industrial centres of the North, but is now increasingly problematic in industrializing states such as China and India (see McCormick, 2017a: Chapter 6). Meanwhile, our new understanding of threats posed to the ozone layer in the 1980s added a global dimension to the problems of the environment, made even clearer as we continue to grapple with the ultimate global and even existential problem of climate change.

The overall effect of these changes has been to produce a dramatically altered global system, where change comes quickly, takes us in directions that are both exciting and alarming, and in which predictions about the future are not always easy to make. Running through all these changes lies the eighth and most far-reaching of current global trends, which is important enough to merit its own section within this chapter: globalization.

GLOBALIZATION

Few pressures have so deeply shaped the new global system, and the place of states within that system, as globalization. This is the process by which the links among humans have tightened, driven and accompanied by increased economic interdependence, changes in technology and communications, the rising power of multinational corporations, the growth of international markets, the spread of a global culture, and the harmonization of public policies in the face of shared or common problems. This is where we most clearly see the distinction between the international and the global discussed in the Introduction: the interactions among states are driven increasingly by trends that are more truly global in nature.

The signs of globalization can be found in many forms and places:

▸ In politics, it is reflected in suggestions that the sovereignty of states is declining as they must work together to address shared or common problems and pressures, and must adjust to the rise of multinational corporations and non-governmental organizations. It can also be found in the habits of cooperation encouraged by the work of intergovernmental organizations.

GLOBAL AND LOCAL 1

GLOBALIZATION AND GLOCALIZATION

The boxes that appear in each chapter of this book under the title Global and Local are designed to take focused topics related to each chapter and use them to contrast global and local perspectives. The goal is to explore the links between the two, to show how each impacts the other, and to offer a more personal perspective on topics that could otherwise seem so large and so broad as to lack a human scale. Just as we reviewed the contrasts between North and South earlier in this chapter, so this is a good opportunity to explore the relationship between globalization and **glocalization**.

Combining the ideas of *globalization* and *localization*, glocalization is recognition that while closer ties are being built at the global level, the importance of meeting local needs should not be forgotten. Consider the following examples:

▶ In politics, not only must national governments work with local governments and communities to shape policies, but those communities can use global links to learn more easily from one another. They have done this on a wide range of topics, from agriculture to education, transport, health care, and the environment. So while it is true that globalization makes it more difficult for national governments to make independent decisions, they make up by learning from experiences in different environments.

▶ In business, products and services can be sold globally, but they should also be adapted or customized to meet the needs of local markets and consumers. Conversely, they may start at a local level, but then be adapted to be distributed at a global level; each level influences the other, and they are connected. An example is offered by the many local menu adjustments made by global fast-food chains. In India (where beef is not eaten), McDonald's sells Maharaja Macs with chicken, lamb or vegetable fillings, KFC offers vegetable burgers and rice bowls, and Subway does not include meat in its sandwiches.

▶ In culture, the concerns about homogenization in the wake of globalization have been offset by the realization that local identities have been helping shape global identities, and that the connections created by globalization give us all more variety; products in local stores come from all over the world, we can listen to music and watch films from many different cultures, and we can eat at restaurants offering a wide range of cuisines.

The key point to appreciate here is that globalization is not a one-way street, and that the global and the local remain intimately connected despite the seeming power and influence of major powers and large economies.

Glocalization: The idea that changes can occur at the global level and at the local level simultaneously, and that both levels are connected, one driving the other.

▶ In economics, it is reflected in the growth of trade, the expansion of international markets, the deepening of economic interdependence, and the globalization of financial institutions as they form new global alliances, and as many financial services reach across borders.

▶ In jobs, it is reflected in the way that borders have ceased to define options in the way they once did. More jobs are being exported or outsourced, old jobs are being lost and new jobs are being created as a result of the opportunities offered by globalization, and more people are moving across borders to follow jobs. Many have no choice but to emigrate (legally or otherwise) because of economic decline or political instability at home, but we should not forget those who willingly follow new opportunities away from home, or retire in other countries.

▶ In culture, it is reflected in the way that much that was once unique to states or communities is being exported, so that we find the same food, music, products and fashions almost wherever we go. Critics worry about the homogenization of global culture along Western lines (see Chapter 3), but glocalization (see Global and Local 1) points to the effects of counter-trends, and cultural change has long involved a process of cross-fertilization. The Western communities often seen as dominating global cultural change have witnessed many of their own changes with an influx of migrants and cultures from many other parts of the world.

The process of globalization is far from new, although just how far back we can reasonably go to find its first steps is debatable. As we saw earlier in this chapter, the era of European exploration may have constituted a first wave. The period between 1870 and 1914 – with its growth of international trade – is seen by some as a second wave (although not everyone agrees; see Chandy and Seidel, 2016). The next wave came between 1945 and 1980, spurred by the growth in international cooperation and the opening of markets within the new Bretton Woods system. The most recent wave (the second, the third, or the fourth, depending on who is doing the counting) rests on the emergence of digital technologies.

Globalization has its supporters (see Bhagwati, 2007, and Goklany, 2007) and its critics (see Cohen, 2007), and its advantages and disadvantages (see Table 1.1 for a summary of opposing arguments). Although it represents support for the universal perspective offered by globalism, and a rejection of the kind of nationalism discussed in Chapter 5, it is far from monolithic, and multiple schools of thought have been

Source: AFP/Getty Images

Riot police hold the line against anti-globalization protesters outside a meeting of finance ministers from the Group of 20 countries in Melbourne, Australia, in November 2006.

Table 1.1: The pros and cons of globalization

Pros	Cons
Created new jobs and economic prosperity in the wake of the opening of markets and expansion of trade.	Resulted in a loss of jobs in wealthier countries, a drain of workers to countries with better wages and prospects, and exploitation of poorer countries with lower wages and weaker regulations. Many barriers to trade remain.
Encouraged international peace by tightening economic links among countries and broadening cultural understanding.	Promoted international tensions through inequalities in trade, income, and opportunity.
Promoted technological innovation by encouraging competition and bigger markets.	Technological innovation would have likely happened even without the pressures of globalization.
Promoted democracy by exerting pressure on authoritarian governments.	Diminished the sovereignty of states at the expense of new power and influence for multinational corporations.
Generated new wealth that has helped expand opportunities, reduced poverty, and offered consumers a wider range of products and services at lower prices.	Greater profits for corporate interests has combined with more competition for poorer countries to increase global economic and social inequalities.
Contributed to improvements in the quality of life, including improved education and health care.	Improvements in the quality of life have come only to elites, while globalization has accelerated environmental decline.

identified within the debate over globalization. Hyperglobalists, for example, believe that we now live in a borderless world and that the role of national governments has been reduced at the expense of multinational corporations. For their part, sceptics argue that the world has not actually changed much over the last century, that the global economy is less open and integrated now than it was before World War I, and that states remain key actors in the global system. Yet others point to the backlash against globalization, the new energy behind arguments that states should place their interests first, and the potential dangers of this approach (see King, 2017). Somewhere in between, there are those who accept that globalization is real, but argue that its effect has not been to reduce the power of states so much as to change the relationships among them, and between states and the market. We will take up some of these themes in Chapters 5 and 9.

DISCUSSION QUESTIONS

1. Is the global influence of the West overstated, or accurate?

2. How might the world look today had there not been two world wars?

3. Are the terms *North* and *South* helpful and useful in describing and understanding the global system, or are they misleading generalizations?

4. Is the American century over? Has the Chinese century begun?

5. Is glocalization a useful analytical tool?

6. Is globalization good for us or bad for us, and how far has it gone?

KEY CONCEPTS

- Bretton Woods system
- BRIC
- Cold War
- Colonialism
- End of history

- Glocalization
- Great power
- Imperialism
- Modern
- Neo-imperialism
- North

- South
- Superpower
- Third World
- West
- Westphalian system
- World war

FURTHER READING

Fink, Carole K. (2017) *Cold War: An International History*, 2nd edn (Westview Press). A study of the Cold War that goes beyond US–Soviet tensions and also looks at its impact on Africa, Asia and Latin America.

Hebron, Lui, and John F. Stack (2017) *Globalization: Debunking the Myths*, 3rd edn (Rowman & Littlefield). An assessment of the different arguments in the debate over globalization, arguing for the need to take a more considered view of its pros and cons.

Marks, Robert B. (2015) *The Origins of the Modern World: A Global and Environmental Narrative from the Fifteenth to the Twenty-First Century*, 3rd edn (Rowman & Littlefield). A broad historical survey that pays more attention than most similar studies to changes outside Europe and the environmental consequences of the modern world.

Sparke, Matthew (2013) *Introducing Globalization: Ties, Tensions, and Uneven Integration* (Chichester: John Wiley). A survey text on globalization, defining the concept and explaining how it has impacted – and been impacted by – economics, law and government.

Williams, Glyn, Paula Meth, and Katie Willis (2014) *Geographies of Developing Areas: The Global South in a Changing World* (Routledge). A study of the global South, offering useful insights into its diversity and its place in the changing world order.

Online Resources

Visit www.macmillanihe.com/McCormick-GS to access additional materials to support teaching and learning.

POPULATION AND RESOURCES

2

PREVIEW

This chapter looks at the links between population and natural resources, as well as some of the key demographic trends shaping (and being shaped by) the global system. It begins with an assessment of key population changes before focusing on the causes and effects of urbanization. It then looks at the challenges of feeding a growing population, noting that the problem is more one of quality than of quantity. The chapter finishes up with a review of how natural resources are used (and misused), focusing on the cases of energy, forests and oceans.

CONTENTS

- **The global population**
- **Feeding the world**
- **The new urban majority**
- **Natural resources**
- **Meeting our energy needs**
- **Managing forests and oceans**

HIGHLIGHTS

- The growth of the global population has accelerated in recent decades, leading to many worried conversations about the mismatch with food and other resources.

- Although the global population is growing, it is levelling out in the North (and even declining in some countries), while Asia continues to build on its numerical dominance.

- One of the most important population developments has been the shift to towns and cities; more than half the people in the world now live in an urban area.

- We currently have enough food to meet global demand, but there are problems with distribution, and climate change poses a threat to future production.

- Achieving the ideal goal of the sustainable use of natural resources has not been easy, as our mixed record with energy, forests and oceans reveals.

- Many of our natural resource problems stem from our failure to take a global approach to their use and planning.

Source: Getty Images

THE GLOBAL POPULATION

In 1798, a book titled *An Essay on the Principle of Population* was published in Britain. Written by the cleric and scholar Thomas Malthus, it quickly became a bestseller. The global population at the time was much smaller than it is today – just under one billion – but Malthus was worried by what he saw. He argued that the natural rate of population growth was geometrical (doubling every 25 years), while that of food production was arithmetical (growing at a constant rate), as a result of which he predicted that population numbers would eventually outstrip the available food supply, leading to widespread famine (Malthus, 1798). For this pessimistic view of the world he earned the sobriquet the 'dismal parson'.

But while his argument was provocative, it was poorly timed, because it came just as Britain was undergoing an industrial revolution that was transforming the economy in general and agriculture in particular: farming techniques were improving, trade was expanding, and new food producers such as Australia and Argentina were becoming part of the global economy. With food supply increasing and the quality of life improving, Malthusian ideas became less relevant.

Jumping forward to the 1960s, a renewed debate over population was sparked by the publication of another book: *The Population Bomb*, written by the American biologist Paul Ehrlich (1968). The global population had by then grown to about 3.5 billion, prompting Ehrlich to warn (somewhat like Malthus) that unless action was taken to control growth, the limits of human capability to produce food by conventional means would be reached, and millions would suffer from starvation. Ehrlich's book was also a bestseller, but again was badly timed, because it was published at the peak of the green revolution, a phenomenon dating back to the 1930s that had led to higher levels of food production – see later in this chapter.

More than 50 years later, the global population has reached 7.5 billion, and is projected to reach 9 billion by mid-century before growth starts to tail off. The kinds of famines that Malthus and Ehrlich warned of are not unknown, but they are rarely the result of a mismatch between population numbers and food supply, and are more often the result of war, conflict, and the disruption of supplies. There is more than enough food and water to meet the needs of the world's people, and more than enough space to go around, even if millions of people live in crowded urban slums and millions more squabble over access to land. Even so, the debate over the relationship between population and resources has never entirely gone away (see Harper, 2016), with worriers pointing to the shrinking gap between milestones in population growth; while it took centuries for human population to reach one billion in 1804, it took only 123 years to reach two billion, and just 13 years to grow from six billion to seven billion (see Figure 2.1). However, projections by the UN Population Fund suggest that thanks mainly to declining fertility rates, global population growth is slowing, and that the total will level off to about 11 billion by the end of the century.

Demography: The study of statistics and trends relating to population, such as birth and death rates, income, disease, age, and education.

The relationship between human numbers and food supply is just one example of the many findings of **demography** (for a brief survey, see Harper, 2018). It shows, above all, that when it comes to understanding population trends, we need to look not just at absolute numbers but at the details behind those numbers. In this regard, there are four key measures to take into consideration:

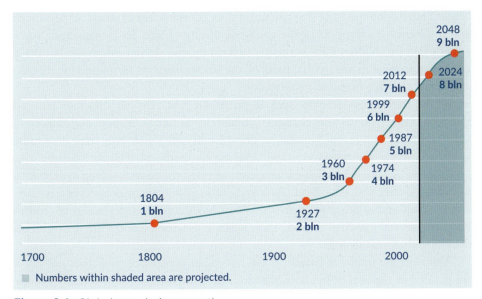

Figure 2.1: Global population growth
Source: UN Population Division (2017).

▶ *Fertility*, or the average number of children to which women give birth. Globally, this number has fallen from 4.5 to 2.5 since 1970, although it ranges as high as 5.0 or more in parts of Africa, and as low as 1.5 in China, Japan, and parts of Europe.

▶ *Mortality*, or the death rate among humans, based on a combination of infant mortality and life expectancy. Thanks to improvements in health care and nutrition (see Chapter 4), infant mortality rates have come down and life expectancy has grown, helping explain the overall growth in human population.

▶ *Replacement*, or the rate at which population numbers remain stable, which – in low mortality communities – has been calculated at 2.1 children per couple. Above that number, a population will increase, while below that number it will decrease.

▶ *Growth*, or the annual rate at which population grows. This had never been greater than 0.5 per cent prior to the industrial revolution, but it reached two per cent after World War II before tailing off to its current rate of just over one per cent. While several African states have rates as high as four per cent, several European counties have achieved **zero population growth**, while the populations of Russia, several Eastern European countries, and Japan are all declining.

Zero population growth: A rate at which fertility and mortality balance each other out so that population neither increases nor decreases.

The overall trends in population change are explained by the **demographic transition** model (see Dyson, 2010), which uses fertility and mortality rates to identify four core stages. In the first – and pre-industrial – stage, both rates are high, because problems such as disease and famine encourage people to have more children in order to ensure that as many as possible survive into adulthood. Fertility and mortality rates offset each other to result in a stable or slowly growing population. In the second stage, as we saw during the industrial revolution, a combination of improved health care, food supply, and living conditions leads to a decline in mortality rates, although

Demographic transition: A model used to explain how population numbers change in concert with changes in economic and social patterns, and improved health care.

fertility rates continue to be high because of a combination of social expectations and a slowness to respond to the changing quality of life. In Europe and North America, more children were surviving beyond infancy during this stage, but often continued to be seen as essential parts of the labour force on farms and in cities. As a result, population began to grow rapidly.

In the third stage, fertility rates begin to drop as families adjust to reduced mortality rates, and to the changes brought by better education and access to contraception. As a result, population growth tails off. The fourth stage sees more women entering the workforce and delaying motherhood. Having children also becomes an increasingly expensive proposition, given the costs involved in providing nutrition, shelter and education. As a long-term result, there is a decline both in fertility rates and in population growth. Most Northern countries are in the fourth stage and several – such as Greece, Italy, Japan, Poland and Spain – are now seeing a decline in their populations.

Although the model is based on the European experience, and does not allow for cultural or regional differences, the kinds of trends seen in 19th-century Europe are now being repeated in Asia and Africa, most parts of which are currently at the second stage of the transition, and witnessing high fertility rates and rapid growth in population. In 1960, about one-quarter of the world's population lived in the North, a share that has since fallen to 15 per cent, and that is projected by the UN to continue falling. Thanks mainly to changes in China and India, the greatest concentration of human population is today found in eastern and south-eastern Asia – see Map 2.1.

Source: Getty Images

Pedestrians negotiate the streets of Shibuya, a major commercial and business centre in Tokyo, the capital of Japan. Shibuya is one of the most densely-populated parts of Tokyo, the biggest city in the world.

More than half the world's
population lives in these countries

Map 2.1: The population dominance of Asia

FEEDING THE WORLD

If there has been one consistent concern stemming from population growth, it is the question of how long the world will be able to feed itself. At first glance, and if Malthus is to be believed, it might be logical to assume that as demand grows – not just in terms of human numbers, but also in terms of the quantity and the variety of food consumed – so supplies will come under increased pressure. But the **green revolution** led to remarkable increases in crop yields in the decades after World War II, ensuring that supplies would keep up with demand. Why is it, then, that about 815 million people went short of food in 2016 (Food and Agriculture Organization, 2017a)? The answer is that we have a problem less of supply than of distribution. We certainly need to keep increasing food production in response to growing population (Gardner, 2013), but – for now at least – the most pressing problem is that food does not always reach the people who need it, and much is wasted along the way.

High up the agenda is the matter of **food security**, which is listed in the UN Declaration of Human Rights (see Chapter 7) as a basic human right. But millions go short, in the worst cases suffering the physical ill effects of **malnutrition** in the form of stunted growth, protein deficiency, cognitive impairment, weakened immunity to disease, and ultimately death from starvation. But this is often less because of food shortages than because many are too poor to buy what they need, or because supplies are disrupted by war or natural disasters. Civil war has been the problem in Yemen, where a conflict that broke out in 2015 between Saudi- and Iranian-backed factions brought an international blockade that prevented food and medical supplies from reaching most of the country's 28 million people. Most medical facilities were closed, an outbreak of cholera in 2017 added to the misery, and even though the major cities had an abundance of food, many Yemenis could not afford to buy it (Craig, 2017).

At the other end of the scale, a new form of malnutrition has come to many countries in the form of obesity. Millions eat more than they need, live sedentary

Green revolution: The post-war growth in global food production resulting from changes in agricultural science, including the use of chemicals, improved water supply, and the development of high-yield crops.

Food security: A condition in which people have access to sufficient, safe and nutritious food.

Malnutrition: A mismatch between supply and demand in nutrition, which may mean having too little food or consuming too much.

COMPARING NORTH AND SOUTH 2

THE CHALLENGES OF POPULATION CHANGE

The broad numbers tell us that world population has been growing rapidly over the last century, and that it will continue growing for several more decades before it starts to tail off. But these numbers miss many of the nuances in rates of growth, fertility, and replacement, a closer examination revealing some important differences in trends in the North and the South – see examples in Figure 2.2.

The concern in much of the North is less with population growth than with population *decrease*. With fewer people having children, and more people delaying parenthood, fertility rates are falling. Meanwhile, people in these countries are living longer, their median age climbing to as high as 40 or more. With populations aging and either declining or remaining static, fewer new workers are being injected into the economy, and younger workers must bear a greater burden of the costs of health care and social security for retirees.

These concerns have spilled over into debates about immigration; some worry that too many immigrants are arriving in North America and the wealthier European countries, and yet the most realistic option for significantly expanding their work forces lies with immigration. Without more babies or immigrants, argue Kassam et al (2015), Europe faces a 'population disaster'. Otherwise, the only options are to increase worker productivity, raise the age of retirement, or require workers to shoulder more of the burden for paying for their own retirement.

In the South, meanwhile, it is the opposite problem: high fertility rates have combined with falling mortality rates to generate high population growth. The conversations are less about how to look after older people than about how to make the kinds of investments in job creation, education, health care, shelter, clean water, food supply, and infrastructure that are needed to keep up with demand. The mixed record is reflected in the problems of slums, congested streets, crime, and inadequate water quality and sanitation found in many Southern cities.

In few places are the pressures greater than in China and India, the two most populous countries in the world. India is projected to overtake China in the next few years, reaching almost two billion before its numbers start to decline after 2050. Considerable growth is also expected in Africa, where many countries – including some of the world's poorest – have high fertility rates. The changes are happening fast: your author was raised in Kenya at a time when the population of the country was about 12 million, and the population of the capital city of Nairobi was about 500,000. By the 1980s, Kenya had the fastest population growth rate in the world (it became the first country to cross the four per cent mark), and there are today more than 50 million Kenyans. Nigeria, meanwhile, is projected to overtake the United States in 2050 to become the world's third most populous country.

lifestyles, and gain weight (genetics and metabolism play a role as well), opening them up to a greater risk of high blood pressure, joint problems, heart disease, diabetes, cancer, and early death. This happens not just in the North but also in several Southern states, particularly in cities. According to estimates from the World Health Organization (2017), the rate of obesity worldwide tripled between 1975 and 2016, leaving about 650 million adults (13 per cent of the total) obese, as well as millions of children. Rates were highest in several Pacific island states (40–50 per cent of the adult population),

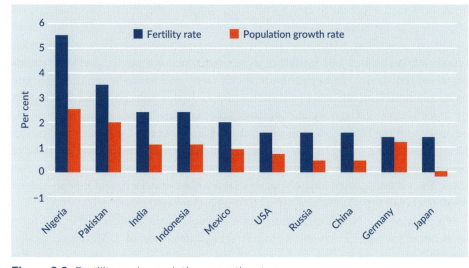

Figure 2.2: Fertility and population growth rates
Source: World Bank Economic Indicators (2018). Figures are for 2016.

as well as several Middle Eastern countries (including Saudi Arabia and Libya), and the United States, Australia, Britain, Mexico, and South Africa (26–33 per cent). The least obese countries include most of sub-Saharan Africa as well as most of south and Southeast Asia, all of which have rates of less than seven per cent.

Another factor in food supply is waste, which happens at every stage of the food production process, from growing to processing, distribution and final consumption. In several wealthier countries, as much as 40 per cent of the food that people buy to eat in restaurants or at home might be thrown away, while the UN's Food and Agriculture Organization (FAO) estimates that about one-third of all the food produced for human consumption is lost or wasted each year; this amounts to 175kg (385 pounds) per person. Figure 2.3 reveals that losses are greatest at every stage in much of the North, but that while there are large losses during production and processing in sub-Saharan Africa, India, China and south-east Asia, consumers in these regions are less wasteful.

Figure 2.3: Food losses around the world
Source: Gustavsson et al. (2012).

A final factor to bear in mind with food supply is the impact of chemicals on improving and guaranteeing our food supplies. The green revolution may have produced astonishing results, but this was in large part because chemical pesticides, fungicides, herbicides and fertilizers were used more intensively, and new strains of wheat, corn, rice, and other basic foods were engineered to yield bigger and more predictable levels of production. Although this was good for the profits of agrochemical companies and of large, mechanized farms, it was bad for the environment, put more chemicals into our food, and was bad for smaller and poorer farmers. Modern farming techniques are also often inefficient in terms of the balance between energy expended in production and calories produced in food (because so much food is transported long distances to reach the consumer), and they also result in more chemical pollution run-off into rivers and groundwater.

In parts of the North there has been a reaction to these problems in the form of support for organic (chemical-free) farming, a rejection of GMOs (genetically-modified organisms, known to their most ardent critics as Frankenfoods), and the popularity of farm-to-table restaurants that champion small farmers, as well as fresh and local ingredients. But rules on organic foods and farm-to-table food are often vague, the science of the effect of GMOs is contested, and none of these developments has much to offer farmers in poorer parts of the world, where simple survival denies them the luxury of the kinds of choices being made by producers and consumers in the North.

The distinction between North and South matters little when it comes to the problems now posed by climate change. With its reliance on chemicals and mass production, and a desire to keep consumers happy, modern farming has resulted in a growth in the output of two key greenhouse gases: carbon dioxide is a by-product of the use of fertilizers, and of the storage and transport of agricultural products, while methane is produced by flatulent livestock and by rice paddies. One estimate (Vermeulen et al., 2012) suggests that as much as 20–30 per cent of global greenhouse gas emissions could now be coming from agriculture.

If agriculture contributes to climate change, it will also likely suffer many of the effects. As temperatures rise, crop-growing patterns might change, farmers might be subject to more serious droughts and flooding, and they might have to change the crops they grow in order to adapt. We have already proven our ability to produce new strains of crops, and science could develop new strains with improved heat tolerance, but much of what might or might not happen is still open to speculation. The Food and Agriculture Organization (2016a) warns that smallholders are likely to feel the effects most seriously, which means that food production will be hardest hit in countries that already have the lowest levels of food security. Food prices might rise, yields might fall, efforts to reduce hunger and poverty might be undermined, and the lives of millions of rural people who depend on agriculture for their livelihoods might be impacted, potentially creating greater numbers of environmental migrants and refugees – see Chapter 11.

THE NEW URBAN MAJORITY

At some time in 2007, according to UN research, a child was born somewhere in the world who nudged the number of people living in towns and cities above those living in rural areas for the first time in human history – see Figure 2.4. After

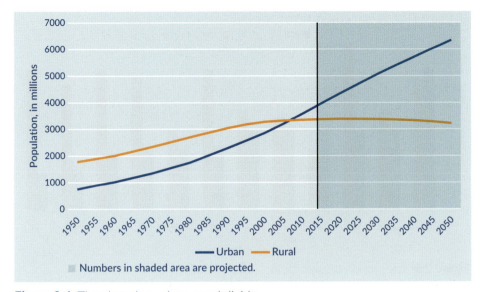

Figure 2.4: The changing urban–rural divide
Source: UN Population Division (2014).

millennia in which most people had lived directly off the land, making their homes in isolated shelters or in villages and hamlets, they had finally been overtaken in number by their urban peers. The switch had been a long time coming, its seeds sown with the industrial revolution, when the rise of factories and mass production drew people from the rural areas of Europe and North America into expanding towns and cities. But even as late as 1960, about two-thirds of humans still lived in rural areas, because industrialization had not yet taken hold in most of the South. Then new industry, improvements in health care, and population growth began to feed off each other in Asia, Africa and Latin America, whose towns and cities began to follow the same growth patterns as their Northern predecessors. By 2050, the urban–rural ratio is expected to the opposite of the number in 1960, with two-thirds of the world population living in towns and cities.

There is little consistency in the definition of the term *urban*, which might be a settlement of a few thousand people or one of millions of people, depending on which government is doing the defining. Nonetheless, UN data reveal some startling developments, as reflected – for example – in the numbers for the world's largest cities. In the 1950s, those cities were almost all in the North, and only two could be classified as a **megacity**: New York and Tokyo, each with about 12 million people. Today there are 28 megacities – all but six of them in the South – and by 2030 there are projected to be 41 (UN Population Division, 2014). The biggest changes have come in Asia and Latin America (see examples in Figure 2.5), but Africa is expected to catch up, with one projection (Hoornweg and Pope, 2014) suggesting that the biggest cities in the world in 2100 will be Lagos in Nigeria and Kinshasa in the Democratic Republic of Congo, each with more than 80 million people. Meanwhile, today's biggest city – Tokyo – will have shrunk to 25 million and fallen to 28th on the global ranking. Only two other Northern cities – New York and Los Angeles – will still be in the top 50.

Megacity: A city with a population of at least ten million people. The list has been growing, and is today topped by Tokyo, Delhi, Shanghai, Mexico City, and Sao Paulo.

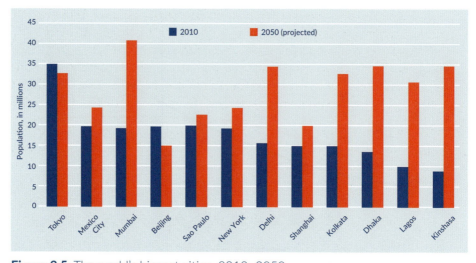

Figure 2.5: The world's biggest cities, 2010–2050
Source: Hoornweg and Pope (2014).

Although cities have grown in part because people have chased the opportunities they offer, the quality of urban life varies. On the one hand, cities provide access to a variety of jobs, schools, hospitals, consumer goods, business opportunities, entertainment, and services, a relatively high standard of living, advanced communication systems, public transport, improved opportunities to engage in civic life, and easier connections to other cities and other parts of the world. On the other hand, many have become nightmares of congestion, the lives of their residents often made worse by crime and pollution, and the distinctions between wealth and poverty clearly evident in the proximity of rich and poor neighbourhoods, and the problem of homelessness. In the fastest-growing cities of the South, and even some in the North, planners have been unable to keep up with the demand for good transport, clean water, and reliable services (Webster and Burke, 2012).

In spite of this mixed record, cities – points out Glaeser (2012:1) – have throughout history been the engines of growth and innovation. In the North, he argues, they have 'survived the tumultuous end of the industrial age and are now wealthier, healthier, and more alluring than ever', while those in the South 'are expanding enormously because urban density provides the clearest path from poverty to prosperity'. Looking at their global impact, the growth of cities and rise of the urban majority have changed the world in many different ways:

▶ Politically, the focus of power is shaped increasingly by the needs, priorities and values of urban residents. Living closer to one another and to the seats of government, they are more motivated to participate in the political process and to use multiple channels for political engagement. Such has been the dominance of cities that it has often led to resentment in rural areas: at least part of the explanation for the recent turn against mainstream political parties in Europe and the United States, for example, stems from a sense among rural voters that they are being overlooked.

▶ Economically, cities swallow up a bigger share of spending (although they also produce a bigger share of government revenues), and they consume more food and energy as well. The cost of living is also higher in cities, because more people are chasing a smaller area of property in which to live or from which to run a business. Differences in wealth and income are evident in the division of most cities into wealthier and poorer neighbourhoods. High prices can combine with congestion to encourage more urban dwellers to move to the suburbs, or even nearby towns, expanding the economic footprint of a city.

▶ Environmentally, cities create more pollution and waste, and some have become so big that they can even impact local weather patterns; they are warmer than the rural areas that surround them, creating heat islands that both radiate more heat back into the atmosphere and generate more precipitation. They also produce more waste, which must either be placed in landfill or recycled, and they create more polluted run-off into rivers and groundwater.

▶ Socially, cities have changed the way in which people relate to one another; they interact with many more other people, which can be good, but the transience of their populations can lead to a decline in the sense of community, encouraging a sense of isolation. City living can also mean higher rates of crime, increased exposure to communicable diseases, and higher mortality as a result of the higher incidences of heart disease and cancer. Urban residents are also likely to be unhealthier as a result of eating more processed or fast food, and getting less exercise.

In summary, cities have changed the relationships among people, greatly influencing the way that they see the world around them. In few ways have urban changes impacted the global system so dramatically as through the rise of the global city – see Global and Local 2.

NATURAL RESOURCES

The mismatch between food supply and population growth is just one example of a broader set of concerns about the consumption of **natural resources**: do we have enough clean water, clean air, energy, minerals, and land to meet the needs of a growing population? As with food, the answer varies from one resource to another, and from one part of the world to another, according to a combination of political, economic and natural circumstances: resources are not always available in the right form, in the right place, and at the right time, and the problems created by imbalances in supply and demand have been compounded by poor management decisions and a failure always to keep up with changing needs. Particularly since the industrial revolution, and in the wake of the rise in human population numbers, the demand for natural resources has grown, but we have not yet learned the skill of managing them sustainably (see Chiras and Reganold, 2009).

> **Natural resources**: Materials or commodities found naturally on earth that have value to humans and other living organisms, including land, food, water, plants, animals, soil, minerals, fuels, and timber.

Part of the problem stems from patterns of ownership: most resources belong to states, which reasonably argue that they have the right to exploit them as national resources without thinking about global trends and demands. In other words, we have tended to approach resources management from a national rather than a global perspective, and have struggled to develop the kinds of universal responses to their management that would better ensure their continued supply. This is why, as we will see later in this chapter, there has been a failure to develop an effective approach to managing forests and fisheries.

GLOBAL AND LOCAL 2

THE RISE OF THE GLOBAL CITY

The effects of urbanization can be seen not just in changing population numbers, but also in the changing roles of cities. The largest among them have long been connected to their neighbouring regions and to one another, and even – in the case of imperial capitals – to the wider world, but a new phenomenon of note is the rise of the **global city** (see Sassen, 2005). These are urban centres that are not just big, but that have attractions and advantages that have helped them exert new influence over global financial, trade, and communications networks. They do not need to be national capitals; instead, they have exploited economic or geographical opportunities to place themselves at the heart of the global system. They have burgeoning economies, they are close to regions of economic growth, they are politically stable, they attract foreign investment, and their global connections have become at least as important to their residents as their connections to their home states. Leading examples of global cities include Dubai, Hong Kong, London, Mexico City, New York, Shanghai, and Tokyo (see Kotkin, 2014).

Source: Getty Images

Most have seen their character changed by the arrival of visitors from all over the world: some doing business, some looking for work, and some just observing as tourists. Many such cities have become homogenized along the way, losing some of their history and personality in the wake of global pressures, even to the extent that they sometimes look the same as one another. Few have gone as far as Dubai (pictured), the capital of the emirate of the same name, which is part of the United Arab Emirates. Although long an important port, it was relatively provincial until it began to grow in the 1980s on the back of international trade and oil revenues. It is today one of the biggest and most expensive cities in the Middle East, a major transport and business hub, and famous for its ambitious architecture and luxury hotels.

But consider this critical assessment of Dubai by Brook (2013: 6):

Whitewashing away its local traditions by speaking English rather than Arabic, shopping in malls rather than souks, selling pork in its supermarkets, and pouring drinks in its hotels, it is a city where the traditions of the Arab world have been intentionally muted to make way for a placeless, tasteless, global future.

He goes on to conclude that while the modern city of Dubai is new, the idea of Dubai is not; it is just one example of an 'instant city' that is modelled on the West and that was built in an effort to pull 'a lagging region into the modern world'. Global cities bring new wealth and influence to the regions of which they are a part, but they also stand as troubling examples of the mixed effects of the confluence of the local and the global.

Another part of the problem stems from the contrasting challenges of managing resources that are renewable and non-renewable. If managed effectively (see discussion in Chapter 11 on sustainable development), renewable resources such as timber, fisheries, cropland, and clean water will continue to meet our needs indefinitely. However, our record in managing and using them wisely has been mixed at best, as illustrated by the choices we have made with commercial energy – see the following section. When it comes to other renewable natural resources – including air, fresh water, forests, and arable land – our record has also been less than stellar. Over-use, misuse and waste have left numerous problems in their wake, including pollution, deforestation, soil erosion, mountains of garbage, and the spread of deserts.

When it comes to management, we are faced with the difficulty of working with different kinds of goods, of which three stand out:

▸ *Private goods* are those that must be bought and owned to be consumed, and whose use by one person excludes others. In other words, those who do not own or pay for them cannot use them. They include consumer goods, food, privately owned homes or road vehicles, and privately owned land, forests, and fisheries.

▸ *Public goods* are those that are accessible without direct cost to all members of a society. They include clean air, public parks, open spaces, scenic views, and national defence.

▸ *Common goods* (or **common pool resources**) are those whose qualities make it hard or impossible to control access. They include the atmosphere, the oceans, fisheries, and water aquifers.

Most decisions on private and public goods are taken by governments, business, and consumers, helped along by market forces. Together, these determine how much is made or built or grown, and where, and at what price it is made available. Decisions on most such goods are approached from a national perspective, with a tendency to exploit them as deeply and as profitably as possible, without much sense of a global approach designed to ensure their wise management and continued availability. But when it comes to common goods, the tendency has been to allow the self-interest of some users to draw more than their share (or to use the air and water as a free sink for wastes), so that they benefit while passing on the costs to other users. If all users take this approach, then the resource is depleted or degraded at the expense of all users, a phenomenon described in an influential 1968 essay by the American ecologist Garrett Hardin (1968) as the '**tragedy of the commons**'.

Hardin used the example of a pasture available for the use of all cattle farmers in a locality. As long as the numbers of cattle were controlled, all was well. But if one of the farmers decided to add one more cow to their herd, calculating that they could increase their profits at the expense of the other farmers, the problems would start: there would be too many cattle in the pasture. The other farmers might then make the same calculation in an effort to keep up with the first, and the number of cattle would further exceed the carrying capacity of the pasture. This was the tragedy, argued Hardin: 'Each man is locked into a system that compels him to increase his herd without limit – in a world that is limited. Ruin is the destination toward which

Global city: A city whose size and political/economic reach is such that it has come to exert an influence beyond the state in which it is located.

Common pool resources: Resources (such as the atmosphere and the oceans) whose size or extent makes it difficult or impossible to prevent individuals from making use of them.

Tragedy of the commons: An economic theory which argues that individual self-interest encourages the over-use of common pool resources, personal gain prevailing over the well-being of society.

all men rush, each pursuing his own best interest in a society that believes in the freedom of the commons. Freedom in a commons brings ruin to all'.

Hardin has since been criticized for being too pessimistic, and for failing to point out that few common goods are entirely unregulated. In research that was to win her the 2009 Nobel Prize in economics, Elinor Ostrom (1990) outlined the design principles that could produce stable use of common pool resources. These included the following:

- Defining clear group boundaries.

- Matching the rules governing the use of common goods to local needs and conditions.

- Ensuring that those affected by the rules could participate in modifying them.

- Making sure that the rule-making rights of community members were respected by outside authorities.

- Developing a system for effective monitoring.

- Using graduated sanctions for rule violators.

- Providing accessible means for dispute resolution.

In short, there is no particular reason why common goods or common pool resources need be degraded or over-used provided that we pursue sensible, coordinated, and collective policies. But in order to achieve this goal, we need to balance economic and environmental considerations, and individual states must work together and take a global view of how best to manage and use resources. But this is much easier said than done, because different pressures and priorities come to bear. From an economic and political perspective, resources are typically defined by their value to humans, who seek to exploit them as quickly and as inexpensively as possible as a source of wealth, profit, and power. In this view, nature is something to be reshaped for our convenience. From an environmental perspective, nature either has its own intrinsic value, whether ecological or ethical, and should either be left undisturbed as far as possible, or else should be used sustainably by exploiting resources in a manner that produces economic and social benefits while recognising ecological value and the importance of management in the interests of ensuring continued supply. As the story of our approach to energy, forests and oceans tells us, however, our track record has not been all that impressive.

MEETING OUR ENERGY NEEDS

We all need energy to cook food, provide heat and cooling, fuel our transport systems, and generate the electricity that provides lighting and that powers the appliances that most people (in the North at least, and in the urban areas of the South) take for granted, including computers, refrigerators, ovens, and televisions. Despite its obvious importance, we have taken a haphazard approach to extracting, managing and using energy, with the result that we have dug ourselves into something of a global energy hole. Before the industrial revolution, most people relied on firewood for cooking and heating, and transport was human or animal powered. When

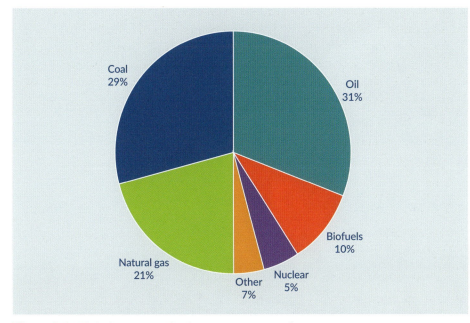

Figure 2.6: Global sources of primary energy supply
Source: International Energy Agency (2016). Numbers have been rounded out.

industrialization came, it took its earliest steps in Britain, which happened to have large and ready supplies of coal that were used to fuel the new technologies of industry (such as the steam engine, and eventually the generation of electricity). Coal was later joined by petroleum (the major source of energy for transport) and – after World War II – by natural gas (used for heating, electricity generation, and transport). The long-term result has been our reliance on **fossil fuels**, which today account for more than 80 per cent of global energy needs – see Figure 2.6.

Although they are cheap and plentiful, they come with a long list of handicaps, prime among them being that they are dirty and often dangerous to extract, transport, and use. Coal-fired power stations may be a major provider of electricity in many Northern countries, but they also a major source of the gases implicated in climate change. Supplies of fossil fuels are also unequally distributed, creating energy superpowers out of those countries that are well endowed in oil (such as Russia and Saudi Arabia) and in coal (such as China and the United States), but leaving many others reliant on imports. Their importance to global industry and economies means that the major producers of fossil fuels – particularly oil – have a strategic advantage that is often out of all proportion to their global role when measured by other resources, or by other kinds of influence. Hence the critical influence of the Middle East, and the long and deep interest shown in the region by Europeans, Americans, and Russians.

Fossil fuels are also finite in supply, and while we still have plenty to keep us going, they are steadily running out, which means that we need to think more actively about future energy plans. It would make more sense in almost every respect to switch to **renewable energy**, the sources of which tend to be cleaner, more widely available, less environmentally harmful, and in most cases infinite in supply (see Boyle, 2012).

Fossil fuels: Fuels formed from the decay of organic matter over millions of years, including coal, oil, and natural gas.

Renewable energy: Energy generated by sources that are potentially or actually infinite in supply, such as solar, wind, and hydro power.

Source: Macmillan New Zealand

An electric power station. Coal has long been a major source of energy in the North, contributing to local and international air pollution, and to climate change.

But we have been slow to invest in renewables, and they currently meet less than one-fifth of global energy needs, in spite of the numerous options available to us.

▶ The biggest investments have been made in nuclear energy, once considered the great new hope of energy production because of its low cost and potentially limitless supplies. But it has been controversial because of concerns about its links with nuclear weapons, worries about the safety of nuclear power stations, the challenges of safely storing radioactive waste, and the cost of building and maintaining nuclear power stations.

▶ The biggest source of renewable energy is biofuels or bioenergy, collective terms for organic material in the form of wood, charcoal or crop residues. Secondary sources come in the form of ethanol made from sugars and starches, and biodiesel made by combining alcohol with vegetable oil or animal fat.

▶ Hydro power is generated by the building of dams that are used to run turbines and generate electricity; solar power uses photovoltaic cells to convert the rays of the sun into electricity; wind power uses windmills to generate electricity; geothermal power uses the heat naturally produced by the earth to provide heating or cooling, or to generate electricity; and ocean power is based on exploiting incoming and outgoing tides, tidal currents, wave power, temperature differences between the surface and the depths of oceans, or salinity differences in estuaries.

Our addiction to fossil fuels is assured mainly because our industries and transport systems were designed around them, because governments and energy companies have deep investments in their continued use, and because energy use and planning is approached from a national rather than a global perspective. Change, however, is upon us: the technological adjustments needed to move us towards renewables are already under way, encouraged in part by market forces; improvements in the performance of batteries, for example, means that we are better able to store energy and to use electricity in road vehicles. Meanwhile, the problems associated with fossil fuels makes them decreasingly popular, encouraging market trends towards cleaner energy.

The North has made the biggest advances in the use of commercial renewable energy, and one of the effects has been cleaner air in most Northern cities, helped by cleaner and more efficient public transport. The sight of electric trams and railways, and of buses powered by ethanol, is increasingly common on the streets of Berlin, Dublin, Moscow, Prague and Vienna, as well as many of the major cities of China and Japan. Metro systems are also found in many European and American cities, but they are more expensive to build and to operate.

In the major cities of the South, meanwhile, rapid population growth has combined with more road traffic and the burning of coal to bring serious air pollution, particularly in China and India. One UN report (World Health Organization, 2014) estimated that about seven million people died worldwide in 2012 as a result of exposure to air pollution, the worst effects being felt in Southeast Asia and the western Pacific, where urban and industrial growth has been fastest and regulations have often been weakest. India alone accounts for 13 of the 20 most polluted cities in the world, with Delhi unenviably occupying the top spot.

Outside Southern cities, there is an energy crisis of a different kind, stemming from a heavy reliance on fuelwood. Although this is a form of renewable energy, and should be cheap and accessible if forests were managed well, demand has been growing and the rural poor are often obliged to travel further to cut down trees and vegetation. As ground cover is removed, soil erosion worsens, leading to the siltation of rivers and lakes, to floods, and to the spread of desert conditions. Few countries have witnessed more serious problems of this kind than Haiti, one of the most impoverished countries in the world. Barely one-third of Haitians have access to electricity, supplies are unpredictable, and power cuts are frequent, obliging many schools and hospitals to rely on their own generators. Outside Haiti's towns and cities, meanwhile, demand for charcoal and firewood has helped cut forest cover from about 60 per cent of the land area in the 1920s and about 30 per cent today.

The most significant energy trend in the world today is the steady move away from oil and coal to electricity. Oil and coal both have many advantages, being energy-rich and relatively easy to ship and to store, while oil can be turned into multiple refined products. But both are dirty to extract and highly pollutive, and supplies are concentrated in a few parts of the world, their production and distribution dominated by large companies such as Saudi Aramco, Sinpec of China, Exxon Mobil, and BP. By contrast, electricity can be produced almost anywhere in the world using a variety of techniques that range from large and expensive nuclear power stations to small and simple hydro-power and wind-power installations. The technological problem of moving from oil-based to electricity-based transport is being addressed, and it is now much easier – for example – to buy electric or hybrid cars than it was even just a generation ago. Political and economic challenges remain, though, in the power of fossil fuel industries and their resistance to giving up their advantages, while the technical means to generate large amounts of electricity still need development.

MANAGING FORESTS AND OCEANS

Forests are a valuable natural resource. They not only serve essential ecological functions as natural habitat, producers of oxygen, managers of water supply, and generators of clouds and rain, but they are also a renewable source of timber for construction and fuelwood. It could reasonably be argued – particularly given their role in shaping weather and offsetting climate change (see Chapter 11) – that they are a global resource, but states persist in seeing them as a domestic resource: they all sit within state boundaries, where they are subject either to public, commercial or private control. As a result, efforts to take a global approach to forestry have failed, while efforts to move states in similar directions on domestic forestry policy have had only mixed results (see Sands, 2013).

Thanks to the spread of agriculture and human settlement, the proportion of the earth's land area covered in forest has fallen from about 45 per cent in the pre-industrial era to just over 30 per cent today. This is still impressive, and the rate of forest removal has fallen in recent years as more governments have made an effort to pursue sustainable forestry practices; the European Union, for example, saw its forest cover increase from 35 per cent to 38 per cent between 1990 and 2015 (Food and Agriculture Organization, 2015). However, the story has not been so positive in sub-Saharan Africa, where the area of forest fell by 11 per cent over the same period; few countries in the region have developed sustainable management policies, and forests face the quadruple threats of growing population, unregulated removal of trees for fuel, logging to meet demand from the North (and increasingly from China), and new demands for access from mining, oil and gas companies.

At the global level, meanwhile, there are no binding international agreements on the management of forests, there has been little input into forestry policy from the major international organizations, and there is a difference of opinion between the North and the South on how to treat forests: most Northern states want them to be seen as a global resource, while most Southern states want them to seen as a national resource. Meanwhile, forests routinely continue to be cut down at a rate that exceeds their replacement, resulting in soil erosion, flooding, the siltation of rivers and dams, the extinction of animal and plant species, and the spread of desert conditions.

Few parts of the global forest landscape are as valuable, or face more substantial threats, as tropical rain forests. Found mainly in the tropical regions of South America, Africa, and Southeast Asia, they cover only about six per cent of the earth's land area but contain about 80 per cent of its vegetation. They attract heavy rainfall that makes them dense and luxuriant, and are home to a multitude of animal and plant species. They also play a key role in helping regulate global climate. However, their universal value barely factors into the calculations of governments, timber companies, miners, and poor farmers looking for farmland, who see them as a barrier to development. As a result, they are being cleared aggressively, satellite imagery suggesting that about five per cent of the world's tropical rain forests were removed between 2000 and 2012 alone (Martin, 2015). Addressing the problem means somehow blending global and local interests, along with those of governments, commerce, and local communities. This is a tall order.

As regards oceans, they are much more clearly a global resource since most of them lie outside national jurisdiction. They cover 71 per cent of the surface of the earth, are home to enormous biological wealth (including plants that produce about half of the planet's oxygen, and fisheries with high nutritional and economic value), play a key role in regulating global weather patterns and climate, are the site of valuable stocks of oil and natural gas, and are a key transport conduit. But we know remarkably little about them, and have treated them poorly. We know that they face threats from overfishing, pollution, and habitat destruction, and we have a list of sound solutions to all three problems, but we have so far failed to develop the will or the means to respond in a coordinated and effective manner.

Source: Getty Images/WaterFrame RM

We know very little about the oceans, but there is growing evidence that coral reefs – home to an abundance of biological wealth – are under threat from pollution and the effects of climate change.

Consider, for example, our failure to agree an effective means for establishing jurisdiction over the oceans. As long ago as 1609, the Dutch jurist Hugo Grotius argued that the seas had to be free, if only because they could not be occupied (quoted by Treves, 2015). This idea of the freedom of the seas was defended by the major European maritime powers, and continues today to explain the manner in which we think about the oceans. Several efforts were made between 1949 and 1982 to develop international maritime agreements, but it was not until 1994 that the UN Convention on the Law of the Sea (UNCLOS) (signed in 1982) won enough support to come into force. The effect of this agreement was to create several zones of control over seas up to 200 nautical miles (370km) from coasts, each involving different rights and obligations – see Table 2.1. Although it was a step in the right direction, UNCLOS is mainly unenforceable, because the oceans are extensive, there is no international body with the power to oversee its enforcement, and – even if there was – the resources that would need to be committed to ensuring enforcement would be substantial. As a result, humans are more or less free to exploit the oceans as they wish, including using them as a handy place to dump waste, and as a mainly unregulated source of fish.

Table 2.1: Maritime zones under international law

Type	Location	State rights
Territorial waters	Up to 12 nautical miles (22km) from coast.	State has sovereignty and jurisdiction.
Exclusive Economic Zone	Up to 200 nautical miles (370km) from coast, regardless of depth.	State controls economic resources, including fisheries, mining, and oil or gas exploration.
Continental shelf	Up to 200 nautical miles (370km) from coast, if water is relatively shallow.	Once claimed, states have sovereign rights over resources on the shelf.
High seas	Outside territorial waters.	None.
International sea bed	Outside territorial waters.	None. Resources must be treated as global common heritage, and used only for peaceful purposes.

The consequences are reflected in global trends on fisheries: the global fish catch grew by a factor of more than 800 per cent between 1950 and 2014 (Food and Agriculture Organization, 2016b), but the number of sustainable fisheries has fallen from 90 per cent to just over 70 per cent of the total. The costs of unsustainable fishing are illustrated by the tribulations of the Peruvian anchovy industry (see Nielsen, 2010). The coastal seas off Peru and Chile were once the site of the biggest fishery in the world, with annual catches of anchoveta topping ten million tonnes in the 1960s. But a combination of overfishing and of changes in ocean temperature brought on by El Niño (a cycle of ocean warming that develops periodically in the Pacific) led to the collapse of the fishery in 1972. With cooler waters and more careful fishing (including avoiding the catching of immature and pregnant fish), stocks recovered, but a new cycle of overfishing and further visits by El Niño had pushed the fishery once again to the brink by 2015. Ironically, little of the catch goes to feeding humans directly (malnutrition is a significant problem among children in Peru), most of it being converted into feed for fish and livestock as far away as the United States and China.

The Peruvian problem is just one among many. In the absence of international agreements on fishing, and with improvements in technology that have allowed fishing boats to range further away from home and to fully process their catch (it can be sorted, gutted, chilled and stored without leaving the boat), more fish are being caught. Even more worryingly, more fish are being caught when they are too young and being thrown away as waste, and more marine species (such as sea turtles, porpoises, albatross, crabs, and starfish) are also being caught in the process and are dying. In short, the management of the oceans and the fisheries present us with a classic common pool resource problem, and we have so far failed to address it effectively.

DISCUSSION QUESTIONS

1. Should we be worried about the global rate of population growth?
2. Is the demographic transition model a useful way of thinking about population trends in the South?
3. What can we do to reduce food waste?
4. What are the likely political, economic and social effects of urbanization?
5. What would it take to move us off our global dependence on fossil fuels?
6. Does the North have an obligation – whether strategic, economic, environmental, or moral – to help tropical countries better protect and manage their forests?

KEY CONCEPTS

- Common pool resources
- Demographic transition
- Demography
- Food security
- Fossil fuels
- Global city
- Green revolution
- Malnutrition
- Megacity
- Natural resources
- Renewable energy
- Tragedy of the commons
- Zero population growth

USEFUL WEBSITES

Food and Agriculture Organization of the UN at http://www.fao.org

International Energy Agency at https://www.iea.org

UN Convention on the Law of the Sea at http://www.un.org/depts/los

United Nations Population Fund at https://www.unfpa.org

FURTHER READING

Balliett, James Fargo (2010) *Forests* and *Oceans* (Routledge). Two brief survey books by the same author in a five-part series on separate environments, each providing scientific background, offering cases from around the world, and discussing human impact.

Gardner, Brian (2013) *Global Food Futures: Feeding the World in 2050* (Bloomsbury). An assessment of current food production patterns, speculating on how matters will evolve over the next few decades.

Glaeser, Edward (2012) *Triumph of the City: How Urban Spaces Make us Human* (Pan). A compelling and readable analysis of the past and the possible future of cities.

Harper, Sarah (2016) *How Population Change will Transform Our World* (Oxford University Press). An assessment of the likely changes in global population, taking into account fertility, mortality, and migration.

Kuzemko, Caroline, Andreas Goldthau, and Michael F. Keating (2015) *The Global Energy Challenge: Environment, Development and Security* (Palgrave). A general survey of the global energy picture, including details on the environmental implications.

Online Resources

Visit www.macmillanihe.com/McCormick-GS to access additional materials to support teaching and learning.

IDENTITY
AND CULTURE

3

PREVIEW

The keyword for this chapter is *identity*, meaning the qualities that determine who we are and what makes us distinctive. The chapter begins with a discussion of the meaning of identity generally, and of the particular place of national identity in global studies. It then looks in turn at culture, race, ethnicity, and religion, beginning with a discussion of the difficulties in defining most of these terms before moving on to a discussion of the different contexts within which they are used. In each case, it reviews the impact of these concepts on global consciousness and global issues.

HIGHLIGHTS

▸ Identity plays a key role in shaping our view of the world, but it is driven by multiple influences, all of which are undergoing change as a result of globalization.

▸ One of the key tensions in identity concerns the conflicting ideas of patriotism and cosmopolitanism.

▸ While culture is hard to define, it is clear that separate cultural identities are increasingly challenged by multiculturalism and the idea of a global culture.

▸ Opinion is divided on the effects of globalization on identity and culture.

▸ The idea of race is important but contested, while the terms *culture* and *ethnicity* are often (and confusingly) used interchangeably.

▸ The spread of religion has long been tied to globalization, a phenomenon that continues to be seen today in the tensions between Islam and Christianity.

Source: ©Royalty-Free/Corbis

IDENTITY AND WORLDVIEW

We are all members of a global human community, and yet few of us actively think of ourselves as such, or as joined by a common experience or sense of togetherness. Instead, we usually think of ourselves as different from one another, moving within our own circles, rarely connecting outside those circles, and having our own sense of **identity**: the qualities that make us who we are, or think we are. These include objective and biological matters of sex and age, and more subjective sociological factors, such as the social class to which we belong, the language we speak, where we were born, where we have lived, the kind of job we do, and so on; see Figure 3.1.

Identity is, in turn, a key influence on our **worldview**, or how we see the world and our place in the world. This is shaped by the experiences, ideas, assumptions, knowledge and biases that we employ when we consider the world we know from direct experience, and the world we have experienced only indirectly. The more we travel, the more we keep up with the news, the more we think about the wider world, and the more we experience people outside our own groups, the wider (usually) will be our worldview and the more we can rely on our own experiences and conclusions. The less we do any of this, the more limited our worldview is likely to be, and the more we will rely on trusted sources or the philosophies of the groups to which we belong to shape how we think. This is why worldviews are often conditioned by modifying adjectives, such as *Islamic*, *Western*, *Russian*, *ecological*, or *feminist*.

As globalization exposes us to new ideas and experiences, as well as new challenges, we can respond in one of three ways:

▶ We can see globalization as a threat to our identity, and opt to associate ourselves more forcefully with the comfortable and the familiar, including culture, race, ethnicity, and religion.

▶ We can see globalization as an opportunity, regard exposure to new cultures and experiences as positive and enriching, enjoy the diversity of the human community, and work to understand what we have in common while being open to the new and the different.

▶ We can recognize the co-existence of multiple identities, and instead of seeing globalization as either a threat or an opportunity, we can take the global view while also retaining our association with the local.

Identity: A concept of self based on attributes that range from age and sex to ethnicity, culture, gender, place of birth, job, and language.

Worldview: The manner in which each of us – as individuals or as members of like-minded groups – perceives the world.

Figure 3.1: Drivers of identity

QUALITY	FEATURES
BIOLOGY	Measurable qualities such as sex and age.
PSYCHOLOGY	Relating to matters of individuality and self-esteem.
SOCIETY	Matters of social class and the social groups to which we belong.
CULTURE	Including history, values, beliefs, and attitudes.
ETHNICITY	Ancestral, social and cultural factors.
NATIONALITY	The sense of belonging to a particular state or nation.

As we will see in Chapter 5, we live in a world of states, and when it comes to the way we define our place in the world, it is usually first and foremost in relation to the state to which we 'belong' through citizenship. When we interact with others who look, speak, or dress differently from us, one of the first questions we might ask is 'Where are you from?', by which we usually mean 'Which country are you from?'. What we expect to hear, based on our initial assumptions, is that they are not from another part of our home country, but from another country altogether.

Although we will see that the term *nation* has a specific meaning, and that most people mistakenly use it to describe a state (or a country), **national identity** has come be the one form of identity that most clearly stands between each of us and the idea of a global community. It goes beyond the legal condition of being a citizen of a state (explained in more detail in Chapter 5), and also involves an association with the values, history, reputation and even the image of the state to which we belong. When an Australian and an Indonesian meet, for example, they will almost certainly make some assumptions about each other based on what they know about their respective countries. And they will almost certainly project some of the qualities associated with their home countries. (For more on the debate about national identity, see McCrone and Bechhofer, 2015: Chapter 1.)

> **National identity**: Identification with a state or nation, as determined by a combination of language, place of birth, and citizenship.

Most people probably do not think much about their national identity until they find themselves celebrating a national holiday, talking to someone from another country, visiting another country, or seeing their home country interacting with another, whether in the form of a sporting event or a matter of foreign policy. They are then reminded of where they 'come from'. The most telling reminders of national differences – according to a survey in 14 countries (Stokes, 2017) – are language, country of birth, country of citizenship, and customs and traditions. Interestingly, missing from this list is accent, despite the fact that people from different countries

Source: AFP/Getty Images

Nigerian fans cheer their team during a qualifying match for the 2018 football World Cup. Nigeria has many ethnic and religious divisions, but its people set them aside when their national sports teams are competing in international tournaments.

that speak the same language will most readily be able to distinguish among themselves by their accents; German-speaking Austrians and Germans, for example, or English-speaking Americans and Australians.

If language is the most telling reminder of national differences, it is also the most important symbol of identity and culture. Try visiting a country whose language you cannot speak, and – unless you can find people who speak your language – you will find it a challenge to manage. Asking even trivial questions, such as the way to a hotel or a restaurant, or how to find a taxi or a bus, not only reminds us of the variety of the human community, but also stands as a barrier to connecting with the people we talk to, or the community in which they live.

Looking globally, the landscape of language is complex, one estimate suggesting that there are more than 7,000 languages divided into more than 150 families (Simons and Fennig, 2017). Figure 3.2 shows the greatest languages in terms of the number of native speakers, but it does not reflect how widely they are spoken. English may not have many native speakers compared to Chinese, but it is by far the most widely spoken language in the world, and the most popular choice as a second language. It began its rise with British colonialism, then expanded on the back of American culture, and has more recently been given a boost by the internet. It is the preferred language of diplomacy, popular culture, business, and mass communication, although there are still many people in the world (about six out of seven by most estimates) who cannot speak English.

National identity is closely tied to the concept of **patriotism**, or love of country. This can be value-based, meaning that it is driven by support for the merits and achievements of a state, or egocentric, meaning that it is driven by a personal association – a patriot loves their country simply because it is theirs (Primoratz and Pavković, 2007). In a positive sense, it can be associated with a **nationalism** based on history, achievements, and symbols, and patriots can rally around the flag in times of need, celebration, or threats to security. But there are also negatives to patriotism, which can spill over into a different kind of nationalism based on superiority regarding other states, or even hostility, reflected in the extent to which

Patriotism: Love of country, identification with country, or devotion to country, as reflected in a pride in the history, symbols and myths of that country.

Nationalism: The belief that nations have the right to determine their own destiny, to govern themselves, to have their own states, to place their interests above those of other nations, and to control movements across their borders.

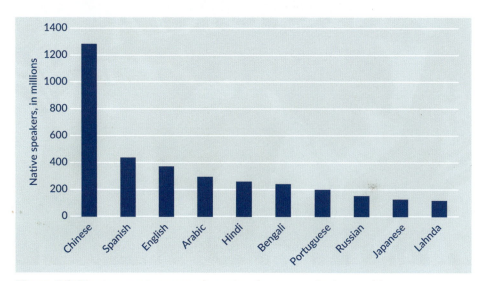

Figure 3.2: The ten most commonly spoken languages in the world
Source: Based on data in Simons and Fennig (2017). Lahnda is a group of languages spoken mainly in Pakistan.

patriotism is most actively exploited during times of international conflict or war. The 'national interest' can be conflated with political or economic interests, so that wars supposedly fought to protect a state may actually be fought to promote a political, economic or social agenda.

Levels of patriotism vary from one state to another, and are impacted by factors such as the age and diversity of a country, the legitimacy of the state, the trajectory of its history (which may sow seeds of pride or doubt, depending on how events have evolved), and the use of myths and symbols. Figure 3.3 shows some comparative data on patriotism, but the research on which it is based offers no explanations for the different figures, leaving us to speculate. The United States, for example, has a culture of patriotism: from a young age, Americans are encouraged to pledge allegiance to the national flag, to stand (with their hands on their hearts) for the national anthem, and to believe that their country is somehow the best, the freest, and the most powerful country on earth, and even that it is exceptional. Europeans, meanwhile, are more suspicious of patriotism because of its historical association with nationalism and war, a particular problem for Germans.

Not everyone is a patriot, or is comfortable with the idea of patriotism. They might agree with the rather cynical suggestion by the French philosopher Voltaire that 'to be a good patriot one must become the enemy of the rest of mankind'. The alternative to patriotism is **cosmopolitanism**, the view that local and global concerns

> **Cosmopolitanism**: Association with the world, with universal ideas, and with the belief that all humans belong to a single community that transcends state boundaries and national identities.

Figure 3.3: Comparing levels of patriotism

Source: Beauchamp (2014). Based on data in World Values Survey, 2010–14.

GLOBAL AND LOCAL 3

CAN YOU BE A CITIZEN OF THE WORLD?

The global and the local can be contrasted in the concept of citizenship. On the one hand, and as we will see in Chapter 5, this is usually defined in legal terms as the idea of belonging to a particular state (or multiple states for the small minority with more than one citizenship). On the other hand, it is often said that we can be good citizens of our local community, whether it is our place of work or the locality in which we live, which implies that we support and contribute to the smooth functioning of that community.

But since we are members of a global community of humans, can we not also be global citizens? When asked where he was from, the Greek philosopher Diogenes (c. 412–323 BCE) declared that he was a citizen of the world (*kosmopolitês*). Similarly, 3rd-century Roman and Greek Stoics argued that all humans belonged to two communities: the community of their birth, and the community of human argument and aspiration. More recently, such ideas were reflected in the Universal Declaration of Human Rights (see Chapter 7) and its focus on rights as the entitlement of all, regardless of race, gender, religion, national or social origin, or the political, jurisdictional or international status of the country or territory to which people belong.

Being a global citizen, and adopting a global identity, however, is less a legal concept than a perception (see discussion in Sterri, 2014). We cannot legally be citizens of the world for the simple and practical reason that there is no global legal authority that can issue world passports and protect the rights of world citizens, and there is no global freedom of movement or residence. But this does not mean that we cannot at least think of ourselves as global citizens if we so choose, and the opportunities to do so continue to grow with changes in the wake of globalization. A global citizen has a broad worldview, takes an interest in global matters, sees the world in global terms, and feels more of a sense of identity with the human race than with a particular state.

The only problem here is that being a global citizen means being globally aware, which in turn means having access to the kind of information and resources that can foster a sense of the place of the individual within the global community. This is mainly available only to those with the necessary education and resources, which is why there is a widespread perception that being a global citizen is associated with elites who benefit from a borderless world and have the means to travel and invest their way into buying new passports; global citizens are sometimes associated with the acronym WEIRD, standing for Western, educated, industrialized, rich and democratic (see Henrich et al., 2010). It has also been argued that global citizens sometimes find themselves able only to associate with others who are like-minded: 'Opportunities to be part of diverse, international communities are predominantly accessible [only] in larger metropolitan cities', suggests Skovgaard-Smith (2017), and those living outside those communities might be unable to develop a sense of belonging, creating a new kind of 'us versus them'.

cannot be separated or divorced, and that rather than the world being separate from the community or state in which each of us lives, it is the only community that matters. Some even suggest that we should try to think of ourselves as citizens of the world – see Global and Local 3. They argue that all humans should be treated equally, and emphasize the importance of drawing on different traditions and cultures, and of remaining open to other ways of life (see Jacob, 2006). As Beck (2006) puts it, if nationalism is based on the principle of 'either/or', then cosmopolitanism is based on the principle of 'both/and'.

UNDERSTANDING CULTURE

As we will see throughout this book, coming to grips with global studies demands that we understand numerous concepts whose meanings are contested. Few are harder to tie down than culture, a term that is typically used in an anthropological or sociological context to describe a community of people with a shared history and common values, beliefs and customs. It can be used to describe the expressions of a community in the form of art, cuisine, literature, or music, but it can also describe a set of assumptions associated with an institution or a society: a model of how it works, of what is considered normal or abnormal, and of the goals that are worth pursuing. Political culture, for example, describes the political personality of a society, reflected in the political norms and values that the community as a whole considers to be desirable and normal.

Culture is learned, and includes rituals, forms of expression, hierarchies, myths, symbols, and the sense of a shared history. Culture is often most clearly revealed in a combination of habits and taboos. Anyone who has tried living in a country other than their own, for example, will soon find themselves having to adapt to new ways of doing things, ranging from different forms of greeting to social expectations in general, and functional norms relating to shopping, travelling, and entertainment. They will also need to understand that values and habits acceptable to one culture might be unacceptable to another. For example, the Vietnamese point with the whole hand, not one finger; food is eaten throughout the Muslim world with the left hand, not the right; you are expected to arrive on time when invited to someone's home in Denmark, but to arrive late in Pakistan; in China, the number four is considered unlucky, in Japan it is nine, and in much of the English-speaking world it is thirteen.

The extent to which cultural differences are barriers to the sense of a global community is reflected in the culture shock that many people face when moving from one culture to another. As often as not, they will struggle to adapt when they find that familiar rules, habits and assumptions no longer apply. They might react by trying to integrate themselves with their new environment, or they might continue to associate with other people from their home culture, or they might hold on tightly to the features of their home culture, seeing their new environment as (at best) different or (at worst) hostile or inferior. Much will depend on the degree of the differences between the new culture and the home culture, and on the extent to which the new culture is receptive to newcomers.

Culture comes in many different forms and is found at multiple levels – see Table 3.1. Taking the broad view, we can talk of human culture, describing the beliefs and values that all humans – regardless of where they come from – have in common, and that help us understand our universal needs and capabilities. Most of us seek, for example, to live as well and as long as possible, to learn, to be inspired, to have a sense of purpose, to love, and to associate with others. Efforts to build a sense of global identity have regularly raised the proposition that in spite of all our differences – visible or not – we are all ultimately humans, and have similar aspirations.

A related idea is that of global culture, suggesting that wherever we go in the world, we can expect to have many of the same experiences, to hear many of the same ideas, to eat similar kinds of food, and to see many of the same brands, products and services for sale. To the extent that there is a global culture, it has so far been

Culture: The values, beliefs, habits, attitudes, and/or norms to which a society subscribes and responds, often unconsciously and even in the face of individual differences.

Culture shock: The discomfort that people might feel when moving to or experiencing a culture other than the one with which they are most familiar.

Global culture: Those aspects of culture (deriving mostly from the West) that have taken on global dimensions.

Table 3.1: Levels of culture

Level	Number of levels	Features
Human	1	The values and aspirations that all humans have in common.
Global	1	The experiences, norms, ideas, brands, products and services found almost everywhere in the world.
Civilizational	Less than a dozen	Broad and collective, but controversial in terms of both definition and implications.
State/ national	Nearly 200	The cultures associated with individual states, often politically motivated.
Local	Thousands	Sub-cultures that are not tied to states, some of which are accepted and others are regarded as a threat.

Western: Ideas and values associated with 'the West', which originally meant Europe but has since broadened to include all societies created and shaped by European colonization.

driven mainly by the inroads made by **Western** ideas into other parts of the world. The terms *West* and *Western* were originally used in a literal geographical sense to distinguish Europe (the Occident) from Asia and the Middle East (the Orient), but they have since taken on a wider set of political, economic and cultural implications associated with Europe, the Americas and Australasia, and distinguished from the Eastern world of India, China, Japan and southeast Asia. 'Western' ideas include the following:

▸ Democracy.

▸ Free market capitalism.

▸ Individualism.

▸ Scientific thinking, in the sense of forming testable hypotheses.

▸ Humanism, or an emphasis on human matters rather than the divine.

▸ Rationalism, meaning that actions and beliefs should be based on reason and knowledge rather than emotion or religion.

This is not to suggest that all or any of these ideas were unique to Europe (free markets, for example, emerged in many other parts of the world before the era of European expansion began), but rather that they have come to be most closely associated with European culture, which is ultimately also Western culture. Discussions about the impact of the West on global culture are frequently peppered with ideas such as **cultural imperialism**, homogenization, assimilation, Americanization, or what Prendergast (1993) describes as Coca-colonization (seeing world events through the prism of corporate profits). But while the West has long had the upper hand in global cultural change, its influence may be on the wane: as the political and economic power of the United States and Europe declines, so Asia – particularly China – is likely to exert an ever-growing influence on the world.

Cultural imperialism: The promotion and imposition of one culture on another, by a dominant power or state over one that is less powerful.

At the very least, we are likely to see less a process of cultural homogenization than one of mixing or hybridization (Nederveen Pieterse, 2015).

At another level, culture can be regarded as civilizational, if we agree with the definition of **civilization** offered by Huntington (1996:43) as 'the highest cultural grouping of people and the broadest level of cultural identity people have short of that which distinguishes humans from other species'. Civilizations have long lives, he argues, but they have no clear beginnings or endings, they have no clear-cut boundaries, and they change over time. He suggests that there are nine such civilizations: African, Buddhist, Chinese, Hindu, Islamic, Japanese, Latin American, Orthodox, and Western (see Map 3.1). But doubts about the existence and qualities of civilization abound, as exemplified by the acerbic observation credited to the Indian leader Mahatma Gandhi, who – when asked 'What do you think of Western civilization?' – is reputed to have answered 'I think it would be a good idea'.

At yet another level, we find cultures associated with states. Since the latter are political creations, state cultures are to a large extent contrived and artificial, and sometimes based on politically motivated myths and symbols. They revolve around claims of a shared history, the depth of such claims varying according to the extent to which the states are culturally homogeneous; histories are often rewritten and shaped to build a sense of unity rather than to acknowledge the differences among the citizens of the state.

Finally, and at the most focused level, we find a world divided into thousands of local cultures and sub-cultures, the precise number being impossible to compute because culture is never static, values regularly evolve, and new sub-cultures come and go. Local cultures are actually more useful than national cultures in terms of understanding what goes on within states, given that they are the most real and

Civilization: An advanced stage of human development, marked by features such as political and social organization. A synonym for *culture*, but with a broader and more collective application.

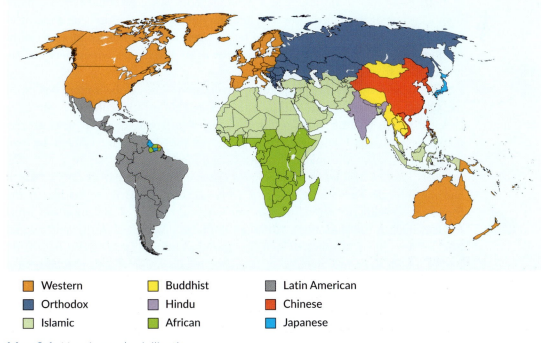

■ Western	■ Buddhist	■ Latin American
■ Orthodox	■ Hindu	■ Chinese
■ Islamic	■ African	■ Japanese

Map 3.1: Huntington's civilizations

immediate to the citizens of those states. Levels of cultural diversity range from a low in countries such as Argentina, Australia, Brazil, China, Japan, and Saudi Arabia, to a high in most sub-Saharan African countries (Gören, 2013). The contrasts are illustrated by Argentina – which is almost entirely white, Spanish-speaking and Catholic – and Nigeria, which is home to dozens of languages and ethnicities (there is no final authority on the exact number), and is divided between a Muslim north and a non-Muslim south. It has been sufficiently concerned about the effect of it divisions as to make the point of opening its national constitution with a statement that Nigerians have 'firmly and solemnly [resolved] … to live in unity and harmony as one indivisible and indissoluble sovereign nation'.

Multiculturalism:
A belief in a society made up of multiple cultures, and recognition of those cultures.

One conversation that several countries have had in recent decades concerns **multiculturalism** (or cultural pluralism), and the extent to which it is recognized, tolerated, or welcomed. The subject does not usually arise in the least culturally diverse countries, but several European countries have had troubled national debates about the extent to which multiculturalism has either failed or succeeded, the spark being the influx over recent decades of migrants from outside Europe who are visibly different from the mainstream image of a European (Chin, 2017) – see Chapter 10. While Europe has long been a region of migrants, it is usually hard to distinguish Finns and Germans and Poles from one another. But with the arrival of immigrants from Africa, the Middle East and South Asia, including many Muslims, the differences have become more visible and tensions have risen.

Some countries have recognized and celebrated the idea of multiculturalism, prime among them being Canada, which in 1988 adopted the Canadian Multiculturalism Act, acknowledging that 'multiculturalism reflects the cultural and racial diversity of Canadian society and acknowledges the freedom of all members of Canadian society to preserve, enhance and share their cultural heritage.' A contrasting view is offered by the United States, which has long pursued the melting-pot idea that immigrants should blend and that a heterogeneous society should become more homogeneous. It has failed, however, and discrimination has long been a factor in American national life, whether driven by race, religion, or ethnicity. More recently, tensions have arisen in the wake of the growth of the Latino community and of immigration from the Middle East.

The relationship between cultures, civilizations and globalization has been the subject of much debate, with questions asked about how cultures might have changed in the face of global influences, and the extent to which new stresses might have arisen. Useful reference points in the debate are offered by two books published in the mid-1990s whose arguments remain relevant today. The first was *Jihad vs. McWorld* by the political theorist Benjamin Barber (1995), which had the sub-title *Terrorism's Challenge to Democracy* but looked more broadly at the forces of consumerist capitalism (on one side) and those of religious and tribal fundamentalism (on the other). Although the term *jihad* refers to the internal and external struggle of Muslims to be believers and to inform others about their faith, Barber used it to convey the idea of dogmatic tribalism that takes a parochial view of the world and rejects modernity. He used the term *McWorld* (borrowed from the McDonald's fast food chain) to convey the idea of free markets, commercialization, secularist materialism, and cultural homogenization, all coming at the expense of independence and separate identities. The two forces, he argued, were both opposed and intertwined, both tearing apart and pulling together the world, with worrying implications for democracy and the state.

The second book was *The Clash of Civilizations and the Making of World Order* by Samuel Huntington (1996). He argued that cultures (as represented in their broadest sense by civilizations, which he defined as 'cultures writ large') were emerging as the leading sources of cohesion, disintegration and conflict in the post-Cold War world. In the pre-modern era, civilizations had little contact with one another. Then came the rise of the West during the modern era (post-1500) and a multipolar international system within which states interacted, competed and fought with each other. Then came the Cold War era, which saw the world divided between the US and its allies, the USSR and its allies, and the Third World. Finally, the end of the Cold War led to the ideological, political and economic differences among states being superseded by cultural differences.

States remained the key actors in the international system, Huntington argued, but the world's major groupings were now civilizational, and we had entered a new era in which the most dangerous and pervasive conflicts would not be between social classes or other economic groups, but between people belonging to different cultures. Culture would be a unifying force in the sense that it would bring together societies united by cultural kinship, but it would be a divisive force in that conflicts would now be civilizational. Huntington argued that these civilizations had contradictory worldviews among which there was little room for compromise, and that while economic conflicts could be bargained away, there were no easy solutions to cultural conflicts. As globalization proceeded, he wrote, tensions would intensify.

Huntington's supporters suggested that he foresaw the tensions that were to arise between the West and Islamic extremism, although whether those tensions are cultural or political in origin remains a matter of debate. His critics, meanwhile, dismissed his generalizations, particularly those he made about Islam and the tensions that he predicted would worsen between Islam and the West. In an article titled *The Clash of Ignorance*, the scholar Edward Said (2001) referred to 'unedifying' labels such as Islam and the West, arguing that 'they mislead and confuse the mind, which is trying to make sense of a disorderly reality that won't be pigeonholed or strapped down as easily as all that'. Other critics rejected Huntington's idea about distinct and monolithic civilizations, and yet others challenged the evidence of clashes between them, and pointed to the problem of differences and tensions within each such civilization, and to evidence that there were actually many points of similarity across civilizational lines.

> **Race**: A grouping or classification of humans based on their heritable physical differences, such as skin colour and facial features.

ACCOUNTING FOR RACE AND ETHNICITY

Just as global studies must account for culture and the differences it imposes on the human population, so it must account for two even more deeply contested concepts: **race** and **ethnicity** (Kivisto and Kroll, 2012). Race is the more troubling of the two because of questions about how the concept is understood and used. Many would argue that is a social construct (a concept that is created and cultivated by society), and there is a high degree of scholarly agreement that it is a biological myth but that it has very real political and social consequences.

> **Ethnicity**: A group of people who identify with one another based on a shared ancestral, social, and cultural background, often determined by a common language.

In its 1950 Statement on Race, issued with an eye to the manner in which racial discrimination had been a foundation for Nazism, the UN Educational, Scientific and Cultural Organization (UNESCO) argued that race was 'not so much a biological phenomenon as a social myth', and that there were so many misconceptions about its meaning that 'it would be better when speaking of human races to drop the term "race" altogether and speak of ethnic groups' (UN Educational Scientific and Cultural Organization, 1969). Building on a habit that subsequently emerged in continental Europe of rejecting race as an analytical category, the European Union in 2000 adopted its Racial Equality Directive, the preamble to which said 'The European Union rejects theories which attempt to determine the existence of separate human races'.

The 'myth of race' is discussed by Sussman (2014), who argues that the belief in the existence of races has become so embedded in culture that most people assume it to be true, and believe that different races can be identified according to physical features such as skin colour and facial anatomy. He also points out that views about race have gone further than the merely physical, with many people making harmful assumptions about members of other races, including that they have different levels of intelligence, contrasting work ethics and abilities, different approaches to family cohesion, and even differences in brain size. 'We have learned', he cynically concludes, 'that races are structured in a hierarchical order and that some races are better than others'. In short, the physical differences among humans have spilled over into psychological and cultural differences, and race is very much part of the discussion about 'us' and 'them', both within countries and at the global level; see Comparing North and South 3.

Source: Getty Images

Children of different races at a school in the United States. Even though race is widely considered to be no more than a social construct, it is still widely used as part of the definition of identity.

COMPARING NORTH AND SOUTH 3

US VERSUS THEM: RACE, ETHNICITY, AND PREJUDICE

Even if race and ethnicity are often seen as social constructs, this does not mean that they are illusory, and they are both real to many people, finding expression – for example – in the prejudice that many show towards others based primarily on their physical differences. We may all be part of a global community of humans, but most of us cannot help but make a distinction between those who look like us and those who do not, and we often change our behaviour and assumptions accordingly. The responses range between a well-meaning (but still conscious) effort to ignore the differences, a conscious or sub-conscious habit of associating and congregating mainly with others who look and act like ourselves, and – at worst – a mix of fear and dislike towards those who look or act differently, resulting in different degrees of discrimination. In the most extreme cases, discrimination is based on pseudo-scientific ideas about the relative worth and substance of different cultures, ethnicities, races, or religions.

Other North and South features in this book contrast the differences between countries of the North and South, but discrimination is a global phenomenon. Whether based on race, ethnicity, culture, religion or some other factor, it typically stems from a complex mix of fear, superiority, ignorance, historical myth, and the teachings of different societies and cultures (see discussion in Garner, 2017). We know all too well of racism directed by white Europeans and Americans against ethnic minorities, but many in China and Japan are also discriminatory towards people from other parts of the world, and Indians are generally more receptive towards white people than black Africans (Stevens, 2017), and ethnic discrimination has been behind numerous conflicts in many African states (spilling over, in the worst cases, into cases of **genocide** in Burundi, the Central African Republic, Rwanda, Somalia, and Zimbabwe).

Concerns about discrimination were the motivation behind the 1965 Convention on the Elimination of All Forms of Racial Discrimination, which came into force in 1969. This obliged signatories to 'condemn racial discrimination and undertake to pursue by all appropriate means and without delay a policy of eliminating racial discrimination in all its forms and promoting understanding among all races'. This was a noble goal, to be sure, but there was little sign of an improvement in the global situation, prompting the UN to convene the 2001 World Conference against Racism, held in Durban, South Africa, and resulting in the adoption of a Durban Declaration and Programme of Action.

Follow-up conferences were held in 2009 and 2011 in Geneva and New York, both of which were boycotted by several countries, much of the controversy at all three meetings arising from divisions over efforts to equate Zionism (belief in the existence of a Jewish state) with racism. The Durban Declaration noted the persistence of racism, as well as outlining its sources, listing its main victims (Africans, migrants, refugees, and indigenous peoples were identified as particular targets), and made numerous recommendations on how racism might be addressed, including changes in national laws, improved education, improved economic opportunities for victims of racism, and improved protection of human rights.

Race may be a social construct, but for many people this does not matter: they still assess each other on the basis of the visible physical differences that have routinely been considered to be indicators of race. Governments do this as well, many of them classifying their populations according to race, a habit which – rather than going away – has been increasingly fine-tuned. In many government and educational institutions

> **Genocide**:
> Intentional efforts to wholly or partially destroy a group of people because of their ethnicity, race or religion.

in the United States, for example, multiple racial categories are recognized, including a distinction between 'Hispanic' and 'non-Hispanic white'. (A related inconsistency is to be found in the use of the terms *Hispanic* and *Latino* as interchangeable, when *Hispanic* actually refers to people from Spanish-speaking countries while *Latino* includes those from Portuguese-speaking countries such as Brazil.) The US Census Bureau (2017) continues to gather information on race, even if it qualifies this by stating on its website that 'the racial categories included in the census questionnaire generally reflect a social definition of race recognized in this country and not an attempt to define race biologically, anthropologically, or genetically'.

A more neutral term that is related to race is ethnicity, but once again we come up against the problem of contested definitions. Not only does it overlap with (and sometimes appear identical to) culture, but it is closely tied to the idea of *nation* discussed in Chapter 5, and can also be used as code for what many would consider race. The UK census, for example, has a section on 'ethnicity' that categorizes people as – among others – white, black or white African, black or white Caribbean, Asian, Arab, or mixed. These are clearly racial categories. Meanwhile, a search of online dictionaries will find many offering a definition of ethnicity in which it is described as a synonym for race. Perhaps the best way to understand the differences is to think of *culture* as combining the anthropological and the sociological, while *ethnicity* and *nation* hover somewhere between the sociological and the political.

The difficulties of reaching an agreement on meaning are illustrated by the effort made by Fenton (2010) to define ethnicity, which takes him through a complex discussion about sociological realities versus social and intellectual constructions, and about the distinction between the imagined and the imaginary. But like many social scientists, he fails to actually define the term *ethnicity* (in a book about the topic), suggesting instead that 'ethnicity refers to the social construction of descent and culture', and that people can and do elaborate an idea of community based on shared cultures and ancestries 'despite the fact that claims to sharing descent and culture are decidedly questionable'. The implication, then, is that ethnicity – like race – is largely imagined.

That may be so, but the term is widely claimed as a point of distinction by people of different ethnic origins, and used in several contexts that show how real it seems to many people. For example, we often talk about eating at 'ethnic' restaurants, the implication being that the food they serve is based on cuisines that are distinct from that of the majority population of a community. We also talk about 'ethnic' minorities, implying that people who look different or who have different cultural heritages are different from the majority. Americans are often hyphenated, based on an inconsistent combination of cultural and ethnic backgrounds: hence African-Americans, Native-Americans, Asian-Americans, Polish-Americans, and German-Americans. We also worry about **ethnocentrism**, and one of the most heinous of war crimes is **ethnic cleansing**. Examples of the latter include the forced removal of different minorities from new states emerging from the break-up of Yugoslavia in the 1990s, or the Burmese removal of the Muslim Rohingya minority in 2017; see Chapter 10.

The world consists of thousands of different ethnicities, but – given the uncertainties about the meaning of the term – it is impossible to say how many for sure. The difficulties are illustrated by the case of Europe, where there are clearly differences

Ethnocentrism: Viewing or judging other cultures from the perspective of the values and norms of one's own.

Ethnic cleansing: The systematic and usually forced removal of an ethnic minority from the territory of another ethnic group with a view to achieving ethnic homogenization.

between Italians, Greeks, Bulgarians, Swedes, and Germans, but the terms *nation* and *ethnicity* are often used interchangeably, and there is no agreement on just how many different nations or ethnicities are found in the region. For example, Minahan (2000) lists 143 nations, or 106 if European Russia is excluded, while Pan and Pfeil (2004) list 160 nations in the European Union (EU) alone. If language is one of the clearest indicators of national or ethnic differences, then the EU states alone speak more than 40 different languages, of which 24 are considered official in the sense that all EU documents must be translated into these languages, simultaneous translation must be offered if requested at EU meetings, and EU citizens have the right to be heard by EU institutions in these languages.

At the same time, regional integration in the European Union has fostered a sense of belonging to Europe that has helped move at least some Europeans away from an exclusive sense of identity with individual states, cultures, or ethnicities. Favell (2008) describes them as 'Eurostars' (borrowing from the name of the high speed trains that link several European cities), referring to people who have taken up, physically or culturally, the new opportunities for mobility offered by integration. One of the more successful EU policies is the Erasmus programme that has provided funding support for university students to study in different EU countries. Members of the so-called Erasmus generation are multilingual, often move permanently to another EU country, and have a strong sense of identification with Europe alongside (or even perhaps in place of) their identification with their home state.

THE CHANGING PLACE OF RELIGION

Following the debates about the meaning of the terms used so far in this chapter, it might be hoped that **religion** – which lies at the heart of both culture and identity – could be relatively easily defined and understood as a belief in superhuman controlling forces. But religion can mean different things to different people, there are few consistencies from one religion to another, and one scholar of comparative religions (Sharpe, 1983) once made the point that 'to *define* religion is ... far less important than to possess the ability to *recognize* it when we come across it'. This brings to mind the argument made before the US Supreme Court by Justice Potter Stewart in 1964 when, in a discussion about pornography, he argued that he would not attempt to define pornography, 'and perhaps I could never succeed in intelligibly doing so. But I know it when I see it' (quoted in Nongbri, 2013, Chapter 1 of which has a useful discussion on the meaning of religion).

However we understand it, religion is an important part of identity for many people, and is tightly connected to culture and worldview. The levels of importance vary, though: according to a Pew Global Attitudes survey (see Figure 3.4), the number who say that religion is important in their lives varies from a high of 98 per cent in Ethiopia to a low of three per cent in China, with a global median figure of 55 per cent. Broadly speaking, religion tends to be more important in poorer countries than in richer ones, and adherence to organized religion is growing fastest in Africa, which is overall the poorest continent.

At first glance, the global religious landscape – unlike the global cultural or ethnic landscapes – looks relatively uncluttered. Among them, Christianity, Islam, Hinduism, and Buddhism are followed by just over three-quarters of the global

Religion: Belief in – and worship of – a superhuman controlling power, usually in the form of a deity or deities, and driven by a combination of beliefs, myths and rituals.

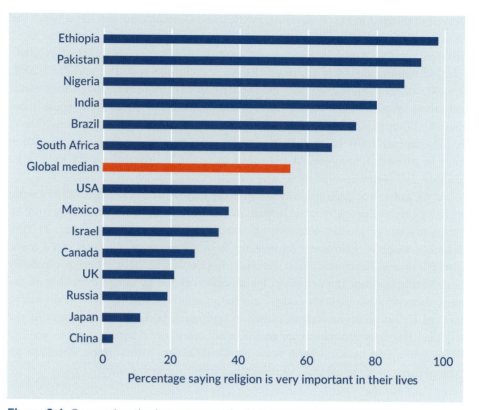

Figure 3.4: Comparing the importance of religion
Source: Pew Research Center (2015b).

population; see Figure 3.5 and Map 3.2. Meanwhile, about 16 per cent of humans have no religious affiliation, while the balance of seven per cent follow numerous smaller religions, such as Judaism, Shinto, Jainism, Sikhism, Taoism, Tenrikyo, and a host of African and Asian folk religions. Most people live in countries in which there is a majority religion, such as the nearly 50 countries where Islam dominates, or the nearly 40 where Christians are in the majority. According to a study by the Pew Research Centre (2017), the percentage share of Christians, Muslims and Hindus is expected to rise (with Muslims reaching near parity with Christians by 2060), while the relative number of Buddhists, members of smaller religions, and those without religious belief is expected to decrease.

But religions are divided within themselves, and come in many different forms with different ideas about the nature of the object of belief. Some (such as Christianity and Islam) believe in only one deity, others (such as Hinduism) in the possibility of more than one, and yet others (such as Buddhism) are more ambiguous about the existence of gods. There are also different ideas about the role of religion in public and personal life, and about its relationship with other aspects of life, including politics and society. Also, the depth of religious belief varies, and there are many people in countries classified as Christian, for example, who no longer believe, or who attend church only for baptisms, weddings, and funerals. **Secularism** has been central to European ideas since the Enlightenment, and there is even evidence now of a move away from religion in the United States, where it has long played a central role in politics and society. But Nongbri (2013) argues that the idea of religion

Secularism: A belief in the separation of religion and the state.

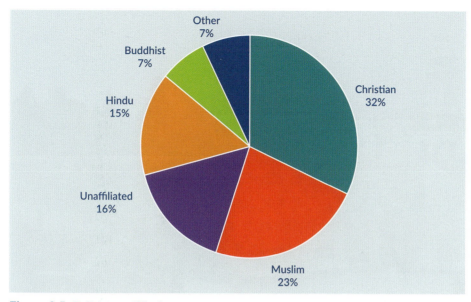

Figure 3.5: Religious affiliations
Source: Pew Research Center (2012). Figures are for 2010, and are rounded out.

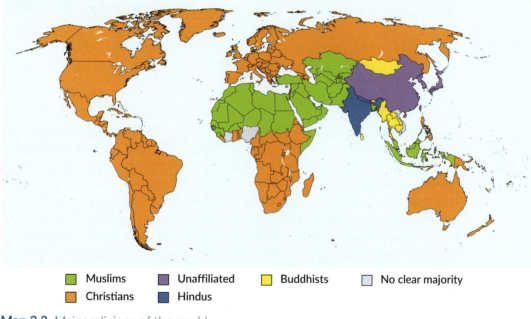

Map 3.2: Major religions of the world
Source: Based on Pew Research Center (2015b).

as a sphere that is distinct from politics or science is a relatively recent European invention; few Muslims make a distinction between the religious and the secular.

Religion impacts global studies through its close relationship with education, the family, social structures, science, and even national identity. Religion has also long had a close relationship with globalization, with one author suggesting that 'no single force can be said to have had a greater impact on propelling globalization forward than religion' (Aslan, 2009, p. 18), because it has always worked to spread its message beyond its point of origin. Foltz (2010) argues that globalization began more than 3,000 years ago as the Silk Road became an important means by which to facilitate

Source: Brand X Pictures

Judaism, Christianity and Islam meet in Jerusalem, home to sites venerated as holy by the different religions, including the Temple Mount, the Wailing Wall, the Church of the Holy Sepulchre, the Dome of the Rock, and the Al Aqsa Mosque.

not just trade but also cultural exchange in the ancient world. The link is also seen clearly in the era of European colonization, which was accompanied by missionary activities and conversion. It continues to be seen today in the work of missionaries, who are often working to spread not just religious beliefs, but a package of related political, economic and cultural ideas. In fact, the debate about religion and religious differences must ask if it stops at belief, or whether it has underlying motives of a different kind. For example, are the tensions between Islam and the West, between Israelis and Palestinians, between Hindus and Sikhs, or between fundamentalist Christians and others in the United States about religion, or are they based on political, economic or cultural differences?

In spite of teaching peace, religion has long been at the heart of conflict and even war, as reflected in the numerous religious wars that plagued Europe for centuries, and this unfortunate tradition continues today with terrorism founded on religious principles (see Juergensmeyer, 2017). The tensions have arisen in part because some have chosen to see globalization as a threat to religion, because globalization is associated with homogenization, which in turn means the spread of ideas that many fear and oppose. The link between religion and homogenization is far from new, and can be found – for example – in efforts to homogenize empires dating from the Romans to the Ottomans. However, we see it today when many Muslims perceive Western values as running against Islamic values and as making too many inroads into Islamic culture, while many in the West view their expanding Muslim populations as a threat to Western culture. This brings us back to the arguments made by Huntington, and quoted earlier in this chapter.

DISCUSSION QUESTIONS

1. What are the most important factors in determining your identity?
2. Can patriotism and global identity coexist?
3. What would it take to be a citizen of the world?
4. Is there is a global culture, and – if so – what are its features?
5. Is race still a useful analytical tool?
6. What distinguishes religion from culture?

KEY CONCEPTS

▸ Civilization
▸ Cosmopolitanism
▸ Cultural imperialism
▸ Culture
▸ Culture shock
▸ Ethnic cleansing
▸ Ethnicity

▸ Ethnocentrism
▸ Genocide
▸ Global culture
▸ Identity
▸ Multiculturalism
▸ National identity
▸ Nationalism

▸ Patriotism
▸ Race
▸ Religion
▸ Secularism
▸ Western
▸ Worldview

USEFUL WEBSITES

Global Citizen at https://www.globalcitizen.org
Global Citizens Initiative at http://www.globalci.org

FURTHER READING

Gannon, Martin J., and Rajnandini Pillai (2016) *Understanding Global Cultures: Metaphorical Journeys through 34 Nations, Clusters of Nations, Continents, and Diversity,* 6th edn (Sage). A study of the variety of cultures around the world, based on cases within and among states.

Kivisto, Peter, and Paul R. Croll (2012) *Race and Ethnicity: The Basics* (Routledge). A survey and discussion of race, ethnicity, their relationship to one another, and the sources and impact of discrimination, inequality, and ethnic conflict.

Nederveen Pieterse, Jan (2015) *Globalization and Culture: Global Mélange,* 3rd edn (Rowman & Littlefield). A book making the argument that we are witnessing the formation of a global mélange culture through processes of cultural mixing.

Richter, Kent E., Eva M. Räpple, John C. Modschiedler and R. Dean Peterson (2005) *Understanding Religion in Global Society* (Wadsworth). A textbook survey of religion and its links with global society.

Lawler, Steph (2013) *Identity: Sociological Perspectives,* 2nd edn (John Wiley). A survey of the debates about identity, exploring the ways in which it is shaped, and how it reveals itself in practice.

Online Resources

Visit www.macmillanihe.com/McCormick-GS to access additional materials to support teaching and learning.

SCIENCE AND TECHNOLOGY

4

PREVIEW

The focus of this chapter is on the intersection between science and technology. It begins with a discussion of the way in which they have impacted our understanding of the global system, before looking at the state of global health, backed up by a case study of the globalization of infectious diseases such as influenza, HIV/AIDS, and malaria. The chapter then turns to technology, with a review of the digital revolution, and a discussion of the global implications of changes in information and communication systems, ending with an assessment of the role of technology in helping foster international travel and tourism.

CONTENTS

▸ Science, technology, and global change

▸ The state of global health

▸ The globalization of disease

▸ The digital revolution

▸ Information, communication, and tourism

HIGHLIGHTS

▸ Advances in science and technology have played a key role in determining the pace of globalization and the shape of the global system.

▸ Connections within the global system have helped make health care a global matter, but access to medical advances is unequal, both within and among countries.

▸ One of the effects of globalization has been greater opportunities for the spread of infectious diseases, many of them controllable with improved access to health care and medication.

▸ The digital revolution has brought changes to the global system that are deep, broad, fast, and still evolving.

▸ Information and communication systems have become global, but even as our choices expand, so many people have been encouraged to use fewer sources of information.

▸ Thanks in large part to changes in technology, international travel has exploded since World War II, allowing more people direct experience of other societies, but also bringing many questionable effects in its wake.

Source: www.imagesource.com

SCIENCE, TECHNOLOGY, AND GLOBAL CHANGE

This book may contain a dozen chapters that each focus on what might seem to be a contained set of topics and ideas, but they all overlap, and cannot be fully understood in isolation. This is certainly true of science and technology. If science is about the pursuit of knowledge, then technology is about the practical application of that knowledge in order to solve problems and to improve the quality of human life. In Chapter 2, we looked at some of the links between science, nutrition, energy supply, and the management of forests and oceans. In this chapter, we look at how science and technology have interacted in the fields of health care, communications, and transportation, and the role of those interactions in shaping the global system. Later, in Chapter 11, we will examine the role of science in understanding the environment, while Chapter 12 will include an assessment of the links between technology and security.

In pinning down the meaning of the term **science**, we must first make a distinction between social science, on the one hand, and the physical and natural sciences on the other. Much of what we define as global studies focuses on matters of **social science**, or the study of human society and the way it works. Because social science is interested in human behaviour, it can rarely be tied down to hard rules, and is often described as the 'softer' and more malleable side of the search for knowledge. One of the effects – as we will see often in this book – is that the meanings of the terms used by social scientists (including *culture*, *ethnicity*, *nation*, *rights* and the *state*) are rarely fixed and routinely contested. This, in turn, is because discussions within the social sciences are often diverted by subjective preferences and biases, which are themselves regularly changing.

This should not distract us from the importance of social science. It helps us make sense of the way that societies function and the way that people relate to one another, it helps us better understand our public options, and – in the sense that it helps broaden our horizons – it lies at the heart of global studies. The social sciences, argues Woodward (2014), help us understand change, demonstrate the links between 'global events and everyday experience', and offer 'critical ways of thinking and of making sense of social, political, cultural and economic life'. Without the work of social scientists, much of what we see happening in the world today – from the rise of nationalism to the tribulations of democracy, the cultural effects of trade, the pressures behind migration, and the debate over climate change – would be hard to understand.

When it comes to the physical or the natural sciences, knowledge takes a different form. Compared to the social sciences, the rules that govern them are more consistent, experiments usually produce the same results time and again, studies are based on quantifiable data, and research deals more with verifiable facts than with subjective opinions. The word *science* derives from the Latin *scientia* (knowledge), and had a much broader meaning until it was restricted in the 19th century to the physical and natural sciences (McLellan and Dorn, 2015). The latter are now often described as 'hard' science, the implication being that they are more certain and objective than social science, and based more on fact than opinion. This, however, is not always the case; while both types of science may be based on the search for objective truth, the choice of our objects of study – and the manner in which we interpret the results – injects an element of subjectivity into both.

Science: The systematic study of the physical, natural and social world with the goal of establishing core truths and developing general laws.

Social science: The study of human society and of the interactions among people within society. Distinct from the natural sciences, such as physics and biology.

As for **technology**, how we live our lives, how we exploit resources, and how human society has evolved are all intimately linked to the way in which we apply science to solve problems. Technology has changed the way we have gathered and processed crops, fought and communicated with one another, manufactured goods, transported ourselves, and generated and stored information. The history of human progress has been in large part the history of changes in technology, whose milestones have included the invention of the wheel, the spear, paper, gunpowder, the printing press, the steam engine, the telegraph, refrigeration, the internal combustion engine, powered flight, radio, television, the contraceptive pill, the personal computer, and the internet. Each in their own way has helped redefine the possibilities of human existence, and most have also been fundamental to the process of globalization. Most have helped make our lives easier, but some have occasionally made them worse, creating – for example – numerous environmental problems, as well as weapons of mass destruction.

> **Technology**: The techniques, skills, methods, and processes used to solve problems, produce goods and services, improve the quality of life, and extend life.

Source: Getty Images

An automated car production line exemplifies the manner in which technology has often replaced human labour, offering convenience and efficiency but also changing the way in which people work.

The value of technology is usually measured in terms of a combination of its utility, simplicity, cost, practicality, and accessibility. Some technological breakthroughs – such as the invention of the wheel – have been simple and inexpensive, and have had universal and timeless effects, while others have demanded much greater investments of time and effort, and are less universally useful; nuclear fission, for example, is not widely available, demands considerable scientific expertise and a large financial investment, and is potentially dangerous. Meanwhile, the capture and exploitation of fossil fuels drove the industrial revolution and created enormous wealth, but also created many problems, and promises to exert ever greater economic pressures until we are able to make significant breakthroughs that can move us into a renewable and non-carbon energy future.

Some technological developments have involved so many steps forward over a distinct period of time, and have had such universal effects, that they have resulted in revolutionary change. The agricultural revolution that happened about 10,000 years ago was made possible by the domestication of animals, and resulted in improved food production and the rise of larger human settlements and more extensive trading networks. But this did not happen overnight. Then came the industrial revolution between approximately 1750 and 1850, based on the invention of the steam engine and the construction of railroads, sparking the factory system, the growth of cities, and mass production. It happened more quickly than the agricultural revolution, but it still took time: more than fifty years were to pass between the building of the first steam engine in 1712 and its transformation by James Watt into something with wider and more practical applications. It took another century for steam engines to spark the creation of railways.

The speed of technological change has accelerated in recent decades, with new methods and products making their way into our lives at a speed that is hard to absorb, and obsolescence kicking in almost before we have had the chance to absorb new developments. Take, for example, the delivery of music: the lives of phonographs (invented 1877), 78 rpm discs (1920s), reel-to-reel magnetic tapes (1930s), 45 and 33 rpm discs (1940s), stereo discs (1960s), compact tape cassettes (1960s), eight-track tape cassettes (1970s), and compact discs and digital audio tape (1980s) were progressively shorter, and they have all been superseded since 2000 by the capacity to download and stream music from multiple sources.

In the section that follows, we will look at some of the ways in which science and technology have intersected in the field of global health. Later in the chapter we will look at the way they have intersected to spawn a digital revolution that has transformed the way we communicate and do business. Finally, we will look at the role of science and technology in changing communications and transport, and the implications for the global tourist industry. In all cases, some of the changes were foreseen, but in many others they were not, and in others they are still emerging. Like the agricultural and industrial revolutions before it, the digital revolution has had global effects, but it has impacted the lives of many more people, and more deeply and quickly, than any earlier period of technological change.

THE STATE OF GLOBAL HEALTH

There is no question that medical science has made enormous progress in recent decades. We understand much more about what afflicts us, we can better treat many diseases and conditions, and – as a result – most of us live longer, have access to improved nutrition, and can be more confident that our lives are not held hostage to many of the kinds of threats to health that were so dangerous to previous generations. At the same time, we increasingly see health not just in local or national terms, but also in global terms. 'The most striking thing about health in the 21st century', argues Crisp (2010), 'is that the whole world is now so interconnected and so interdependent'. However, he goes on, Western scientific medicine is no longer capable by itself of continuing to improve our health, and without a paradigm shift towards a global perspective, we are in danger of continuing to use old ideas to tackle new problems.

Even more fundamentally, one of the primary problems we face is that the benefits of advances in medical science have not been equally spread. Consider the results of two core indicators of the quality of health:

▶ *Life expectancy* is a measure that is affected by a wide variety of factors, from the quality of health care to nutrition and even public safety (rates are lower, for example, in cities with violent crime problems, or countries suffering from civil war). Overall life expectancy improved between 1960 and 2015 from 52 years to 72 years, but the numbers vary considerably both within and among states, and even between men and women (see examples in Figure 4.1). Someone born to a middle-class family in the North can expect to live longer than someone born into poverty in the North or the urban South, who can in turn expect to live longer than someone born in one of the poorer rural areas of a country such as Afghanistan or Sierra Leone.

▶ *Infant mortality* is a measure of the quality of health care; a society that cannot ensure the health of newborns and their mothers clearly has deeper problems. Rates are expressed as deaths per thousand live births, and while the ideal would be a figure of zero, there are always newborns suffering from genetic or other problems for which there is no solution. Overall, rates between 1960 and 2015 fell from 65 per 1,000 live births to 30, but again there are differences within and among states: the countries with the best health care systems – including Finland, Iceland, Japan and Sweden – are down to just two deaths per thousand live births, while those with the worst systems – including Chad, Mali, Nigeria, and (once again) Sierra Leone – have rates of 70–90.

Japan and Sierra Leone are worth looking at in more detail, since they are at opposite ends of both scales. For Japan, the advantage is not just universal health care, but good habits: most Japanese see their doctors often (sometimes monthly), stay in hospital (if needed) longer than most other patients in the North, enjoy price-controlled medicines, and eat healthy and balanced diets that results in comparatively

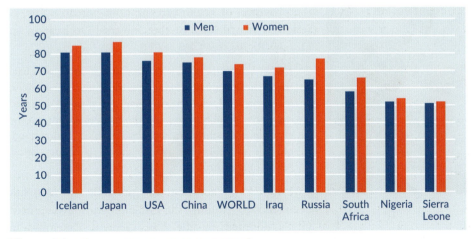

Figure 4.1: Life expectancy rates compared
Source: World Bank Economic Indicators (2018). Figures are for 2016.

low rates of obesity, hypertension, and heart disease. The Japanese situation is far from perfect, however, with concerns about a cumbersome health care bureaucracy, a shortage of doctors, and growing pressures on the health care system from an aging population (Organization for Economic Cooperation and Development, 2015). Nonetheless, good health care is a central feature of life in Japan.

In Sierra Leone, by contrast, the problems are rife. There is no universal health care system, there is a shortage of health clinics and medical staff, poverty remains a widespread problem, and the country is still recovering from the effects of a civil war that ran from 1991 to 2002. Many people become ill or die as a result of problems that could be prevented with improvements in nutrition, public education, and the provision of clean water and sanitation, which would reduce rates of malaria, pneumonia, tuberculosis, diarrhoeal diseases, and HIV/AIDS. The country's health problems were exemplified by a state of emergency there in the wake of the outbreak of Ebola virus disease in West Africa in 2014–16; with more than 14,000 cases and nearly 4,000 deaths, Sierra Leone was the worst affected country after Liberia.

The main international body with an interest in health matters is the Paris-based World Health Organization (WHO), whose tasks include coordinating approaches to health care within the UN system, setting standards, encouraging research, and monitoring health trends. It was WHO, for example, which in recent years coordinated responses to the outbreak of Lassa fever in Nigeria and the spread of yellow fever in parts of Brazil, and in 2018 classified Video Game Addiction as a disorder, organized an international conference on the problem of violence directed at children, and published a report warning about the rise in the number of cases of resistance of bacterial infections to antibiotics. WHO has also been a long-time advocate of both **primary health care** and **universal health care**, calling on all its member states to adopt the latter as the best way of guaranteeing health for all. WHO defines good health as going beyond the mere absence of disease or infirmity, and including 'a complete state of physical, mental and social well-being' (World Health Organization, 2018a).

There is a widely held view that good health and the provision of health care are both human rights, as reflected in Article 25 of the Universal Declaration on Human Rights (see Chapter 7):

> Everyone has the right to a standard of living adequate for the health and well-being of himself and of his family, including food, clothing, housing and medical care and necessary social services, and the right to security in the event of unemployment, sickness, disability, widowhood, old age or other lack of livelihood in circumstances beyond his control.

Progress on applying this principle, though, has been mixed. Among the Millennium Development Goals adopted by the UN General Assembly in 2000 (see Chapter 8), health and health care featured prominently: infant and maternal mortality were to

Primary health care: Health care that is basic, personal, and general, and geared towards initial treatment rather than dealing with specialized or advanced problems.

Universal health care: Health care made available to everyone at little or no direct cost, regardless of pre-existing conditions or ability to pay.

Source: Getty Images

Medical science has made much progress in recent decades, but access to modern surgical techniques and health care is unequal, both within and among countries.

COMPARING NORTH AND SOUTH 4

ACCESS TO HEALTH CARE

Few points of comparison bring out the differences between the richest and poorest countries of the world quite so clearly as access to quality health care. The residents of most Northern states (the USA being a notable exception) have access to universal health care, provided at little or no direct cost by highly qualified medical staff using the most advanced medical technology and a wider array of medications. In the more successful Southern states, health care and medical science are both catching up quickly; many – including Argentina, Botswana, Brazil, China, Cuba, India, Mexico, and Sri Lanka – offer their residents both free and universal health care, the benefits reflected in improving longevity and a higher quality of life. But in many Southern states, health care is free only at the primary level, and in many others – including Afghanistan, Cambodia, Haiti, Kenya, and Nigeria – it is neither free nor universal.

At the same time, differences in the quality of health do not come down simply to wealth and poverty, or the nature of health care systems. Marmot (2016) writes of the global health gap, which he argues is often a function of the place of a person or of a community on the social ladder. In every country, he argues, those who suffer a relative social disadvantage also suffer a relative health disadvantage, often regardless of their comparative wealth; hence someone with a low social status in a wealthy country is likely to live a shorter life than someone with a high social status in a poor country. Improved health care and changes in behaviour only go so far in addressing health needs, which must also take into account social inequalities.

There is also a curious inverse relationship at work by which many residents of the North find their health suffering the costs of affluence. Although most live longer and generally healthier lives than ever before, many experience new problems related to increased life expectancy (including dementia) and sedentary lifestyles (including diabetes and obesity). These problems are starting to be felt among the wealthier residents of the urban South as well.

In the rural South, meanwhile, many people suffer not just from limited access to health care, but also lack the kinds of often inexpensive medicines that leave them prone to illness or death from preventable sources, including contaminated water, inadequate sanitation, and infectious disease (see later in this chapter). Even where access to health care is strong, social attitudes might sometimes get in the way. Consider the case of HIV/AIDS, which in most parts of the world is no longer the death sentence it once was. In many parts of sub-Saharan Africa, religious and cultural taboos about sex education, contraception and homosexuality have combined with poor governance and corruption to mean that many people are discouraged from talking about HIV or AIDS, or taking the necessary action to contain its spread (see Lomborg, 2012).

be cut, the spread of disease was to be halted and reversed, more people were to have access to clean water and more of those in the South were to have access to affordable medicines. Noble goals, to be sure, but the ongoing problems faced by many parts of the world are reflected in the different levels of access to health care discussed in Comparing North and South 4. In spite of all the advances in medical science, the global community remains clearly unbalanced in the extent to which it benefits from those advances. The causes and the effects are illustrated in the case of infectious diseases, which remain a global problem in spite of our improved capacity to control them.

THE GLOBALIZATION OF DISEASE

A distant relative of mine by the name of Henry McCormick fought in the British Army during World War I. He was a member of the Royal Field Artillery, and saw action in Gallipoli and Egypt before moving to the Western front in early 1917. He survived the devastation of the Third Battle of Ypres and the German spring offensive of March 1918 on the Somme, took part in the August offensive against the Germans on the Somme, and survived to celebrate the end of the war on 11 November 1918. But barely four months later, before he could be shipped home, he fell ill and died in Belgium at the age of 24. Having survived some of the most violent battles of the Great War, he had fallen victim to the world's first great influenza **pandemic**, which lasted from early 1918 to late 1920. About one in three humans were thought to have come down with the disease, which resulted in an estimated 50–100 million deaths, far surpassing the death toll of the war, in which an estimated 18 million people died (Spinney, 2017).

The particular virus involved, H1N1, returned in a new version in 2009, originating in Mexico and taking an additional 200,000 lives in a second pandemic. Also known as swine flu, because it is similar to a virus that afflicts pigs, H1N1 is different from seasonal influenza: while the latter is most serious for the elderly or those with pre-existing chronic diseases, and is most active during the northern and southern winters, H1N1 is active during the summer and has higher fatality rates among young adults. Seasonal flu is serious enough, being caught by an estimated 5–10 per cent of adults and 20–30 per cent of children annually; H1N1 is that much more threatening, and exemplifies the wider problem of **infectious disease**.

Even as medical science continues to make breakthroughs, and individual countries make progress in health care, the problem of diseases spread by microorganisms (many of which can be transferred from one human to another) persists. In the 1960s, on the back of successes such as the eradication of smallpox, there was a view that medical science had almost reached its limit in addressing infectious diseases, and research instead began to focus on chronic (persistent) diseases such as cancer. But then the emergence of HIV and AIDS in the 1980s drew attention back to infectious diseases, whose effects were being exacerbated by urbanization, trade, international travel, and migration: more people live closer to one another, and move across borders, allowing for the easier spread of disease. Globally, infectious diseases are now among the leading causes of death among humans, accounting for about 12 per cent of deaths globally in 2016, but taking much higher tolls in low-income countries.

With some of these diseases, such as influenza, we have a long familiarity, but others are unfamiliar – see Table 4.1. Some have become more serious as a result of changes in medical science, such as the rise of resistant strains of bacteria in the wake of the over-use of antibiotics. Others were either controlled or geographically restricted, but began to spread in the wake of globalization. When Europeans moved to the Americas, for example, they took with them many diseases to which natives had no immunity, including malaria, chickenpox, measles, syphilis and even the common cold. More recently, as cities have grown and as people have become more mobile on the back of migration and international travel, so diseases have been able to spread more widely. Consider, for example, the case of West Nile virus. First discovered in Uganda in the 1930s, it spread to North Africa, central Asia, and

Pandemic: An outbreak of an infectious disease over a large region, spilling over borders and perhaps spreading globally.

Infectious disease: One caused as a result of contamination by microorganisms capable of hosting and transferring the disease, such as bacteria, viruses, and parasites.

Table 4.1: Examples of infectious diseases

Disease	Qualities	Status
Smallpox	Deadly in 25 per cent of cases, killing as many as 500 million people in the 20th century.	Eradicated in the late 1970s.
Influenza	A viral disease transmitted by touch or coughing/sneezing, that occasionally evolves into pandemics.	Preventable and treatable, but mutagenic (its genetic form can change) and often deadly: 3–5 million cases annually, and 300,000–650,000 deaths.
Malaria	Caused by parasites transmitted through bites of *Anopheles* mosquitoes.	Once widespread, eradicated in most of the North, but remains a major cause of illness and disease in tropical Africa: 216 million cases in 2016, and 445,000 deaths.
Cholera	Acute diarrhoeal infection caused by ingestion of contaminated food or water. Linked to poor sanitation.	Can be controlled with improved water supply and sanitation. Up to four million cases annually, with as many as 150,000 deaths.
HIV/AIDS	Spread through bodily fluids, the virus almost always progressing to AIDS, and long being fatal.	Became prominent in the 1980s. Preventable and treatable, but remains a major cause of death in Africa and Southeast Asia.
Tuberculosis	Spread through the air, mainly infecting the lungs.	1.7 million deaths in 2016, mainly in the South.

Source: Based in part on World Health Organization (2018b).

Europe, and was first identified in North America in 1999, the suspicion being that it was introduced by infected visitors from Israel, which was then experiencing an epidemic (Gubler, 2007).

Meanwhile, many parts of the South continue to suffer from diseases that are controllable, but which persist because health care systems are underdeveloped, or sanitation is poor, or the necessary medications are either too expensive or not available in sufficient quantities. Consider the example of malaria, transmitted when people are bitten by mosquitoes carrying the malaria parasite; the symptoms include a high fever, headaches and vomiting, leading in the most serious cases to death. It can be prevented by the use of netting over beds (mosquitoes are most active at night) or by taking anti-malarial medication. Victims can even be treated fairly easily once they have the disease if they have access to good health care, but this has become more difficult as the parasite has developed resistance to drugs. Long ago eradicated in North America, Europe and the Caribbean, malaria remains endemic (common) in much of tropical Africa, and is responsible for several hundred thousand deaths annually, including one in five deaths of children in sub-Saharan Africa.

Another disease, which affects fewer people, but is more deadly, and has recently expanded far beyond its point of origin, is Ebola. First discovered only in 1976, in a village near the Congolese river for which it is named, it is transmitted from wild animals to humans, and then from humans to humans. Its symptoms include fever, muscle pain, vomiting, diarrhoea, rash, and both internal and external bleeding. On average, about half of all victims die from the disease, for which there is as yet no proven treatment, although there are many ways of containing it once cases have been identified. There were limited outbreaks in several central African countries in the 1970s and 1990s, but it first made wider headlines with the 2014–16 outbreak in several West African countries (Guinea, Liberia, and Sierra Leone were worst affected). It was eventually contained, but not before nearly 28,000 people were infected and more than 11,000 people died (data from World Health Organization, 2018c).

A new element in the globalization of disease is environmental change. As human population has grown, so people have moved into regions once considered too hostile for settlement, both exposing themselves to new diseases and encouraging the spread of others. The building of dams has encouraged the spread of water-borne diseases such as malaria and sleeping sickness, the growing of crops has encouraged the spread of parasite-carrying rodents, and the killing of predators has allowed disease-carrying pests to proliferate; the latter was behind an outbreak of Lyme disease in the north-eastern United States, when the expansion of suburbs pushed back predators such as wolves, allowing an increase in the number of deer carrying ticks infected with the disease. Climate change is now bringing wider problems; as global temperatures rise and weather patterns change, disease-carrying insects and animals are moving outside their natural boundaries, pushing tropical diseases further north and south.

In summary, then, while medical science has been making enormous progress in terms of its understanding of what ails us and how to respond, we continue to face the challenge of inequalities in access to health care. Meanwhile, the spread of infectious disease brings together many of the core themes in global studies, including the effects of globalization, urbanization, economic inequality, and environmental change. Many of those themes are also reflected in other areas at the confluence of science and technology, few of which are more immediate to more people than the implications of the digital revolution.

THE DIGITAL REVOLUTION

In mid-2012, a song was released by the South Korean rapper Psy that commented ironically on the privileged lifestyle of the residents of Gangnam, a suburb of the capital city of Seoul. *Gangnam Style* was an immediate hit, and within months the accompanying video had become the first to receive one billion hits on YouTube. (It had topped three billion views by early 2018.) Psy was transformed from being all but unknown outside his home country to becoming a global figure, hailed – somewhat hyperbolically – by UN Secretary-General Ban Ki Moon (also from South

Korea) as 'a force for world peace', and credited for bringing unparalleled new levels of attention to his country. The popularity of the music video underlined not just the power of social media, but also their global reach, and their capacity to rapidly distribute images, songs and ideas at a global level.

We saw earlier in the chapter that technological change can sometimes happen quickly, and nothing has made this clearer than the case of the **digital revolution**. Founded on the development of computers and the management of information, it has brought change that is faster, deeper, and wider than that seen in any previous era of sustained technological development. It has also been more truly global, and to a large extent has come to define not just what we mean by *technology* but also what we mean by *global*; for the first time in history, almost every part of the world is connected, even if the depth of those connections varies according to access to electricity, the internet, personal computers, and cell phones.

Digital revolution: The revolution in the generation, storage, and sharing of digital information.

Source: Getty Images/Hero Images

The digital revolution has helped change the way in which many people work, redefining the nature of work life and home life.

Schwab (2016) considers the digital revolution to be the third industrial revolution, the first having been based on the invention of the steam engine and the second on mass production. He argues that we could be on the verge of a fourth industrial revolution that promises to go beyond 'smart and connected machines and systems' and to move into new areas ranging from gene sequencing to nanotechnology, renewable energy, self-drive vehicles, and quantum computing. These technologies, he predicts, will be fused with one another and will interact across physical, digital and biological boundaries, and the overall effect will be to 'change everything'. But he also warns that we lack the necessary levels of leadership and understanding to respond to the changes that might come, and that we lack the kind of narrative needed to outline the resulting opportunities and challenges, and to avoid a popular backlash against these changes; people can adapt to change, but if it happens too deeply and too quickly, it can spark resistance. In short, we do not fully understand what is happening or how to respond.

Timeline: Key events in the development of the internet and the Web	
Date	**Developments**
1969	Military-funded ARPANET project connects four sites in the United States.
1970s	Expansion of networking; foundation of Apple (1976).
1980s	Commercial internet service providers founded; foundation of AOL (1985) and creation of World Wide Web (1989).
Mid-1990s	Email and internet access become more widely available, commercial use restrictions lifted on web browsers, search engines expanded, file sharing becomes possible. Foundation of Amazon (1994), eBay and Yahoo! (1995), Expedia (1996), Netflix and Priceline (1997), Google and PayPal (1998), Alibaba and Salesforce (1999), and Baidu (2000). Wi-Fi named 1999.
2000s	Rise of online shopping, personal websites, blogs, the mobile revolution (Android launched 2007, iPhone released 2007 and iPad released 2010), e-books, social media, tweets, apps, memes, the cloud, and the 'internet of things' (the integration of the physical and the digital, including power grids, smart cars, and smart homes). Foundation of Facebook (2004), YouTube (2005), Twitter (2006), and Uber (2009). Cloud computing starts to become widely available 2009.

Digital divide: Differences in levels of access to information and communication technology, whether between individuals, communities, geographic areas, or countries.

The internet and the Web offer prime examples of the speed, depth, and breadth of technological change – see Timeline. The former dates back only to the 1960s, and the latter to 1989, but changes and developments followed quickly, spawning numerous related offshoots and tying in to changes in computer and phone technology that are all taken for granted now by those who have access to them. It is easy to forget that it took barely a generation to take us from manual typewriters and rotary phones to the electronic and digital options that are now available, and the ubiquitous sight of people mesmerized by their mobile devices. The result has been not just an information and communication revolution, but a revolution in the way we work, do business, relate to one another, undertake research, engage in politics, make our purchases, and pay our bills. But once again we face global inequality: only about half the population of the world has immediate access to the internet, creating a **digital divide** both between and within countries, drawing a line between the global and the local, and between the rich and the poor – see Global and Local 4.

GLOBAL AND LOCAL 4

THE DIGITAL DIVIDE

Many have hailed the effects of the digital revolution, but it is far from achieving its full potential, because so many people remain cut off from the opportunities it provides; there is a digital divide between those who are globally connected and those who still define their lives around the local. The former can use the internet to exploit opportunities at the global level, while the latter become more marginalized, with a view of life and its opportunities that has not changed much in scale since before the digital revolution.

Globally, just over half of people have internet access at home, which means that they have the kinds of connections made available by the internet to news, education, jobs, banking, and buying goods and services online. But while the figure for Europe is nearly 85 per cent, for Africa it drops to less than 20 per cent – see Figure 4.2. And not only is internet connectivity highest in the North, but Northern states have also led the way in the development of digital technology, and are home to the major internet companies, such as Google, Amazon, and Facebook; the South – mainly in the form, so far, of Chinese companies such as Alibaba and Baidu – is still some way from catching up. As a result, argues Srinivasan (2017), 'ninety-nine percent of the world's population remains excluded from most decisions made around the future of the Internet and digital technology'.

The digital divide is not just a problem between the North and the South, but also within countries, including those parts of the North that do not yet have broadband access. As so much of daily life moves online, those without connections are left behind: the people with the highest levels of access tend to be the wealthiest, the best educated, and those who live in urban areas. Meanwhile, low levels of access are often equated with poverty, lower levels of education, and living in rural areas that might not have broadband access or cell phone services, or even – in some cases – electricity.

Those who are already cut off politically and economically will find themselves even more marginalized, a problem that ties in to debates about the extent to which traditional notions of citizenship have spilled over into **digital citizenship**. The UN has even gone so far as to declare access to the internet to be a basic human right. Prompted by efforts in several European countries to pass laws that would allow for the suspension of internet access to those accused of illegal file sharing, a special report to the UN Human Rights Council argued that internet access was an 'enabler' of other rights (such as freedom of expression and assembly) and critical to economic and social development (La Rue, 2011).

Friedman (2007) argues that the internet has 'flattened' the world by making national borders less significant, weakening territorial government, allowing countries to compete and collaborate with one another as never before in a global market, and allowing us to move more freely (at least, in cyber terms) across those borders. But Goldsmith and Wu (2008) disagree, arguing that national governments are continuing to maintain their sovereignty in the age of the internet, largely because they are continuing to protect and promote their economic interests, and many – particularly authoritarian countries such as China and Russia – are controlling access to information on the internet.

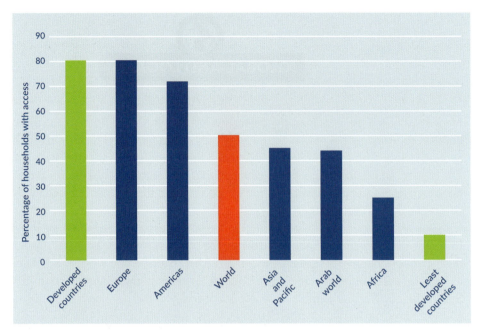

Figure 4.2: Contrasting levels of internet access
Source: International Telecommunications Union (2017).

Digital citizenship: Using information technology in order to engage with politics, government, society, and community.

The pace of technological change promises to continue to proceed rapidly, bringing remarkable changes to communication, transport, manufacturing, education, the workplace, and health care. In his book *Thank You for Being Late* (which is subtitled *An Optimist's Guide to Thriving in the Age of Accelerations*), the *New York Times* columnist Thomas Friedman (2016) writes of the 'tectonic movements that are reshaping the world', which he clusters under three groups: globalization (addressed in Chapter 1), climate change and loss of biodiversity (see Chapter 11), and technological change. In the case of the latter he refers to Moore's Law, named for a pioneer of microchip development (Gordon Moore), who in a 1965 article predicted that microchips would become exponentially smaller, more powerful, and cheaper (Moore, 1965). In order to grasp how far microchip technology has advanced, engineers at Intel drew an analogy with the Volkswagen Beetle; had it evolved at the same speed as microchips between 1971 and 2016, they calculated, it would now be able to achieve speeds of 500,000 km per hour, would run for three million kilometres on five litres of fuel, and would sell for four American cents (Friedman, 2016: 38).

It is important to think not just about how such technologies are evolving, but also about their impact on shaping the world. 'Digital technologies are not neutral', Srinivasan (2017) reminds us. New technologies and old technologies alike are tools created by particular people in particular places, he argues, and are therefore socially constructed in the sense that their designers approach them with a particular set of values and presumptions. Hence it is important to think of new technology not as fixed but as 'open to voices and perspectives that otherwise remain confined to the side-lines'. So far, as noted earlier, much of the digital revolution has been driven by Northern needs and preferences. As the South plays a greater role in driving technological change, we are likely to see exciting new developments.

INFORMATION, COMMUNICATION, AND TOURISM

In few arenas have science and technology combined to bring such revolutionary change as in the field of long-distance communication. It once took years to travel around the world, and weeks or even months for news from one part of the world to reach another. As a result, most people knew little about what happened outside their local communities, and had little or no sense of global consciousness. Today, we live in a world in which news is routinely broadcast globally as it happens and from wherever it happens, and in which we can talk to almost anyone who owns a phone or a computer (often at no cost), and in which – with enough money and the right documents – it is possible to travel thousands of kilometres to see that world for ourselves.

We should not forget that levels of access are unequal; in the poorest and most isolated parts of the world, the rest of the world can still seem as alien and distant as it ever did. We also need to make a distinction between quality and quantity; access to information, and multiple channels of communication, does not necessarily make us better informed or better able to understand the world. And there is a clear irony in the way that most of us are now connected more deeply and widely than our ancestors could have ever imagined, yet loneliness and a sense of isolation are widespread problems. Nonetheless, we have all been changed by these developments.

At first, changes in the technology of communications came slowly. The first printed book was produced in China in 686, but another 800 years were to pass before the Gutenberg press started printing with moveable type, and the first newspaper did not appear for another 150 years after that. It took another 250 years or so before the first mass circulation newspapers began to appear, at which point the changes accelerated, taking us rapidly into the age of **mass media** (see Kovarik, 2016). This allowed quicker, wider, and more immediate communication than ever before:

> **Mass media**: Channels of communication – such as television, radio, and websites – that reach a large number of people.

- ▸ Radio entered the equation in the 1930s, greatly cutting the time it took news to spread internationally.

- ▸ We saw the advent of television in the 1950s, but television audiences had already begun to fragment by the 1980s with the rise of cable and satellite broadcasting.

- ▸ International communications broadened during the 1990s with the arrival of the internet and 24-hour global television news.

- ▸ Mobile phones began to replace landlines in the early 2000s.

- ▸ We find ourselves now in an era of social media and interactive news, with newspapers falling by the wayside, and structured television choices being replaced with the personalized programming offered by streaming.

Some of the changes were foreseen in the early 1960s by Marshall McLuhan, a Canadian professor of media studies who coined the term **global village** to describe the way in which the rise of electronic media was metaphorically shrinking the world. 'As electrically contracted,' he argued, 'the globe is no more than a village. Electric speed in bringing all social and political functions together in a sudden implosion has heightened human awareness of responsibility to an intense degree'. Different groups in society could no longer be contained, he suggested: 'They are now involved in our lives, as we in theirs' (McLuhan, 1964).

> **Global village**: A metaphor conveying the idea that electronic media have reduced the size of the world by tightening the connections among humans.

The expansion of mass media still had a long way to go when McLuhan was writing, and that process continues today as we try to keep up, and to think about what it has meant for the way we see the world and interact with each other. It took about a month for news of the American declaration of independence in 1776 to reach Britain, and several more weeks for the British reaction to filter back to the colonies (Martelle, 2014). Today, we can expect coverage of important news live from anywhere in the world, accompanied by often elaborate analysis from multiple quarters and perspectives. As a barrier to communication, physical distance has all but gone.

But while the distances have closed and the choices have expanded, the advent of the internet, social media and streaming has also made it possible for us to cut ourselves off from news and analysis that we find disagreeable or distasteful, allowing us to shape our view of the world to fit our preferences. This leaves us living in an **echo chamber**, being less exposed to competing ideas and opinions. Just as the metaphorical global village has started to become more real for more people, so many of its inhabitants have been opting to shut themselves away in their metaphorical homes. They talk electronically only with those of their neighbours with whom they agree, and choose only the news they wish to read or hear. The effect is to make us less informed about global and domestic trends.

At the same time, though, changes in technology have allowed humans to be more mobile than ever before, travelling across borders and experiencing different societies and cultures – in person – in ever greater numbers. In 2017, a record four billion passengers boarded an aircraft somewhere in the world and were flown safely to their destinations (International Air Transport Association, 2018). To be sure, many of them were repeat travellers, they were flying for reasons that ranged from business to pleasure, and there are still billions of people in the world who have never flown. Still, this was an astonishing development, representing a 990 per cent increase on the number of people who flew in 1950, but still being less than half the number of people who are projected to fly in 2036.

What does this mean? Personal experience is theoretically the best way to see the world in its variety and to witness the growth of global connections, but what motivates tourists? Does travel broaden people's worldviews, and do they use their visits to learn more about other societies, or are they simply looking for the opportunity to relax by a pool, indulge themselves with food and drink, and visit popular sites along with thousands of other tourists? And is tourism good for those parts of the world that attract the most visitors, or are they being loved to death? The industry certainly creates jobs and encourages investment, but it also threatens to overwhelm local cultures, to homogenize the world as tourists seek to replicate the comforts of home, and contributes to environmental damage and climate change.

For better or for worse, the combination of science and technology has brought great change to patterns of travel, with developments in transport broadening our access to parts of the world that were once far out of the reach of most people. Consider these changes:

▸ The first known single-voyage circumnavigation of the world – an expedition initially led by Ferdinand Magellan, and that set out in 1519 – took three years.

▸ Even when Europeans left home in larger numbers to trade, fight, colonize, or emigrate, it took them weeks to reach the Americas, months to reach Asia and Australasia, and for many of them it was a journey of no return.

Echo chamber: A metaphor describing the manner in which ideas circulate within a closed system, and are amplified and reinforced by repetition.

▶ The advent of the first commercial jet aircraft in the 1950s cut international travel to a matter of hours.

▶ In 2011, a Boeing 787 flew around the world – from Seattle to Seattle, via one stop in Dhaka, Bangladesh – in 43 hours.

▶ Today, if we can afford the price of a ticket, we can have breakfast, lunch and dinner on different continents.

Of course, not everyone is able (or wants) to travel, and international travel is still the preserve of those who can afford it, or whose jobs require it. Even so, it is much more common than it once was. As we will see in Chapter 10, the (usually) permanent movement involved in migration was once available only to those who had the motivation and the means to move. Shorter-term travel was usually for practical reasons such as exploration, conquest, or settlement, and it was geographically limited by the available maps and means of transport. It was only in the early 19th century that the idea of travel for pleasure – to go on a tour, to be a tourist, or to engage in **tourism** – became more common, but it was still the preserve of the wealthy few. The era of mass international travel only began after World War II, but it has grown quickly to become one of the world's most important economic activities, worth an estimated $7.6 trillion in 2016 – or about 10 per cent of the value of all global economic activity – and accompanied by implications that are political, financial, cultural, educational, and environmental.

> **Tourism**: Short-term travel for business or pleasure.

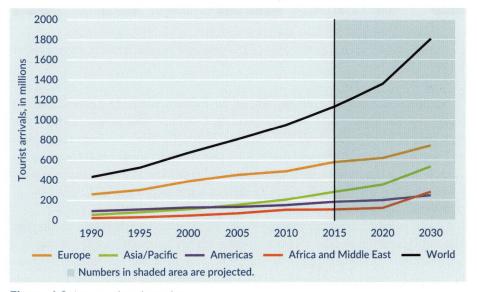

Figure 4.3: International tourism
Source: Based on World Tourism Organization (2017).

The World Tourism Organization – the Madrid-based UN agency responsible for promoting and monitoring trends in tourism – defines tourism as 'a social, cultural and economic phenomenon which entails the movement of people to countries or places outside their usual environment for personal or business/professional purposes' (World Tourism Organization, 2018). Based on this definition, there were just 15 million international tourist arrivals in 1950. By 1990, that number had risen to 435 million, by 2015 it was up to just over 1.1 billion, and it is projected to rise by 2030 to just over 1.8 billion – see Figure 4.3. Travel for leisure has even continued growing in the face of economic downturns in several countries and of concerns about terrorism.

Source: John McCormick

Tourists swarm the ruins of Tulum, one of the last cities built and occupied by the Maya, on the Caribbean coast of what is now Mexico. The growth of the global tourist industry has had mixed benefits.

Europe is the target of about half of all tourists, while the Chinese and the Americans dominate as measured by spending. It is important to note, though, that most people travel within their own regions. Hence the high numbers for Europe are explained in part by the fact that it is an area in which many small countries are situated next to each other, with well-developed connections by road, train and air. Intercontinental travel is still relatively rare, accounting for about 20 per cent of tourist arrivals (all data from World Tourism Organization, 2017).

Global tourism, suggest Lyon and Wells (2012), may have become 'the largest-scale movement of goods, services, and people in human history', making it a significant catalyst for change and economic development. But questions arise about the impact of tourism on culture and the environment. It is now almost impossible to travel to the more popular destinations in the world without running across large numbers of other tourists, and finding purpose-built facilities catering for tourist convenience rather than based on connecting to genuine local life and culture. The demands of tourists have resulted in the building of hotels, restaurants, transport networks, and other supporting infrastructure, all of which have brought new income and opportunities to tourist destinations.

But these developments have also meant overcrowding, damage to popular tourist sites, the swamping of local culture, and environmental problems arising from changes to ecosystems and the heightened production of greenhouse gases.

And when it comes to cultural exchange, a visitor to a popular destination will likely find few opportunities to mix with local people (other than those selling souvenirs and tours) and little opportunity to experience what life is like for local residents. As a result of global interconnectedness, note Lyon and Wells (2012), the differences between 'everyday places' and 'tourism places' have become increasingly blurred.

In summary, we live in a world in which information is more easily available in larger volumes, in which we can communicate more easily and keep up with developments in almost every part of the world, and in which it is much easier to experience and witness the variety of human society and physical environments directly. And yet, as this is happening, we are also witnessing the narrowing of options: people are being exposed less to a variety of ideas and opinions, and even when they travel there is a good chance that they will experience only what has been provided to cater for their tastes and convenience, rather than the variety of the human experience.

DISCUSSION QUESTIONS

1. What part do the social, physical and natural sciences play in helping us understand the global system?

2. Is universal health care for everyone in the world an achievable or desirable goal?

3. To what extent do Northern countries and their pharmaceutical industries have a moral or practical obligation to help Southern countries control the spread of infectious diseases?

4. Are you excited, encouraged, concerned or worried about the possibilities of the digital revolution?

5. What are the features of the global village? Does it even exist?

6. Is international tourism a good thing?

KEY CONCEPTS

▶ Digital citizenship
▶ Digital divide
▶ Digital revolution
▶ Echo chamber
▶ Global village

▶ Infectious disease
▶ Mass media
▶ Pandemic
▶ Primary health care
▶ Science

▶ Social science
▶ Technology
▶ Tourism
▶ Universal health care

USEFUL WEBSITES

World Health Organization at http://www.who.int
World Tourism Organization at http://www2.unwto.org

FURTHER READING

Crisp, Nigel (2010) *Turning the World Upside Down: The Search for Global Health in the 21st Century* (Royal Society of Medicine Press). A comparison of health care in rich countries and poor countries, with an assessment of what it will take to even out the differences.

Friedman, Thomas L. (2016) *Thank You for Being Late: An Optimist's Guide to Thriving in the Age of Accelerations* (Picador). An assessment of the 'tectonic' changes taking place in the world, with a focus on the effects of technology, globalization, and environmental change.

Hamelink, Cees J. (2015) *Global Communication* (Sage). A study of the changes that have come to global communications, and of their effects on culture and politics.

Reisinger, Yvette (2012) *International Tourism: Cultures and Behaviour* (Routledge). A textbook assessment of the links between tourism and globalization, assessing the ways in which international tourists and host cultures influence each other.

Srinivasan, Ramesh (2017) *Whose Global Village? Rethinking how Technology Shapes our World* (New York University Press). A critical assessment of the dominance of the West in the development of digital technology, and of the importance of considering other voices and cultures in its future applications.

Online Resources

Visit www.macmillanihe.com/McCormick-GS to access additional materials to support teaching and learning.

STATES
AND GOVERNMENT

5

PREVIEW

We cannot fully understand the global system without appreciating the qualities and the changing nature of states. The chapter begins with a survey of the meaning and features of the state (including authority, legitimacy, and sovereignty), looks at the meaning of citizenship, compares and contrasts states and nations, and then looks at the evolution of states (emphasizing their proliferation since 1945). It then discusses the nature and role of government, compares democratic and authoritarian states, and reviews the current condition of the state system, contrasting arguments that it is declining, strengthening, or simply changing form.

CONTENTS

▸ **Understanding states**

▸ **States vs. nations**

▸ **The evolution of states**

▸ **Understanding government**

▸ **Challenges to the state**

HIGHLIGHTS

▸ The building blocks upon which the global system is based are the world's nearly 200 independent states.

▸ States are distinct from nations, the former being a legal and political concept while the latter is mainly a cultural and historical concept.

▸ The modern state system was born in Europe, but its reach has gone global mainly since 1945 and the creation of many new states in the wake of decolonization.

▸ Governments have the authority to administer the people and the territory of states, and to make the decisions that impact the relations between states.

▸ About half the world's people live in democracies, while the other half live in authoritarian systems.

▸ Opinion is divided over whether states are becoming stronger, or weaker, or are simply changing form within an evolving global system.

Source: shujaa_777

UNDERSTANDING STATES

If you have ever travelled internationally, you will have been reminded of the state almost every step of the way. You will have had to carry a passport from the state of which you are a citizen, you will have shown the passport both at your port of departure and your port of arrival (you might even have had to apply for a visa before you travelled), you will have gone through customs and immigration controls at your port of arrival, and the government of your target state will have made it clear that – without special permission – there was a limit on how long you were going to be allowed to stay.

This all happens because we live in a world of states. They have primary authority over the world's territory and over the residents of that territory, and they together make most of the decisions that define and shape the nature of the global system. True, that system is also defined by the numerous decisions of individuals, corporations, and interest groups, and the place of the world's nearly 200 independent states in the global system is changing: they are not as independent as they might at first seem, and some argue that they are becoming weaker. Regardless, we cannot fully understand the dynamics of the global system without first understanding what states are, how they work, and how they interact.

Defined simply, a **state** is a territory marked by borders, that contains a population, and that is overseen by a government whose authority is recognized by the citizens of the state and by the governments of other states (see Jessop, 2016). States are often referred to as countries, but this is a term with geographical connotations that is too vague for the tastes of most social scientists and legal scholars. States are also often and wrongly referred to as nations, a term that has a separate meaning, explored later in this chapter.

In order to understand how states work, we need to be clear on the meaning of four key concepts. First, states have **authority**, meaning that they have the

State: A territory with a population and a government whose existence and independence are recognized under international law.

Authority: The acknowledged right of a state to act or to rule.

Figure 5.1: Six features of a state

TERRITORY	A geographical area marked by borders.
POPULATION	A permanent population of citizens and non-citizens.
AUTHORITY	The acknowledged right of a state to act or to rule.
LEGITIMACY	Recognition that a state has the right to wield authority within its borders.
SOVEREIGNTY	The principle that a state answers to no higher political or legal authority.
GOVERNMENT	The system of institutions, processes and laws responsible for addressing the needs of the residents of a state.

acknowledged right to act or to rule, a condition that exists when subordinates accept the capacity of superiors to give legitimate orders. If power is the capacity or the ability to control, and to bring about intended effects, then authority is the right to wield power. Someone who points a loaded gun at you may have the power to make you do as they say, but they only have the authority to use that gun if they are in the police or the military, and are using the gun in the execution of their legal duties. By acknowledging the authority of a state, we accept its right to make decisions (even if we might not always agree with those decisions) and we accept our own duty to obey (Huemer, 2013).

Second, states have **legitimacy**, meaning that their existence and the authority they wield within their borders is generally recognized by the people who live there, and by the governments and citizens of other states. Legitimacy is a political and moral concept, based on whether or not the authority of a state is accepted, a topic about which there has been much debate in recent years (see Gilley, 2009). States might face questions about the legitimacy of their actions (have they gone too far, for example, in invading the privacy of their citizens?), while others face questions about whether they have a right to exist at all. An example of the latter is Kosovo, a region of Serbia that declared independence in 2008, but whose international status is disputed: as of 2018, fewer than 60 per cent of UN member states recognized Kosovo, the exceptions including neighbouring Bosnia and Serbia, as well as China, Greece, Russia, and Spain.

> **Legitimacy**: Recognition that a state has the right to wield authority within its borders.

Third, states have **sovereignty**, meaning that they answer to no higher political or legal authority, and are legally independent in the sense that they can make all their own decisions (Jackson, 2007). In practice, states are so heavily interconnected in so many ways that true independence is a myth; states might have the power to make laws and impose taxes, but their decisions are often impacted by the decisions of other states or by the pressures of the global system of which states are a part.

> **Sovereignty**: The principle that a state answers to no higher political or legal authority.

Finally, all states have a **government**, made up of the institutions, processes and laws that are needed to keep states running, and to represent them in dealings with other states. A government is made up of political leaders, including the executive (president or prime minister), the members of the legislature, and judges in the courts, as well as the bureaucracy needed to implement law and public policy. This means we can extend the idea of government to include the police, the military, and all the employees of government institutions, from the national to the local.

> **Government**: The system of institutions, processes and laws responsible for addressing the needs of the residents of a state.

None of these four qualities is always absolute or directly measurable: states are sometimes involved in political disputes that create uncertainties about their borders, populations change as they grow and as people move across borders, states periodically face challenges to their authority and legitimacy (some more so than others), the sovereignty and independence of states has always been qualified by external economic and political pressures, and governments come in many different forms that often have different relationships with their citizens and with each other. And states do not act in isolation; they are deeply interconnected, and are subject to pressures from their citizens and from other states – see Global and Local 5. But one way or another, all states have all four qualities.

Source: Getty Images\Victor Cardoner

The Houses of Parliament in London, UK. The institutions of government, and the people who fill them, are a key feature of the state.

Armed with this knowledge, it should be easy to identify all the world's states and to determine how many there are; in a neat and tidy world, all territory would come under the jurisdiction of states, and all states would have the same core features and powers. Unfortunately, the world is not a neat and tidy place, and the innocent question 'How many states are there?' is hard to answer. The most complete listing of states can be found in the membership roster of the United Nations, which currently includes 193 states. But there are several problems with this list:

▸ Four UN members in Europe (Andorra, Liechtenstein, Monaco, and San Marino) are no more than microstates that are in almost every way integrated within the bigger states that surround them.

▸ Several of the world's territories do not appear on the list, either because they are not independent territories (Bermuda, the Cayman Islands and Puerto Rico come to mind), or because they are not internationally recognized as states. Consider the case of Taiwan, which was a member state of the UN until 1971 when it was expelled in the wake of a decision to admit China to the UN. It exists, it has territory, a population, authority, sovereignty and a government, but it lacks legitimacy. Meanwhile, membership of the UN is not obligatory: Switzerland is one of the oldest states in the world, but did not become a full member of the UN until 2002.

▸ Several states have separatist movements whose activities have brought about a break-up of an existing state and a redrawing of state boundaries. This happened in the 1990s, for example, with the former Yugoslavia (which is now seven separate states), and in 2011 with the independence of South Sudan from Sudan. Several European countries – including Britain and Spain – contain significant separatist movements, and several others have separatist movements

GLOBAL AND LOCAL 5

STATES: THINKING GLOBALLY, ACTING LOCALLY?

At some time in the 1970s the phrase 'Think globally, act locally' began to appear in the titles of books and conferences, and even on bumper stickers. The sentiment it expressed was that people should take the global view by considering the health and welfare of the entire planet, and their place in the global system, while taking action within the local communities in which they lived. The sum of millions of positive individual local actions, ran the logic, would have global effects. While the phrase probably grew out of concerns about the environment, it has since been applied to education, commerce, finance, farming, marketing and town planning, among others.

States are central to this idea, because they are an intermediary between the global and the local: the global system is defined to a large extent by the powers and the interaction of states, but states also reach down to the local interests of their citizens, and ideally reflect those interests back to the global level. In short, the work and status of citizens must be understood from both a top-down perspective and a bottom-up perspective.

At the global level, states decide how to relate with one another, reach agreements on everything from trade to military cooperation, and make many of the decisions that shape how we think about human rights or deal with migration. They might want to take the global view and try to address shared problems together, or they might pull back and give priority to their national interests. We have seen much cooperation among states since the end of World War II, but in recent years we have also seen many governments arguing that they need to protect home industries and clamp down on immigration; examples include the United States under President Donald Trump, India under Prime Minister Narendra Modi, and several European countries under conservative governments.

While it is hard for most people to have a direct impact at the global level, actions taken at the local level can accumulate, with global effects. We might think of climate change, for example, to be far too big a problem to be solved by individuals, and yet if everyone was to change the way they consumed energy (by using public transport, recycling, avoiding bottled water, and reducing their electricity consumption, for example), the production of greenhouse gases would decline – see Chapter 11. Broader political and economic changes are also taking place at the local level, and these are having global effects, sometimes in spite of choices made by national governments. Migration is a good example: local communities are often at odds with national government on migration policy, in some cases being more welcoming and in others being less welcoming. Their attitudes help shape national policy, which in turn helps shape global policy.

that are only kept in check thanks to authoritarian governments, as in the case of China and Tibet.

▶ States vary in the extent to which they actually have control over their land and people. While the vast majority of UN members have both sovereignty and legitimacy, some – such as Iraq and Somalia – are quasi-states, meaning that they exist but have lost control over much of their territory. Others are *de facto* states, meaning that they control territory and provide governance but are mainly unrecognized by the international community and are not UN members; examples include Abkhazia, Kurdistan, Nagorno-Karabakh, Transnistria, and the Turkish Republic of Northern Cyprus (see Caspersen, 2011).

Source: AFP/Getty Images

Weeks before a secession referendum in 2017, demonstrators wave flags during a rally in Barcelona in support of independence for the Spanish region of Catalonia.

As a result, when we look at the membership roster of the UN – from Afghanistan to Zimbabwe – we find only those countries that meet all the standard definitions of a state. They might vary in population size, economic size, geographical area, and internal homogeneity, but they almost all have the kind of authority and legitimacy that makes them autonomous actors within the global system. In turn, their interactions are the fuel that drives that system.

Almost everyone in the world lives under the authority of a state, and is directly impacted by the work of a state, feeling its effects in several important ways – see Figure 5.2. In order to be legally associated with a state, we must have **citizenship**, which gives us the full right to live in – and participate in the public life of – our home state (see Bellamy, 2008). More specifically, those rights include the following:

> **Citizenship**: The idea of legally 'belonging' to a given state as a result of birth or being given citizenship, and having related rights and responsibilities.

▸ The right to live in that state.

▸ The right to vote or run in elections for political office.

▸ The right not to be removed from that state, unless extradited for a crime in another state, nor to be denied entry upon returning from another state.

▸ The right to hold a passport issued by our home state, and to travel across borders backed by the protection of our home government.

But citizenship goes beyond this by also including a set of duties. As good citizens, we are expected to engage in the civic life of our home state, to vote, to obey the law, to undertake jury service, and to serve in the military if required. Being a citizen, in short, means that we can take part in the political life of a state, and enjoy all the same rights and opportunities as our fellow citizens, including the full

Figure 5.2: Seven responsibilities of a state

LAW AND ORDER	Providing and maintaining the police and criminal justice system.
REGULATION	Adopting regulations and standards on everything from environmental management to food safety, price controls, working conditions and access to alcohol and drugs.
WELFARE	Providing welfare in the form of public health care, unemployment benefits, educational subsidies, and assistance to farmers.
MONEY	Managing the money supply and interest rates.
TAXES	Collecting taxes and overseeing the spending of public funds.
INFRASTRUCTURE	Providing and maintaining basic services such as roads, schools, water and energy supply.
NATIONAL SECURITY	Maintaining armed forces.

protection of the law and the legal system, and a minimum standard of economic and social welfare. But these are sometimes hard qualities to measure and quantify, a process that is complicated by at least three other realities:

▶ The legal non-citizen residents of a state have almost all the same rights as citizens. They may not be able to vote or run for public office, and they can be deported if they break state laws, but otherwise they have the same opportunities to participate in public life as full-fledged citizens. About 244 million people (three per cent of the world's population) are legal residents of a state other than their home state.

▶ Dual citizenship is increasingly common, with some people holding two, three, or even more passports, muddying the waters of rights and obligations. (And we should not forget the questions asked by some about why citizenship should be tied to states, and why – as we saw in Chapter 3 – we cannot be citizens of the world.)

▶ There are – as we will see in Chapter 10 – many people living in states who are doing so without authorization, which means that they have none of the rights enjoyed by citizens, but are still part of the way that peoples and states interact with one another.

In spite of their separate legal existences, states are far from isolated from one another. They trade and do business, they invest in one another, their citizens move across borders, they learn from one another, they react to political and economic developments in other states, and – as we will see in Chapter 6 – they are bound together by the work of international organizations and the signature of international treaties. We can understand many of them in terms of their individual histories and separate social circumstances, but we must also look beyond national borders if we are to fully understand the changing circumstances in which each them functions.

STATES VS. NATIONS

A foreigner looking at Britain might think of it as a single political and cultural unit. It has clearly defined borders, it has a national flag, it has a government, it has a seat in the United Nations, and it has almost everything else that it needs to function as a state. But look a little closer, and you soon find that it has many internal divisions. It is, to begin with, a united kingdom of three other entities – England, Scotland, and Wales – with Northern Ireland thrown in for good measure. Each of these entities has its own languages, political parties, educational systems, and religions. These divisions make it harder for the UK to think of itself as a unified state, but this is not an unusual problem; many countries have an identity problem based on internal national divisions.

Although the terms *state* and *nation* are often used interchangeably, they have quite different meanings: while a state is a legal and political concept, involving a territory with sovereignty and legitimacy, a **nation** is a cultural and historical concept. Because states exist under law, they are relatively easy to identify. A nation, however, is a looser concept, and might even be what Anderson (1983) once described as an 'imagined community'. To complicate matters, the term *nation* is not used equally everywhere in the world, and is often seen as interchangeable with the concept of *ethnicity*: while Europeans might talk of their national differences, for example, Africans would talk of their ethnic differences. (But it is also worth remembering – as we saw in Chapter 3 – that ethnicity and race are also quite different.)

In most cases, nations coincide with states to form what is called a **nation-state**. But there are few states that are home to a single nation, among the few examples being Japan and Iceland. In Japan, thanks to its centuries of physical and cultural isolation, about 98.5 per cent of the population is Japanese, most of the balance being made up of small Chinese, Korean, and Filipino minorities. In Iceland, again thanks to its physical isolation, the population of 330,000 people shares such a well-documented descent from within a compact community that the state's birth records provide a perfect laboratory for genetic research.

The world has many more **multinational states**, particularly in Europe and Africa, the former because of their long histories of interactions with one another, and the latter because most of their borders were set for them by colonial powers in the 19th century. Consider the examples of Belgium and Nigeria. The former may be small (with a population of just over 11 million), but there is no Belgian language and only a modest Belgian culture; about 60 per cent of Belgians are members of the French-speaking Flemish community, about 30 per cent are Dutch-speaking Walloons, the capital of Brussels is bilingual, and about 10 per cent of the population consist of national minorities, including native German-speakers and a large foreign-born Italian community. Meanwhile, Nigeria is divided into dozens of different ethnic groups (as few as 250, as many as 400, depending on how they are defined), most of them speaking different languages, living in different parts of the country, and preferring to mingle with their own when they move to cities.

Nation: A group of people who identify with one another on the basis of a shared history, culture, language, and myths.

Nation-state: A state whose citizens share a common national identity.

Multinational state: A state consisting of multiple different national groups living under a single government.

Alongside the national (or ethnic) diversity we find within states, we also find national or ethnic diversity globally, raising the phenomenon of the **diaspora**. The term was once used in connection with a mythical or actual homeland, was particularly associated with the Jewish people, and was based on the assumption that the members of a diaspora still identified with that homeland and hoped one day to restore or return to that place (Safran, 1991). Its meaning and use has since been broadened to describe a group of people with a common heritage, whether or not they still identify with 'home' and/or plan to return there. Examples include Irish immigrants who moved to the United States in the wake of the 19th-century potato famines, and Indians sent by the British as labourers to eastern and southern Africa.

Diaspora: The scattering or movement of a population beyond its geographical or native homeland, or the population that lives over an extended area outside its homeland.

Perhaps the biggest modern diaspora is the African example, made up of the descendants of the slaves taken to the Americas between the 15th and the 19th centuries. While few have more than a passing relationship with those parts of mainly West Africa from which their ancestors were taken, they continue to bring distinctive qualities to the cultures of the states in which they now live, particularly Brazil, Cuba, and the United States. Europe has also been the source of major diasporas, including the Spanish and Portuguese settlers who moved to the Americas, displacing or intermarrying with native populations. More recently, as we will see in Chapter 10, conflict and war have created new diasporas in the wake of the displacement of large numbers of refugees from countries such as Syria, Colombia, Afghanistan, Iraq, South Sudan, and Zimbabwe. Many see their displacement as temporary, pending the return of peace to their homelands, but for many others the displacement is permanent.

Yet another kind of diaspora concerns people who live in their traditional homeland but who lack formal control over that homeland. The creation of Israel in 1948 involved expropriation of territory already occupied by Palestinians, who have since – without success – sought a Palestinian state. While the numbers are disputed, an estimated 1.7 million Palestinians live in Israel, another 4–5 million live in the neighbouring lands of the Palestinian Authority, while perhaps another 6 million live elsewhere. Nearby, an estimated 30 million Kurds live in or around what many hope will eventually become the state of Kurdistan, the territory of which is currently divided between Iran, Iraq, Syria, and Turkey – see Map 5.1.

In summary, then, there is general agreement on the characteristics of a state, the membership roster of the United Nations is the authoritative list of the world's states, and states play the dominating role in defining the features of the global system. But not all the world's territory is part of a state, states are not as independent as they and their leaders might like to think, and nations are at least as important as states in understanding how people identify themselves. States do not exactly coincide with nations, and the dispersal of nations has created diasporas, leaving us with a fluid situation that becomes more fluid as migration patterns become more complex.

THE EVOLUTION OF STATES

The world's biggest state by population is China. It is also one of the oldest states in existence, its origins dating back several thousand years, although its boundaries have changed constantly, achieving their modern form only during the

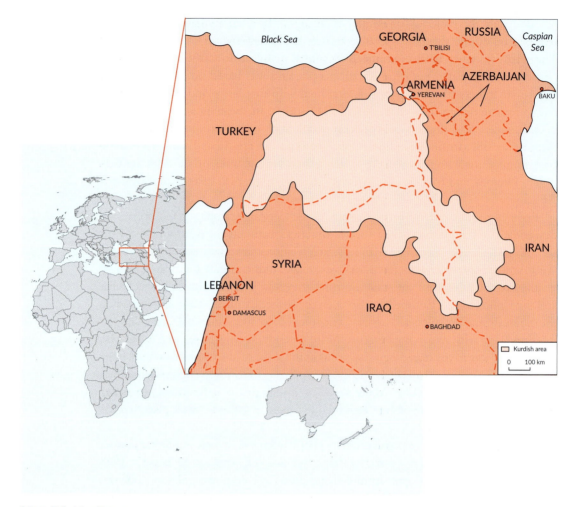

Map 5.1: Kurdistan

20th century. China also has a long history of being relatively isolated and of failing to make much in the way of a global impression; this is why the global system as we understand it is founded so much on Western ideas and influences. All, though, is about to change. China has been emerging from the isolation and introspection of the era of Mao Zedong (1949–76), its economy is growing rapidly, its military is building, the reach of its technology is expanding, and its political influence is deepening. Its emergence is just the latest dramatic shift in the reordering of global power, which has revolved for centuries around the creation, reshaping, and elimination of states.

Although the origins of the modern state system can be traced back about 300–500 years (see Anderson, 1998), most of today's states are much younger than that. As we saw in Chapter 1, there was no single event that marked the emergence of modern states, although their roots lie in medieval Europe, and particularly in war. Where governance had been dominated until then by monarchs, feudal lords, and the Catholic Church, the introduction of gunpowder in the 14th century transformed the scale and tactics of armies, with organized infantry and artillery replacing knights on horseback. The result was an expensive European arms race, which obliged rulers to employ administrators to recruit, train, equip and pay for standing armies, laying the foundation of modern bureaucracies. Political units became larger, and local patterns of administration and justice became more uniform. Trade grew, and rulers began to establish formal diplomatic relations with their foreign counterparts. At the same time, the Reformation undermined the religious foundations of the medieval system.

The 1648 Peace of Westphalia confirmed the development of centralized authority in much of Europe, but there was still a need for its theoretical justification. The crucial concept here was sovereignty, as later conditioned by the idea that citizens should consent to be ruled. The idea that the sovereign should be subject to limits and controls was given a firmer basis by the English philosopher John Locke (1632–1704), who argued that citizens possessed natural rights to life, liberty and property, and that these rights must be protected by rulers governing on the basis of the law. Locke suggested that citizens agreed to obey the law, but that if rulers violated the natural rights of citizens, then citizens had the right to resist; see Chapter 7.

During the 19th century, the outlines of European states were clarified and strengthened as borders were tightened and more controls were exerted over movement across borders in the interests of security. It is hard to believe today, but prior to World War I there were few limits on cross-border travel, mainly because few people had the means or the reason to visit other countries. Passports were introduced in Europe during World War I, allowing governments to control cross-border movement, and states exerted more control over their economies by pursuing protectionist policies. Income taxes were introduced, and the functions of states expanded to include education, factory regulation, and policing.

The reach of states expanded still further during the 20th century as a result of war, which achieved new levels of breadth and depth with the two world wars, fought between entire countries rather than just between specialized armed forces. To equip themselves meant that states had to engage in an unparalleled mobilization

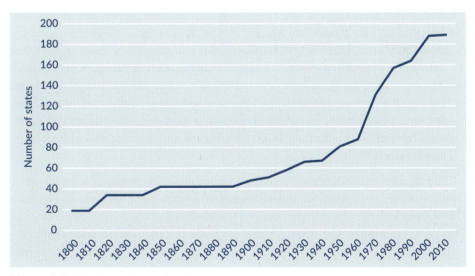

Figure 5.3: The formation of states
Source: Based on appendix in Crawford (2007). Includes only those states internationally recognized as sovereign and independent in mid-2018. Excludes European microstates.

of citizens, economies and societies, which meant an expansion in the ability to tax effectively and systematically, which meant a need to expand the size of government and the reach of government into the lives of citizens. When they were not fighting each other, meanwhile, European states in particular were taking on more responsibility for protecting their citizens from illness, illiteracy, unemployment and old age. The warfare state gave way to the welfare state.

The expansion of the state system globally can be seen as taking place in four distinct waves:

▶ The first came in the early 19th century, with the independence of Spanish and Portuguese territories in Latin America. This created 15 new states, including Argentina, Brazil and Mexico. The constitutions of these new states were neither democratic nor fully implemented, and the result was a tradition of authoritarian and often military government, and the creation of political and economic inequalities that are still evident today.

▶ The second wave took place as a consequence of World War I, leading as it did to the final collapse of the Austro-Hungarian and Ottoman empires. This spawned 12 new states, including Austria, Czechoslovakia, Hungary, Poland, Turkey, and Yugoslavia, many of which were drawn into the orbit of the new Soviet Union and failed to develop the same record of democratic and capitalist development experienced in Western Europe.

▶ The third and biggest wave came after 1945 as a result of the dismantling of their empires by European states exhausted by war; see Figure 5.3. The new United Nations began life in 1945 with just 51 members, but over the next forty years, nearly 90 new states (almost half the UN's current membership roster) emerged in Africa, the Caribbean, Asia and the Pacific. Most lacked a record as coherent entities, and statehood was often superimposed on populations with major ethnic, regional and religious divisions, the destabilizing effects of which often continue to be felt even today.

▶ The fourth wave came in the 1990s, triggered by the collapse of communism. This led to the dissolution of the Soviet Union into 15 successor states, including Russia, Ukraine, and Kazakhstan. It also meant new freedom for more than a dozen Soviet satellites in Eastern Europe, such as Hungary and Poland. The experience of these new post-communist states has been mixed, with the Baltic states gaining economic and political stability as well as membership of the European Union, but Belarus remaining authoritarian and several states torn between retaining their links with Russia and exerting themselves more independently.

The changes have continued, with the reunification of Germany, the break-up of Czechoslovakia and Sudan, the independence of Eritrea from Ethiopia and of East Timor from Indonesia, the departure of Montenegro and Kosovo from Serbia, and secessionist movements in several European countries that raise the possibilities – for example – of an independent Scotland and an independent Catalonia. Meanwhile, the pressures on the state system have become more complex, in many ways reducing the barriers that divide them, and in many other ways making them stronger – see later in this chapter.

UNDERSTANDING GOVERNMENT

If states are the building blocks of the global system, it is mainly because they have governments with the authority to administer the people and the territory of states, and to oversee relations among states. As we saw earlier, a government is a structure consisting of institutions, processes and laws that is responsible for addressing the needs of the people who live under its jurisdiction. As we will see in Chapter 6, there is no world government, meaning that governments exist in a substantive form only at the level of states and of the subsidiary political units that make up states, such as regions, provinces, counties, and cities. Meanwhile, a **political system** describes the features of the structure of government: how its institutions are designed and function, how rules are made and enforced, how citizens participate, how elections are organized, and how the parts fit together.

> **Political system**: The interactions and organizations (including government) through which a society reaches and enforces collective decisions.

Ideally, citizens should have the right to choose their own government (usually through electing representatives) and the government should be responsive to the needs of all the people under its jurisdiction. The ideal, though, rarely happens. Even in the most democratic systems, there are always unanswered questions about how best to arrange for people to choose their governments, about how best to structure governments, and about how governments can best measure the needs of the people, and best resolve conflicting needs and demands. Governments do not just answer to the wishes of citizens, but are also driven by their own ideological leanings, by the influence of those in society with power and resources, and by the actions and demands of other governments.

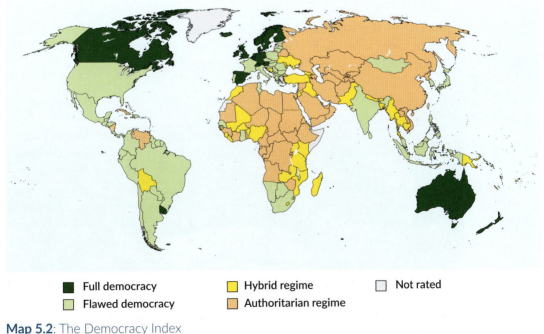

■ Full democracy   ■ Hybrid regime   □ Not rated
□ Flawed democracy   ■ Authoritarian regime

Map 5.2: The Democracy Index
Source: Economist Intelligence Unit (2016).

We have no universal system for classifying states according to their different levels of democracy, but a useful guide through the maze is offered by the Democracy Index, compiled by the news weekly *The Economist*. This divides most of the states of the world into four clusters: full democracies, flawed democracies, hybrid regimes, and authoritarian regimes – see Map 5.2. Simplifying this still further leaves us with two categories.

> **Democracy**:
> A political system in which government is based on a fair and open mandate from all qualified citizens of a state, and is based on the rule of law.

Democracies. There is no generally agreed definition of **democracy**, which is a variable measure rather than a fixed and absolute condition: some states are more or less democratic than others. At a minimum, a democracy must have representative government, free elections, respect for the rule of law, and the protection of individual rights. But each of these concepts is subject to multiple questions: what does 'representative' mean, what constitutes a free election, and how can we be sure that all individual rights are equally protected? Winston Churchill once famously said that democracy was the worst form of government, except for all the others. The implication was that while it is full of imperfections, it is the best political system we have been able to develop.

Even the most efficient democracies still suffer from elitism, from limits on representation, from inequalities, from inefficiency and corruption, from failed policies, and from the impingement of the rights of individuals and groups upon one another. Even so, about half the world's people can reasonably claim to live in a democracy, and the idea has spread from its European origins to many other parts of the world, including Australia, Brazil, Canada, India, Japan, Mexico, New Zealand, and the United States. The Democracy Index gives about 20 states the ranking of full democracies, and nearly 60 the ranking of flawed democracies. The latter have

> **Democratization**:
> The process by which states build the institutions and processes needed to become stable democracies.

most of the qualities of a democracy, but suffer from weak governance and an underdeveloped political culture, and include among their number the United States, Japan, France, South Korea and India. Several flawed democracies are undergoing a process of **democratization**, where political institutions and processes are becoming more stable, individual rights are better protected, and the voice of the people is heard more clearly (Grugel and Bishop, 2014).

Source: Hindustan Times/Getty Images

A candidate gives an address during an election campaign in India, often described as the world's largest democracy. Elections are the lifeblood of democracy, allowing voters to help choose their government.

Authoritarian systems. The typical features of an **authoritarian system** include government by an elite, manipulated elections, a failure to support and respect the rule of law or to protect individual rights, and intolerance of opposition. Although authoritarian rule is usually associated with a dictator or a single dominant leader, such leaders cannot win and keep power by themselves, which means that they must rely on others to stay in power, and those others – whether the military, the wealthy, or members of a particular ethnic group or religion – will demand benefits in return for their support, but will also likely be jockeying among themselves for influence.

There are constitutions in authoritarian states, but they are only inconsistently applied, laws are vague and contradictory, the executive is usually powerful while the legislature and the courts are marginalized, minorities are often poorly treated, and 'the people' are expected to go through the motions of supporting the government while doing nothing to rock the boat or to challenge the establishment. The Democracy Index gives about 40 states the ranking of hybrid regimes, and just over 50 the ranking of authoritarian regimes. While the former still have some vestiges of democracy, political pluralism has all but disappeared from the latter. Most authoritarian states are found in Africa, the Middle East and Asia, prime examples being Belarus, China, Iran, North Korea, and Russia.

> **Authoritarian system**: One in which power is concentrated in the hands of a ruling elite, which manipulates society in order to remain in power.

Table 5.1: Comparing democracies and authoritarian systems

	Democracies	Authoritarian systems
Elections	Regular, fair, secret, and competitive.	Often accompanied by fraud, manipulation, and violence.
Political institutions and processes	Well-defined, stable, and predictable, based on a distribution of powers and a system of political checks and balances.	Weak, immature, or poorly defined, with a centralization of power in the hands of leaders and elites.
Political participation	A wide variety of institutionalized channels, including multiple political parties with a variety of platforms.	A limited selection of channels, and no guarantees that the voices of citizens will be heard effectively.
Powers of government	Limited, with protection of individual rights and freedoms under the law, sustained by an independent judiciary.	Fewer limits, with a mixed record on the protection of individual rights and freedoms under the law, with no independent judiciary.
Political opposition	Active, effective, and protected.	Constrained, and subject to threats and even violence.
Media	Diverse and independent, subject to few political controls and free to share a wide variety of opinions.	Limited and controlled, subject to political controls and free to share only officially sanctioned opinions
Examples	Australia, Brazil, Canada, India, Japan, Mexico, South Korea, the United States, and most of Europe.	China, Iran, North Korea, Russia, and most of the Middle East, North Africa, and sub-Saharan Africa.

COMPARING NORTH AND SOUTH 5

THE PERFORMANCE OF STATES: NORWAY AND SOMALIA

In understanding the records of states, the performance of their governments and economies, and the structures of their societies, we need to look at them both individually and comparatively. There are many comparative ranking systems available to us, which assess states according to a wide variety of political, economic and social criteria – several are used in this book. While the results vary, there is a high degree of overlap and coincidence among them, as illustrated by taking two states that routinely rank at the extremes of all these scales: Norway often ranks in the higher reaches, and Somalia often ranks in the lower reaches (to the extent that it can be ranked at all – see Table 5.2). It is worth comparing them so as to give us some insight into what success and failure mean in state terms. Before doing so, though, it is also worth noting that their relative records cannot all be explained by domestic decisions and circumstances, but is also a reflection of their different places within the global system.

Norway is a relatively homogeneous society with a history that dates back hundreds of years, even if it only became fully independent in 1905. It also has a wide range of natural resources, including oil, natural gas, forests, and minerals, and a small population of just over five million people. On only one measure – economic freedom – does Norway not top the polls, and this is because Norwegians and other Scandinavians support strong systems of welfare and redistribution, paying relatively high rates of tax. But for this they receive some of the best public services in the world, including education, health care, and generous social security.

Somalia is quite different on almost every count, suffering so much disarray that its condition cannot even be fully measured. It became independent in 1960 when British and Italian colonies were combined into a single new state. Ethnic divisions made it difficult to build stability, and the northwest region declared independence in 1991 as the Republic of Somaliland. A humanitarian mission in 1992 ended in failure, after which the fracturing of the state among warlords and religious factions worsened.

Somaliland has had a relatively stable history, but its independence is not generally recognized. Meanwhile, the rest of Somalia has been a land of lawlessness, poverty and disorder, its southern region of Puntland functioning autonomously and being the home of many of the pirates who have infamously been active off the Horn of Africa. Somalia has one of the highest population growth rates in the world, a problem that places ever more pressure on its land and resources. It also has one of the highest infant mortality rates in the world, widespread poverty, an economy that barely functions, a major refugee problem, and suffers high risk for infectious disease because of its lack of clean water and an effective health care system.

Democracies and authoritarian systems do not just have contrasting internal features (see Table 5.1), but also have contrasting positions within the global system: the former are mainly more open and engaged while the latter are more closed and protective. Both types worry about threats, both place self-interest at the top of their agendas when negotiating with other states, and both seek either to encourage other states to their point of view or to prevent unwelcome ideas from other states influencing their own. Overall, however, democracies have stronger records of

Table 5.2: Ranking Norway and Somalia

Index	Originator	Number of states ranked	Norway	Somalia
Freedom in the World	Freedom House	195	1=	189
Democracy Index	The Economist	167	1	Not ranked
Fragile States Index	Fund for Peace	178	2	177
Corruption Perception Index	Transparency International	176	6	175
Per capita GDP	World Bank	190	1	Not ranked
Index of Economic Freedom	Heritage Foundation	178	27	Not ranked
Human Development Index	UN Development Programme	168	1	Not ranked

Sources: 2017 issues of each index.

cooperation and of taking the lead in the work of international organizations, or the agreement of international treaties.

We saw in Chapter 1 that Francis Fukuyama was premature in declaring the end of history (the global triumph of democracy) in 1989. Since then, there have been signs in democracies of a reaction against the elitism represented by a class of professional politicians, against a growing gap between the rich and the poor, and against what are widely seen as the threats posed by globalization and immigration. Many of the citizens of democracies that had long been so open to the global system now seem to be reacting against that system, giving support to new political parties on the right that oppose immigration and globalization, and electing leaders running on a nationalist platform. Brown (2010) notes the symbolism contained in the proliferation of walls marking national borders, such as those dividing Israel from Palestine, South Africa from Zimbabwe, and the United States from Mexico. She also suggests that they are often little more than frequently breached 'theatrical props', projecting an image of sovereign power while also raising questions about the inability of states to address many of the effects of globalization.

Gilley (2009) wonders about the declining faith of citizens in the ability of states to rule, and points to indicators of a crisis in the legitimacy of states, posing threats to their stability. Even such established democracies as France and India are losing their moral claims over society, he argues, while authoritarian states such as China and Iran enjoy strong showings of public support. These states, argue Diamond et al. (2016), have recently won new influence in the global arena, as they develop new tools and strategies to contain the spread of democracy and to challenge the liberal international political order. Meanwhile, the advanced democracies have retreated, failing to respond to the threat posed by the authoritarians.

In its annual report on the state of freedom in the world in 2017, the New York-based think-tank Freedom House noted that 67 countries had suffered net declines in political rights and civil liberties (continuing a trend dating back more than a decade), and summarized the year as follows:

> In 2016, populist and nationalist political forces made astonishing gains in democratic states, while authoritarian powers engaged in brazen acts of aggression, and grave atrocities went unanswered in war zones across two continents. All of these developments point to a growing danger that the international order of the past quarter-century—rooted in the principles of democracy, human rights, and the rule of law—will give way to a world in which individual leaders and nations pursue their own narrow interests without meaningful constraints, and without regard for the shared benefits of global peace, freedom, and prosperity (Freedom House, 2017).

These are trends that are drawing wide concern, both generating and reflecting the debate about the post-Cold War uncertainties discussed in Chapter 1.

CHALLENGES TO THE STATE

Even though we take states for granted, and almost all of us live in one, as well as being citizens of one, questions have long been asked about their stability and future. As the number of states has grown since 1945, so also have the links that have bound them. The problems they face have also changed, intensifying the debates about how well equipped they are to address those problems. Opinion is divided between those who believe that states are becoming stronger, those who believe they are becoming weaker, and those who think they are simply changing form within an evolving global system.

The strength of states can be found in their continued monopoly over the control and use of militaries, their ongoing role as the key actors in the management of economic production and international trade, and in the fact that their citizens still identify mainly with their home states, whose authority they recognize. In the face of such challenges as international terrorism and immigration, states are exerting new controls that make it more difficult (or, at least, more complicated) to travel across state borders. We have also seen the rise of the **security state**. Combined with new initiatives by business to learn the habits of consumers, and by social media to develop algorithms based on those habits, this has sparked a reaction as citizens express concerns about surveillance, threats to civil liberties, the activities of intelligence services, and limitations on the right to privacy (see Chapter 7).

The changing role and power of states can also be seen in increased support for nationalism (see Chapter 3). This has always been a factor in the actions of nations and of states, but the new nationalism is an effort to conflate the interests of states and nations and to assert state interests at the regional or global level. States still cooperate, they are still members of international organizations, and they still reach international agreements, but many are re-asserting themselves as large blocs of their voters support policies critical of globalization and immigration. This is reflected in the election of leaders such as Donald Trump in the United States and Rodrigo Duterte in the Philippines, the domestic popularity of Vladimir Putin in Russia, the

Security state: A state that follows the activities of its citizens through closed-circuit television, the monitoring of phone calls and internet use, and other means.

Source: Brand X

Symbolizing the rise of the security state and the spread of public surveillance, a security guard monitors coverage from closed-circuit television cameras.

2016 British decision to leave the European Union, and support for nationalist parties in France, Hungary, India, the Netherlands, and Turkey during the same period.

On the other hand, there are many who argue that the state is in trouble, an argument made as long ago as 1946 when it was described as a 'leviathan in crisis' (Browne, 1946). Critics charge that states are too often at odds with one another, driven by their habits of placing narrow interests above the broader interests of humanity, of imposing artificial political divisions on human society, and of reminding humans of their differences rather than their similarities. On the economic front, states are sometimes criticized for protecting domestic markets in a fashion that interferes with the functioning of the free market, imposing limits on trade that handicap innovation and efficiency, and failing to manage their economies and national resources to the benefit of all their residents. (But some are also criticized for being enslaved to the free market, and for failing to impose enough regulation, for example on the banking industry.) Finally, states are criticized for being too concerned with protecting and promoting their own interests to be able to deal effectively with problems such as terrorism, unauthorized immigration, and climate change. In short, critics charge that they are unable to meet the demands of their residents for security, justice, and prosperity.

Another pointer to the reduced role of states in the global system can be found in the growth of international cooperation. Critics of globalization and immigration may have prompted a nationalist backlash in many states, but – as we will see in Chapter 6 – the work of international organizations continues, the obligations of international treaties expand, and states continue to work together on a wide range of problems. Terrorism, for example, has encouraged nationalism, but it has also underlined the importance of cooperation on intelligence gathering and sharing.

An additional indicator of the weakening of states can be found in the breadth and depth of the global marketplace. Humans have traded with one another for as long as organized society has existed, but the extent and the effects of the global marketplace have ballooned since the end of World War II – see Chapter 9. Many of the underlying dynamics of that market are determined less by governments (and, therefore, states) than by multinational corporations, whose decisions – influenced by the demands of consumers – impact developments in new technology, changes in the nature of the workplace, trade flows, and investments.

Finally, the weakened position of states can be found in a combination of increased migration (both legal and unauthorized) that has watered down the cultural differences among states, and led to declining public loyalty to states. Where once most people did not travel far from where they were born, immigration – as we will see in Chapter 10 – has become more common, aided and abetted by the rise of international tourism. More people are more aware of the many options available to them for education and work, this might take them to new countries and cultures, they learn more about the variety of human society, and they are less inclined to see the world solely in terms of their home states and nations.

In the most extreme cases, some states – variously labelled weak, fragile, failed, or **failing states** (there is no agreement on the best term) – have so many domestic structural problems, and such a marginal place in the global system, that they have teetered on the brink of collapse. Estimates of the number of such states vary from about 20 to about 60, depending on how they are defined. One useful point of reference is the Fragile States Index produced annually by the US-based Fund for Peace, using a series of political, economic and social measures to rate different countries. In its 2017 index it described most democracies as being either sustainable or very stable (Finland alone earned the label 'Very Sustainable'). It issued warnings for China, India, Indonesia, Mexico, and Russia, and alerts for several African and Middle Eastern states, including Afghanistan, Iraq, Somalia, South Sudan, Sudan, and Syria (see also discussion in Collier, 2007). Among the measures it uses are the following:

Failing state: A state with deep structural problems, often major internal divisions, weak governing institutions, and failed or failing economies.

▸ Security threats.

▸ Schisms between different groups in society.

▸ Economic decline and high levels of poverty.

▸ Uneven economic development.

▸ Levels of state legitimacy.

▸ Quality of public services.

▸ Respect for human rights and the rule of law.

The future of the state is about as clear or as unclear as it has ever been. States will continue to be needed to manage many basic services, to provide their citizens with security, to prepare their citizens with the education and skills needed to address global economic pressures, to fight international terrorism, and to provide the driving force needed to respond to shared global problems such as disease and environmental degradation. Rather than declining, states may instead be undergoing a process of reform as they respond to the impact of globalization and to changes in the distribution of global resources. But whichever way they are headed, they continue to be at the heart of the definition of the global system.

DISCUSSION QUESTIONS

1. Which is more important to your identity: being a citizen of a state, or being a member of a national group?

2. Are state borders as important as they once were in terms of defining the global system?

3. Is the idea of thinking globally and acting locally realistic, or is it just a handy slogan?

4. Is Freedom House justified in its concerns about the possible emergence of a new international order in which states pursue their own narrow interests without meaningful constraints?

5. Why are some states stable and successful, while others are not?

6. Are states becoming stronger, weaker, staying about the same, or merely changing form?

KEY CONCEPTS

▶ Authoritarian system
▶ Authority
▶ Citizenship
▶ Democracy
▶ Democratization
▶ Diaspora

▶ Failing state
▶ Government
▶ Legitimacy
▶ Multinational state
▶ Nation
▶ Nation-state

▶ Political system
▶ Security state
▶ Sovereignty
▶ State

USEFUL WEBSITES

Democracy Index at http://www.eiu.com/topic/democracy-index

Fragile States Index at http://fundforpeace.org/fsi

Freedom in the World at https://freedomhouse.org/report-types/freedom-world

Membership of the United Nations at http://www.un.org/en/member-states

FURTHER READING

Delanty, Gerard, and Krishan Kumar (eds) (2006) *The Sage Handbook of Nations and Nationalism* (Sage). An edited collection on the idea of nations, with chapters looking at cases from around the world.

Diamond, Larry, Marc F. Plattner, and Christopher Walker (eds) (2016) *Authoritarianism Goes Global: The Challenge to Democracy* (Johns Hopkins University Press). An edited collection that reviews the efforts of undemocratic states to become more assertive on the global stage, and the failure of democracies to respond.

Diener, Alexander C., and Joshua Hagen (2012) *Borders: A Very Short Introduction*; Richard Bellamy (2008) *Citizenship: A Very Short Introduction*; and Steven Grosby (2005) *Nationalism: A Very Short Introduction* (Oxford University Press). These three books in the series have topics relevant to this chapter.

Jessop, Bob (2016) *The State: Past, Present, Future* (Polity Press). This offers a survey of the state, with chapters on its structure, its relationship to the nation, and speculation on where the state system is headed.

Hague, Rod, Martin Harrop, and John McCormick (2016) *Comparative Government and Politics: An Introduction*, 10th edn (Palgrave). A comparative survey of political systems and of the governmental institutions and processes found in states.

Online Resources

Visit www.macmillanihe.com/McCormick-GS to access additional materials to support teaching and learning.

LAW AND INTERNATIONAL ORGANIZATIONS

6

PREVIEW

The chapter looks first at the nature of international law, and at how international treaties are developed and implemented. It then looks at the work of international organizations, reviewing the structure and goals of intergovernmental organizations such as the United Nations, and then at the work of non-state actors such as international non-governmental organizations, multinational corporations, religious organizations, and those working outside the law. The chapter ends with a study of regional integration and its particular role in the global system.

CONTENTS

HIGHLIGHTS

▸ In the absence of a system of world government, international decision-making is made within a process of global governance.

▸ The work of international organizations and the effects of international laws often combine into regimes that define and outline activity.

▸ International law is typically based either on treaties signed between states or on the terms of membership of an international organization.

▸ There has been a dramatic increase in the number and reach of international organizations since 1945.

▸ Understanding the global system also means understanding the work and the reach of non-state actors that are not part of the structure of states.

▸ Many states in the world have gone beyond conventional cooperation and have engaged in regional integration, developing new systems of law and common policies.

Source: Courtesy of the ICJ. All rights reserved.

UNDERSTANDING GLOBAL GOVERNANCE

Every year, leaders of twenty of the world's biggest and wealthiest countries convene at an international summit meeting. They call themselves the Group of 20, or the G20, and they fly to the meeting from the Americas, Africa, Asia, the Middle East, and Australasia. They stay at the best hotels, are accompanied by security details and communications staff, meet in plush conference centres, and will be aware of the demonstrators that often gather nearby to express their opposition to the work of the leaders. Economic and financial matters are high up the agenda, and participants are conscious both of the exclusivity of their club and the presence around the table of leaders with a poor record on democracy. In spite of the contradictions, the group will set time aside to pose for a group photo, the smiles on everyone's faces belying their frequent differences and the challenge of trying to make decisions that benefit not only their own citizens but the world at large.

We saw in the last chapter that government consists of the institutions, processes and laws by which societies are governed, and that it exists in a substantive legal form only within states. In spite of organizations such as G20, there is no such thing as a world government (the operative term to describe the global system is **anarchy**) but states can never be entirely independent because of the ties that connect them. What we find when we look at political relationships involving two or more states, and at the systems, rules, and institutions that have been created in their wake, is a process of **governance**. In contrast to the formal institutions and procedures associated with government, governance describes a process or a style of governing. For example, we can talk about corporate governance, good governance, e-governance, or corrupt governance.

We can also talk about **global governance**, describing the way in which decisions are reached among states via a mix of governmental and non-governmental forces. It is reflected in declarations of intent, the agreement of treaties, and the membership of international organizations. It can also be seen in the countless decisions, events and actions that determine how goods and services are moved across borders, how the departures and arrivals of international travellers are managed, and how cooperation evolves on everything from health care to education, police investigations, research, environmental management, and the technological developments that help us communicate quickly and effectively (see Weiss, 2013). These are the 'good' aspects of global governance and globalization, but we should not forget the 'bad and the ugly', found in the activities of global criminal networks and international terrorism (see Chapter 12), which must be addressed by states, ideally working together.

At the state level and below, governments are expected to reach and execute decisions for the community over which they have jurisdiction, a process that – in democracies, at least – involves direct public accountability: voters make demands of governments, while governments claim to be responsive to those demands. At the global level, matters are quite different: there are institutions, but they lack sovereignty, have only as much authority as states give them, and have no direct political relationship with voters. There are laws in the form of treaties, but they do not have the same effect as national laws, because there is rarely a meaningful mechanism for enforcement, and signatories can opt out of their obligations – or work around them – without much fear of punishment.

Anarchy: A condition in which organized government is absent. Anarchists argue that governments are unnecessary and harmful, and favour self-governed societies based on voluntary associations.

Governance: The sum of the many ways in which collective decisions are made and implemented, with or without the input of formal institutions.

Global governance: The accumulation of institutions, processes, agreements, procedures, norms and actions that help us address transboundary needs and problems.

Focusing first on institutions, these are created when states (or interest groups within states) see opportunities for mutual benefits arising out of international cooperation, and set up bodies to help guide that cooperation. **Institutions** have been defined by Young (2002) as sets of rules, decision-making procedures, and programmes that define practices, assigning roles to participants in these practices and guiding interaction among those in the different roles. Institutions can be both formal, as in the case of the United Nations or the World Trade Organization, and informal, as in the case of the family, schools, and religions. They can also be governmental, with states as members, or non-governmental, meaning that they are made up of national or local interest groups, professions, private associations, or individuals.

> **Institution**: An informal or formal set of rules and procedures that define practices, assign roles, and guide interactions.

At the global level, the study of institutions and law is closely tied to the study of **regimes**, a term which (Krasner (1983) describes as the 'principles, norms, rules, and decision-making procedures' around which the expectations of actors converge in an area of concern. There is no hard and fast template for a regime, the elements of each changing according to how much structured action has been taken on a particular problem. Regimes are also, as much as anything, about citizen action. So while they are usually described as consisting of the cluster of institutions, treaties, proclamations, and actions that define and outline activity in different areas at the international and global levels, they also include the actions of groups and individuals working outside government. In later chapters, we will be looking at regimes focused on human rights, finance, trade, migration, the environment, and security, and finding that they are all structured differently, and have had varying levels of success and failure.

> **Regime**: A set of rules, norms, institutions and agreements surrounding a given issue and around which the expectations of interested actors converge.

Regimes are not necessarily based on specific international treaties or the work of dedicated institutions, although it gives them more focus if they are. Nor are they exclusively driven by the work of state governments. Instead, the 'actors' involved in a regime include non-governmental organizations (NGOs), international organizations, multinational corporations, and mass movements (see Breitmeier et al., 2006). Regimes can also be contrasted with non-regimes, where goals and policies are pursued across borders without formal multilateral agreements (Dimitrov, 2006). While the existence of a regime is not necessarily an indication of progress (as the often-stalled talks on dealing with climate change reveal), the absence of a regime is usually an indication of a lack of progress; little in the way of identifiable global regimes have yet formed – for example – around tactical nuclear weapons, the management of forests and fisheries, or information privacy.

The use of the term *regime* implies a uniformly structured and organized approach to a problem, but – as we will see in the chapters that follow – the performance of global regimes varies from one topic to another. For example, there is a substantial trade regime, made up of numerous trade agreements and given depth by the work of the World Trade Organization. But when we talk of an environmental regime, it is an accumulation of multiple international and regional organizations and treaties that have varied levels of achievement. There are global regimes for climate change and biodiversity, but (as we saw in Chapter 2) none for energy or fisheries, and efforts to build a global maritime regime have not moved far beyond the mixed results of agreements to control pollution at sea.

INTERNATIONAL LAW

A law is a rule that imposes limits and obligations on people or institutions, and that is enforceable by designated authorities, including courts and the police. At the state level and below, laws take the form of statutes written and adopted by legislatures, of case law that arises out of court decisions, and of regulations created by administrative agencies. We all know approximately how this works; if we are caught breaking a state or local law, we can expect to be punished with a fine or jail time, determined and enforced by police forces and courts that are part of the institutional fabric of government. The body of law constantly evolves, and often contains loopholes and contradictions, but its sources and effects are relatively clear, as are the obligations of those to whom it applies, and the punishments they face if they break the law.

Rules and regulations can also be found at the international level, but with two main differences: **international law** is targeted at states rather than individuals, and it is not supported by the same kinds of political, judicial, and police systems that we find with state or local law. International law is not drawn up by legislatures, there are few international courts in which legal cases can be tried, there is no international police force that can monitor application of the law and chase down law-breakers, and there is no unified system of sanctions that can be used to punish law-breakers (Shaw, 2014). All of this raises the question of the significance of international law; what good is a rule if it cannot be enforced? To answer that question we need to look first at the sources and forms of international law, and then at the means for making sure that it is followed.

International law is typically based either on treaties signed between states or on the terms of membership of an international organization. A **treaty** (otherwise known as a convention) can have goals that range from the broad to the narrow, it is voluntarily agreed by signatory states, it brings these states together to achieve a consensus on their shared goals, and it ties these states into a policy community where action, achievement, and failure are all closely monitored and the results shared among members of the community. Treaties mainly follow a standard format, beginning with a preamble describing the general goals, a series of articles containing the substance of the agreement and the means for resolving disagreements, and the list of signatories. Some are bilateral (signed between two parties) while others are multilateral (involving three or more parties).

There are tens of thousands of treaties in existence, dealing with numerous different topics (see Table 6.1 for some examples). But quantity does not necessarily translate into quality, and while many international treaties are both ambitious and respected, many others are more general and have resulted in little or limited change, or slow progress in bringing about change. Even before they come into force, treaties are often subject to a long and arduous process of drafting and discussion that can result in a watering down of goals (see Figure 6.1), the outcome depending on the breadth and complexity of the problem being addressed and the number of parties involved. It may take years for states even to agree that a problem should be addressed by a treaty, more years to reach agreement on the content of the treaty, and yet more years for the treaty to be given teeth in the form of meaningful targets. Some are sufficiently controversial that they never achieve enough ratifications to bring them into force, and yet others set targets that are politically difficult to achieve.

International law: The set of rules governing relations among states, and consisting of a combination of customs and formal agreements.

Treaty: An agreement between or among states that holds them responsible for upholding specified principles or meeting specified goals and deadlines.

Table 6.1: International treaties: Some examples

Year signed	Where signed	Topic
1864–1949	Geneva	Four conventions on the humanitarian treatment of prisoners, civilians, and the sick and wounded during times of war.
1919	Versailles	Treaty formally ending World War I.
1944	Bretton Woods, New Hampshire	Agreement among wartime allies on post-war international economic system.
1949	Washington DC	Created North Atlantic Treaty Organization.
1957	Rome	Established European Economic Community.
1963	Various	Banned atmospheric nuclear tests.
1979	New York	Defined states' rights and responsibilities with regard to use of the world's oceans.
1992	Rio de Janeiro	Established general agreement to address climate change.
1997	Ottawa	Agreement to eliminate anti-personnel landmines (those designed to injure or kill people, as opposed to blowing up tanks or ships).
2003	Geneva	Protection of current and future generations from dangers of tobacco consumption and exposure to tobacco smoke.

Figure 6.1: Stages in the development of an international treaty

STAGE	CONTENT
PROBLEM RECOGNITION	Problem defined as needing international agreement and action.
NEGOTIATION AND AGREEMENT	Terms and goals discussed and treaty drafted, usually focusing on definition of a problem rather than committing parties to specific obligations.
SIGNATURE	States sign, usually committing them to little more than good faith efforts to refrain from acts that would undermine goals of treaty.
RATIFICATION	States commit to terms of treaty. Specified number of ratifications usually needed before treaty comes into force.
GIVING TREATIES TEETH	Detailed commitments worked out in subsequent Conferences of Parties, where protocols to the treaty may be discussed and agreed.

Treaties are important, but they are not always a solution to a problem. In his study of global environmental law, for example, Selin (2014) suggests that the negotiation and implementation of environmental agreements 'is a process that encourages and enables, but does not require, cooperation. Treaties can play a constructive role in establishing common rules and standards, but they cannot be the sole problem-solving mechanism.' At the same time, he points out that compliance is not the only measure of effectiveness, and that treaties should also be assessed according to the extent to which they mitigate a problem, change common practices, and shape norms and decisions beyond the confines of the treaty process.

The extent to which treaties make a difference depends on the extent to which two conditions are met. First, treaties need to have realistic targets. The most successful tend to be those with focused interests and goals, strong political support, and limited geographical reach. The 1963 Partial Test Ban Treaty, for example, brought an end to atmospheric nuclear tests, leading to a sharp reduction in the concentration of radioactive particles in the atmosphere. Its goals were made more achievable by the fact that only five states had carried out such tests up to that point (the US, the Soviet Union, China, France and Britain), but even non-signatories China and France have abided by the terms of the treaty, as have newer nuclear powers such as India and Pakistan. It has been much more difficult to win support for the 1996 Comprehensive Nuclear Test Ban Treaty, which has yet to enter into force because it has not been ratified by enough countries (see Zartman et al., 2014).

The second, and most important, factor influencing the success of a treaty is that enforcement is critical. If a government signs and ratifies a treatment, then there is an assumption that it will live up to its obligations, and all is well and good if it does. But there is little that can be done to punish a state if it breaks or bends the terms of the agreement it has signed. It could be named and shamed, or it might even be expelled from the agreement or the international organization whose membership terms it is not respecting. Efforts can also be made to prevent such outcomes, including the holding of regular meetings of parties to a treaty (which remind signatories of its provisions), the establishment of secretariats charged with managing treaties

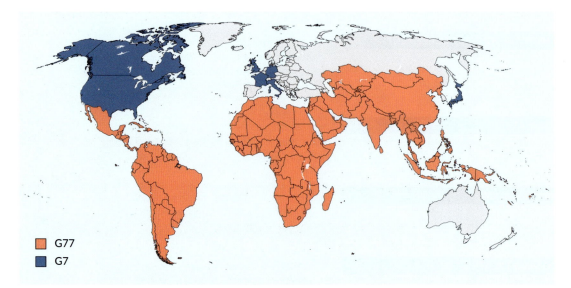

G77
G7

Map 6.1: The Groups of 7 and 77

COMPARING NORTH AND SOUTH 6

THE CHANGING BALANCE OF INTERNATIONAL INFLUENCE

In 1945, when the United Nations began work, it had 51 member states, and the interests of the UN were defined by the dominating role in the global system of the victors of World War II: the United States, the Soviet Union, Britain, France and China. It seemed reasonable and logical to many that these states should have permanent membership and veto powers in the UN Security Council. But much has changed in the intervening years: the membership of the UN has climbed to 193, the Soviet Union no longer exists (Russia inherited its seat), Britain and France are no longer the leading world powers they once were, China is on the rise in both political and economic terms, and the case for the retention of veto powers by World War II victors – or, indeed, any countries – has weakened. The balance of influence in the world has changed, the South exerting itself in ways that many in the North do not yet fully understand.

The North still wields much power because its members include most of the world's biggest economies, because they operate most of the world's biggest militaries, and because they generally agree on the benefits of democracy and free markets. These factors give them advantages when it comes to negotiating the terms of treaties, or defining the goals of intergovernmental organizations. But the global role of the United States is on the wane, most European countries exert influence only through their work within the European Union, and globalization has seen the centre of gravity pulled increasingly towards China, India, Brazil, Nigeria, and other countries in the South with the fastest-growing economies and populations.

The changes are reflected in the work of international organizations bringing together clusters of countries with shared political and economic interests. The seven wealthiest democracies – the US, Canada, Japan, France, Germany, Britain and Italy – have worked together since 1975 in the Group of 7 (otherwise known as G7), whose leaders meet annually at summits designed to talk about pressing issues and to build coordinated responses. It briefly expanded between 1998 and 2014 to become G8 when it admitted Russia, which was then expelled following the Russian annexation of Crimea.

The South, meanwhile, had already tried to offset the global influence of the wealthier states by creating the Group of 77, or G77, in 1964. This was founded by 77 African, Asian and Latin American members of the UN in an effort to enhance their negotiating capacity in the UN, but while its membership has since expanded to more than 130 members, it has faced internal divisions and finds itself unable to exploit its potential influence. More effective, because it is smaller, is the Group of 15 that was created in 1989, and now has 17 Southern members, including Brazil, India, Iran, Mexico, and Nigeria. The interests of G7 and G77 are meanwhile straddled by the work of the Group of 20, or G20, formed in 1999 to bring together the world's biggest economies regardless of their political position; it includes the G7 along with Argentina, Australia, Brazil, China, the European Union, India, Indonesia, Mexico, Russia, Saudi Arabia, South Africa, South Korea, and Turkey.

Leaders of the G7 – arguably the most collectively powerful group of people in the world – gather during their annual summit in Germany in 2016.

Source: AFP/Getty Images

(see later in this chapter), and regular reporting requirements. Beyond that, the obligation to respect agreements stems mainly from an understanding of playing the game, and the benefits of reciprocity: if a state respects the terms of an agreement, then it can reasonably expect all others to do the same. If it fails to respect those terms, then there is a risk of jeopardizing the goals of the agreement, and of the state establishing a reputation as one that does not cooperate. Similarly, cooperation can attract rewards in the sense that cooperative states are more likely to win the cooperation of other states.

Although there is no international court system of the kind found at the state and local level, there are a few international courts whose job is to adjudicate and support the work of their related institutions (see Mackenzie et al., 2010). For example, the International Court of Justice – based in The Hague – is the judicial organ of the United Nations, and can hear cases involving state members of the UN. Meanwhile, the Strasbourg-based European Court of Justice is the judicial organ of the European Union, and can issue rulings on cases involving the treaties upon which the EU is based. Equivalent courts fulfil the same role for other regional bodies such as the African Union, the Caribbean Community, and the Andean Community. In the field of human rights (see Chapter 7), the European Court of Human Rights issues judgements on cases within its 47 member states, while the International Criminal Court holds perpetrators accountable for serious violations of human rights, including genocide, crimes against humanity, and war crimes. But what all these courts have in common is the weakness or the absence of enforcement mechanisms to back up their judgements.

INTERNATIONAL ORGANIZATIONS

On the eastern shore of Manhattan, overlooking the East River that cuts through the city of New York, stands the imposing headquarters of the United Nations. Built in 1952, it often shows its age, and many of the interior spaces could benefit from some modernization and updating. Nonetheless, it remains almost constantly busy, with delegates arriving from nearby embassies and from many distant parts of the world, security making sure that no one uses the building to make a political statement, and groups of tourists winding their way through the building on self-guided tours. Occasionally there will be a major gathering in the Security Council at which representatives of the five permanent members of the Council and its ten rotating members will speak out on matters of urgency and importance, or nearly 200 delegates in the General Assembly will take votes on resolutions. The UN is the most senior and prominent of the world's network of **international organizations** (IOs), their work standing at the heart of the process of global governance, while stopping short of being a global government.

> **International organization**: A body set up to promote cooperation between or among states, with either governments or non-governmental actors as members.

Although states are the building blocks of the global system, they do not work in isolation, and one way in which they cooperate is through the work of international organizations such as the UN. These are bodies whose members consist either of state governments or of non-governmental organizations, and that have been created to bring their members together to work on a focused set of interests (Karns et al., 2015). Name almost any field of human endeavour and there is likely to be at least one IO serving its interests, but probably many more – see Table 6.2 for some examples.

Table 6.2: International organizations: Some examples

Name	Founded	Headquarters
International Telecommunication Union	1865	Geneva, Switzerland
Universal Postal Union	1874	Bern, Switzerland
International Olympic Committee	1894	Lausanne, Switzerland
International Federation of Association Football (FIFA)	1904	Zurich, Switzerland
Baptist World Alliance	1905	Falls Church, VA, USA
Interpol (International Criminal Police Organization)	1923	Lyon, France
United Nations	1945	New York, USA
International Association of Universities	1950	Paris, France
Organisation for Economic Co-operation and Development	1960	Paris, France
International Union of Geological Sciences	1961	Beijing, China
World Tourism Organization	1975	Madrid, Spain
Islamic Development Bank	1975	Jeddah, Saudi Arabia
International Trade Union Confederation	2006	Brussels, Belgium

The oldest IOs trace their origins back to the 19th century, but their numbers have exploded since the end of World War II on the back of new enthusiasm for international cooperation. According to data maintained by the Brussels-based Union of International Associations (UIA), there were fewer than 220 IOs in existence in 1909, and still only about 1,000 in 1951. The number had nearly quadrupled by 1970, had grown again to nearly 27,000 by 1990, and by 2013 stood at just over 66,000 – see Figure 6.2. The growth has been biggest among non-governmental organizations, which are less stable because most rely on public donations and the work of volunteers; hence, notes the UIA, about 1,200 new organizations are added to its records each year, but just under half the organizations in those records in 2013 were described as dormant.

The motives behind the creation and the work of IOs range from broad goals such as promoting peace or security to more focused goals such as the promotion of research, the setting of professional standards, the management of international programmes, the reduction of duplication, or the gathering of data. They come in multiple shapes and sizes:

▶ They may be global, regional or bilateral in scope.

▶ They may or may not have significant resources.

▶ They will have different levels of support and input from their participating members.

▶ They will have varied levels of specialized knowledge about their issues of concern.

▶ They will often use different methods to achieve their objectives.

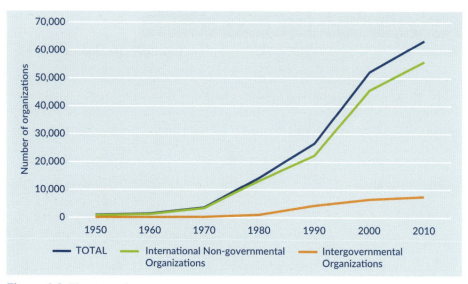

Figure 6.2: The growth of international organizations

Source: Based on data in Union of International Associations (various years).

Intergovernmental organization:
A body that promotes or facilitates cooperation among states, and consists of state members.

A specific kind of IO – an **intergovernmental organization** (IGO) – is the kind of body that most readily come to mind when we think of international organizations. As their name implies, IGOs are set up by governments, their members are states, and their goal is to promote cooperation among states. The grandparent of them all is the United Nations, together with its family of specialized agencies and programmes. Other IGOs include the World Trade Organization (see Chapter 9), which has a global membership focused on trade issues, and the North Atlantic Treaty Organization (see Chapter 12), which brings most of Europe into a security alliance with Canada and the United States.

The term *intergovernmental* should not always be taken too literally, because many IGOs do not actually bring together governments, so much as – for example – bureaucrats, scientists, or experts speaking on behalf of those governments. Also, while governments make the ultimate decisions and pay the financial costs of membership, the positions they take may be shaped and even implemented by groups and people who work outside government.

The work of IGOs is based on three principles:

▸ *Voluntary cooperation.* While states have laws that can be used to compel or force their citizens, IGOs must rely on consent and voluntary cooperation. They do not usually have much authority beyond the requirements of the terms of membership, which rarely provide them with the ability to enforce their rulings.

▸ *Shared interests.* While states will usually make decisions on the basis of self-interest, IGOs provide a forum within which members identify and work on shared interests. Their main job is to act as facilitators or as venues through which states can negotiate or cooperate with one another, using a range of methods that vary from gathering information to setting standards, carrying out research, and hosting conferences, all designed to help shape the international policy agenda.

▶ *Minimal autonomy*. The staff appointed to manage or coordinate the interests of IGOs have few, if any, independent powers, and can typically do only what the member states allow. They lack, for example, the power to impose taxes or enforce their rulings, have few assets, and do not control territory.

IGOs vary widely in terms of their age, size, reach and effectiveness. They might have political, military, economic, financial, social, cultural, religious or educational interests, they might have just two member states or they may be open to global membership, they might have a clearly defined functional responsibility (such as police cooperation or the management of whaling) or a broader set of interests (such as economic cooperation), and their powers and roles will vary from setting standards to gathering information, making rules, and monitoring the performance of states. A particular kind of IGO whose work is closely related to international law is the **treaty secretariat**. These are usually created under the terms of a treaty, their influence depending on the number of states that have signed the treaty they are monitoring, the depth of the goals involved, the size and visibility of the problem addressed by the treaty, the amount and speed of progress achieved in implementing the goals of the treaty, and the level of credibility they establish with their state members.

> **Treaty secretariat**: A body charged with monitoring the application of an international treaty, and with encouraging negotiations among signatory states.

The earliest IGOs were founded in Europe in the 19th century, and include the Commission for the Navigation of the Rhine (founded 1831), the International Telegraph Union (founded 1865 to establish international standards, and since renamed the International Telecommunication Union), and the General Postal Union (set up in 1874 – also to establish standards – and since renamed the Universal Postal Union). The more ambitious goals of promoting peace and preventing international conflict were behind the creation in 1920 of the League of Nations. In spite of its problems and its short life (see Chapter 1), it helped promote the kind of international perspective that was later behind the formation of the ultimate IGO: the United Nations (UN).

Founded in 1945, the purposes of the UN (Article 1 of the UN Charter) are to maintain international peace and security through the removal of threats to peace, to encourage good relations and cooperation among states, and to encourage respect for human rights. It is the closest we have come to creating a truly global organization, but it is not a world government; it can only do as much as the member states allow it to do, and sovereignty still clearly lies with the member states, as made clear in Article 2 of the UN Charter: 'The Organization is based on the principle of the sovereign equality of all its Members'.

There are five parts to the UN:

▶ The *General Assembly* is its major meeting place, where all states are equal and have the power to discuss and pass resolutions.

Source: ImageSource

The headquarters of the United Nations in New York. The prime example of an intergovernmental organization, the UN has worked to promote peace and international security since 1945.

▸ The *Security Council* is more focused, with 15 members: the five permanent members that were on the winning side of World War II (the US, Russia, the UK, France, and China) and that have the power of veto, and ten rotating members.

▸ The *International Court of Justice* (see earlier in this chapter). Based in The Hague (the Netherlands), it has 15 judges appointed to renewable nine-year terms.

▸ The UN also has an extensive family of *programmes and specialized agencies* dealing with a variety of issues, ranging from education to health, the environment, food security, monetary stability, the status of women, industrial and agricultural development, and intellectual property (see Table 6.3). Several of these are dealt with in detail in later chapters.

▸ The UN pulls together and manages international *peacekeeping forces* that are committed to global trouble spots – see Chapter 12.

While opinion is divided on its value (see Table 6.4), the UN is probably the best kind of global IGO that is possible given the variety of demands and expectations made by states in their interactions with one another. It suffers many of the standard problems faced by large organizations, including waste, inefficiency, differences of opinion about priorities, and a failure of the parts always to communicate effectively with one another. It faces the additional problem of having to rely on political support and budgetary contributions from countries that often disagree with each other and with the directions taken by the UN. But in spite of its problems, it is better that we have the UN than we do not.

Table 6.3: Selected agencies and programmes of the United Nations	
FAO	Food and Agriculture Organization of the UN
IBRD	World Bank (International Bank for Reconstruction and Development)
ICAO	International Civil Aviation Organization
ILO	International Labour Organization
IMF	International Monetary Fund
IMO	International Maritime Organization
UNESCO	UN Educational, Scientific and Cultural Organization
UNEP	UN Environment Programme
UNIDO	UN Industrial Development Organization
ITU	International Telecommunication Union
UNWTO	UN World Tourism Organization
UPU	Universal Postal Union
WHO	World Health Organization
WMO	World Meteorological Organization

Table 6.4: The pros and cons of the United Nations

Pro	Con
The universality of its membership; it is the only intergovernmental organization that encompasses almost the entire world and that deals with a broad range of global matters.	No powers of enforcement.
Offers a forum within which international disputes can be discussed and hopefully resolved.	Outdated distribution of powers of membership, particularly veto powers in Security Council.
UN has helped promote peace and democracy in many parts of the world.	UN peacekeeping operations tend to stabilize conflicts rather than ending them.
UN resolutions help give support to international actions, and discourage those where there is no global consensus.	Suffers from the waste and inefficiency often associated with large bureaucracies.
Specialized agencies and programmes offer helpful means by which states can address more focused problems and needs.	Has found it hard to offer a means to dealing with non-state actors, such as terrorist groups.

NON-STATE ACTORS

International cooperation does not just take place among governments, but also takes place outside the hallways of government with expanding networks of **non-state actors** (Higgott et al., 2011). Whether they work at the local, state, or international level, they can influence the way that states behave internationally or globally, and often have functions that fill the gaps in the work of states, or act in a way that forces a reaction from states. Examples include multinational corporations or industries (particularly the financial, banking and energy industries), economic interests (such as labour unions and consumers), social interests (such as ethnic groups or retired people), religious groups (particularly in states that are home to multiple religions), and those – such as organized crime and terrorist organizations – that work outside the law.

Non-state actor: Institutions that are not part of the structure of states (although they may have state members) but that influence policy, whether at the local, national, international or global level.

The key non-state actors are **international non-governmental organizations** (INGOs), which bring together interests that work outside government, including individuals, national non-governmental organizations (NGOs) or interest groups, professions, or private associations. Examples include Amnesty International, Greenpeace, and the International Red Cross (each of which is covered in more detail in later chapters). In terms of their goals and methods, most INGOs reflect the work of groups active at the national level, whose goal is to influence policy without becoming part of government. They do this using a variety of methods, including coordinating pressure on governments, undertaking research, raising and spending funds, promoting media coverage of the issues they care about, and blowing the

International non-governmental organization: A body that works to encourage international cooperation through the work of non-state members such as individuals or private associations.

whistle on the performance of states, corporations, or individuals. They come in many different sizes and forms:

▶ Some are local grassroots organizations, others have strong international connections.

▶ Some have focused interests, others have a wide range of interests.

▶ Some work out of modest offices with limited means, others work out of plush offices in capital cities.

▶ Some use direct action, others can be seen working alongside governments at major international gatherings.

In many ways, INGOs make up for the failures of governments to agree responses to regional or global problems, so they are effectively taking up the slack. Some also have the advantage of being created and run by ordinary citizens unlimited by political baggage, which gives them greater flexibility and freedom to work with like-minded citizens from other states. Often, an NGO will be created in one country and will inspire the creation of equivalent national offices in other countries, the network being held together – and kept on the same track – by the creation of an international coordinating office. This is the case, for example, with Friends of the Earth, an environmental group founded in the United States in 1969, but now active through national offices in 75 countries, coordinated by an international headquarters in Amsterdam.

Multinational corporation:
A private enterprise that has facilities and income-generating assets in two or more countries, managing its global activities from its home state.

Another kind of non-state actor is the **multinational corporation** (MNC), also known as a transnational corporation or a multinational enterprise. While MNCs are not always thought of and assessed in the same ways as conventional INGOs, multinational corporations are both international and non-governmental. Just as corporations play a key role in making and implementing policy at the state level, so MNCs are an important part of the system of global governance. This is particularly true of the biggest multinationals, such as banks, energy companies, automobile manufacturers, and pharmaceutical companies, whose reach is often both broad and deep, placing many at the heart of globalization. They differ most obviously from standard INGOs in that they seek to make a profit, a motivation that makes them inventive, ambitious, and influential, particularly in a system of global governance that lacks the same kinds of formal institutions with responsibility to voters and public opinion that we find within states.

Multinationals impact the global system in several ways: they drive international trade, lead decisions about targets of foreign investment, have control over often large financial or natural resources, drive the production of goods and services, help change consumer tastes and choices, help determine how we use energy, have a major impact on environmental policy, take the lead in the development of new technologies, help shape policies on workers' rights, provide new jobs, decide where those jobs will be located, and play a key role in the economic health of states.

An example is offered by IKEA, which is far from the biggest multinational in the world, but which has had a near-global impact on the way people shop for home furnishings. Founded in Sweden in 1943 by the 17-year-old Ingvar Kamprad (the name is an acronym based on his initials and the first letters of the farm where he grew up, and his hometown), IKEA soon became famous for the variety and the

GLOBAL AND LOCAL 6

CIVIL SOCIETY

This chapter looks at global governance, international regimes, and international law. But while it is important to understand their qualities, and to appreciate how they work, it is equally important to realize that the global system is also impacted by the activities of people and organizations working outside government in what is known as **civil society**. These might be driven by the work of a single influential leader such as Nelson Mandela or the Dalai Lama, or of a community of non-governmental organizations working on issues such as human rights or environmental protection, or of mass movements that coalesce behind a popular issue such as workers' rights or women's rights.

At the global level, the growth in the number and reach of INGOs in the wake of expanded international cooperation reflects the emergence of a **global civil society**. When we study global governance, we quickly realize that it is shaped and driven by millions of local decisions. Such has been their impact that Mathews (1997) wrote of a power shift in global politics, coming in the wake of the rise of 'non-traditional' threats such as environmental decline, and the advent of new concerns about human security rather than national security. She concluded that national governments were 'not simply losing autonomy in a globalizing economy . . . [but were] sharing powers – including political, social and security roles at the core of sovereignty – with businesses, with international organizations, and with a multitude of . . . non-governmental organizations'.

The conventional view is that NGOs and INGOs are created as a result of 'bottom-up' societal responses to needs and problems, and to a large extent this is true; most INGOs have been created as the result of local initiatives by ordinary people rather than by governments. But Reimann (2006) argues that there has been a 'top-down' dynamic at work as well: new sources of funding and new channels for political access have created new international political opportunities that have encouraged the formation and growth of NGOs and INGOs, while Northern states and IGOs have actively promoted the spread of NGOs in the South. The European Union and UN agencies, in particular, have sub-contracted some of the responsibility for their projects to INGOs, have provided funding to INGOs, and have created networking agencies designed to encourage national NGOs to work with one another.

low cost of its products. It opened its first store outside Sweden in 1963, and by the time Kamprad died in 2018, it had more than 400 stores in nearly 50 countries, and was attracting more than two billion visitors to its website. Its products have a distinctly Scandinavian feel to their design, meaning that IKEA not only has an impact on trade and the creation of jobs, but is also something of a trader in style.

MNCs have not been with us all that long, their number and reach growing only in recent decades in tandem with the growth of the global system (Chandler and Mazlish, 2005). The first such organizations were the trading companies set up by British, Dutch and other European entrepreneurs in the wake of imperialism and industrialization; one of the world's first MNCs was the East India Company, created in London in 1600, which eventually became so big that it had its own military and almost single-handedly ruled the Indian subcontinent. The first broader wave of MNC activity did not come until the 1880s, however, and the second has been under way since the 1970s. According to data maintained by the UN, the number of MNCs

Civil society: The arena within which citizens engage with one another to address problems of shared concern, reflected at the global level in the features of **global civil society**.

Customers visit an IKEA store in Shanghai, China. Since its creation in 1943, the Swedish company has opened stores all over the world, helping change consumer habits and tastes.

grew from about 35,000 in 1990 to about 63,000 in 2002 and about 100,000 in 2012 (UN Conference on Trade and Development, various years). Some are so big that they have become what Khanna (2016) describes a 'metanationals' in the sense that they are truly global, and no longer headquartered in a single state. They control such large assets and employ so many people that some have become more influential than states, leading Khanna to assert that 'the world is entering an era in which the most powerful law is not that of sovereignty but that of supply and demand'.

The location of the biggest MNCs tells us much about the changing balance of economic and financial power in the world. Where they were once based mainly in the North, there has been a rapid increase in the number of MNCs based in the South, notably in China. In 2005, just 18 of the world's 500 biggest corporations listed in the *Fortune* Global 500 were Chinese, a share that had grown to 103 in 2016. Between 2001 and 2012, the number of North American companies on the list fell from 215 to 144, while the number of Asian companies grew from 116 to 188 – for examples, see Table 6.5.

Much of what we hear about the work of MNCs is controversial at best, and negative at worst. They are accused of placing profits above social concerns, and of exploiting differences in national environmental and worker standards by closing down operations in countries with higher standards and moving them to those with lower standards and wages. They are also implicated in efforts by poorer countries to exploit natural resources at almost any cost, bringing to mind tales of multinational oil companies and their environmentally harmful extraction of oil in countries such as Nigeria. On the other hand, there is evidence that many MNCs have adopted the principle of corporate social responsibility: the idea that companies should place social and environmental issues at the core of their decision-making because it is in their financial interests so to do. (See Chapter 11 for more details.)

Table 6.5: The world's ten biggest multinationals

Rank	Name	Home state	Sector	Revenue $ billion
1	Walmart	USA	Retail	485
2	State Grid	China	Energy	315
3	Sinopec Group	China	Energy	267
4	China National Petroleum	China	Energy	263
5	Toyota	Japan	Vehicles	255
6	Volkswagen	Germany	Vehicles	240
7	Royal Dutch Shell	UK/Netherlands	Energy	240
8	Berkshire Hathaway	USA	Financials	223
9	Apple	USA	Technology	215
10	Exxon Mobil	USA	Oil	205

Source: Fortune Global 500 (2018).
Note: Based on annual revenues for 2016.

Much like multinational corporations, religious organizations are not usually thought of as international organizations, and yet the choices made by governments, and by millions of adherents to religion around the world, are often influenced by organized religion. This is particularly true in the cases of the world's two largest religions, Christianity and Islam, which together are followed – as we saw in Chapter 3 – by more than half the people in the world. Those who believe are influenced not just by their different doctrines, but also by the work of many religious IOs; for Christians, these include the Baptist World Alliance, the World Council of Churches, and the Friends World Committee for Consultation. There are also many inter-faith organizations that work to encourage cooperation among religions, and others that work to achieve peace in divided societies.

Few religious organizations have had longer or wider influence than the Catholic Church, whose political and social role predates the rise of the Westphalian system. Catholics today make up only about 16 per cent of the world population, but the reach of Catholicism is felt as widely as Latin America, the United States, Ireland, Spain, Italy, Poland, and the Philippines. The Catholic Church even has its own state in the form of the Vatican City, and while this may be a pale shadow of its former self (the Papal States once covered much of what is now northern Italy, and popes once wielded enormous power throughout Europe), its reach is widely felt: the Pope is one of the few religious leaders with global influence, and the opinions of the Vatican have helped shape attitudes towards human rights, birth control, nuclear proliferation, climate change, and poverty.

While most non-state actors are relatively easy to identify, and work within the law, there are two other darker sides to this part of the discussion about governance: organized crime and terrorist movements. Both problems have been with us much longer than most people might realize, but the response of states to both has had to be tightened as their reach has expanded. Almost all of us have been affected by terrorism, even if only to the extent to which we have to go through security checks when boarding a plane or attending a concert or sporting event – see Chapter 12. The effects of organized crime tend to be more restricted, but they have expanded to the point where agreement has had to be reached on how to define organized crime: it boils down to crime carried out as a form of business by a group. Examples of organized crime groups include the Sicilian mafia, the Russian mafia, the Yakuza of Japan, and successors to the triads of China. In 2000 the UN Convention against Transnational Organized Crime was agreed in an effort to encourage cooperation on the control and suppression of their activities, including human trafficking and smuggling.

REGIONAL INTEGRATION

Intergovern-mentalism:
A theory/model based on the idea that key cooperative decisions among states are made as a result of negotiations among representatives of those states.

Supranationalism:
A theory/model based on promoting the joint interests of cooperating states, with a transfer of authority to those IGOs.

Regional integration: The promotion of cooperation and collective action among a group of neighbouring states based on the identification of shared interests and goals, and the development of common policies and collective laws.

Most international organizations focus on cooperation, the idea being to have states work together while also retaining their sovereignty. With IGOs, this is based on the principle of **intergovernmentalism**, meaning that governments cooperate among themselves. But in some cases the depth of that cooperation has gone further, and states have created new regional organizations that include shared institutions that have more legal authority than is the case with standard IGOs; in working to encourage collective action, they develop common rules on shared interests. This moves them into the realm of **supranationalism**, meaning the creation of new levels of cooperation which work in the interests of the whole rather than just the parts. The work of these new bodies is based on the agreement of treaties that usually carry many more obligations than most conventional treaties, and involve the creation of administrative bodies that have the authority to make new laws and help encourage the development of common policies in areas where their members have agreed to cooperate.

This takes them far beyond the obligations involved in the membership of bodies such as the UN or the World Trade Organization, although the institutions are designed in such a way that the governments of the member states have a key role in the adoption and execution of those rules and policies; the arrangement is one of a pooling rather than a surrender of sovereignty. How far they are prepared to go with this pooling depends on public and political opinion; the most enthusiastic supporters of the idea see it as part of a process that could lead eventually to economic and political union, while critics see integration as a threat to the independence of states.

The idea of supranational bodies is far from new, the earliest examples being found in the alliances once made among monarchs and emperors, particularly in Europe. In the modern era, the first major exercises in integration date from the 19th century, and include the customs union among German states in the 1820s that laid the foundations for the eventual unification of Germany, and the 1848 constitution that formed the basis of the Swiss Confederation (Mattli, 1999). The process of integration might begin with the creation of a free trade area within which the internal barriers to trade are eased, then evolve into the creation of an open single market (with free movement of people, capital, goods and services), then move to the creation of a single currency, and finally – at least theoretically – move to the creation of a new and federal political union, which has yet to happen anywhere.

The most prominent example of **regional integration** at work is the European Union (see McCormick, 2017b). Tracing its roots back to the early 1950s and efforts to promote peace in western Europe by bringing down economic and political barriers, it evolved in 1958 into an effort to build an open European market. Its membership and reach has since expanded: it now has more than two dozen members, a population of half a billion people, and common or shared policies on agriculture, asylum, competition, education, the environment, external relations, immigration, security, terrorism, and trade. The idea has been far from uncontroversial, however, particularly among those Europeans who worry that integration is undermining national sovereignty and that open borders mean more migration. A backlash against the idea has been brewing since at least the early 1990s, feeding in to the rise of right-wing anti-immigrant and anti-EU political parties, and a groundswell of opinion in favour of reforming or even – in some countries – leaving the EU. Shockwaves were caused by a vote in Britain in 2016 to leave the EU, the first time such a decision had been taken.

In spite of the doubts about its merits and effects, many examples of regional integration can be found around the world, and there are few countries that are not involved in at least one, and sometimes two or more (see Figure 6.3). How far each of these groups is likely to succeed with its goals depends on what Nye (1970) once described as their integrative potential, which depends on several conditions:

▸ The economic equality and compatibility of the states involved.

▸ The extent to which the elite groups that control economic policy in the member states think alike and hold the same values.

▸ The presence and work of a network of interest groups to provide support and information.

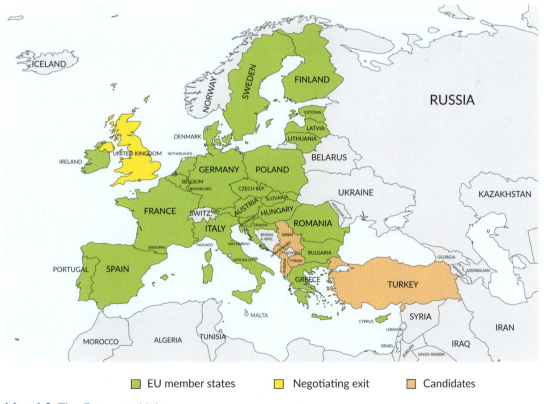

Map 6.2: The European Union

Figure 6.3: Regional integration: Some examples

NAME	YEAR FOUNDED	MEMBERSHIP
EUROPEAN UNION	1952	28, including Germany, France, Spain, Poland, Sweden, Greece.
ASSOCIATION OF SOUTHEAST ASIAN NATIONS (ASEAN)	1967	10, including Indonesia, Malaysia, Thailand.
CARIBBEAN COMMUNITY	1973	15, including the Bahamas, Guyana, Jamaica.
ECONOMIC COMMUNITY OF WEST AFRICAN STATES (ECOWAS)	1975	15, including Ghana, Ivory Coast, Nigeria.
SOUTH ASIAN ASSOCIATION FOR REGIONAL COOPERATION	1985	8, including Afghanistan, India, Pakistan.
NORTH AMERICAN FREE TRADE AGREEMENT (NAFTA)	1994	3: Canada, Mexico, United States
AFRICAN UNION	2002	55: every African state.
UNION OF SOUTH AMERICAN NATIONS	2011	12, including Argentina, Brazil, Venezuela.

▶ The capacity of the member states to adapt and respond to public demands, which depends in turn on levels of domestic stability and the capacity – or desire – of decision-makers to respond.

The EU has had problems because of the different size of its member states, their different levels of democratic and economic development, and their different attitudes towards cooperation. Even greater challenges are faced by the African Union, created in 2002. Using institutions and procedures similar to those found in the EU, it includes all 55 states on the continent of Africa, which vary in terms of their wealth, size, stability and internal unity, as well as being home to numerous ethnicities and religions, and including both democracies and authoritarian regimes. Even much smaller exercises in regional integration have had challenges; the North American Free Trade Agreement (NAFTA) has only three members (the US, Canada, and Mexico), but the political and economic conditions in Mexico are different from those in the two other partners, and NAFTA has been strained by the twin threats posed by unauthorized immigration from Mexico and the shift of jobs to Mexico with its lower wages and weaker environmental standards.

DISCUSSION QUESTIONS

1. The governments of states are held to expectations about their duties and performance. Is there an equivalent set of expectations for institutions working at the international or global level?

2. What does the rise of China mean for the balance of international influence?

3. Is it time to remove veto powers from the Big Five UN members, or to redistribute powers to reflect the new realities of the world today?

4. Is the rise of non-state actors good or bad for the global system?

5. Is there such a thing as a global civil society?

6. What does regional integration have to offer in terms of meeting global needs?

KEY CONCEPTS

▸ Anarchy
▸ Civil society
▸ Global civil society
▸ Global governance
▸ Governance
▸ Institution
▸ Intergovernmental organization

▸ Intergovernmentalism
▸ International law
▸ International non-governmental organization
▸ International organization
▸ Multinational corporation

▸ Non-state actor
▸ Regime
▸ Regional integration
▸ Supranationalism
▸ Treaty
▸ Treaty secretariat

USEFUL WEBSITES

European Union at https://europa.eu

Group of 77 at http://www.g77.org

International Court of Justice at http://www.icj-cij.org

Union of International Associations at https://www.uia.org

United Nations at http://www.un.org

FURTHER READING

Hanhimäki, Jussi M. (2015) *The United Nations: A Very Short Introduction*, 2nd edn (Oxford University Press). A brief survey of the UN, with chapters on its history, structure, work on potential future development.

Karns, Margaret P., Karen A. Mingst, and Kendall W. Stiles (2015) *International Organizations: The Politics and Processes of Global Governance*, 3rd edn (Lynne Rienner). A general survey of the nature, structure and work of international organizations.

Lowe, Vaughan (2015) *International Law: A Very Short Introduction* (Oxford University Press). Part of a series of brief introductions on different topics, this one looks at the meaning and effects of international law.

Shaw, Malcolm N. (2014) *International Law*, 7th edn (Cambridge University Press), and Malcolm Evans (ed) (2014) *International Law*, 4th edn (Oxford University Press). Two of several general surveys of international law, looking at its structure, reach, and types.

Weiss, Thomas (2013) *Global Governance: Why? What? Whither?* (Polity Press). An assessment of the origins, qualities and possible future directions of global governance.

> **Online Resources**
>
> Visit www.macmillanihe.com/McCormick-GS to access additional materials to support teaching and learning.

HUMAN RIGHTS

7

PREVIEW

The focus of this chapter is human rights. It begins with an outline of the Universal Declaration of Human Rights, and examples of rights violations. It then discusses the evolution and expansion of human rights, tracing the story from the issue of slavery to emerging views about LGBT and intergenerational rights. The chapter goes on to outline the dimensions of the global human rights regime, based mainly on a series of focused treaties, UN bodies, international courts, and international NGOs. The chapter ends by discussing the difficulties of measuring and comparing human rights records, using the case of women's rights and the insights it provides.

HIGHLIGHTS

▸ Human rights are the universal and inalienable rights to which all humans are entitled.

▸ The definition of such rights has been in a new phase of intensity since the adoption in 1948 of the Universal Declaration of Human Rights.

▸ Even as the definition of human rights deepens and broadens, many countries continue to impinge upon the rights of their citizens and residents.

▸ The body of international human rights agreements has expanded to include women, children, tribal peoples, migrant workers, people with disabilities, and sexual orientation.

▸ Efforts to bring prosecutions for the abuse of civil rights at the international level have had only mixed results.

▸ Democracy is no guarantee of the protection of human rights, but limits on democracy do not necessarily mean consistent limits on rights.

Source: EyeEm/Getty Images

UNDERSTANDING HUMAN RIGHTS

In 1998, an announcement in a Spanish newspaper listed the names of several people whose homes had been foreclosed and put up for auction. The announcement soon became available on the internet. One of those affected was a man named Mario Costeja González, who soon became frustrated that while the foreclosure on his home had been resolved, and his debt to society paid, anyone searching for him online would learn of his misfortune. He asked the newspaper to remove the information, claiming that the forced sale had been concluded and was no longer relevant. In short, he felt that he had the 'right to be forgotten', as did anyone else in a similar situation. Leaving this information online meant that it could continue to be found and used against him indefinitely, by employers, banks, or insurance companies, for example. The newspaper refused to accede to his request, as did Google, so he began legal proceedings, and in 2014 the European Court of Justice sided with Costeja against Google, instructing the internet company to comply with EU law on data privacy. As a result, it is now possible under certain circumstances to ask Google to delete troublesome internet links, or face legal action.

Is the right to be forgotten a legitimate human right? Costeja certainly thought so, as did many in the legal community, but this marked a novel new twist on the concept of human rights, arising from the emergence of the Web and social media. It was just the latest in an ongoing public debate about the meaning of human rights, whose heritage dates back centuries, and whose definition continues to change as new groups of people seek protection, and new developments bring new questions to the surface. As humans, it is argued, we are all afforded certain rights relative to each other and to the states of which we are citizens. But where do those rights begin and end?

The conversation begins with two types of rights that are determined mainly by political decisions:

> ▶ **Civil liberties** are the rights and freedoms we have relative to government, and that are granted or conceded by government. These include freedom of speech, association, religion and assembly, the legal principle being that government cannot abridge such rights.

> ▶ **Civil rights** are the rights and freedoms we have relative both to government and to other individuals, and that offer protection against discrimination based on such characteristics as race, gender, religion, age, and sexual orientation. Different states and societies will often have different ideas about the list of protected groups.

Overarching these, and often overlapping as well, are **human rights**. These are distinct in the sense that they are not regarded as having a political origin, but are instead defined as the rights to which humans are entitled simply by virtue of being human. In this sense, they are rights from 'below', deriving not from government or states but from human existence. They are regarded as universal (everyone has them) and inalienable (they can neither be given nor taken away). Expressed differently, they are considered as negative rights in the sense that they only require governments to refrain from doing anything (such as limiting the freedom of association, for example), as distinct from positive rights that require action on the

Civil liberties: The rights and freedoms that humans have relative to their governments.

Civil rights: The rights that protect humans from discrimination based on who they are.

Human rights: The natural, universal and inalienable rights to which all humans are entitled.

part of governments, such as protecting rights to education by building schools. Negative rights include freedom of speech and religion, while positive rights include food, shelter, employment, and health care (see Langlois, 2016).

The authoritative source on the definition of human rights is the **Universal Declaration of Human Rights** (UDHR), which was adopted in December 1948 by the UN General Assembly. But there were only 56 member states of the UN at the time, so the vast majority of today's 193 member states were not involved directly in the discussions over the UDHR or in the final vote, and the debate over human rights has taken new directions since thanks in part to the views of societies and states with often different ideas about what constitutes a human right. The UDHR remains our key source of reference, though. It contains 30 articles, the first sentence of the Preamble emphasizing that 'recognition of the inherent dignity and … equal and inalienable rights' of all humans is 'the foundation of freedom, justice and peace in the world'. It then goes on to list the multiple specific rights and freedoms to which humans are entitled – see Table 7.1.

One of the most fundamental disagreements in the debate about rights centres on perspective (see Donnelly, 2013: Chapter 3). While **universalism** holds that everyone possesses an equal set of rights regardless of who they are, **relativism** holds that there must be exceptions based on culture, religion, or tradition, and thus that ideas about rights must be seen in relative terms. Cultural relativists have often argued that the definition of human rights has been driven too much by Western ideas, which – for example – emphasize the rights of the individual over those of the community. Universalists might respond that this argument is too often used as an excuse for the denial of human rights to selected groups.

Take, for example, the denial of power to women in many societies, and the cultural expectations imposed on women. While universalists would quote and support Article 16 of the UDHR ('Marriage shall be entered into only with the free and full consent of the intending spouses'), many societies – including some in rural areas of Africa, Asia and Latin America – would argue that it is right and proper (or financially necessary) that marriages can be arranged without consideration of the feelings of the partners, least of all young girls who are betrothed this way. Similarly, the UDHR and public opinion in Western societies would abhor female circumcision, but it remains part of the culture of many African and Middle Eastern societies, where supporters uphold it as a coming-of-age ritual that ensures chastity and promotes fertility (Abusharaf, 2006), and argue that protection against this practice is not a universal human right.

Regrettably, human rights are often violated even in those democratic states that most enthusiastically support the principles contained within the UDHR. Not everyone has equal protection under the law, for example, with discrimination leaving some individuals and groups treated differently, as in the case of LGBT communities (see later in this chapter). And while the UDHR says that equal pay for equal work is a human right, women were still earning only 59 per cent as much as men globally in 2017 (World Economic Forum, 2017). This is because they are paid less, work longer hours, have less chance of reaching senior positions, and are often expected to take a greater role in raising children. Meanwhile, human rights are violated in the case of **political prisoners**, although it can be difficult sometimes to distinguish political prisoners from common criminals, the idea of imprisonment

Universal Declaration of Human Rights: The definitive outline of human rights, adopted by the UN General Assembly in 1948.

Universalism: The view that all humans possess an equal sets of rights, regardless of who they are, where they live, or where they come from.

Relativism: The view that human rights are culturally relative, and that there is no one-size-fits-all set of rights.

Political prisoner: A person who is imprisoned because their actions or beliefs run counter to those of the government of the day.

Table 7.1: Rights listed in the Universal Declaration of Human Rights

Life, liberty and security of person.	Freedom of opinion and expression.
Not to be a slave.	Freedom of peaceful assembly and association.
Not to be subjected to torture or to cruel, inhuman or degrading treatment.	To take part in government.
Recognition as a person before the law.	Equal access to public service.
Equal protection before the law.	To social security.
Effective remedy for acts that violate fundamental rights.	To work, with just and favourable work conditions.
No arbitrary arrest, detention or exile.	To protection against unemployment.
Fair and public hearing by impartial tribunal in event of a criminal charge.	Equal pay for equal work.
To be presumed innocent until proved guilty.	Just and favourable remuneration ensuring an existence worthy of human dignity.
No arbitrary interference with privacy, family, home or correspondence.	To form and to join a trade union.
Freedom of movement and residence within borders of a state.	Rest and leisure, including periodic time off with pay.
To leave any country and return.	A standard of living adequate for health and well-being., including food, clothing, housing, and medical care.
To seek and enjoy asylum from persecution.	Security in the event of unemployment, sickness, disability, or old age.
To a nationality.	To education.
To marry by consent and found a family.	To freely participate in the cultural life of the community.
To own property alone or with others.	To protection of interests in intellectual property.
Freedom of thought, conscience and religion.	To international order in which human rights can be fully realized.

Prisoner of conscience: A person who is physically prevented from expressing or holding opinions by a government or a state.

for political reasons depending on how those reasons are defined and understood. A related term is **prisoner of conscience**, coined by Amnesty International founder Peter Benenson (1961), who defined it as follows:

> Any person who is physically restrained (by imprisonment or otherwise) from expressing (in any form of words or symbols) any opinion which he honestly holds and which does not advocate or condone personal violence. We also exclude those people who have conspired with a foreign government to overthrow their own.

Undoubtedly the most famous political prisoner of the 20th century was Nelson Mandela of South Africa, although he was also a controversial figure because of his early association with violence. Known for his activism against his country's system of apartheid (organized racial segregation), he was jailed in 1962 for his participation in a sabotage campaign. He spent 27 years in jail, much of it in the Robben Island prison off the coast near Cape Town, becoming a symbol for the resistance to apartheid. He was released in 1990, helped negotiate the end of apartheid, served a term as president of South Africa, and became a global icon for social justice. A more recent example of a prisoner of conscience was Burmese opposition leader Aung San Suu Kyi, who spent many years under house arrest between 1989 and 2010 because of her resistance to the military government of Burma (Myanmar). Her party won a landslide victory in the 2015 elections, allowing her to become the equivalent of the prime minister. Unfortunately, she later undermined her reputation by failing to speak up when the Burmese regime worked to expel members of the minority Muslim Rohingya from the country – see Chapter 10.

The most egregious violations of human rights can be found in cases of genocide or ethnic cleansing. Even if both terms are relatively new (see Chapter 3 for discussion), the actions they describe are not, and history is littered with examples of both; Adam Jones (2017) describes genocide as 'one of humanity's enduring blights'. The more infamous historical examples include the 13th-century invasions of Genghis Khan, genocide directed by European settlers at the native populations of the Americas, the attempted extermination of the Herero and Namaqua peoples of present-day Namibia when it was German Southwest Africa, the systematic efforts to destroy Armenians in the Ottoman Empire during and after World War I, and – of course – the Holocaust that resulted in the deaths of more than six million Jews and Roma in Europe between 1933 and 1945. Recent examples of ethnic cleansing include the gassing of Kurds in Iraq by Saddam Hussein, the massacre of nearly one million Tutsis and anyone who might be harbouring them in Rwanda in 1994, and attacks on Croats, Bosniaks, Serbs, Kosovo Albanians and other ethnic minorities during the wars that followed the break-up of Yugoslavia in the early 1990s.

THE EVOLUTION OF RIGHTS

Rights have been part of the human experience for as long as organized society has existed, but the definition of those rights has broadened and become more legalized and homogenized only relatively recently. (For a study of the history of human rights, see Hunt, 2007.) Among the earliest recorded outlines of rights were those found in religious texts: the Judeo-Christian Ten Commandments could be seen as a form of protection of selected rights when they forbade murder (the right to life), adultery (marriage rights), or stealing (property rights), while the Muslim Quran includes arguments in favour of equality, the right to life, and the right to own property.

In broader legal terms, key principles were established by Magna Carta, signed in England in 1215 and giving barons and the church rights relative to the monarch. Prior to Magna Carta, monarchs were considered to be above the law and to derive their authority from God; Magna Carta made the monarch subject to the laws of the land, and also proclaimed that there were certain rights enjoyed by individuals, including *habeas corpus*, preventing people from being arbitrarily detained by the government.

While there would be few significant legal developments for several centuries, the idea of **natural law** emerged from the writings of thinkers such as Thomas Aquinas (1225–74), Thomas Hobbes (1588–1679), and John Locke (1632–1704).

Natural law: The view that certain rights are derived from nature rather than the rules of government or society.

Their views suggested the existence of a common human morality in that everyone had an inherent sense of right and wrong, and that rights were not dependent upon states to declare them or documents to legitimize them. For Locke, **natural rights** included those to life, liberty and property. A later and competing school of thought was represented by those, such as Jeremy Bentham (1748–1832) and John Austin (1790–1859), who argued that there was nothing natural about natural law, because of differences that people and governments might have about the meaning of the word *natural*. Instead, they argued that human rights existed because states consented to them, and thus defined those rights.

> **Natural rights**: Rights that exist as a result of the universal law of nature, and that cannot be given or taken away by government.

Human rights were given new expression with the passage in 1689 of the English Bill of Rights, which provided more powers and protection for ordinary people relative to the monarch. Exactly a century later, the Declaration of the Rights of Man and the Citizen placed on record the new post-revolutionary relationship in France between the rulers and the ruled; it proclaimed that 'Men are born free and remain free and equal in rights', and included mention of specific rights such as freedom from arbitrary arrest and execution, the freedom of religion and expression, and the right to protection of private property. This statement reflects related ideas in the 1776 US Declaration of Independence, whose opening sentence famously read as follows:

> We hold these truths to be self-evident, that all men are created equal, that they are endowed by their Creator with certain unalienable Rights, that among these are Life, Liberty and the pursuit of Happiness.

The 1791 US Bill of Rights, a set of amendments to the new US constitution, later laid out such rights such as the freedom of religion, speech, the press and assembly, but also – more controversially – implied that there was also a right to keep and bear arms. This belief is almost unique to American gun owners, and is by no means supported universally. In fact most countries have strict limits on the ownership of guns.

While the theory and practice of human rights had taken several centuries to evolve, such rights were still some way from being universally applied and protected, with even the most advanced democracies of the 19th century denying them to women, for example. The suffragist movement grew out of efforts to win voting rights for women, which were not achieved in most Western states until the early part of the 20th century. Meanwhile, one of the more flagrant disregards for human rights was found in the persistence of **slavery**. Few conditions reflect the limits on human freedom quite as comprehensively as being a slave, which means being defined as the personal property of the slave-owner, and losing control over all but the most routine of life's decisions and choices.

> **Slavery**: An arrangement by which humans are defined as property, and individuals can be owned, bought and sold.

The British movement against slavery resulted in the abolition of the slave trade throughout the British Empire in 1807, and of slavery in 1833. Slavery remained legal in many parts of the world, though, prompting the holding in 1840 of the First Anti-Slavery Convention in London, and the creation that year of the Anti-Slavery Society, the world's first global human rights NGO. The Russian equivalent of slavery – serfdom – was only finally abolished in 1861, while internal slavery remained legal in the United States until 1863. Although slavery is now universally illegal, many millions of people remain enslaved, with the biggest numbers in India, China, Pakistan, and Bangladesh (Global Slavery Index, 2016). It is found most often in the form of bonded labour (working to pay off a debt), forced migrant labour, child labour, and sex slavery.

While most attempts to protect and promote human rights were focused on states, an international initiative began after World War I with the creation of the League of Nations, whose founding charter included reference to the protection of minorities within states. But little was achieved, the work of the League was disrupted by war, and it was not until the end of World War II that the international movement to protect human rights began to move into high gear. Inspired by the horrors of the war, the founding charter of the United Nations included the aspirational idea that member states sought to 'reaffirm faith in fundamental human rights, in the dignity and worth of the human person, in the equal rights of men and women and of nations large and small'. Article 1 of the charter listed one of the purposes of the UN as that of 'promoting and encouraging respect for human rights and for fundamental freedoms for all without distinction as to race, sex, language, or religion'.

At one of the first meetings of the UN in early 1946, a draft document on human rights was introduced, leading to the creation in June 1946 of the UN Commission on Human Rights, which – chaired by former US First Lady Eleanor Roosevelt – began work on what would become the Universal Declaration on Human Rights (see Glendon, 2002). This was accepted by the UN General Assembly in December 1948, but it was only a declaration, and not a legally binding document, so work continued on the development of additional agreements, which would eventually focus on women, children, tribal peoples, migrant workers, people with disabilities, and sexual orientation – see later in this chapter.

While it might seem as though agreement was reached fairly quickly once the UN was in place, and that thinking about the definition of rights began to accelerate in a newly receptive post-war atmosphere, the debates over those rights have been far from straightforward, and complications persist. During the Cold War (see Chapter 1), for example, the US and the Soviets were often prepared to overlook abuses of human rights by their client states in return for guarantees of support. On the US side, some of those states were led by some of the worst abusers of human rights of their time, including 'Papa Doc' Duvalier of Haiti, Ferdinand Marcos of the Philippines, Mobutu Sese Seko of Zaire, the Shah of Iran, and Saddam Hussein of Iraq.

This dynamic was further complicated by the end of the era of colonialism, which saw the membership roster of the UN expanding and the injection of the views of newly independent countries. While the West focused on the importance of individual rights, such as freedom of speech and religion, the Soviets argued that the socialist model was more conducive to the idea of rights to employment, education, and health care. Those in the v, meanwhile, were interested in the broader human condition rather than individual rights alone.

The 1982 African Charter of Human and Peoples' Rights (the Banjul charter) offers some interesting contrasts with the definition of human rights offered by the UDHR and related documents. While the Banjul charter overlapped in many ways with the UDHR (it includes the right to life, and the freedoms of conscience, expression, association, and assembly), it also makes mention of the right of self-determination, and of being able to 'freely determine their political status and … [to] pursue their economic and social development according to the policy they have freely chosen'. This traces back to concerns about the manipulation of developing countries by the major powers during the Cold War through support for corrupt governments and the provision of weapons.

The Banjul charter also mentions the right to the 'free disposal of wealth and natural resources', calls on signatories to 'undertake to eliminate all forms of foreign exploitation particularly that practised by international monopolies so as to enable their peoples to fully benefit from the advantages derived from their national resources', and refers to the 'right to economic, social and cultural development with due regard to their freedom and identity and in the equal enjoyment of the common heritage of mankind'. Combined, these ideas can be taken to refer to efforts by African states – in the face of globalization – not to be restricted by international efforts to protect forests, fisheries, air and water quality, or biodiversity, or by the efforts of multinational corporations to exploit African resources, and to have equal access to the wealth derived from those resources.

THE EXPANSION OF RIGHTS

The Universal Declaration of Human Rights may be the foundational guide for how we define rights, but it can also be seen as a picture of a particular point in time, and of the opinions of the 56 countries that were members of the UN in 1948. The debate about rights never ends, and as more voices have entered the debate, and as globalization has changed the dynamics of the global system, the list of rights has expanded. Consider the following examples.

Intergenerational rights. Although human rights are normally understood in terms of people who are alive today, it has also been argued that the present generation has an obligation to protect the rights of future generations by not engaging in any activities that would negatively impact the lives of anyone not yet born (Thompson, 2009). In a sense, present generations hold power over future generations through their control of resources and the making of decisions that might impact future generations, potentially limiting their options or setting back their interests. Present generations can even ultimately decide if there will be any future generations at all (an all-out nuclear conflict, for example, would probably wipe out the human race), how many people will exist in the future, and what kind of quality of life they will have. In short, humans should make sure that they leave the world in at least no worse a condition than they found it (but ideally in a better condition).

These ideas are behind the concept of sustainable development discussed in Chapter 11. Living sustainably means doing so in a way that does not reduce the natural capital of resources such as forests, fisheries, clean air, and fertile soil, but allows them all to regenerate in a way that ensures their continuing availability in future, and even cleaning up the damage generated by past generations. Climate change is the ultimate example of a violation of the rights of future generations: unless we work to address it, and quickly, we will leave behind global systems that are compromised, impinging on the quality of life of all those who follow.

Sexual orientation and gender identity. Another new aspect of individual rights concerns sexual rights, including not just focused issues such as arranged marriages, but broader questions relating to lesbian, gay, bisexual and transgender (LGBT) rights, such as the right to choose a partner of the same sex, and the right to alter one's own sex or choose one's own gender identity. Such matters come up against sometimes difficult religious questions, ideas about the protection of cultural values and traditions, and

COMPARING NORTH AND SOUTH 7

COMPARING APPROACHES TO LGBT RIGHTS

The rights of lesbian, gay, bisexual and transgender (LGBT) people have drawn new attention in recent decades, with many changes coming in the North (although discrimination is still widely found), but resistance continuing in socially conservative parts of the South (see Keating and Burack, 2016). There is an ongoing debate about whether such rights are human rights or civil rights, and changes to law and policy have led to a patchwork quilt of legal provisions: these range from the nearly two dozen countries (mainly in Europe and the Americas) that now recognize same-sex marriage, to the nearly four dozen countries (mainly in Africa and the Middle East) where same-sex intercourse is illegal, or even – as in the cases of Saudi Arabia and Iran – punishable by death. Even in many progressive Northern states, the change of heart has been relatively recent; while same-sex male intercourse has been legal in France since 1791, and in the Netherlands since 1811, it has been legal in Britain only since 1967, and nationwide in the United States only since 2003.

At the heart of the debate over LGBT rights has been the question of whether or not to regard marriage as a right that should be extended to same-sex couples, giving them the standard entitlements of married couples in matters of social security, taxation, immigration, and inheritance, and the adoption of children. The Netherlands in 2001 became the first country in the world to recognize same-sex marriage, and it has been followed by ten other European countries, along with (among others) Argentina, Brazil, Canada, New Zealand, South Africa, and the United States.

LGBT rights came relatively late to the agenda of the United Nations, where it was only in 2011 that the Human Rights Council passed its first resolution calling for a report on discrimination based on sexual orientation and gender identity, Support for LGBT rights has come from nearly 100 countries, covering Australasia, Europe, and almost all of North and South America, along with Japan, the Philippines, South Africa, and South Korea. But more than 50 mainly north African and Middle Eastern countries oppose such rights, while the balance of just over 40 mainly central/southern African and Asian states (including China, India, and Russia) have taken no formal position in the UN either for or against LGBT rights. Opinions on homosexuality vary enormously, based on a combination of religious, social and political arguments – see examples in Figure 7.1 – and standing as a prime example of the tensions between relativism and universalism.

An Australian couple celebrate their marriage on the day that Australia joined many other states in legalizing same-sex marriage on 9 January 2018.

Source: Getty Images News/Getty Images

the legal provisions for same-sex unions or marriages, and gender reassignment. Opinion is divided even within states about how far LGBT rights should extend, and the global conversation is complicated by widely varying opinions on the matter – see North and South 7.

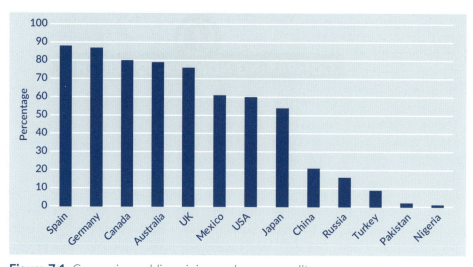

Figure 7.1: Comparing public opinion on homosexuality
Source: Pew Research Center (2013). Percentage answering Yes to the question 'Should society accept homosexuality?'

The right to clean water. Access to clean water is not something that most people in the North much think about, but freshwater resources are not equally distributed, water can be contaminated by lead and other pollutants even in wealthy countries, and most supplies of water are controlled and sold by private water companies. As corporations, cities, and local governments strive to expand their ownership of the rights to water supplies, critics respond by arguing that water is a global resource that cannot and should not be owned.

The availability of clean water has improved, such that 90 per cent of the world's population now has access to uncontaminated water, but while this is a marked improvement since 1990, when only 76 per cent of people had access, the rates vary by country, from 100 per cent in most of Europe to 50–75 per cent in Africa. Data collected by the World Health Organization (2016) suggest that as many as 660 million people have no access to uncontaminated water. If, as the UDHR suggests, humans have the right to 'a standard of living adequate for health and well-being', then anything that supports that goal could reasonably be considered an additional right. The UN General Assembly was moved to resolve in 2010 that access to safe, clean water was 'essential for the full enjoyment of the right to life' (Sultana and Loftus, 2012), but critics ask who would be responsible for ensuring the right to water, and what impact this might have on international security given unequally distributed supplies.

DNA rights. Medical and scientific advances have revealed the value of deoxy-ribonucleic acid (DNA) as a marker in criminal cases, and many governments have collected large DNA databases. While this information can help solve crimes, and absolve those wrongly charged with a crime, its collection has raised concerns about the potential for abuse, and infringements on the right to privacy. In a 2008 case, the European Court of Human Rights ruled that Britain had violated the rights of its citizens by storing the DNA of people who had been arrested for a crime but then either acquitted or had the charges against them dropped. Given the nature and the amount of information contained in the samples, the Court argued, their retention 'had to be regarded as interfering with the right to respect the private lives of the individuals concerned'. On a related note, genetic testing can help people identify risks and take remedial action to avoid future health problems, but questions have been raised about how such information might be used by insurance companies or employers.

THE GLOBAL HUMAN RIGHTS REGIME

At the state and local levels, the protection and enforcement of rights is based on constitutions and extensive bodies of law, with responsibility falling to a combination of government, courts, and the police, watched closely by the media and interest groups, intertwined with public opinion. At the global level, meanwhile, the human rights regime – like all other regimes discussed in this book – is based on a combination of international treaties and intergovernmental bodies to which states have only voluntary obligations, backed up by pressures from other states, international NGOs, and public opinion. While the pressures of globalization have moved states closer to one another in many different ways, they have so far failed to produce a level playing field in the area of human rights.

The first post-war treaty on human rights was the Convention on the Prevention and Punishment of the Crime of Genocide, adopted by the UN General Assembly in 1948 as a direct response to the horrors of the Holocaust. Efforts to agree a broader treaty on human rights were handicapped by differences of opinion between the US and the Soviet Union, which led to the adoption in 1966 of two covenants with contrasting philosophies: the International Covenant on Civil and Political Rights (favoured by the US) stressed negative rights, while the International Covenant on Economic, Social, and Cultural Rights (favoured by the USSR) stressed positive rights. Both eventually came into force in 1976, and the combination of three documents – the Declaration of Human Rights and the two covenants – have since constituted the International Bill of Rights and the ultimate exposition of those rights. As the debate over human rights broadened and deepened, new agreements were reached that focused on the rights of more targeted groups – see Figure 7.2.

In organizational terms, the lead body is the United Nations, which provided a baseline in the form of the Universal Declaration of Human Rights, and has since overseen the setting of standards, promoting knowledge and awareness, drawing attention to violations, and acting as a forum within which states can define the debate as well as press and encourage other states. Central to the work of the UN from 1946 to 2006 was the UN Commission on Human Rights, but it spent its early years promoting rather than investigating, turning to a more interventionist approach from the 1960s. It was joined in 1993 by the Office of the UN High Commissioner for Human Rights (UNHCHR), which is based in Geneva and has worked to draw attention to human rights violations and to exert pressure on abusive governments. It previously worked with the UN Commission on Human Rights, but following an outcry when several countries with poor human rights records were elected to serve on the Commission, a decision was taken to replace the latter in 2006 with the UN Human Rights Council, supervised by the High

Figure 7.2: International human rights agreements

YEAR SIGNED	NAME
1948	Convention on the Prevention and Punishment of the Crime of Genocide
1965	International Convention on the Elimination of All Forms of Racial Discrimination
1979	Convention on the Elimination of All Forms of Discrimination Against Women
1987	United Nations Convention Against Torture
1989	Convention on the Rights of the Child*
1990	International Convention on the Protection of the Rights of All Migrant Workers and Members of their Families
1991	Convention Concerning Indigenous and Tribal Peoples in Independent Countries
2006	Convention on the Rights of Persons with Disabilities
2011	UN Resolution on Sexual Orientation and Gender Identity

*Only two countries have failed to ratify this treaty: Somalia and the United States. In the case of the latter, ratification has been blocked – as have several key treaties in other areas of endeavour – mainly because of opposition from conservative Republican Senators concerned about questions of national sovereignty.

Commissioner and empowered to carry out periodic reviews of the human rights situation in all UN member states, and to receive complaints from states as well as from individuals and organizations.

In spite of the progress in defining human rights, there has been only a mixed record in terms of monitoring the record of different states in honouring their obligations, and there is little available in the way of following up with enforcement. Attention can be drawn to violations, diplomatic pressure can be brought to bear, and states can take unilateral or collective action to cut off trade or investment with the worst offenders. International tribunals can also be organized to try and punish perpetrators of war crimes and other more heinous violations of human rights, but these have been rare: the Nuremberg Trials and the Tokyo Trials were held after World War II to investigate dozens of war criminals in Germany and Japan, and both resulted in multiple prosecutions as well as executions. More recently, the UN

Security Council set up a tribunal to look into violations of humanitarian law in the former Yugoslavia, and others were set up to investigate genocide and other crimes in Rwanda, Sierra Leone, Lebanon, Cambodia and East Timor.

States have also occasionally argued that they have a 'right' to intervene directly, and without UN approval, in the event of gross violations of human rights, based on the 'doctrine of humanitarian intervention'. This was used, for example, to justify a US invasion of the Dominican Republic in 1965, India's invasion of what is now Bangladesh in 1971, Tanzania's invasion of Uganda in 1979, the use of force by NATO in Kosovo in 1999, and the US-led invasion of Iraq in 2003. The problem here lies not just with the potential contravention of international law, but also with the way in which almost any actual or perceived threat can be defined as humanitarian in order to justify an invasion. A more recent debate has surrounded the idea of the doctrine of the 'responsibility to protect', which argues that when states cannot protect their own citizens from genocide, ethnic cleansing, or similar violations of human rights, the international community has an obligation to step in, ideally with UN approval. (The term **humanitarianism** implies a general concern for the welfare of humans, but has often overlapped with human rights concerns.)

Humanitarianism: A general concern for the welfare of humans.

While many of the instances of mass human rights abuses during the Cold War were overlooked by the superpowers in the interests of currying the support of client states, the end of the Cold War changed the landscape. The abuses could not be ignored so easily, and yet ad hoc tribunals to prosecute criminals were cumbersome, as was shown by the creation of tribunals to investigate crimes against humanity in Rwanda and the former Yugoslavia. Proposals began to circulate to set up a permanent International Criminal Court (ICC) that could try perpetrators for the most serious violations of human rights, including genocide, crimes against humanity, and war crimes. The treaty setting up the court was adopted in 1998 and came into force in 2002, giving the new court – based in The Hague in the Netherlands – the power to step in as a last resort should states be unable or unwilling to take action. It issued its first arrest warrants in 2005, aimed at Ugandan warlords, and indicted its first head of state in 2009 when Omar al-Bashir of Sudan was charged with supporting a programme of rape and murder by paramilitary groups in the western region of Darfur.

The ICC was not universally welcomed, and only 124 countries have been party to the court's founding statute. It has faced stiff opposition not just from states that might be the target of its work, such as Israel and Russia, but also from the United States. Complaining that its soldiers might be subject to politically motivated or frivolous prosecutions, the US worked with China to have the Court subordinated to the UN Security Council, where it has the power of veto (see Elsea, 2002). When it failed, President George W. Bush threatened to pull US personnel out of peacekeeping operations unless they were given immunity from prosecution, and negotiated illegal 'impunity agreements' with individual governments under which they agreed not to surrender US nationals to the Court. Finally, in August 2002, Bush signed a new law prohibiting US cooperation with the ICC, and allowing punishment of states that signed the treaty. Its refusal to ratify the ICC treaty places the US in the company of China, Iraq, Iran, Israel, Russia, and Turkey.

Criticism of the court has since continued, particularly from African states that accuse it of focusing too much on African targets. Since its creation, it has investigated potential violations of international law in the Central African Republic, the

Source: Anadolu Agency/Getty Images

Photos of victims on display outside the International Criminal Court during the trial in late 2017 of former Bosnian military chief Ratko Mladic, known as the 'Butcher of Bosnia' for his role in the war crimes that accompanied the break-up of Yugoslavia in the 1990s.

Democratic Republic of the Congo, Ivory Coast, Kenya, Libya, Mali, Sudan, and Uganda, but has failed to investigate similar concerns in Colombia, Palestine, Venezuela or the actions of British troops in Iraq. Investigations, however, do not mean successful prosecutions: even following the commission of numerous war crimes – including rape and the use of child soldiers – during civil unrest in northern Mali in 2012–16, the ICC was able to prosecute only one case, involving the destruction of sites of cultural heritage. Supporters argue that the Court has only opened investigations into situations that fall within its jurisdiction, and that even the prospect of an investigation has been enough to encourage improved respect for international law. Critics disagree, and several African states – including Burundi, the Gambia, and South Africa – say that they plan to leave the ICC.

If many questions still remain about the efficacy of international efforts to monitor and enforce human rights, more progress has been made at the regional level with the work of the European Court of Human Rights, based in Strasbourg, France. The court includes all members of the Council of Europe, a cooperative regional body that was founded in 1949, and that now has 47 members, including Iceland, Russia, and Turkey. The Court was founded in 1959 under the terms of the 1950 European Convention on Human Rights, which was in turn adopted under the auspices of the Council of Europe in order to promote the protection of human rights and fundamental freedoms. The Court was a temporary body until 1998 when it became a permanent institution to which direct access was available to citizens of the member states. It now receives tens of thousands of applications each year, and issues as many as 1,000 judgements annually. Turkey, Russia and Italy top the list of violators of human rights (see Figure 7.3), the most common judgements being for problems with the length of legal proceedings, the right to a fair trial, and the

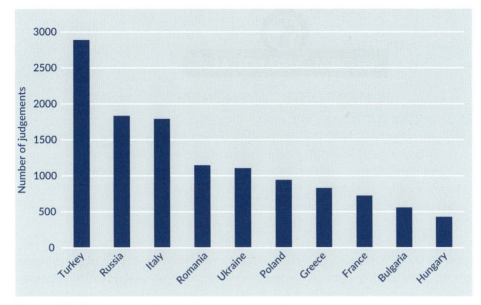

Figure 7.3: Europe's ten biggest human rights offenders
Source: European Court of Human Rights (2017).
Note: Figures are for judgements issued between 1959 and 2016 where at least one violation was found.

protection of property. Like all similar international bodies, however, the Court has no powers of enforcement.

In the world of non-state actors, there is an active community of NGOs campaigning for human rights at both the local and the international level, either directly or as part of their other work, and either focused on the rights of particular groups of people (such as women, children, indigenous peoples, political prisoners, or the disabled) or on rights more broadly defined.

▶ Perhaps the oldest such organization is Anti-Slavery International, which traces its roots back to the creation in London in 1839 of a committee to work for the abolition of slavery throughout the British Empire. It continues to work today against the most common forms of contemporary slavery, including bonded labour, forced marriage, and human trafficking.

▶ In 1922, the International Federation of Human Rights was founded in France to bring together ten national human rights organizations. Today it has nearly 200 affiliated organizations in nearly 100 countries.

▶ The best known human rights INGO is Amnesty International, which was founded in 1961 – see Global and Local 7. It was joined in 1978 by Human Rights Watch, which was founded in the United States and has gone on to generate reports and briefings on the human rights situation around the world, including an annual summary *World Report*.

▶ One INGO that started out with a particular goal in mind but then developed a related interest in human rights is Médecins Sans Frontières (Doctors Without Borders), founded in France in 1971. Its primary goal is to provide volunteer medical services in war-torn regions of the world, but this also sometimes leads to it speaking out against corruption and war crimes. It won the 1999 Nobel Peace Prize in recognition of its humanitarian work.

GLOBAL AND LOCAL 7

HUMAN RIGHTS CAMPAIGNERS

Although there is a significant global human rights regime, the record on human rights from one state or community to another depends in large part on the work of local campaigners and organizations. Global agreements can help us define human rights (even if there is a difference of opinion concerning what is a right and what is not), there is a body of international treaties outlining the rights of targeted groups, and we have a modest set of legal institutions to back them up. But it is often on the front lines of the struggle over human rights that the goals are most clearly defined and changes most effectively achieved.

At the global level, the best known INGO is Amnesty International, which works to draw attention to the plight of prisoners of conscience, campaigns to end torture and the death penalty, and promotes the rights of women, children, and minorities. It was founded by a British lawyer named Peter Benenson (1921–2005), who was reportedly shocked by a report he read in a newspaper while commuting to work one day about two Portuguese students who had been sentenced to long terms in prison for giving a toast 'to liberty' against the authoritarian regime of Antonio Salazar. He wrote an article titled 'The Forgotten Prisoners' that was published in the weekly newspaper *The Observer*, asking for readers to write letters in support of the students. To coordinate further letter-writing campaigns, he founded Amnesty International in July 1961. The organization went on to win the 1977 Nobel Peace Prize, and to become the biggest human rights INGO in the world, with more than seven million members.

At the local level, there are hundreds of national and local bodies working directly with the problems they seek to solve, but in many cases the campaign for human rights revolves around the work of committed individuals, who must often place themselves in danger in order to work for their goals. A good example is offered by Tawakkol Karman (pictured), a Yemeni journalist and human rights campaigner who set up a group named Women Journalists Without Chains in 2005. She helped lead a campaign for press freedom in Yemen, for which she earned multiple death threats, and was deeply involved in anti-government protests arising out of the Arab Spring in 2011, the same year that she was both arrested and won the Nobel Peace Prize. The Nobel citation recognized her 'non-violent struggle for the safety of women and for women's rights to full participation in peace-building work', and she became the first Arab woman and only the second Muslim woman to win the prize.

Source: AFP/Getty Images

Meanwhile, many tireless individuals have taken enormous personal risks to campaign for human rights, their names often found in the lists of winners of numerous national and international human rights awards, such as the European Human Rights Prize, the UN Prize in the Field of Human Rights, and occasionally the Nobel Peace Prize. Winners of such awards include former US President Jimmy Carter, Sérgio Vieira de Mello (a Brazilian diplomat and special UN representative who died in an al-Qaeda bomb attack in Baghdad in 2003), Malala Yousafzai (who campaigned for equal access to education for girls in Pakistan, and was injured in an attempted murder by a Taliban gunman), and several campaigners against apartheid in South Africa, including Albert Luthuli, Helen Suzman, and Nelson Mandela.

COMPARING RECORDS ON HUMAN RIGHTS

Broadly speaking, the more democratic a society, the better its record on human rights is likely to be. Conversely, the less democratic a society, the worse its record on human rights is likely to be, because authoritarianism involves curtailing individual rights and freedoms. However, democracy is no guarantee that all will be well in the field of human rights, nor do limits on democracy necessarily mean consistent limits on rights. Cuba, for example, has long been classified as an authoritarian system, and yet it has performed relatively well in the provision of basic services such as education and health care, and has outperformed many democracies in encouraging equality between men and women; on the Global Gender Gap Index (see Map 7.1), it ranks ahead of Canada, the United States, and Australia.

Measuring performance on human rights is not easy, because the extent to which different societies are performing well or badly is not always easy to quantify, and can be influenced by the subjective perspective of those doing the measuring. Nonetheless, there are several ranking systems available to us, which correlate closely in terms of their results, and if taken collectively can give us a good idea about how different countries perform on human rights:

▶ The UN High Commissioner for Human Rights maintains a *Human Rights Index* that summarizes the situation in different countries around the world.

▶ Amnesty International publishes an annual *State of the World's Human Rights*, while Human Rights Watch maintains an annual *World Report* on the state of human rights around the world, with assessments of the situation in the most troubled countries. In its 2017 report (Human Rights Watch, 2017) it reflected on the 'dangerous rise' of populism in the United States and Europe, new authoritarianism in Egypt and Turkey, and the 'overreach' of counterterrorism activities.

▶ Verisk Analytics, a US data analysis company, maintains an HR Risk Index that evaluates the risk to business in almost every country in the world, using criteria such as human rights and a range of political, economic, and environmental risks.

▶ A group of three NGOs – the Cato Institute of the US, the Fraser Institute of Canada, and the Friedrich Naumann Foundation of Germany – maintain the Human Freedom Index that goes beyond human rights, looking at a combination of personal, civil and economic freedoms.

Human rights is so varied a topic, and the situation changes so much with time and place, that it is hard to make many generalizations. More detailed insight into the dynamics of the matter is offered by looking at the particular issue of women's rights. Although the situation varies by state and occupation, women generally have

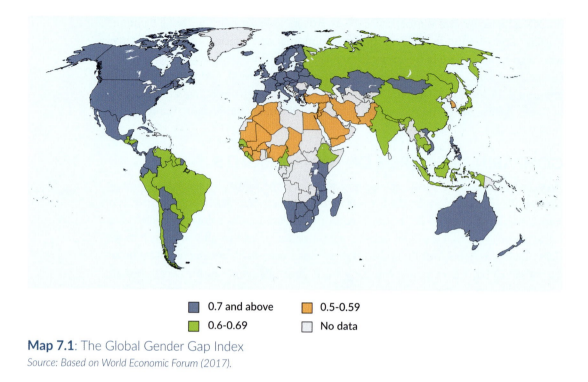

Map 7.1: The Global Gender Gap Index
Source: Based on World Economic Forum (2017).

Legend:
- 0.7 and above
- 0.6-0.69
- 0.5-0.59
- No data

fewer economic opportunities and political power than men, meaning that their rights are circumscribed related to those of men:

▸ Women do not hold as many positions of power in government or business as men.

▸ Women are not paid as much as men for the same kind of work.

▸ There are still many social expectations that keep women out of the workforce.

▸ Questions of **reproductive rights** are often shaped by men rather than women.

▸ Women are often the target of violence and abuse perpetrated by men, a problem brought to international attention in 2017 by an avalanche of charges in the United States against men prominent in politics, the media, and entertainment, and famously spawning the hashtag #MeToo.

> **Reproductive rights**: The right of an individual to decide whether or not to reproduce, and to have access to appropriate information and health care.

A revealing comparative assessment of the relative place of women globally can be found in the Global Gender Gap Index, maintained since 2006 by the World Economic Forum, and providing insight into the magnitude of gender-based disparities using economic, educational, health and political criteria. Focusing on gaps in access rather than different levels of development, recent reports have found that while the gaps in access to education and health care have been closing, they are still large when it comes to economic opportunity and political participation. The broad results of the 2017 index are shown in Map 7.1: the Nordic countries have done best, while African and Middle Eastern states have generally done worst. Rwanda is one of the notable exceptions to the African rule, thanks to a quota system that results in a large number of women being elected to its national legislature and its efforts to close the gap on economic opportunity. Japan, meanwhile, is an outlier among democracies, thanks mainly to the relatively low numbers of women in the workforce and in positions of economic and political leadership.

DISCUSSION QUESTIONS

1. Are human rights truly universal, or are they best seen as culturally relative?

2. Why did it take so long for states and communities to define and build on the idea of human rights?

3. Why do some people persist in curbing the human rights of others?

4. Do we have a 'right to be forgotten' for past indiscretions?

5. Is the International Criminal Court a good idea?

6. Why are men and women still not afforded equal rights?

KEY CONCEPTS

▸ Civil liberties

▸ Civil rights

▸ Human rights

▸ Humanitarianism

▸ Natural law

▸ Natural rights

▸ Political prisoner

▸ Prisoner of conscience

▸ Relativism

▸ Reproductive rights

▸ Slavery

▸ Universal Declaration of Human Rights

▸ Universalism

USEFUL WEBSITES

Amnesty International at https://www.amnesty.org

European Court of Human Rights at http://www.echr.coe.int

Human Rights Watch at https://www.hrw.org

International Criminal Court at https://www.icc-cpi.int

UN High Commissioner for Human Rights at http://www.ohchr.org

UN Human Rights Council at http://www.ohchr.org/en/hrbodies/hrc

Universal Declaration of Human Rights at http://www.un.org/en/universal-declaration-human-rights

FURTHER READING

Clapham, Andrew (2015) *Human Rights: A Very Short Introduction*, 2nd edn (Oxford University Press). A short survey of the meaning and history of human rights, with chapters on issues such as free speech, torture, discrimination, and the death penalty.

Demick, Barbara (2010) *Nothing to Envy: Real Lives in North Korea* (Granta). A journalist's take on life in North Korea, the most extreme example of a society that ignores basic human rights.

Donnelly, Jack (2013) *International Human Rights*, 4th edn (Westview Press). A survey of the meaning, development, and application of human rights, with chapters on their global implications and relationship to contemporary issues.

Goodhart, Michael (ed) (2016) *Human Rights: Politics and Practice*, 3rd edn (Oxford University Press). An edited collection on the link between human rights and politics, with chapters on focused topics such as gender identity, human trafficking, and genocide.

Jones, Adam (2017) *Genocide: A Comprehensive Introduction*, 3rd edn (Routledge). A textbook survey of one of the more heinous examples of the abuse of human rights.

Online Resources

Visit www.macmillanihe.com/McCormick-GS to access additional materials to support teaching and learning.

ECONOMY

8

PREVIEW

This chapter offers a survey of the global economy. It begins with a review of the way in which economies are measured, compared, and understood. It then looks at the changing global economic landscape, assessing the changing balance of the North and the South, the debate over development, the European Union, the emergence of the BRICs, and the effects of the 2007–9 global financial crisis. The chapter goes on to discuss the global financial regime before contrasting the effects of wealth and poverty, and reviewing some of the ways in which global poverty and inequality are being addressed or overlooked.

CONTENTS

- Understanding the global economy
- The changing global economic landscape
- The global financial regime
- Wealth and its effects
- Poverty and its effects

HIGHLIGHTS

- Economies can be measured by size, structure, and contrasting levels of freedom and equality.
- The global economic landscape has undergone dramatic changes since 1945, the dominance of the North having been challenged by the emerging economies of the South.
- The global financial regime revolves around exchange rates, debts, and foreign investment.
- The key actors in the global financial regime include central banks, regional banks, and international organizations such as the World Bank and the IMF.
- Wealth allows the countries of the North to invest heavily in infrastructure, education, health care, and shelter, while also giving them considerable global influence.
- In spite of global economic growth, poverty and inequality remain pervasive problems, both within and among countries.

Source: onurdongel

UNDERSTANDING THE GLOBAL ECONOMY

Every year, a gathering takes places in the Swiss ski resort of Davos hosted by a foundation named the World Economic Forum. In attendance are national leaders, chief executives of major multinationals, economists, and celebrities, and they claim to be interested in improving the state of the world by sharing ideas. Critics note that Davos is a resort that is too expensive for most people to enjoy, and that many of the participants fly in on private jets; the conference has reportedly been described as the place 'where billionaires tell millionaires what the middle class feels' (Freed, 2016). It not only seems to overlook the direct interests of the global poor, but also – for its critics – exemplifies the power and influence of rich countries, and the unequal effects of globalization.

> **Economics**: The study of the production, distribution, and consumption of goods and services, including such matters as money, markets, supply, demand, costs, competition and efficiency.

Although **economics** is concerned with the production, distribution, and consumption of goods and services, these topics are all so much a part of human life that their impact is felt in many other areas, including politics, national security, public health, education, environmental quality, crime, land use, transport, and shelter. In addition to the challenges of understanding these relationships, we also need to understand the causes and effects of global economic change. The roots of that change can be dated back to the emergence of the modern era, and traced through the impact of the industrial revolution, but the global economic system is mainly a product of developments since 1945: new influences and trends have made economics more complex and diverse, and have broadened and deepened the connections among states.

As we saw in Chapter 1, the global economy before World War I was dominated by a few European powers, much of whose wealth was based on manufacturing often using imported raw materials. After 1945, the United States moved quickly to

Source: AFP/Getty Images

Participants in the annual World Economic Forum, held in Davos, Switzerland. Although they discuss trends in the global economy, they are seen by critics as representing only the viewpoint of wealthy countries and interests.

Figure 8.1: Four measures of economic activity

SIZE	The value of goods and services produced (gross domestic product).
STRUCTURE	The balance between industry, services, and goods.
FREEDOM	The extent of government intervention in the marketplace.
EQUALITY	The balance of income distribution.

global pre-eminence on the back of the Bretton Woods system, the relative influence of European powers declined, the oil-based power of the Middle East began to grow, and the foundations were laid for the rise first of Japan and of South Korea, and then of China and India as new economic forces. At the same time, new patterns of trade and consumerism emerged, and markets became increasingly global, both driving and being driven by globalization. The balance continues to change today as the older industrial powers face more competition from Asia and Latin America. At the same time, however, many parts of the world remain mired in poverty, and inequalities grow both within and between states.

In order to appreciate the dynamics of the global economic system, and to identify trends within that system, we can use four comparative measures as a guide (see Figure 8.1). First, we need to consider economic activity as measured by **gross domestic product** (GDP). This tells us the relative size and health of economies, allowing us to rank them from the biggest to the smallest – see Table 8.1 for examples. (See Fioramonti (2013) for insight into the debate over GDP, which he describes as 'the world's most powerful number'.) Other measures are sometimes used, such as gross national product (GNP), which measures the output of all means of production owned by the residents of a country, and gross national income (GNI), which measures income.

GDP tells us the absolute size of economies, but since countries vary dramatically in terms of the sizes of their populations – from more than a billion each in China and India to a few tens of thousands in the smallest countries – it only gives us part of the picture. A more accurate comparison of levels of productivity is found in per capita GDP, where production is divided by population. The differences in the results are reflected in Table 8.2, whose lists of the most and least productive countries are very different from those found in Table 8.1. States with large service sectors –

> **Gross domestic product**: The core measure of the size of economies, calculated by giving a monetary value to all goods and services produced within a country in a given year, regardless of who owns the different means of production.

Table 8.1: The world's biggest and smallest economies

Five biggest	GDP	Five smallest	GDP
United States	$ 18.6 trillion	Palau	$ 293 million
China	$ 11.2 trillion	Marshall Islands	$ 183 million
Japan	$ 4.9 trillion	Kiribati	$ 165 million
Germany	$ 3.5 trillion	Nauru	$ 102 million
United Kingdom	$ 2.6 trillion	Tuvalu	$ 34 million

Source: World Bank Economic Indicators (2018). Figures are for 2016, and are rounded out.

Table 8.2: The world's most and least productive economies			
Five most productive	Per capita GDP	Five least productive	Per capita GDP
Luxembourg	$ 103,000	Central African Republic	$ 380
Switzerland	$ 79,000	Mozambique	$ 380
Norway	$ 71,000	Niger	$ 360
Ireland	$ 62,000	Malawi	$ 300
Iceland	$ 60,000	Burundi	$ 290

Source: World Bank Economic Indicators (2018). Figures are for 2016, and are rounded out.

particularly in banking and finance – move to the top because of the relatively high value of such activities, while those with large and less profitable agricultural sectors move to the bottom.

Our second comparative measure is economic structure, which tells us what different countries produce. This, in turn, offers us insights into the nature of different economies, and how they fit into the global system. In making these comparisons, we start from the assumption that all economic production falls into one of three categories:

▸ *Industry* produces commodities or tangible goods such as road vehicles, building materials, and consumer goods.

▸ *Services* consist of intangibles such as retail activity, financial services, health care, and utilities.

▸ *Agriculture* consists of anything produced off the land (or out of the oceans), including crops, timber, meat and dairy products, and fisheries.

As a general rule of thumb, most Northern states are post-industrial, because they started their process of industrialization earliest, and most of their domestic economic activity is now based on services. Meanwhile, the wealthiest emerging states are still industrializing, while the poorest states in the South still rely heavily on agriculture and basic industry. This is illustrated in Figure 8.2, which contrasts service-based economies such as Britain and France with the rising industrial powers of India and China, and the still-developing economy of Sierra Leone, where agriculture accounts for 61 per cent of GDP.

As a third indicator, we can compare different levels of economic freedom, which gives us insight into the extent to which governments play a role in the economy. Levels of intervention vary within a scale between two core types of economic management:

▸ **Capitalism**, or economic liberalism, is based on leaving as many economic decisions as possible to the market. This means less government intervention in the form of taxes, regulations, price controls, subsidies, and public ownership of industries and services (see Clark, 2016).

▸ Social democracy and **socialism** are varieties of state-centred economics, because they see free markets working alongside government programmes aimed

Capitalism: An economic philosophy based on leaving as many decisions as possible on production, distribution, and prices to the free market.

Socialism: An economic philosophy based on redistributing opportunity and wealth through greater government involvement in the marketplace.

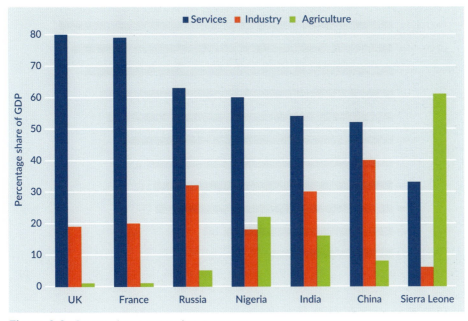

Figure 8.2: Comparing economic structures
Source: Based on data in World Bank Economic Indicators (2018). Figures are for 2016.

at promoting social justice through redistribution. Policies include progressive taxes (those who earn more pay more), state welfare, and state-run health care and education.

All governments shape and control economies in some fashion, typically mixing elements of capitalism and socialism with a combination of taxes, regulations, health and safety standards, price controls, subsidies, and the provision of welfare. Northern states have opted for different levels of economic liberalism and social democracy, many of them opting for **neo-liberalism**, an approach to the economy based on privatization, deregulation and free trade, and associated initially with leaders such as Ronald Reagan and Margaret Thatcher. It has been widely criticized for its focus on efficiency at the expense of equality, and for making the rich richer while overlooking the needs of the underclass.

Neo-liberalism: An economic philosophy based on economic liberalization that has been adopted by many Northern countries since the 1980s.

For their part, the fastest-growing Asian and Latin American states have adopted increasingly free-market policies, while the less-developed states of the South have often failed to develop economic stability because of a trying combination of historical, external, and internal factors – see later in this chapter. Authoritarian states are less predictable in the way they manage economies, policies often being based on the capricious views of leaders and ruling elites, and typically revolving around the accumulation of control in the hands of such elites.

One insight into the comparative differences is offered by the Index of Economic Freedom maintained by the Fraser Institute, a conservative Canadian think-tank (see Gwartney et al., 2016). The index is based on 42 measures that rate countries according to such factors as the size and reach of government, approaches to property rights, levels of access to sound money, and regulation of credit. Each country is given a score out of 10, with the freest economies earning the highest scores and the more controlled economies earning the lowest scores. Figure 8.3 gives examples from the 2016 index, which gave Hong Kong and Singapore the highest

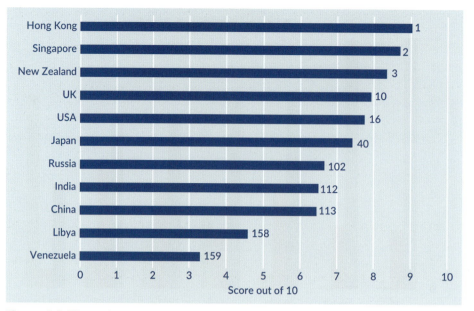

Figure 8.3: The Index of Economic Freedom
Source: Based on data in Fraser Institute (2016). Ranking indicated at the end of each column.

ratings, placed most democracies in the range of 7.5 or higher, and ranked India and China at 112th and 113th respectively, among a cluster of Asian, African, and Latin American states. Venezuela was placed last, while more than 30 countries were not ranked at all because of a lack of reliable information.

The fourth comparative economic measure is income distribution, which tells us much about how people fare within and among countries. In both cases there is unequal distribution, with the wealthiest countries accounting for the biggest shares of GDP, and the wealthiest people in most countries owning or controlling large amounts of national wealth. The global situation is reflected in the numbers for GDP: Figure 8.4 shows the dominance of the older post-industrialized economies,

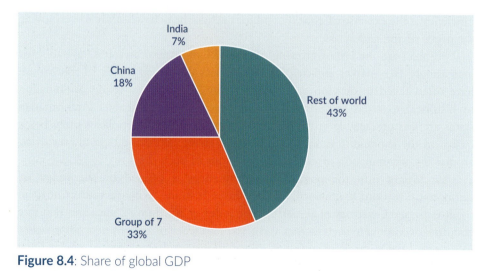

Figure 8.4: Share of global GDP
Source: Based on data in World Bank Economic Indicators (2018). Figures are for 2016.

particularly those that are members of the Group of 7. Both globally and domestically, income inequality is reflected in the **Gini coefficient**, a measure created in 1912 by the Italian statistician Corrado Gini.

Based on the simple premise of giving a value of 0 to a state where everyone has equal income and a value of 1 to a state where one person owns all the wealth, it shows that the global figure has been growing as countries have become richer, reaching its current level of about 0.65 (Bourguignon, 2015). Meanwhile, national figures range from a low of about 0.25 (Finland, Slovakia, Ukraine and Sweden) to a high of about 0.60 (Haiti, South Africa and Lesotho) (CIA World Factbook, 2017). The Gini coefficient has the advantage of being simple, but it has been criticized for being a measure of income rather than of opportunity, for being based on sometimes unreliable GDP and income data, for failing to take into account the informal market (a key source of income in poorer countries), and for measuring current income rather than lifetime income. Concerns about its accuracy have led to the development of a new measure, the Palma ratio, based on the ratio of the income share of the wealthiest 10 per cent to that of the poorest 40 per cent.

> **Gini coefficient**: A measure of income inequality, used to show the distribution of wealth in a given population.

THE CHANGING GLOBAL ECONOMIC LANDSCAPE

The global economic system has undergone dramatic change since 1945, as the connections among countries have grown and the effects of globalization have been felt, for better or for worse. The pre-war dominance of Europe was exemplified by Britain, which – at the height of its power in 1914 – accounted (with its Empire) for 25 per cent of global GDP and 44 per cent of global foreign direct investment (De Keersmaeker, 2017), and controlled the world's most powerful currency, the pound sterling. The United States had begun to emerge as an economic power between the two world wars, but would not fully assert itself until after 1945, while China and Japan were only regional powers at best, and most of the rest of the world was either under colonial control or still economically developing.

As we saw in Chapter 1, the changes that came after 1945 grew out of the Bretton Woods system, based as it was on plans to open the global economy, underpinned by stable exchange rates and the new power of the US dollar. Governments were interested in free trade and in bringing down barriers to trade, such as tariffs and quotas. More change came with the wave of decolonization that began immediately after the war, bringing many newly independent states into the global system. At first, it was tempting to see the world as being divided into two large blocs:

▸ A developed world of wealthy, capitalist economies. These included Canada and the United States, Western Europe, Japan and South Korea, and Australia and New Zealand. Among them they were the most productive, controlled the most wealth, were home to the biggest corporations, had the highest incomes, and were the most tightly bound into the global economy. Most had gone early through their industrial revolutions, and were now moving into service-based economies.

▸ A developing world of emerging and poorer economies. These included most of Africa, Asia and Latin America. Among them they were the least productive, had the least wealth, were suppliers and markets for corporations headquartered mainly in the developed world, had the lowest incomes, and were the least tied into the global economy. Some were, at best, at an early stage of their industrial revolutions, and many still relied heavily on agriculture.

But this picture was always too simplistic, not just because there were major variations within each group of countries, but also because the two categories overlooked the place in the global system of communist states such as the Soviet Union and its allies, along with China and much of Southeast Asia. The Soviet brand of communism meant centralized control, inefficiency, little attention to environmental concerns, and economic production that was dominated by military interests. Meanwhile, the Chinese brand of communism meant most of these along with a focus on rural development; urban industrial development was still at an early stage in China, Vietnam, Laos, Cambodia, and those parts of Africa where China tried to exert its influence, including Angola, Mozambique and Tanzania. The bigger point, though, was that communism also meant marginalization for much of the world during the Cold War, leaving most of these countries with the challenge – after 1990 – of restructuring their economies and revising their place in the global system.

The Middle East was also becoming more economically and politically important, but mainly because it had large stocks of a single commodity that the rest of the world needed: oil. Europeans, Russians, and Americans had long been active in the region as they sought to control oil supplies. Those interests continued to grow after 1945 as global demand for oil grew, as the strategic tensions of the Cold War entered the equation, and as the conflict between Israel and the Arab world spilled over into economic tensions. This had its deepest effects during the energy crises of 1973 when Arab oil states cut production in the wake of Western support for Israel during the Yom Kippur war of that year. Arab–Israeli tensions and US policy in the region fed into the later rise of international terrorism and its association with Islamic extremism.

Development: The improvement of the economic and social well-being of peoples, communities, or states. Often used only in the context of poorer states.

With the end of the colonial era, **development** moved up the global economic agenda, with questions raised about how those countries variously described as developing, less developed, or underdeveloped could best improve their place in the global system, in both absolute and relative terms (see Todaro and Smith, 2016). Just how to identify and understand these countries has been the topic of a long debate, with suggestions that we use measures such as GDP, literacy rates, and health care, all combined into the idea of quality of life, however that is measured. As a means of comparing economic and social development, the Human Development Index (started by the UN Development Programme in 1990) is helpful. This uses three core measures: health care as represented by life expectancy, education as represented by the number of years of schooling, and standard of living as represented by per capita GNI. It then generates scores out of 1.0 for most of the countries of the world, rating them as either Very High, High, Medium, or Low – see Map 8.1.

The end of the Cold War in about 1989–91 not only brought about the collapse of the communist bloc as a distinctive actor in the global system, but also emphasized and accelerated the emergence of Asia and Latin America. The potential of countries such as Brazil, China, India, Indonesia and Mexico had long been understood, but their strengthening global positions now became more obvious,

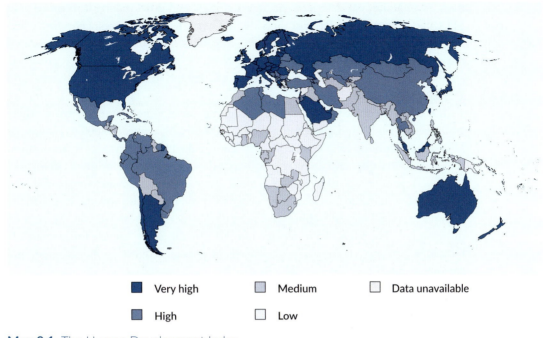

Legend:

■ Very high   ▨ Medium   ☐ Data unavailable

■ High   ☐ Low

Map 8.1: The Human Development Index
Source: UN Development Programme (2017).

helped by trends towards greater democracy in several of them. No longer were the Americans or the Western Europeans as dominant as they had been since the 1950s, and many of the old assumptions about their relative power and advantages had to be reviewed. Asia's prospects were underlined – as we saw in Chapter 2 – by its population growth.

Meanwhile, the European Union (see Chapter 6) continued its rise as a global economic force. Its membership increased in stages, beginning with its six founding members in 1958, and doubling to 12 members by 1986. The end of the Cold War released Eastern Europe from the grip of the Soviet Union, and in 2004 the character of the EU changed when ten mainly Eastern European states (including the three former Soviet republics of Estonia, Latvia and Lithuania) joined the EU; in 2013, Croatia became the EU's 28th member state. Along the way, the EU had removed many of its internal barriers to trade and to the free movement of people and money, overtook the United States as the biggest economic actor in the world when measured by GDP, and came to account for the largest share of global trade and foreign investment. Mergers and acquisitions across EU borders meanwhile led to the rise of large and competitive new European multinationals such as Airbus, Volkswagen, AXA, Total, and Allianz. (For a brief survey of the economics of the EU, see McCormick, 2017b: Chapter 7.)

The South also asserted itself as the balance of global economic power continued to move away from the North. As we saw in Chapter 1, the acronym BRIC was invented in 2001 to summarize the strengthening roles of Brazil, Russia, India and China. The clear leader in this group was China, whose economy (when measured by GDP) grew by more than 300 per cent between 1990 and 2000, and then by an additional 900 per cent between 2000 and 2015 (taking it to more than $11 trillion), overtaking Japan to become the world's second largest economy when measured by GDP. By 2012, Jim O'Neill – the investment banker who had invented the acronym BRIC – was talking of the Next 11, or N11: a secondary group of emerging markets that included Bangladesh, Egypt, Iran, Mexico, Nigeria, and Vietnam (Martin, 2012).

But while there were positive trends in some developing countries, many others continued to lag behind, prompting the UN General Assembly in 2000 to publish its Millennium Development Goals (MDG). These called for progress in the eradication of extreme poverty and hunger, the expansion of universal primary education, improved gender equality, reduced child mortality, and greater environmental sustainability, all by 2015. On almost every front there was improvement, but many communities still lagged behind and poverty has persisted (as we will see later in this chapter). The MDG were replaced in 2015 by the 2030 Agenda for Sustainable Development, with 17 new goals focused on poverty, education, health care, and climate change.

Global financial crisis: The crisis sparked in 2007 by financial deregulation and speculation in the United States, which spread quickly to Europe.

A shock came to the international system in 2007 with the breaking of a **global financial crisis** that was the worst of its kind since the Great Depression of the 1930s. More a North Atlantic crisis than one with truly global proportions, it had its origins in the sub-prime mortgage industry in the United States, where banks and financial companies – seeking new profits, and encouraged by growing home prices and weak financial regulations – had lent to low-income home-buyers. These loans could be turned into securities and sold off, earning large profits while also passing on the risk. When the US housing bubble burst, the value of assets held by banks and financial institutions fell, and with few reserves to back them up, many either went bankrupt or turned to the government for help, stock prices plummeted, many people lost their jobs and their homes, and shrinking consumer demand led to financial woes for business.

Because many of these so-called toxic assets had been sold to financial institutions in other countries (particularly Europe), the crisis quickly spread, generating a full-blown international banking crisis. Its rapid spread emphasized not just the extent of one of the major risks of globalization, but also the extent to which Northern states had failed to develop and implement effective domestic financial regulations. Emerging economies were relatively unaffected, emphasizing the extent to which they were achieving their own momentum; between 2008 and 2009, German GDP fell by eight per cent and US GDP by two per cent, but Chinese GDP grew by 11 per cent (World Bank, 2017). The fallout from the crisis seemed to confirm the ongoing shift of economic power from the North to the South.

The cumulative result of all these changes is a global economic landscape that is hard to summarize simply, that is transforming rapidly, that is increasingly globalized, but that still contains enormous inequalities. While the world's population is today just over twice what it was in 1960, GDP grew more than 50-fold over the same period, more than half that growth coming since 2000 – see Figure 8.5. There has been a liberalization of trade (see Chapter 9), cross-border flows of investment have grown, and the reach of the digital economy has expanded. But while there are many 'haves' in the world, there are still many 'have nots'; the rich become richer and consume more, while hundreds of millions of people in the South are still denied even basic necessities such as shelter, clean water, and sanitation.

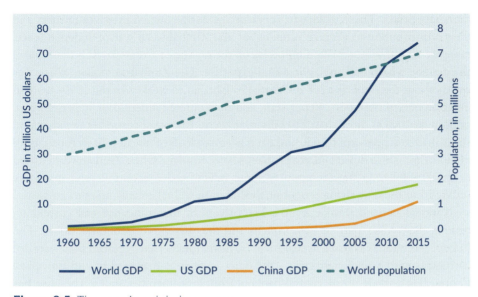

Figure 8.5: The growing global economy
Source: Based on data in World Bank Economic Indicators (2018).

THE GLOBAL FINANCIAL REGIME

Global economic connections, then, are both broad and deep. Countries trade with one another, investments flow back and forth, people move across borders in search of jobs and economic opportunities, and events in one part of the world have knock-on effects in others. We might be able – if we so choose – to mentally ignore or isolate ourselves from much of what happens outside our immediate communities, but when it comes to economics, the ties that bind us are tight, and the effects are felt everywhere. There is a substantial financial regime (discussed here) as well as a substantial trade regime (discussed in Chapter 9), both built by a combination of deliberate government action and – more importantly – the numerous decisions of thousands of multinational corporations working across borders.

The global financial regime is based on money, in the form of national currencies. A key power of states is the creation and management of such currencies, and the way they relate to one another – and the way the global system works – is based centrally on the **exchange rates** among currencies. Their value was once based on the **gold standard**, which meant mainly static exchange rates, but – as we saw in Chapter 1 – the final link between gold and currencies ended in 1971, and currencies are now mainly valued against each other according to floating exchange rates; these tell us how much we will be given if we exchange dollars for euros, or roubles for yen, and so on. Every international financial exchange is based on these rates, which fluctuate according to levels of confidence in national currencies, markets and economies. The US dollar has been the world's most credible and stable currency since the 1950s, its global role exemplified by its attractions as a **reserve currency**.

By contrast, poorer, more unstable, or more badly managed economies have weaker and less credible currencies, few having surpassed in recent decades the unhappy tale of Zimbabwe. Entering independence in 1980 with a sound economic base, its government made a series of bad decisions on land ownership and

Exchange rate: The value of one currency relative to another.

Gold standard: An arrangement by which countries fixed the value of their currencies to gold. Abandoned by Britain and the United States in the 1930s, and no longer used.

Reserve currency: A foreign currency that is held by governments, and is used to help them pay off debts or to reduce exchange rate risks.

monetary policy. These included the seizure of farms owned by white farmers and their redistribution to alleged 'veterans' of the Zimbabwean war of independence, many of whom were actually supporters of the regime of President Robert Mugabe, and few of whom had any agricultural expertise. The Zimbabwe dollar, which was worth about the same as a US dollar in 1980, began to weaken in the 1990s with an inflation rate of about 10–40 per cent, and then entered a period of hyperinflation, peaking in 2008 at more than 230 billion per cent. Imports became more expensive, shops had few products to sell, and even a simple loaf of bread cost as much as 10 million Zimbabwe dollars. Many problems were resolved when Zimbabwe switched to the US dollar, giving the country some much-needed economic and monetary stability, but the underlying economic dysfunction will take many years to go away.

National **central banks** are the key players in managing national currencies, making them a key part of government and the shaping of economic policy. The European Union is unusual in that most of its members have replaced their national currencies with a single currency – the euro – which is managed by the European Central Bank, made up of central bankers from euro member states. The euro has undergone many teething troubles since its introduction in 1999, not least being the debt crisis that hit several euro states beginning in 2009. Even so, it remains the second most powerful currency in the world, after the US dollar.

At the global level, the two major financial organizations are the World Bank and the International Monetary Fund (IMF), both of them specialized agencies of the UN, both created in 1945 as part of the Bretton Woods agreement and both headquartered in Washington DC. The immediate task of the World Bank was to help with the post-war reconstruction of Europe. As Europe recovered, the Bank

Central bank:
A national bank responsible for maintaining the value of a state's currency, limiting the amount of money in circulation, setting interest rates, and guarding against inflation.

Source: Getty Images/iStockphoto

The world's newest reserve currency is the euro, launched in 1999. It is now used in most of the member states of the European Union, where it replaced national currencies that often dated back centuries.

moved its attention to other parts of the world, and as decolonization accelerated, it focused on the South. It makes low-interest loans to help countries meet their debt obligations, and to encourage adjustments designed to improve efficiency and to open markets. Like all banks, it often requires conditions for its loans, which has opened the bank to charges of neo-imperialism, further emphasized by the large shares held in the bank by the world's wealthiest countries, and a tradition of appointing Americans to the presidency of the bank. The bank has also been criticized for the environmental costs of many of the projects it supports, and has altered its policies accordingly.

For its part, the IMF has the more specific task of helping countries that are having difficulties with their balance of payments with the rest of the world. Like the World Bank, it makes loans and usually requires conditions for those loans, voting power is dominated by the wealthy countries (the US, Japan, Germany, France and Britain among them have more than one-third of the votes), and the IMF's managing director has always been a European. Replacing gold as a world standard in 1969, the IMF created the **Special Drawing Right** as a reserve that can be exchanged for national currencies. With its value determined by a basket of key currencies (the US dollar, the euro, the Chinese renminbi, the Japanese yen, and the British pound), it is the closest we come to having a global currency, but it can only be used by states, most often as a line of credit by poorer countries.

> **Special Drawing Right**: An artificial currency created and maintained by the IMF, supplementing standard reserve currencies.

One of the effects of the concerns about rich-country financial dominance has been the creation of **regional development banks**, including those in Asia, Africa, and Latin America, and the Islamic Development Bank (IDC) based in Jeddah, Saudi Arabia. Although rich countries – notably the United States and Japan – are shareholders in several of these banks (but not the IDC), the majority of shares are held by countries in the respective regions in which the banks operate. They are more familiar with – and invested in – local needs, the banks provide a bigger voice to borrowers in the South, and they are more able to use peer pressure to encourage policy changes (see Griffith-Jones et al., 2008). Looking more globally, the five BRICS countries decided in 2013 to set up the New Development Bank, headquartered in Shanghai, China. This was prompted by a concern about the inability of these countries to have a voice in the work of the World Bank and the IMF commensurate with their economic growth, and by a desire to build on the rapid growth in South–South economic cooperation (Desai and Freeland, 2014).

> **Regional development bank**: A bank set up and run within a given region, pooling contributions from its shareholders to offer low-interest loans to countries in the region.

Much like individual consumers who must often borrow in order to make large purchases, states also must borrow. They might do this because they are running a trade deficit (importing more than they are exporting), or because they have found it politically difficult to raise taxes in order to cover their expenses. They borrow from a combination of banks, businesses, the public, and foreign governments, not just creating critical global links in the form of **national debts** but also global risks; should they find that they can no longer repay their debts, they will be obliged either to renegotiate the terms of the debt, seek help from the IMF, or default (fail to repay).

> **National debt**: The amount that a government owes as a result of running a budget deficit and/or a trade deficit, much of it often owed to foreign investors.

Wealthy countries have enough in the way of resources that they have little difficulty either borrowing or servicing their debts, but large debts interfere with their domestic economic choices (because so much of their income is spent on interest payments) and impinge upon their sovereignty by leaving them obliged to

GLOBAL AND LOCAL 8

SMALL BUSINESSES IN THE GLOBAL MARKET

We can travel almost anywhere in the world and still see the same global brands, such as Coca-Cola, HSBC, IKEA, McDonald's, Nike, Toyota, Samsung and Starbucks. But while the big multinational corporations (MNCs) dominate the global market and drive many consumer choices, they all began as small businesses, and perhaps even as the inspired creation of a single person. Small companies deserve attention not just because they often become the basis of brands that reach all over the world, but also because they continue to outnumber the large ones and employ a majority of the global workforce, giving them a critical role in driving economies. They are known collectively as **small and medium enterprises** (SMEs), and while they are defined differently by different governments, the definition used by the European Union is representative: small companies are those with fewer than 50 employees and a turnover of less than €10 million, while medium companies have fewer than 250 employees and a turnover of less than €50 million.

The Northern origins and bases of so many MNCs reflects not just the dominating role of the North in global economic matters, but also the circumstances that allowed small companies to grow into big companies: good ideas, large domestic markets, business-friendly laws, and a large element of good luck. (It should not be forgotten, however, that many small companies either remain small, or fail – commerce can be a cut-throat business.)

In large parts of the South, meanwhile, SMEs are among the leading drivers of economic development, and in many ways are helping make up for the failures of decades of policies that have done little to create new jobs or to promote economic independence. Improved investment opportunities and regulatory support from governments would help more operators of small businesses flourish and sell their products more widely, and would also help the South stave off the cultural inroads made by the spread of Northern-based companies. Many Southern entrepreneurs have been encouraged by hostile policies at home to emigrate and to take their skills to the North, leading to a brain drain that undermines the prospects of progress in their home countries; see Chapter 10.

Small and medium enterprises: Independent companies with small numbers of employees and small turnovers, making them distinct from larger (and often multi-national) corporations.

Foreign direct investment: Any large-scale investment made in a business by foreign governments, businesses, or individuals.

other countries. No country has pushed itself into such serious debt problems as the United States, which has for decades had both a budget deficit and a trade deficit, as a result of which its national debt grew from $900 billion in 1980 to more than $21 trillion at the beginning of 2018. While the US has a high standard of living in spite of this, its debts are strategically worrying; just under half are held by foreign investors, and just over $1 trillion each by China and Japan.

Another element of the global financial system is **foreign direct investment** (FDI), consisting of all the investments made by governments, businesses and individuals in countries other than their own. A company might expand from one country to another, or a government might buy land or a business in another country, or an individual might invest in assets in another country. With investment driven by the hope of achieving strong returns, the most popular targets will be countries with open economies, valuable resources, and skilled work forces, so there is an understandable bias towards countries that are stable, and against those that are unstable, poor, or badly governed. The biggest sources and targets of FDI are the 35 members of the Organization for Economic Cooperation and Development

(OECD), an intergovernmental organization whose original goal was to coordinate policy during the rebuilding of Europe after World War II. It now works to encourage free markets and trade among its members, which include non-European countries such as Australia, Canada, Japan, Mexico, and the United States (see Woodward, 2009).

WEALTH AND ITS EFFECTS

In that imaginary global community of 100 people outlined in the Introduction, just 17 account for more than 60 per cent of total economic output, and almost all are Europeans, North Americans, Japanese or South Koreans, or Australasians. They not only account for the most production overall, but for the most per capita production (see Figure 8.6), and the most consumption. The relative **wealth** of their economies – much of it founded on the advantages of imperialism and of a global system weighted in their favour (see section on poverty) – has also allowed them to invest heavily in infrastructure, education, health care, and shelter, and has given them considerable power; the global marketplace and the forces of globalization are shaped to a large degree by the interests and the actions of the governments and corporations of these states.

> **Wealth**: An abundance of money, material possessions, and opportunity, which can be measured in both quantity and quality.

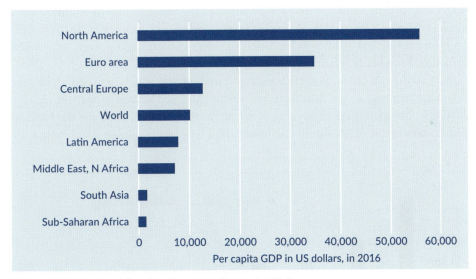

Figure 8.6: Regional levels of economic productivity
Source: Based on data in World Bank Economic Indicators (2018).

But not all is well in the world of the wealthy, and barely a day goes by without worried discussions about the crisis of capitalism, which brings both opportunities and problems:

▸ The opportunities include the creation or expansion of businesses and jobs, the capacity to invest in infrastructure and technological development, the provision of dependable services (clean water, sanitation, energy supplies, and transport, for example), investments in high quality education and health care, and philanthropy.

▸ The problems include excessive and/or careless consumption, driven by greed or laziness and leading to waste, malnutrition (in the form both of too little and too much consumption), maldistribution of wealth, inequality, a sense of entitlement, and environmental decline.

On the one hand, many of the most important and valuable advances in technology have been tied closely to wealth, which provides the perfect combination of opportunity, need, and resources. But, on the other hand, the history of industrialization in particular has also been one of dirt and waste: it has created air pollution, water pollution, and waste in multiple forms (municipal, agricultural, toxic, and hazardous). The search for profits has long meant a careless approach to development, with too little attention being paid to fair and equal wages, worker safety, public health and safety, and environmental quality.

Economic inequalities are illustrated in Figure 8.7, which shows how much wealth and income is controlled by the top ten per cent of households in selected states: as much as 76 per cent of wealth and 28 per cent of income in the United States, easing off to 39 per cent and 24 per cent, respectively, in Greece. Taking a more global approach, the anti-poverty INGO Oxfam has long monitored and shared information on the distribution of wealth, and concluded that 82 per cent of the wealth generated globally in 2017 was controlled by one per cent of the world's population, while the poorest 50 per cent saw no increase in their wealth. 'Living wages and decent work for the world's workers are fundamental to ending today's inequality crisis', Oxfam argued. 'All over the world, our economy of the 1% is built on the backs of low paid workers, often women, who are paid poverty wages and denied basic rights' (Oxfam International, 2018).

Just as the effects of poverty are deeply studied and widely worried about (see following section), so are the effects of wealth. And just as we are not entirely sure what circumstances lead to poverty, so we are not sure what allows for the creation and accumulation of wealth in the hands of a few, beyond some combination of

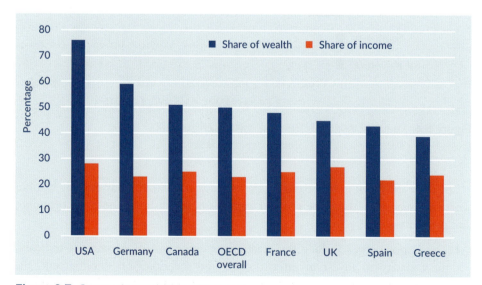

Figure 8.7: Comparing wealth and income
Source: Murtin and d'Ercole (2012). Data are for the wealthiest ten per cent of households in 2010.

creativity, energy, ambition, hard work, advantage, and good fortune. As to how best to encourage a more equitable distribution of wealth, we are also uncertain, the opinions ranging between the trickle-down idea of allowing the wealthy to keep their riches in the hope that they will invest them in new business and new jobs (on the one hand) and redistribution through taxing and spending (on the other). Clearly we have not pinned down the magic formula of wealth creation, given that there are still many people who live in poverty even in the wealthiest countries, and given that the gap between the rich and poor continues to grow.

POVERTY AND ITS EFFECTS

In spite of the rapid recent growth in the size of the global economy, and the particularly rapid rise of new economic powers such as China, poverty and inequality remain pervasive problems. In the imaginary global community of 100 people described in the Introduction, 80 would live on less than $10 per day and would consume just 14 per cent of resources, while 70 would be either malnourished or undernourished, and 23 would lack shelter. This is a matter not just of differences between wealthy states and poor states, but also of differences within states: there is still a high degree of poverty even in the wealthiest countries, and a small but growing class of wealthy people even in the poorest states. The mismatch in levels of wealth also means a mismatch of opportunity and influence: the wealthiest countries have the most power in large part because they also have the most wealth. The poorest countries, meanwhile, tend to find themselves carried along on economic and political tides generated in other parts of the world, and must react to international developments rather than shaping them.

Measuring **poverty** is not easy – the definition of those who are poor can be either relative or absolute, depending on the overall wealth of the economies in which they live, and their different experiences; see Comparing North and South 5. Relative poverty is determined by circumstances, meaning that poor people living among other poor people might not feel as deprived as those who live within sight of wealth. Absolute poverty, meanwhile, is based on setting a threshold and defining all those who live below that threshold as poor. Finally, extreme poverty is the most obvious and visible, describing those who live at the lowest margins of the wealth and income scale, in both absolute and relative terms.

> **Poverty**: A scarcity of money, material possessions, opportunity, and basic needs, which can be measured in both quantity and quality.

The causes of poverty are complex, including both domestic and international factors, and their variations by time and place making it difficult to generalize (see Cosgrove and Curtis, 2018). They include the following:

▶ The legacy of colonialism and slavery.

▶ Political instability.

▶ High population growth.

▶ War and conflict.

▶ Social and political discrimination, and gender inequalities.

▶ Inadequate investment in education, job creation, health care, or infrastructure.

▶ Social or geographical marginalization.

COMPARING NORTH AND SOUTH 8

THE DIFFERENT MEANINGS OF POVERTY

Because of differences in laws, regulations, living costs, patterns of consumption, and culture, poverty has different definitions in the North and the South. In the United States, for example, people are defined as poor if they live below a threshold established by the government: about $24,000 for a household of four, for example, or about $12,000 for someone living alone, with 'deep poverty' defined as household income that is less than half the poverty threshold. On that basis, about 13–15 per cent of the US population lives in poverty, and about 5 per cent in deep poverty. But incomes of this kind would make residents of the poorest countries relatively wealthy; in India and South Africa, for example, someone is considered to be living in poverty if they earn less than $2 per day, while the World Bank has set the international poverty line at $1.90 per day. Using this measure, about 700 million people around the world – or 10 per cent of the world's population – are poor.

In the North, poverty is cushioned to some extent by welfare programmes that provide a safety net in the form of unemployment benefits, free or subsidized education, and subsidized health care, and by regulations that provide protection for workers, provide for clean water and sanitation, and outlaw abuses such as child labour and slavery. Not all are caught by the safety net, however, while welfare and wage levels often guarantee little beyond a minimum quality of life, and homelessness remains a widespread problem. Meanwhile, the gap between the rich and the poor continues to grow.

In the poorest parts of the South, meanwhile, the poor have fewer legal protections and much less in the way of organized welfare. Living conditions are often dire, with many obliged to live in slums that may lack clean water or sanitation, and where life is disrupted by crime and long commutes through clogged city streets to poorly paid jobs. Those jobs might involve being obliged to work for long hours in factories making products for consumers in wealthy countries. For the urban and rural poor alike, the lack of good schools means that many grow up to be illiterate, keeping them within the cycle of poverty, while many lack adequate health care, leaving many with debilitating health problems, and many others die from diseases such as malaria that could be prevented with a modest investment on the part of government.

- ▸ Familial or marital instability.

- ▸ Vulnerability to natural disasters.

- ▸ Bad economic or political decisions.

- ▸ Corruption.

Poverty brings with it a host of problems that make the prospects for successful development more distant: it is often accompanied by hunger and malnutrition, health problems, illness or death from often preventable diseases, low levels of literacy, inadequate shelter and sanitation, poor environmental quality, underinvestment, and psychological problems that range from humiliation to a lack of energy and motivation. The best way to address all these problems has been the subject of a debate among sociologists dating back decades, but their failure to reach agreement or to offer definitive answers is reflected in the persistence of poverty and inequality. We can all wish and hope for more efficient government and more effective economic policies, but these targets are too broad and general, and the answer lies in more focused solutions. These include investments in education and family planning, policies that encourage small businesses and the creation of jobs, and improvements in infrastructure.

Investing in women is a particular priority. One of the key sources of poverty all over the world is gender discrimination, and when women are poor, the societies in which they live suffer disproportionately; women will likely have the least access to health care and education, are more often trapped in poorly paid or unpaid domestic work, are more dependent upon their spouses, have fewer options than men to start and build businesses, have less access to land and other assets, have a reduced political voice, are often the least engaged in economic development, and might be subject to sexual exploitation. While the income and poverty gap between men and women is closing in some countries, in others it persists, leaving half the population subject to oppression and in a state of greater need. Women are better off in the North (although still face much economic and social discrimination), but in the South are among the poorest of the poor, with levels of inequality being highest in those countries that are the least globalized.

Another priority lies in investing in, and lending to, small business through what is known as **microfinance**. Family farmers and businesses cannot usually hope to attract support from large banks or financial institutions, and nor can they usually meet the terms of loans set by those institutions. But the experience of the Grameen Bank in Bangladesh shows how thinking small can work. Created in 1983 by Muhammad Yunus (who won the 2006 Nobel Peace Prize for his efforts), this makes small loans available to those who would otherwise find it impossible to borrow or to take the first steps out of poverty (Yunus, 2007).

Microfinance: Lending and investing at a small scale to help small businesses in developing countries.

Source: Getty Images

A mother and her children in India. Women in the Global South are more likely to be trapped in poverty than men, and efforts to improve their economic situation often come up against the barrier of gender discrimination.

Just as the causes of poverty vary by time and place, so – too – do the roots of inequality among states. Among the most often touted causes are the heritage of colonialism and the creation of an unbalanced global economy. There are many who argue that the effects of colonialism continue to linger long after the end of Europe's empires. Those empires were built on exploitation, the imperial powers becoming rich at the expense of their colonies, and the spirit of that exploitation continues today as poorer states find it hard to compete, to develop large multinational corporations, or to profit as fully as they might from their labour and resources.

A second cause of inequality is poor domestic policy choices. There are examples of poorer countries that are well endowed in resources – whether land, oil, minerals, or labour – but that have made bad choices in the way they have managed or exploited them. Many suffer from the **resource curse**, by which their national economy is dominated by a single resource (such as oil in Nigeria), leaving them susceptible to changes in price and in supply and demand. Others have simply allowed themselves to be driven by corruption or incompetence, as in the case of Zimbabwe.

Resource curse: A situation in which the value of a single profitable resource can create economic problems for a country.

Third, many poorer countries have suffered from political instability. Many countries that have the potential to build strong economies have been undermined by political instability, conflict, or civil war, with roots often dating back to the colonial heritage of states that were created without any heed to cultural, political or religious realities. This has been a particular problem in many African countries, where borders were drawn around multiple ethnic groups that have since competed with each other for power; examples include Angola, the Democratic Republic of the Congo, Kenya, Mozambique, Sierra Leone, and Sudan (which split in two in 2011 after a long civil war).

Finally, inequality has been promoted by misfortune in the form of geography and natural disasters. Many of the poorest African states straddle the desert or semi-desert regions of the Sahara, leaving them with limited agricultural land and often weak connections to global markets; Burkina Faso, Chad, Mali and Niger, for example, are dry inland states with no coasts or ports. Meanwhile, most Caribbean states are too small and too lacking in natural resources (as well as being subject to hurricanes) to have built economies that go much beyond tourism, while the latter is not much of an option for the even smaller (and more isolated) states of the Pacific, such as the Marshall Islands, Kiribati, Palau, and Tuvalu. The last has a population of 11,000 people who mainly make a living off the export of copra (dried coconut kernel) and the sale of the .tv internet suffix, and worry about the prospects of having their homes swamped by rising sea levels in the wake of climate change.

Outsourcing: The process by which a company uses an external vendor to provide a service that the company might normally have provided for itself. This happens on a global scale as companies outsource to countries with cheaper labour and weaker regulations.

The poorest states are clearly unequal in terms of their political and economic power, but this does not mean that they do not have cards to play. For example, many of them have natural resources that are important to wealthier countries, perhaps the most important of which is cheap labour. In order to cut costs and maximize profits, business in Europe and North America has been **outsourcing** jobs, giving poorer states a new role in the economic decisions of wealthy states. However, the costs are considerable: While outsourcing is good for corporate profits, it has been bad for the environment, for worker safety, and for worker wages. Meanwhile, the poorest states also have two more negative powers over wealthy countries: many are sources of unauthorized immigration and of terrorism, both of which problems – as discussed in Chapters 10 and 12 – have moved high up the political agenda of wealthy countries.

One approach to reducing poverty and inequality involves the provision of **development aid**, whether channelled from governments or from private groups. The flows are from the wealthy countries to the poorer ones, most come in the form of bilateral aid from one country to another (the rest is multilateral, given by countries to international organizations, which then distribute the aid), and most is targeted at providing technical assistance, building infrastructure, and investing in education and health care. The biggest sources are the 28 members of the Development Assistance Committee of the OECD, with the European Union collectively providing about half the global total (just under $90 billion in 2016), and the biggest recipients including the poorest states of Africa and Asia. The UN in 1970 set a target for donor countries of making sure that they gave at least 0.7 per cent of their GNI as aid, but few have met the target: they include Norway, Sweden, Luxembourg, Denmark, and the UK. The United States gives the most in absolute terms, but it amounts to only 0.2 per cent of GNI, and much American aid takes the form of weapons and military advice.

Opinion on the value of development aid is divided, with critics arguing that recipient countries have not seen much economic improvement as a result of aid, that it encourages a form of dependency, that it often comes with strings attached since it is frequently directed at strategic allies of donor countries, that it provides new opportunities for corruption, and that it is based on donor ideas about where help is needed rather than taking into account local culture and needs (see Moyo, 2009). The potential benefits of development aid are also undermined by policies pursued by wealthy countries, such as the higher tariffs imposed on manufactured goods from developing countries relative to developed countries, and the large subsidies given to farmers in developed countries, making it more difficult for farmers in poorer countries to compete.

Development aid: Assistance provided by wealthier countries to poorer countries, in the form mainly of technical aid targeted at the long-term alleviation of poverty.

DISCUSSION QUESTIONS

1. Is gross domestic product an adequate measure of economy productivity?
2. Given current trends, how is the global economy likely to change over the next century?
3. In the face of the pressures of globalization, do states any longer have much in the way of economic independence?
4. Is capitalism in trouble?
5. What are the optimum conditions for the creation of wealth and the equal distribution of opportunity?
6. How is poverty best defined, and what are the strengths and weaknesses of conventional measures?

KEY CONCEPTS

- Capitalism
- Central bank
- Development
- Development aid
- Economics
- Exchange rate
- Foreign direct investment
- Gini coefficient
- Global financial crisis
- Gold standard
- Gross domestic product
- Microfinance
- National debt
- Neo-liberalism
- Outsourcing
- Poverty
- Regional development bank
- Reserve currency
- Resource curse
- Small and medium enterprises
- Socialism
- Special Drawing Right
- Wealth

USEFUL WEBSITES

Fraser Institute Index of Economic Freedom at https://www.fraserinstitute.org

International Monetary Fund at http://www.imf.org

Organisation for Economic Cooperation and Development at http://www.oecd.org

UNDP Human Development Index at http://hdr.undp.org/en/content/human-development-index-hdi

World Bank at http://www.worldbank.org

FURTHER READING

Clark, Barry (2016) *The Evolution of Economic Systems: Varieties of Capitalism in the Global Economy* (Oxford University Press). A survey of the different kinds of modern economic systems, with chapters offering cases from the US, several European countries, Russia, China, and emerging economies.

Collier, Paul (2009) *The Bottom Billion: Why the Poorest Countries are Failing and What Can Be Done About It* (Oxford University Press). A study of the roots of the problems in the world's poorest countries, arguing that the wealthy countries need to change their policies on trade, corruption, and even military intervention.

Sumner, Andy (2016) *Global Poverty: Deprivation, Distribution, and Development since the Cold War* (Oxford University Press). An assessment of poverty around the world, including a discussion of why some people remain poor despite economic growth.

Timmerman, Kelsey (2012) *What Am I Wearing? A Global Tour to the Countries, Factories, and People That Make Our Clothes* (Wiley). A journalist's assessment of the connection between Northern consumers and the lives of garment workers in some of the poorest parts of the world.

Todaro, Michael P., and Stephen C. Smith (2016) *Economic Development*, 12th edn (Pearson). A textbook on economic development, with chapters on its key principles and on its domestic and global policy implications.

Online Resources

Visit www.macmillanihe.com/McCormick-GS to access additional materials to support teaching and learning.

TRADE

9

PREVIEW

This chapter builds on Chapter 8 by looking at the specific subject of trade. It begins with a review of the global trading picture, and of the recent and rapid rise in trade volume. It then looks at the changes that have come to the global trading system since 1945, before reviewing the qualities of the global trading regime, including the role of the World Trade Organization, the implications of changes in technology, and the rise of multinational corporations and global cities. The chapter ends with a discussion about free trade, comparing different levels of trade cooperation and the pros and cons of free trade.

CONTENTS

▸ **Understanding trade**

▸ **The evolution of global trade**

▸ **The changing global trading landscape**

▸ **The global trade regime**

▸ **Free trade**

▸ **Trade and inequality**

HIGHLIGHTS

▸ Trade has played a key role in shaping the global system.

▸ Global trade volumes have increased dramatically since 1945, creating a new and complex system of trade networks, challenges, and opportunities.

▸ Approaches to trade have long been driven by the competing views of protectionists and liberals.

▸ Although the North has long dominated global trade, the South is on the rise, led by China.

▸ The global trade regime is guided by the World Trade Organization, opinions on whose performance are divided.

▸ Free trade has long been at the heart of debates about the nature of global trade, but opinion on its advantages and disadvantages is divided.

Source: Getty Images/Westend61

UNDERSTANDING TRADE

Trade: The exchange of goods and services among producers and consumers, whether through barter or using a medium of exchange such as currency.

Trade has been part of the human experience since the emergence of the earliest organized societies. No state is self-sufficient, and most need access to a variety of goods and services that they cannot always provide for themselves, leaving them either to buy what they need using the intermediary of cash, or – more rarely – to barter or trade with one another. At the international level, individuals, companies, and states trade with one another, in some cases participating in regional blocs within which the barriers to trade are eased or removed. The process is not limited to economics, because the items and services that are traded, and the trade balances that ensue, have political, social, cultural, and health implications. Trade is both a cause and an effect of globalization, and a conduit for the exchange and spread of influence, both good and bad. Trade patterns have – to a very large extent – shaped the global system and the nature of the world in which we live.

In the pre-modern era, trade was carried out by individual entrepreneurs who would often take great personal risks to accompany their commodities from source to market (Bernstein, 2008). But as trade volumes grew and networks expanded, so did the sophistication of technology and communications; almost everything from the most ordinary cargoes to the highest-value items is today conveyed by fleets of highly automated container ships and climate-controlled jet aircraft, in many cases reaching their destinations in a matter of hours. We live in a global marketplace tied by numerous pathways, whether physical, financial, or digital. It is not a fully open marketplace, to be sure, because governments never stop working to promote what they define as their national interests and to protect their home industries, with everyone seeking the ideal combination of the highest profits and the lowest costs.

In spite of the remaining barriers, one of the most notable developments of recent decades has been the dramatic growth in the volume of global trade: the numbers have exploded as trade links have broadened and deepened, and as the means of buying and selling across borders have grown. Figure 9.1 shows that the value of merchandise exports and imports (each of which has closely followed the other) grew by nearly 13,000 per cent between 1960 and 2015, even in spite of some volatility after the global financial crisis in 2007–11. Changes in technology have made it easier to buy, sell and transport goods and services, and new options and buying habits based on the internet have greatly expanded the world of **e-commerce**. This is particularly true for individuals, who play an ever-greater role in the forces behind trade: if you have access to credit and the internet, you can buy almost anything you want from almost any corner of the globe, and many items that were once considered exotic are now easily available wherever there is a means of purchase and delivery.

E-commerce: The buying or selling of goods and services online.

As with economies, there is a league of trading powers, the biggest economies tending also to be the biggest sellers and buyers of goods and services. But the numbers vary by trade in tangible goods or merchandise, as distinct from trade in services such as tourism, insurance, financial services, communications, and construction. The patterns of trade are also complex, with some countries running a trade surplus (they export more than they import), and some running a trade deficit

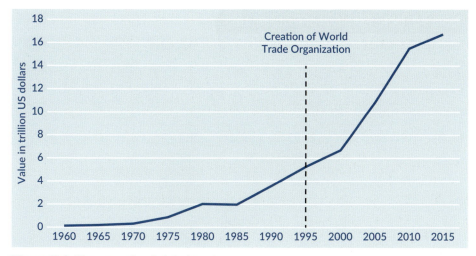

Figure 9.1: The growth of global trade

Source: Based on data in World Bank Economic Indicators (2018). Figures for imports and exports are similar.

(they import more than they export). The size and content of trade flows differs in tandem: individual countries are more or less important to one another according to a combination of their relative histories, what they need to buy, what they have to sell, the value of the commodities they trade, the trade agreements they reach, and the health of their political and economic relationships.

Without question, the three biggest trading powers are China, the European Union, and the United States, which among them account for about 40–45 per cent of imports and exports (see Table 9.1). (Although the EU is a multi-state regional organization rather than a state, it has a single trade policy and a single internal market, so it is best understood within the global system as a unit.) Were the Americans, the Chinese, and the Europeans to be on the same page in terms of their trading goals and principles, they would exert an almost unassailable level of influence over the global trading system. But while the Americans and the Europeans (at least) might agree on the broad goals of trade, they are also ferocious competitors, and both cast worried eyes at the rapidly expanding place of China.

Table 9.1: The world's biggest traders

MERCHANDISE				SERVICES			
Exports	**%**	**Imports**	**%**	**Exports**	**%**	**Imports**	**%**
China	17	USA	18	European Union	25	European Union	21
European Union	15	European Union	15	USA	20	USA	13
USA	12	China	12	China	6	China	12
Japan	5	Japan	5	Japan	5	Japan	5
South Korea	4	Canada	3	India	4	Singapore	4
Total share	53		53		60		55

Source: World Trade Organization (2017a). Figures rounded out.

Table 9.2: Different kinds of trade controls

Type	Effect	Examples
Tariffs	Taxes on imports that make them more expensive to consumers, and are usually designed to protect a home industry.	China levies a high tariff on imports of poultry, while the United States levies tariffs on most vegetables, as well as woollen clothes and vehicle parts.
Quotas	Limits imposed on the quantities of selected goods that can be imported into a country in a given period of time.	The European Union has more than 120 agreements with trading partners regarding imports of a variety of agricultural goods, such as chicken, beef, and butter.
Embargos or sanctions	Block or limit the ability of another country to import or export. Usually designed to punish that country or achieve political change.	The sanctions imposed by many countries on North Korea following its first nuclear test in 2006.
Subsidies	Financial aid to businesses, agriculture, or particular industries, designed to help them survive or to encourage changes in the way they function.	Government contracts to manufacturers, as in the case of defence contracts from the US government to Boeing.
Import and export licences	Limit the amount of specified products that can be bought or sold across borders.	Export licences imposed on trophies and furs for sports hunters.

In shaping their trade policies, countries broadly take one of two approaches:

Protectionism: The view that domestic markets should be protected from the kind of competition often posed by international trade.

▶ *Protectionism* involves efforts to protect the home market or domestic producers by imposing controls on imports. It stresses national interests (sometimes spilling over into an 'us first' attitude of nationalism), and relies on government regulation and the expansion of the powers of a state at the expense of rival states.

Liberalism: The view that open markets and fewer trade controls are in the broader interest of everyone.

▶ *Liberalism* is based on the idea that open markets are best, and that efforts should be made to reduce restrictions on trade. This idea is behind the development of free trade, discussed later in this chapter.

Several different controls are available – see Table 9.2 – with opinion differing on their relative value and impact. The differences in the combination of the controls used from one country to the next depends on a variety of political factors and the particular industries that different countries want to promote or protect.

THE EVOLUTION OF GLOBAL TRADE

History is replete with examples of sophisticated trading networks, such as those involving the Sumerians, the Romans, and the Persians. Among the most famous was the Silk Road, a trade route established in the 3rd century BC between China and the West, supplying silk, slaves, and spices, and providing a commercial and a cultural bridge between the two. Later, the spread of Islam in the 8th and 9th centuries was accompanied by expanded trade connecting the Middle East and the northern half of Africa. Trade first began to develop global dimensions with the era of European exploration, as the Portuguese, the Spanish, the Dutch, the British and other western Europeans used their technological and military advantages to develop ties with the Americas, Africa, and Asia. Trade connections evolved into the building of empires, leading in turn to the harnessing of the advantages of colonial dominance to build preferential trade networks: in the case of Britain, for example, all commodity trade was required under law to take place using British ships, manned by British crews, and trading between ports in Britain and the empire.

Mercantilism (controlling trade so as to promote exports over imports) was popular in parts of western Europe between the 16th and the 18th centuries, but its principles were challenged by influential British economists such as Adam Smith and David Ricardo. They argued that removing barriers to trade would allow countries to specialize in certain economic activities, based on their relative levels of labour, resources, capital and skills. This notion of **comparative advantage** would allow everyone to do what they did best, optimizing the use of resources globally, and allowing everyone to benefit provided they traded freely. But comparative advantage works best with an even playing field, and neither Smith nor Ricardo could have foreseen the rise of the multinational corporations that have created much unevenness, nor the scale of the differences in trading power between a few large actors – such as the United States, the EU and China – and many mid-sized and smaller actors.

Encouraged by the lead of Britain, which in 1846 repealed some of its more protectionist laws, many trading powers adopted free trade policies during the 19th century. There was a massive expansion of trade and capital flows, breakthroughs in technology and communications, a reduction in the costs of transport, and an explosion of migration, setting off what Ikenberry (2000) has described as 'the first age of globalization'. But by the end of the century there had been a move back towards protectionism, and the global trading system was dominated by European powers, particularly those with empires. The lack of leadership and of an international system for encouraging trade led countries to steer away from open markets, with the result that trade volumes declined after World War I, a trend that accelerated as many countries – led by the United States – opted to protect home industries in the wake of the Great Depression.

When it came to deciding how best to proceed after World War II, the negotiators at Bretton Woods chose to emphasize liberalization. As we saw in Chapters 1 and 8, the IMF and the World Bank were created to help with exchange rate stability and post-war economic recovery. There were also plans to create an International Trade Organization (ITO) that would have been the trade agency of the UN and the third pillar of the Bretton Woods system. However, the United States was opposed to the restrictions that would have been imposed by the ITO, so governments instead opted to create the General Agreement on Tariffs and Trade (GATT), designed to be a forum in which they could negotiate over the progressive reduction of barriers to trade. Seven rounds of negotiations took place under the auspices of GATT, usually named for the place in which they began: hence the Geneva, Tokyo, and Uruguay rounds, while the Kennedy round that begin in 1964 was named in honour of the assassinated president, John F. Kennedy. The rounds varied in length from as little as five months to as long as several years, and each resulted in a new set of trade agreements.

Comparative advantage: The theory that if countries specialize in producing goods and services in which they have advantages (such as bigger endowments, or cheaper labour), and if they trade freely with one another, then everyone will benefit.

The era was deeply influenced by the rise of the United States as a trading power, building upon its military and political power. These qualities gave the US a Cold War advantage over the Soviet Union, whose power rested almost entirely on its military, and whose economy was relatively backward. The US used its influence to support post-war economic reconstruction in western Europe and Japan, then invested heavily in both regions, then played a key role in building free trade agreements first with Canada and Mexico, and later across the Atlantic and the Pacific.

The decades after the war also saw the independence of former European colonies, whose new place in the world built on changes in their older neighbours to alter the place of the South in global trade calculations. The South took the view in the 1950s and 1960s that it needed to protect its manufacturing from competition from the North. But this approach failed, and the records of open economies such as South Korea provided an example of the benefits of liberalization, encouraging many other Southern states to move away from protectionism (Bhagwati et al., 2016). Although no countries in the South except China and India yet comes close to playing the same kind of global role as the bigger trading powers, several middle-range trading countries are asserting themselves, including Brazil, Indonesia, Malaysia, Mexico, Singapore, South Africa and Thailand. Meanwhile, several others with large populations – such as Pakistan, Nigeria, and Bangladesh – underperform, and the gap between the wealthiest and poorest economies continues to grow.

The long-missing international trading body finally arrived in 1995 (see later in this chapter) with the establishment of the World Trade Organization (WTO), one of whose responsibilities is to oversee ongoing negotiations under the terms of GATT. The **Doha round** (named for the capital of Qatar) was launched in 2001 but broke down seven years later following disagreements between the North and the South over agricultural trade, industrial tariffs, and non-tariff barriers to trade, and a disagreement between the US and the EU over agricultural subsidies. Efforts to revive Doha failed, and it had been all but abandoned by the end of 2015, casting a pall over the future of the global trading system. Nonetheless, South–South trade has grown, and the role of the South in blocking agreement under the Doha round of negotiations hints at its possibilities.

> **Doha round**:
> The most recent (and failed) set of negotiations aimed at further developing the global trading system.

THE CHANGING GLOBAL TRADING LANDSCAPE

The global trading system is today undergoing rapid and remarkable change. To begin with, we have seen the rise of regional trading blocs on the model of the European Union (see Chapter 6). These often go beyond simple efforts to promote free trade, and in the European case it has meant three major changes:

▸ The creation of a single market, with almost entirely free movement of people, capital, goods and services.

▸ A common external trade policy, meaning that the EU now negotiates as a whole in its dealings with other countries.

▸ For most but not yet all of its members, a single currency in the form of the euro.

Almost every country in the world is now a member of at least one regional integration block, and while none has yet gone as far as the EU, many have aspirations in that direction.

A second major change is evident in the rise of China as a global trading powerhouse. Until the first efforts were made to modernize its economy in the late 1970s, it barely registered on the global scale, doing most of its trade with the Soviet Union, but it has since quickly caught up; where it accounted for less than 2 per cent of world trade between the world wars, it now has a share of more than 15 per cent. Among the developments that transformed China:

▸ The US lifted its ban on trade with China in the early 1970s (and has since built a large trade deficit thanks to the growth in imports of Chinese consumer products).

▸ Large investments were made in manufacturing in the 1980s.

▸ China joined several international organizations such as the World Bank and the IMF, and – after several unsuccessful efforts – was allowed to join the WTO in 2001 in return for opening its market.

▸ It reorganized its domestic trade organizations.

▸ It created special economic zones that were geared towards exports, such as Hong Kong.

▸ It made new efforts to attract foreign investment.

▸ It transformed itself from an importer of manufactured goods to a major exporter.

The influence of China is exemplified by the extent to which the Europeans and the Americans have changed their approach to trade dealings with China, and by its support for a New Silk Road linking East and Central Asia. Sometimes known

Source: AFP/Getty Images

The Chinese foreign trade minister signs the documents for China's accession to the World Trade Organization in 2001, an event that confirmed the rise of China as a modern global trading power.

COMPARING NORTH AND SOUTH 9

THE CHANGING BALANCE OF TRADE POWER

Trade opportunities are regarded differently by rich countries and poor countries, big ones and small ones, and by those that are resource-rich and resource-poor. Logic suggests that wealthier, bigger, and more resource-rich states will have an advantage, but matters are not always that simple. To be sure, the North still dominates global markets, but changes in the nature of the global trading system have worked to the advantage of the South in ways that might not have been expected.

For several millennia, the great trading powers were based in Asia and the Middle East. But in a matter of two centuries, in a phenomenon that historians call the 'great divergence', they were displaced by what we think of today as the North. Europeans had the initial advantage, having been pioneers first in the opening of global trade routes and then in the technological developments that helped them exploit trade advantages, domestic resources, and labour to spark the industrial revolution. But the dissolution of their empires after 1945 meant the end of their privileged access to raw materials and markets, and new competition from the United States and Japan. Then, in the space of just a few decades, in what Baldwin (2016) describes as a 'great convergence', the balance changed again: a combination of rapid industrialization in parts of the South and deindustrialization in parts of the North has resulted in a rising share of income for the South and a falling share for the North.

One of the driving forces in the change has been information technology (IT). Its development has made it easier and cheaper for companies to move labour-intensive work from the North to the South, and – as this happened – they have also been able to move marketing, managerial, and IT jobs. This has accelerated the economic development of a few leading countries in the South – such as China and India – while the older Northern countries have deindustrialized, leaving both sets of countries with new policy challenges and economic uncertainties. For now, the richer Northern states have the advantage in exporting services, high technology products, and capital, while poorer Southern states have the advantage in raw materials and labour. But the balance is changing, a trend that ties in to worries in the North about the effects of globalization.

The South today is an expanding consumer and producer of the commodities that are at the heart of global trade, its newly assertive role in global trade exemplified by the failure of the Doha round of trade negotiations between 2001 and 2015. Although the major cause of that failure was the inability of the EU and the US to agree on agricultural subsidies, it did not help that China, India and Brazil were inclined to negotiate hard and to hold their ground, while poorer countries generally sought special treatment in order to protect their farmers. The end of Doha also coincided with the rise of the BRICs, with China's expanding place in the global trade system, and with the decline of US economic leadership.

as the Belt and Road Initiative, the goals behind this are to streamline China's trade interests in the region, to ensure stable energy supplies, to promote the development of Asian infrastructure, and consolidate Chinese regional influence (McBride, 2015). The ultimate goal is a new trading network centred on China. At first there were concerns that tensions between China and the United States would grow as the two actors expanded their interests in the region, but the 2017 decision by the Trump administration to pull out of the Trans-Pacific Partnership (a 12-state trade agreement signed in 2016) seemed – at least temporarily – to hand the initiative to China.

Finally, and cross-cutting countries and regions, we have seen two developments that have taken more control over trade out of the hands of governments: the ongoing rise of multinational corporations (MNCs), and changes in technology. As we saw in Chapter 6, the number of MNCs has nearly tripled since 1990, and many of them have become enormous, with a global reach, weaker association with individual countries, and a critical role in shaping trade decisions and patterns of trade. The world's biggest multinational is Walmart, which operates in nearly 30 countries and has more outlets outside its home country of the United States than inside. Its international profits and revenues are smaller than those from the United States, however, and it has been working to expand its international operations, particularly targeting China, India, and Japan. Meanwhile, the economic rise of China is reflected in the growth of Chinese multinationals such as State Grid, Sinopec, and Chinese National Petroleum.

Change has also come in the wake of efforts by MNCs to alter the way they are structured. They were once associated with the integration and standardization of **Fordism**, and even when they began expanding outside their mainly American and European home states in the 1970s, MNCs often took the same approach as they did at home, making them relatively inflexible and unwilling to adapt to local pressures and opportunities. More recently, post-Fordism has seen MNCs become more decentralized and transnational, using new technologies and business practices to gear themselves more towards the needs of multiple markets (see discussion on glocalization in Chapter 1), working harder to compete with local businesses, and moving production to countries with cheaper labour and looser regulations.

> **Fordism**: A term inspired by the Ford Motor Company, describing mass production of standardized goods on an assembly line, using specialized and semi-skilled labour.

As for technology, the way in which goods and services are made, transported, and sold continues to be transformed. Industry is increasingly automated, technology changes what we make and how it is designed, and goods are moved more quickly and in larger quantities. Until the 1950s, most goods for transport were known as 'break bulk cargo', meaning that they were loaded, transported, and unloaded in individual bags, crates, or boxes. Containerization began to take hold in the 1950s, with goods packed in standard-sized containers that can be carried by road, train, or container ships, saving both time and cost. More than 90 per cent of so-called non-bulk cargo (packaged cargo) is now transported by containers, the ships that carry them loading and unloading at ever bigger terminals such as those in Shanghai, Singapore, Busan, Rotterdam, Hamburg and Los Angeles.

Developments in technology have also meant that consumers – at least in the North – are moving away from bricks-and-mortar stores to shopping online, greatly increasing the variety of products and sources available to them, and creating a global digital mall. (But vendors are also encouraged at the same time to more actively increase or reduce prices according to supply and demand.) International sales have grown on the back of the expansion of internet payments systems such as PayPal, or – for those without bank accounts – mobile

Source: Getty Images

The switch to containers has been one of the most notable developments in global trade, the standardization involved helping move goods around the world more easily.

wallets such as M-Pesa, launched in Kenya in 2007. Delivery options have also broadened, giving more business to couriers such as FedEx and DHL, more downloading options for products such as books and streaming for music, and the expanded possibilities inherent in 3D printing (otherwise known as additive manufacturing).

There has always been a close relationship between trade and innovation, thanks to the pressures and opportunities created by competition, new markets, and **technology transfer**, by which inventions are spread from their source to other users. Ideally, invention leads to patenting and copyrighting, and then to commercialization and marketing as access to new inventions is licensed or sold to other users. Less ideally, technology is stolen by other users, China having developed a particularly poor reputation, with accusations that it has counterfeited fashion designs, pirated movies and video games, infringed on patents, and stolen trade secrets and proprietary technology and software over a period of decades (Blair and Alexander, 2017).

Looking more widely, changes in technology have always had their most immediate impact on jobs, which are lost or transformed as technology changes. Entire new industries, for example, are being created out of digital technology, and high technology products have accounted for a greater share of global trade. Meanwhile, outsourcing has been made easier by the internet, sophisticated logistics systems, and easier international travel. The transfer of jobs has been one of the most consistent complaints in the North about the effects of globalization.

Whatever approach is favoured by different governments at any particular time, most of them – not surprisingly – continue to pursue self-interest, seeking to protect their home industries and consumers, and to achieve maximum profit at minimum cost. As a result, the global trading system remains far from a level playing field, with

Technology transfer: The transfer of technology from a creator to a secondary user, for example through licensing.

large and often growing gaps in income, opportunity, and equality, and poorer states struggling to compete against the enormous power and reach of the world's biggest economies and multinationals.

THE GLOBAL TRADE REGIME

Trade is typically good for economic growth, and bigger markets are typically good for economic expansion. At the same time, it is natural for buyers and sellers to work to outwit one another by exploiting opportunities and advantages, and unless governments and corporations are careful, they can find themselves undercut and undermined by unfair and unscrupulous trading practices. Hence the need for rules and norms, and hence the rise of the global trade regime, at the heart of which lies the World Trade Organization (WTO).

The WTO traces its roots back to efforts in the late 1940s to set up an International Trade Organization, whose failure left in its wake the looser GATT process. In 1995, the obligations of GATT were integrated into the new WTO, headquartered in Geneva, Switzerland. The WTO is a stand-alone organization that is not part of the United Nations, and whose job is to oversee the global system of trade rules and treaties, provide a forum in which members can negotiate the terms of international trade, and operate a resolution mechanism by which countries engaged in a trade dispute can make their cases before the WTO, which then issues a judgement (see Hoekman and Mavroidis, 2016). It has no powers of enforcement, but all countries joining the WTO agree to abide by its rules and decisions, to support its principles of a freer, more predictable and competitive global trading system, and to treat each other equally by granting all other WTO members **most-favoured nation status**. While the latter might sound like an effort by states to give special trade deals to other states, it is actually an agreement not to discriminate, and to treat all other countries equally as 'most favoured'.

> **Most-favoured nation status**: An agreement under the terms of membership of the WTO by which all members agree to treat each other equally.

The WTO has a director-general and a large staff, but all decisions are taken by a consensus of the membership. Its original members were the 128 parties to GATT, since when it has grown to 164 members. A country that wants to join must apply and negotiate the terms of membership, and will be assessed by the existing members on the basis of its level of economic development and its trade policy. Notable non-members include Algeria, Ethiopia, Iran, Iraq, and Syria (all of which are observers with membership applications pending), and Eritrea, North Korea, South Sudan, and six Pacific island states, none of which are either observers or applicants. China and Russia had both long been kept out of the WTO, mainly because neither of their economies was sufficiently open; Russia achieved the required recognition as a market economy by the EU and the US only in 2002. China eventually joined in 2001, and Russia in 2012. As a country lacking much experience in global trade (beyond its exports of oil and natural gas), Russia has since had problems adjusting to the requirements of the WTO.

The rulebook agreed under the terms of membership of the WTO now runs to more than 30,000 pages and includes more than two dozen separate treaties and agreements. Rulings by the WTO, meanwhile, have generated an extensive body of trade law designed – at least in theory – to prevent restrictive trade measures, to provide consistency, to encourage equity, and to protect consumers, workers, and the environment (see Van den Bossche and Prévost, 2016). The original focus of GATT on trade in goods has expanded to include services (prompting the development of a new General Agreement on Trade in Services) and **intellectual property**, including the example of 'geographical indications'. These are products (mainly food and drink) that are identified by their geographical name, and which Europeans have been particularly active in protecting. For example, champagne, cognac, tequila, Darjeeling tea, Roquefort cheese, and Vidalia onions can only be named as such if they come from the associated regions. Unless it is actually made in the Champagne region of France, for example, 'champagne' must be described as 'sparkling wine'.

> **Intellectual property**:
> Inventions and creations of the mind, including designs, copyrights, trademarks, and patents.

Opinion on the impact of the WTO is divided. Its supporters credit it with promoting global economic growth and raising living standards by making trade easier and more open, with reducing the barriers to protection, and with promoting healthy competition. But its critics charge that it reduces the sovereignty of its members by limiting their freedom of action, that its bigger members have too much power to shape its agenda, that its decision-making procedures are not sufficiently transparent, and that its promotion of free trade has meant a weakening of labour unions and environmental standards as jobs are moved from wealthier countries to poorer countries with weaker worker rights and environmental quality.

One of the WTO's most important responsibilities is to act as a forum in which trade disputes can be heard, argued, and hopefully resolved. While GATT included a relatively weak dispute settlement procedure, the WTO has a stronger and binding system. It has heard many disputes since 1995, most of which have been resolved and have cleared the way for more open trade or for clearer definition of rights and responsibilities. Perhaps not surprisingly, the bigger trading powers have been the most active in either lodging complaints or being the target of complaints (see examples in Figure 9.2), although China has been much less active than its size might suggest, and has brought many fewer complaints than have been brought against it. There could be more disputes in future as China and other emerging economies become more assertive, but there might also be fewer disputes simply because WTO members are learning more from experience, and fine-tuning the terms of global trade.

Although the WTO lacks the power to enforce its decisions, it is understood that membership comes with an obligation to follow the organization's rules, and if a member fails to respect a decision on a dispute, the complainant country or countries can ask the WTO for the authority to retaliate. Trade is ultimately about quid pro quo, and governments usually want to avoid harmful, costly and time-consuming trade wars. A country that failed to honour WTO rules could soon find itself and its companies suffering from tariffs on its exports and limitations on its companies doing business abroad.

Among the list of recent disputes, three in particular stand out:

▸ The world's biggest trade dispute by value has been one between the United States and the European Union over subsidies to their respective major civilian aircraft manufacturers, Boeing and Airbus. The dispute dates back to 2004, and to charges by Boeing that Airbus benefitted from government subsidies

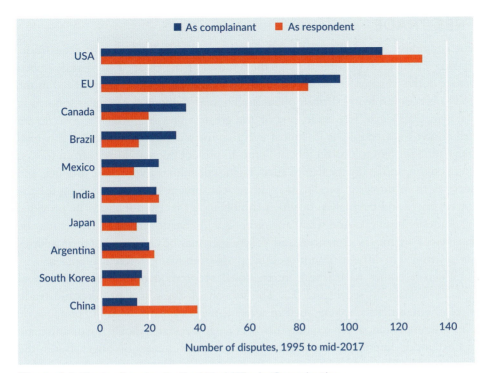

Figure 9.2: Trade disputes in the World Trade Organization
Source: Based on data in World Trade Organization (2017b).

to develop new aircraft models. Airbus countered that Boeing benefitted from tax breaks and US government defence contracts. Despite several rulings from the WTO, the dispute was still under way in 2018, while both companies are beginning to cast nervous glances at potential new competition from the state-owned Commercial Aircraft Corporation of China, or Comac.

▶ Two tripartite disputes among the EU, the US and China. In one case, China alleges that the other two have imposed unfair duties against **dumping** on its products, while – in the other – the EU and the US allege that China imposes unfair export restrictions on raw materials used in the manufacture of vehicles, aircraft, computers and cell phones. In the first case, the US and the EU are concerned about protecting home producers from an influx of cheap Chinese products, and in the second they are concerned about protecting profits for their manufacturers.

> **Dumping**:
> Exporting a product and selling it in large volumes at a price that is lower than the price charged in the originating market.

Since trade takes place between individuals or companies, and not between countries, much of the global trading regime is a matter of states promoting and protecting the interests of their domestic industries. Those industries are the building blocks of the regime, which in turn means that multinational corporations are at the heart of global trade. They take the lead on the development of new technology, on decisions about investment and the creation of jobs, and play a key role in determining trade flows. To a large extent they have taken the initiative on trade out of the hands of states, emphasizing once again the declining reach of states.

FREE TRADE

Free trade: The condition under which all barriers to trade are removed, creating an open and competitive marketplace, either between two countries, or among three or more.

For centuries, one of the primary themes in trade has been that of **free trade**: making it as open as possible through the removal of the kinds of barriers described earlier in this chapter. It has always been controversial, a view encapsulated in the 1824 observation by the British politician Thomas Babington Macaulay (quoted in Baldwin, 2016) that 'free trade, one of the greatest blessings which a government can confer on a people, is in almost every country unpopular'. There is a natural inclination to want to protect jobs at home, to protect home industries from foreign competition, and to 'fly the flag' in encouraging consumers to purchase products and services from domestic producers. And yet consumers are always looking for the lowest prices and the highest quality, a combination that cannot always be provided by domestic business. And what, any more, is a 'domestic' product? Toyota may be Japanese, Ford may be American, and Volkswagen may be German, but their vehicles are assembled in different countries using parts from many different suppliers.

Preferential trade agreement: Gives preferential access for specified products from members of a trading bloc by reducing but not eliminating tariffs.

When it comes to reaching international accommodations, there are several options available – see Figure 9.3. The loosest of these is a **preferential trade agreement**. Strictly speaking, such an agreement goes against the WTO principle of non-discrimination, which requires that WTO member states should not discriminate against goods entering their countries based on their country of origin. But in the face of difficulties with reducing trade barriers, more countries have opted in recent decades for this softer route to liberalization. Supporters argue that preferential trade is a complement to free trade, but critics charge that it stands as a barrier (Bhagwati et al., 2016). A prime example of such an agreement is the Africa Caribbean Pacific initiative maintained by the EU, which has generated a series of programmes (the most recent running from 2000 to 2020) designed to give 80 countries, mainly former colonies of EU states, preferential access to EU markets.

Figure 9.3: Degrees of trade cooperation

TYPE	QUALITIES	EXAMPLES
PREFERENTIAL TRADE AGREEMENT	Gives preferential access for specified products from members of a trading bloc by reducing but not eliminating tariffs.	Global System of Trade Preferences among Developing Countries, with 42 members.
FREE TRADE AGREEMENT	Reduces or removes mutual barriers to trade among participating countries, while retaining barriers to the movement of people and capital.	South Asian Free Trade Area involving 8 countries.
ECONOMIC UNION	A single market among participating countries, with free movement of people, capital, goods and services, and a common external trade policy.	European Union.
MONETARY UNION	A single currency among participating countries, and a joint policy on controlling money supply and interest rates.	Euro, Eastern Caribbean dollar, Central African CFA franc, and West African CFA franc.

Bigger commitments are involved in **free trade agreements** (FTAs), which typically involve freer trade rather than free trade, because the market among their members is never fully open. The earliest ideas about free trade date back to ancient Greece and Rome, although what they achieved were not formal FTAs so much as systems in which free trade was supported and pursued. Since the end of World War II, and encouraged by the new atmosphere promoted by GATT, the number of FTAs has grown exponentially, to the point where the WTO website in 2017 listed more than 300 in force; see Map 9.1 for examples. Almost every country in the world is now part of one or more free trade agreements or areas, most are bilateral while some are multilateral, some focus on goods alone while others include goods and services together, and some are narrow and modest in their goals while others are broad and far-reaching. In short, there is no universal template for an FTA, and in many cases countries agree freer trade rather than truly free trade.

A deeper form of integration involves the creation of an **economic union**, or a single market within which there is free movement of goods, services, people and capital, and all member states have a common external trade policy. The European Union is the leading example, although – to be accurate – not all its economic policies are integrated; its members still go their own way, for example, on taxes and on fiscal policy (borrowing and spending). Nonetheless, a citizen of one EU state can move easily to another to continue their education, take a new job, or retire, and can expect to be treated the same as a citizen of the other state in almost every respect except voting in national elections or running for national office. (For more details, see McCormick, 2015, Chapter 19.)

Short of a full-blown political union, the deepest form of economic agreement with trade implications is a **monetary union**, in which all members of the union give

> **Free trade agreement**: Reduces or removes mutual barriers to trade among participating countries, while retaining barriers to the movement of people and capital.

> **Economic union**: A single market among participating countries, with free movement of people, capital, goods and services, and a common external trade policy.

> **Monetary union**: A single currency among participating countries, and a joint policy on controlling money supply and interest rates.

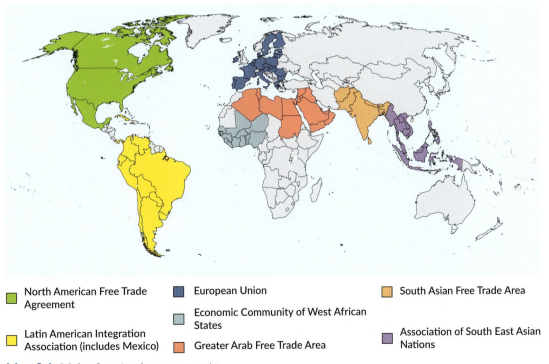

■ North American Free Trade Agreement	■ European Union	■ South Asian Free Trade Area
	■ Economic Community of West African States	
■ Latin American Integration Association (includes Mexico)	■ Greater Arab Free Trade Area	■ Association of South East Asian Nations

Map 9.1: Major free trade agreements

up their national currencies and create a single currency. Examples include the euro (19 countries), the Eastern Caribbean dollar (seven countries), the Central African CFA franc (six countries), and the West African CFA franc (eight countries). With all members of the group using the same currency, they need no longer worry about the effects of exchange rate fluctuations on mutual trade. At the same time, they surrender a significant part of their economic independence, obliged as they are to work in unison on matters such as the setting of interest rates.

Opinion on the advantages and disadvantages of free trade is mixed (see Table 9.3), the main question being less about the idea in principle (most people would agree that open markets are better than closed markets) than about the terms of trade, the relative economic balance of the members involved in an agreement, and the extent to which they play by the rules. Free trade works best where each of the participants derives clear benefits, is similarly based in terms of their levels of economic development, and brings something valuable to the bloc. It works worst where none of these conditions apply.

Table 9.3: The pros and cons of free trade

PROS	CONS
Encourages development, innovation, prosperity.	Heightens the effects of economic imbalances among countries.
Helps create new businesses, jobs, and profits.	May benefit only the wealthy, and jobs are lost in one country as they move to countries with cheaper labour.
Encourages a more dynamic business environment through competition.	Smaller or poorer countries are hurt by loss of income from taxes and tariffs.
Encourages foreign direct investment.	Investment might flow only to countries with the most dynamic economies.
Encourages the transfer of technology.	Heightens the danger of the theft of intellectual property.
Encourages greater global economic output.	Levels of economic output might vary.
Helps promote the sense of a global community.	Undermines cultural diversity by promoting homogeneity.
Encourages states to specialize, removing duplication.	Works only if states are capable of specializing and reaping balanced rewards.
Encourages peace, since states that trade are less likely to go to war with each other.	Reduces the sovereignty and independence of states.
Has helped promote a substantial increase in global standards of living since 1945.	Makes states more prone to the effects of economic downturns in other states.
Creates bigger markets to which business can sell their products and services.	Benefits only states that are able to compete in those bigger markets.

TRADE AND INEQUALITY

In an ideal world, trade should bring wealth and opportunity in its wake. By being able to sell to a larger international or global market, entrepreneurs and businesses should be able to improve their chances of making better products and greater profits, which would mean improvements in the quality and variety of products, the creation of new jobs, and higher wages for workers. But commerce is an endeavour fraught with risk, many new ideas and products fail, and handicaps built deliberately or accidentally into the global trading system are both a cause and a result of imbalances in wealth, opportunity, and equality.

In many ways, success in business and trade is based on three qualities: creativity, infrastructure, and survival (as well, perhaps, as an element of luck). The first of these comes into play when an entrepreneur has the foresight to develop a new product or service that meets a clear need, and sells well and widely. Infrastructure plays its role when the maker of the product (or the provider of the service) has access to the means needed to convey the product to potential consumers. Survival comes into play when the entrepreneurs with the most advantages and backing are able to overcome their competition.

In many respects, poorer countries suffer disadvantages on all three fronts:

▸ Creative ideas are more likely to be capitalized upon in economies with large and ready potential markets, and business-friendly laws. This is why so many companies such as Apple, Microsoft, Amazon, and Uber began in the United States rather than in Russia, China, or India. In Southern states, these essential qualities are often missing or reduced.

▸ If the infrastructure is not there to get a product or service to market – the necessary machinery, or raw materials, or energy supply, or reliable transportation systems, for example – then a product will more likely fail.

▸ Survival is difficult when the rules are loaded in favour of the biggest and most powerful players, meaning a greater reliance on luck for everyone else.

While increased trade should bring new opportunities to poorer countries, most of the evidence suggests that it can close wealth gaps between rich countries and poor ones, but not necessarily among poor ones, and not necessarily within poor countries. Those who have benefited least from the growth of world trade are the poorest and the most vulnerable: the rural poor are worst off because they often live in areas cut off from key markets, and perhaps undermined by conflict or civil war. The urban poor are often relatively better off, but they are still often paid little, suffer often dire working conditions, are usually unable to convert jobs and wages into improving their lives, and are usually unable (or unwilling) to exert much political pressure for change.

Workers in the North often worry about the impact of globalization on their jobs, but while many of those jobs have moved to countries with cheaper labour and weaker regulations, the opportunities this has created have not always been for the best. Consider the case of the garment industry in Bangladesh (see Manik and Yardley, 2013, and Yardley, 2013). In 2013, it was the world's second biggest garment exporter after China, having grown rapidly as Western retailers looked for ever-cheaper sources for their products. More than 5,000 garment factories employed

GLOBAL AND LOCAL 9

FREE TRADE VERSUS FAIR TRADE

When we think about free trade at the global level, we think mainly about the biggest trading powers, the trade blocs that some of them have formed, and the expanding reach of the big multinationals. We can see their presence all around us, in the vehicles we drive, the electronic products we buy, the clothes we wear, and the toys with which our children play. Many of the profits on the sale of these goods go to large manufacturers that are active in multiple countries, whose reach and size means that they can lack a human scale. As the final target of a sometimes long supply chain, we as consumers routinely fail to appreciate the remarkable confluence of ideas and hard work by which many people in many locations have converted raw materials into the products we seek out. We see only the brand name, and perhaps the country of manufacture, but have little idea of what it took to make sure that the goods we seek are available where we want them, when we want them, and at a price we can afford.

One phenomenon that has helped draw more attention to the ethics of trade and to the distribution of profits is **fair trade**. This is a process designed to make sure that the local producers of goods in poorer countries are given a fairer share of the profits from the sale of those goods, rather than having most of them accrue to the global multinationals or to companies in the wealthier consumer countries.

Although it has only drawn wider attention since the 1990s, the idea dates back to western Europe in the 1960s, and to efforts to encourage so-called solidarity trade: radical students and labour unions sought to make a gesture against what they saw as neo-imperialism. It was an idea reflected in the adoption in 1968 of the slogan 'Trade, Not Aid' by the UN Conference on Trade and Development, and the launch that same year in the United States of the *Whole Earth Catalog*, promoting the interests of independent producers from around the world. The International Federation of Fair Trade (now the World Fair Trade Organization) was founded in 1989, and efforts were made in the 1990s to give fair trade more consistency by launching certification schemes aimed at guaranteeing the origins of products sold in this spirit.

Since then, fair trade has expanded to focus on agricultural commodities such as coffee, chocolate, cocoa, cotton, and fruit, the underlying argument being that to give them a fairer price is an effective way of helping poorer states develop, and is a more effective alternative to foreign aid. Supporters of fair trade argue that it helps offset some of the inequalities created by globalization, bringing more balance into the mismatch between the global and the local (see Brown, 2013). Critics, however, are not so sure about the equity of the redistribution, suggesting that few of the benefits actually reach their targets and that there is little evidence of much impact (see Wydick, 2016).

Fair trade: A social movement designed to give producers in poorer countries a bigger share of the profits from the sale of their commodities.

about 3.2 million people, many of them women, and most of them paid as little as $40 per month. Advocates argued that the industry had helped pull people out of poverty and provided the country with badly needed foreign exchange, but critics pointed to low wages, unsafe working conditions, and a routine failure to meet local construction codes.

On the morning of Wednesday, 24 April 2013, hundreds of workers took their accustomed places in a garment factory in the capital city of Dhaka. The day

Bangladeshi garment workers protest low salaries during a protest in the capital city of Dhaka. Recent events have drawn attention to the poor conditions in Bangladeshi garment factories, most of whose production is for export to Europe and the Americas.

Source: Barcroft Media/Getty Images

before, an inspection team visiting the factory had found cracks in its structure, and warned that the eight-storey building violated several construction codes. Their findings prompted the worried owners of stores and a bank on the lower floor to close, but the managers of the garment factory on the upper floors insisted that business continue as usual. The workers had barely settled to their tasks before there was a loud cracking sound and the concrete floor of the factory began to roll, beams and pillars collapsed, and the building seemed to implode. Initial reports placed the death toll at about 70, but as rescue workers combed the wreckage of the factory, the numbers rose into the low hundreds. The final official toll was 1,127, making the collapse the deadliest disaster in the history of the global garment industry.

Several of the major Western retailers for whom workers had been making clothes expressed immediate regret and sympathy after the disaster, but also claimed to be unaware of the working conditions, and promised to take action. Meanwhile, millions of consumers around the world had bought clothing bearing the label 'Made in Bangladesh' without too much thought to the link between their purchase and the export of jobs to Bangladesh, and the working conditions and pay scales in Bangladeshi garment factories. The Western companies who retailed that clothing could have had it made much closer to home, but that would have meant paying higher wages and meeting more demanding worker safety regulations, which would have pushed up the price of the clothing, making it less attractive to consumers. Far better for the bottom line to move the jobs elsewhere, taking advantage not just of lower wages, but also of the new ease of moving goods from distant factories to stores in wealthy Western cities.

DISCUSSION QUESTIONS

1. Protectionism or liberalism: which is the best approach?

2. What does the rising power of China portend for the future of the global trading system?

3. Is the work of the WTO an indication of the advantages or of the disadvantages of globalization?

4. Considering all its pros and cons, is free trade good for us, or only for some of us?

5. Are the goals of fair trade achievable?

6. What can be done to help poorer countries benefit more from increased trade?

KEY CONCEPTS

- ▸ Comparative advantage
- ▸ Doha round
- ▸ Dumping
- ▸ E-commerce
- ▸ Economic union
- ▸ Fair trade

- ▸ Fordism
- ▸ Free trade
- ▸ Free trade agreement
- ▸ Intellectual property
- ▸ Liberalism
- ▸ Monetary union

- ▸ Most-favoured nation status
- ▸ Preferential trade agreement
- ▸ Protectionism
- ▸ Technology transfer
- ▸ Trade

USEFUL WEBSITES

World Fair Trade Organization at https://wfto.com

World Trade Organization at https://www.wto.org

FURTHER READING

Bernstein, William J. (2008) *A Splendid Exchange: How Trade Shaped the World* (Atlantic Monthly), and Kenneth Pomeranz and Steven Topik (2015) *The World that Trade Created: Society, Culture, and the World Economy, 1400 to the Present*, 3rd edn (Routledge). Two studies of the history of trade and its impact on shaping the global system.

Bhagwati, Jagdish N., Pravin Krishna, and Arvind Panagariya (eds) (2016) *The World Trade System: Trends and Challenges* (MIT Press). An edited collection of studies of the opportunities and problems inherent in the way global trade is conducted.

Hoekman, Bernard M., and Petros C. Mavroidis (2016) *The World Trade Organization*, 2nd edn (Routledge). A survey of the WTO, with chapters on its history, methods, impact, and future prospects.

Irwin, Douglas A. (2015) *Free Trade Under Fire*, 4th edn (Princeton University Press). A discussion about the nature of free trade and the misconceptions from which it often suffers, written from an American perspective but with broader lessons included.

Rivoli, Pietra (2015) *The Travels of a T-Shirt in the Global Economy: An Economist Examines the Markets, Power, and Politics of World Trade*, 2nd edn (John Wiley). A study of the life of a T-shirt, tracing each step in its production and consumption, and making a number of observations about the nature of the global economy along the way.

Online Resources

Visit www.macmillanihe.com/McCormick-GS to access additional materials to support teaching and learning.

MIGRATION

10

PREVIEW

This chapter looks at one of the most controversial issues in global matters. It begins with a review of the dimensions of migration and how they have changed over the last century, then looks at migration patterns, at the major sources and destinations of migration, and at recent trends such as increased mobility and the contrasting effects of more migration and greater efforts to control the movement of people. It assesses the global migration regime, and ends with a discussion about the effects of migration, the pros and cons of migration, and a comparison of approaches and attitudes in Europe and the United States.

CONTENTS

- Understanding migration
- The causes of migration
- The global refugee problem
- The global migration regime
- The effects of migration

HIGHLIGHTS

- Migration is as old as human history, but has recently grown in both breadth and complexity, both within and across borders.

- In spite of the political, economic and social significance of migration, there is no consensus on how to define a migrant.

- There are many different causes of migration, combining a variety of push factors and pull factors, ranging from the political to the environmental.

- In the most troubled cases, migration is caused by political or economic factors that create refugees and asylum-seekers.

- The global migration regime is modest, focusing mainly on the needs of refugees and migrant workers.

- Migration has both costs and benefits, the emotional qualities of many of the recent debates in Europe and North America often distracting from reasoned analysis.

Source: EyeEm/Getty Images

UNDERSTANDING MIGRATION

Migration is as old as human history, and a natural part of the human condition. For as long as they have been able, humans have often sought new places to live, and the new opportunities that have come with moving. In other cases they have been forced to move by deliberate government policy, or encouraged by changing circumstances: the motives for migration have ranged from the political to the social, and from the voluntary to the forced, while the scale of the movement has varied in size and distance: it might involve a single **migrant** moving for personal reasons or an entire community displaced for broader political or economic reasons, and the movement might happen within a country, across borders to a neighbouring country, or across oceans to a new continent; see examples in Table 10.1.

For most of human history, the scale of migration was determined by a combination of economic, geographical, and resource factors; people needed the motivation to move, the necessary modes of transport, an absence of natural barriers, and the means to support their migration. Over the last century and a half, the process has been complicated by the strengthened enforcement of state borders. As we saw in Chapter 5, these are nothing new, but they have been protected more rigorously as governments have made more efforts to control transnational immigration; passports are required, visas must often be bought, quotas are imposed,

> **Migration**: The movement of people from one place to another, including outward movement (**emigration**) and inward movement (**immigration**).

> **Migrant**: Someone who has moved from one region of a country to another, or from one country to another.

Table 10.1: Examples of migration from history

Place	Time	Features
Europe	35,000–45,000 years ago	Colonization of Europe as people moved from the Middle East.
Atlantic	1840–1914	Great Atlantic Migration of about 30 million people to the United States, mainly from Ireland, Germany, Italy, and Eastern Europe, many driven out by poor economic and social conditions.
Brazil	19th century	Mainly from Portugal, Germany and Italy, pushed out by poverty at home and new opportunities abroad.
Australia	19th–20th centuries	Migration of Europeans, encouraged by a White Australia policy that was rescinded only in 1973, since when there has been more immigration from Asia.
Soviet Union	1920–52	Forced transfers of workers to underpopulated areas.
India–Pakistan	Late 1940s	Exchange of Hindus and Muslims following the partition of India in 1947, displacing 10–12 million people.
China	1980s	Movement from rural to urban areas, spurred by economic development and urbanization; probably the largest migration in human history.
Middle East	Since 2011	Displacement of millions as a result of the instability created by the Syrian civil war.

'undesirables' are blocked, and walls have sometimes been built. 'We may live in an era of globalization,' argues Reece Jones (2017), 'but much of the world is increasingly focused on limiting the free movement of people'. Imposing those limits has become more difficult, though, as the dimensions of migration have changed:

▶ Globalization has brought new economic patterns and opportunities that have prompted people to move for many different reasons. Once they might have moved internally, or from rural to urban areas, but migration has become increasingly transnational in its scope.

▶ International travel is much easier and cheaper. While once only the rich or the privileged could travel, and the poor could migrate only in organized and government-sanctioned programmes, the post-1945 era of mass tourism and cheap international travel has – as we saw in Chapter 4 – widened the options.

▶ Patterns of migration have become more complex, as increased **mobility** has combined with changing political and economic pressures to encourage more people to move from a wider variety of source countries to a wider variety of destination countries.

Mobility: The capacity to move, whether from one location to another, one job to another, or even one social class to another.

▶ The global refugee problem has worsened, with war and instability in several parts of the world forcing people to move against their wishes, whether within or between countries.

▶ More people are moving out of free choice, whether seeking to further their education, or to live in a more amenable culture or a warmer climate.

▶ While legal migration has grown, so has unauthorized migration, presenting governments with the challenge of protecting the former while limiting the latter.

▶ There has been new tension between the migration of skilled and unskilled workers, with governments preferring the former, but finding the latter useful for seasonal or cheap labour of the kind that is less attractive to local citizens.

As all these changes have taken place, the migration picture has become more complex – see Table 10.2. Migration has become more common and more controversial, its pros and cons are more vigorously debated, it has raised questions about security and threats to national identity, and it has tested the tolerance of previously progressive societies as they watch their communities becoming more racially and religiously diverse. In multiple European countries, for example, conservative political parties have been formed with opposition to immigration at the heart of their policies, and candidates for public office have won support by advocating policies in favour of limits on immigration. Meanwhile, the home countries of many immigrants have suffered a brain drain (see later in this chapter) as their most ambitious and talented citizens have left to seek new opportunities elsewhere.

In spite of all this, we are not agreed on exactly how to define a migrant. Is a migrant someone who holds foreign citizenship (living legally in one country while having the citizenship of another country), someone who is foreign born (living legally in one country but born in another), or does the term include both? What about people who were born in another country while their parents were living or

Source: Universal Images Group/Getty Images

Muslim women in a subway train in Paris, France. The increasing tide of anti-immigration rhetoric across Europe has fed concerns around multiculturalism and integration.

working abroad, and have returned home? What about people living temporarily in a foreign country, for work or for education? How long must they live in their new country before they can be classified as a migrant? (One year, says the UN.) What about people who hold the citizenship of two or more countries? What about internal migrants who do not cross borders, or rural-to-urban migrants, or seasonal migrants? And where do unauthorized immigrants fit into the scheme?

The UN migration agency – the International Organization for Migration (2017) – defines an international migrant as follows:

> [A]ny person who is moving or has moved across an international border or within a State away from his/her habitual place of residence, regardless of (1) the person's legal status; (2) whether the movement is voluntary or involuntary; (3) what the causes for the movement are; or (4) what the length of the stay is.

This is a remarkably broad definition, however, that does not make a distinction between short-term and long-term movement. The Population Division of the UN has a narrower definition, including only people who hold foreign citizenship or who are foreign born. On that basis, there were about 244 million migrants in the world in 2015, a 60 per cent increase since 1990 and a 41 per cent increase since 2000 (UN Population Division, 2015). Given that the global population is about 7.4 billion, this means that just over three per cent of the world's population consists of legal immigrants, a proportion that has remained steady for several decades even while the number of migrants has grown (International Organization for Migration, 2015).

What are we to make, meanwhile, of those immigrants who are living without authorization in a country other than their own? Although they are often described in the media as illegal immigrants, this term is contested, and is best restricted to cases

Table 10.2: Types of migration

Type	Qualities	Examples
Internal	Takes place within states.	Italians moving from poorer southern regions of the country to wealthier northern regions.
Rural-to-urban	People leaving declining small towns and rural areas to seek opportunities in cities.	Historically common in the North, and increasingly common in Africa and China.
Regional	Movement to neighbouring states in search of work.	Men from Zimbabwe, Mozambique, and Botswana moving to South Africa to work in its mines.
Seasonal	Based on seasonal demand for labour.	Agriculture and the tourist industry in Europe and the United States.
Temporary	Migration for a limited period of time, for work or education.	Students living in another country to continue their education.
Unauthorized	Migration without the authorization of the receiving country.	India may be the biggest target in the world, with an estimated tens of millions of unauthorized immigrants from neighbouring states.
Transit	Moving through a country on the way to another.	Unauthorized migrants from Central America moving through Mexico on their way to the United States.
Forced	Migration against the will of those being moved.	Shipment of African slaves to the Americas and the Middle East.
Return	Migration back to the country or area of origin.	British immigrants to Australia returning to Britain.

of migrants who are smuggled or trafficked across borders. For those migrants who cross borders without legal authority or documentation, there is a host of additional terms, including *undocumented*, *clandestine*, *unlawful*, *non-compliant*, *irregular*, and the term chosen for this book: *unauthorized*. These are people who have moved from one state to another without permission, and may or may not have been detected by the governments of destination states. Their numbers are hard to pin down given that they do not report their presence to authorities, but three examples give some idea of the scale of the problem:

▶ In the United States there are 47 million authorized immigrants and an estimated 11 million unauthorized immigrants (Passel and Cohn, 2015).

▶ In the EU there are about 35 million legal immigrants from outside the EU, and estimates of the number of unauthorized immigrants range between 1.9 and 3.3 million (Triandafyllidou, 2009). The EU border agency Frontex reported a surge in 2015 of detected crossing of EU borders, with more than 1.8 million people entering the EU without authorization.

▶ India is both one of the biggest sources and destinations for migrants, but data on the number of unauthorized immigrants are even harder to confirm than in the US or the EU. Numbers are thought to run into the low millions, with most coming from Bangladesh and Pakistan (see Shamshad, 2017).

The distribution of migrants is unequal both in terms of the source and destination countries, thanks to a combination of deliberate policy, different levels of opportunity, and geographical location. Unsurprisingly, the two parts of the world with the most immigrants are the European Union and the United States, which are also the two wealthiest regions in the world. At the same time, there are many other parts of the world that are magnets for migrants, including the oil-rich states of the Middle East, and the mining industry of South Africa. Australia and Canada have become more welcoming to migrants (although they set tough educational demands of applicants), while Japan – at the opposite end of the scale – has imposed a near-total ban on immigration. Meanwhile, we need to be careful how we read the numbers: the United States, Germany and Russia may be the biggest destination countries for migrants in absolute terms, but the biggest migrant populations as a percentage of the domestic population are found in the United Arab Emirates, Qatar and Kuwait. Figures 10.1, 10.2, and 10.3 offer some insights into the complexity of the migration picture.

Push factors: Problems and pressures that encourage people to leave their home region or state. The opposite of **pull factors**, or opportunities that draw people to a new region or state.

THE CAUSES OF MIGRATION

Why do people migrate? There are many different reasons, combining a variety of **push factors** and **pull factors**. The former encourage people to leave their home region or state and include a lack of opportunity, persecution, social instability, high

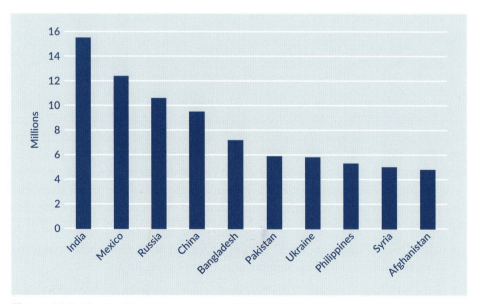

Figure 10.1: The ten biggest source countries of migrants
Source: UN Population Division (2015).

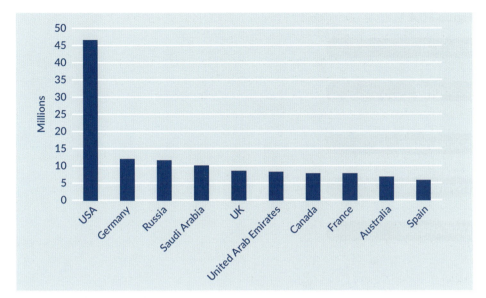

Figure 10.2: The ten biggest destination countries for migrants
Source: UN Population Division (2015).

crime rates, economic decline, overpopulation, natural or man-made environmental problems, and war. Meanwhile, pull factors are the kinds of attractions that encourage migrants to move to a particular country or region, or encourage employers in those countries to seek out migrant workers; these include better economic opportunities, higher wages, greater demand for service-sector and low-skill workers, more personal security, stronger political freedoms, furthering their education, re-joining family members, and even something as simple as better weather or a more comfortable social environment.

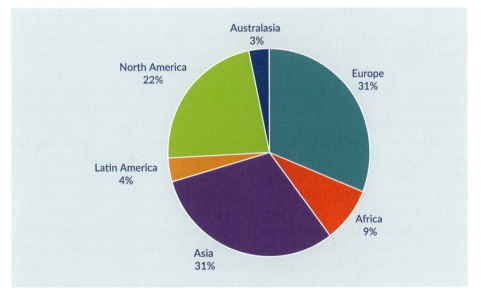

Figure 10.3: Distribution of migrants by region
Source: United Nations (2015). Numbers refer to share of global total, and are rounded out.

Figure 10.4: Causes of migration

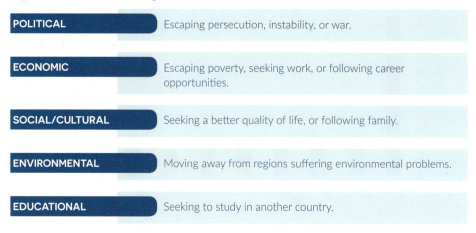

POLITICAL	Escaping persecution, instability, or war.
ECONOMIC	Escaping poverty, seeking work, or following career opportunities.
SOCIAL/CULTURAL	Seeking a better quality of life, or following family.
ENVIRONMENTAL	Moving away from regions suffering environmental problems.
EDUCATIONAL	Seeking to study in another country.

Broadly, the motivations for migration can be placed into five major groups:

Political. The most serious push factors in migration are typically political, ranging from human rights abuses to discrimination, persecution, instability, and all-out war. In the most modest cases, migrants may be leaving home because they find political circumstances uncomfortable or threatening; they might be concerned about instability, or even about the dominance of a government whose policies they oppose. In the most extreme cases, migrants are compelled to leave home out of fear for their own security, and they become either an **asylum-seeker** or a **refugee**. The former is someone who seeks permanent residence in another country because they face concerns about their personal safety if they return home. If they can prove their claim, they will usually be given a fast-track to permanent residence in their new home state. Germany and the United States have been among the biggest destinations for asylum-seekers in recent years. (See later in this chapter for more discussion about refugees.)

Economic. The economic causes of migration may either push someone away from home because of a lack of opportunities, or may pull someone to a new home that offers better opportunities, or may see a combination of push and pull pressures working at the same time. Economic factors have long been behind internal migration, encouraging people to move from declining rural areas to growing cities, for example, but they have also been behind international migration to countries with strong economies, such as Australia, Canada, Germany, the United States, and the major oil producers of the Middle East. In some cases it has been the natural pull of the market, but in some cases there has been a deliberate government effort to recruit workers: this was true, for example, of British efforts in the 1950s to recruit workers from the Caribbean to address a shortage of labour, and of German efforts to recruit guest workers from Turkey and several European countries in the 1960s.

Wealthy countries sometimes make an effort to encourage the best-educated workers, while both discouraging but acknowledging the importance of unskilled workers. The United States has long had a system by which a Green Card (allowing permanent residence) can be issued to migrants who bring valuable skills to the country, and holders of these cards are allowed to apply for US citizenship after

Asylum-seeker: Someone who seeks permanent residence in another country out of fear for their personal safety if obliged to return home.

Refugee: Someone who is forced to move from their home as a result of local political, economic, social or environmental disruption.

five years. The European Union began issuing Blue Cards in 2009 with the same underlying goal. Australia, Britain and Canada use a points system for expectant immigrants, giving preference to those with qualifications such as strong work experience, a good education, language proficiency, and a strong financial foundation.

Social and cultural. In some cases, migration is prompted by social or cultural factors, such as a desire to join family or community members already in another country (sometimes known as **chain migration**), or – more nebulously – to seek out a better or different quality of life. Family reunification is one of the pressures that leads migrants to move to the same region or suburb as others from their home country, which is why many Algerians have congregated in the same suburbs of France, many Indians and Pakistanis have congregated in the same suburbs of London and other major UK cities, and why there are so many Cubans and Haitians in the same neighbourhoods of Miami.

> **Chain migration**: The long-term process by which immigrants linked by social networks follow pioneer immigrants from the same community or family.

The search for an improved or different quality of life is hard to measure, because its definition is so subjective. It is relatively easy to understand why a retiree from Sweden might want to move to Portugal or Spain, or a retiree from Canada to Mexico (warmer weather combine with a more diverse culture to make for an irresistible push/pull combination, for some at least), but other quality of life factors are harder to pin down; everyone has their own definition of the ideal circumstances and environment in which to live.

Environmental. Less thoroughly studied, but nonetheless compelling, are the effects of environmental change and natural disasters on migration. This has been a common motivation throughout history, a famous example being the Dust Bowl of the 1930s in the United States, when the cumulative effects of decades of soil mismanagement was made worse by drought, sparking massive dust storms, leaving farmland that was once arable bare and unproductive, and forcing tens of thousands of people to abandon their farms. Uncontrolled deforestation, leading to soil erosion, flooding, and the spread of deserts, have created similar problems in different parts of the world, and climate change is now seen as the major actual or potential cause of displacement. The number of 'climate refugees' is contested, but there is little question that rising sea levels, more extreme weather events, and changing patterns of crop production are likely to lead over the long term to new movements of population. One comprehensive study (Hsiang et al., 2013) concluded that there was 'strong causal evidence linking climatic events to human conflict across a range of spatial and temporal scales and across all major regions of the world'.

Educational. A common motivation for someone to move from one country to another is to pursue an education. And while the plan for most students may be to return home, many end up staying in their adopted country and eventually becoming citizens. The opportunities and motives behind international education have grown on the back of globalization, and the number of international students has grown rapidly as it has become easier to enrol at universities in foreign countries. Universities have also made more efforts to recruit foreign students, ostensibly because they want to foster a diverse learning environment but also because they can charge them higher fees.

More than three million international students were enrolled in higher education in the 35 member states of the OECD in 2014 (Organization for Economic

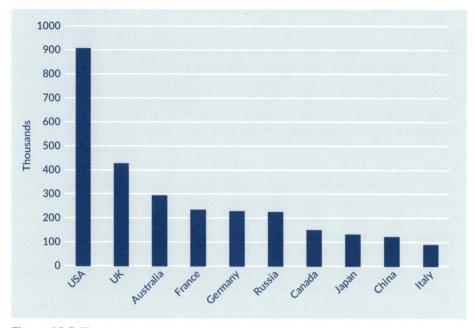

Figure 10.5: The ten biggest destination countries for international students
Source: UN Educational Scientific and Cultural Organization (2017). Data are for 2013–15.

Cooperation and Development, 2017), a number that is expected to keep rising as universities continue to work to attract foreign students. The United States is the most popular destination for international students, attracting just over 900,000 in 2015 alone – see Figure 10.5. Other English-speaking countries are also popular, including Australia, Britain, and Canada, but France and Germany are also in demand, and China is growing in the rankings. Looking at individual universities, a survey produced by *Times Higher Education* in the UK found in 2017 that 72 of the top 200 universities attracting overseas students were in the UK, 27 were in the United States, and 22 were in Australia (Bhardwa, 2017).

The effects of such movements are important not just for the educational opportunities offered: having large numbers of foreign students expands the international impact of the destination countries, and – since many students stay on permanently in those countries – brings new ideas and skills to the workforce. The movement of students is an example of the wider relationship between a **brain drain** from source countries and a **brain gain** for destination countries (a principle which also applies to the movement of skilled workers). This has to be thought about carefully, though, because it is not a simple binary choice: the movement of students can actually be a gain for source countries, which can benefit from the new skills learned by their citizens overseas, and from remittances sent home to families – see later in this chapter.

Brain drain:
The emigration of trained and talented individuals from one country to another, resulting in a loss of skills resources in the former. The obverse is a **brain gain** or the addition of skills resources in destination countries.

THE GLOBAL REFUGEE PROBLEM

Much of the debate about migration revolves around refugees, who – unlike migrants – have been displaced against their will and forced to seek refuge elsewhere. The world is currently undergoing one of its most serious ever refugee crises,

Table 10.3: Displaced people in the world

Number	Category	Features
22.5 million	Refugees	More than half under the age of 18, and nearly half from five countries (Syria, Colombia, Afghanistan, Iraq, South Sudan).
40.3 million	Internally displaced persons	Biggest populations in Colombia, Syria, Iraq, Democratic Republic of Congo.
2.8 million	Asylum-seekers	The number of asylum claims lodged globally grew almost six fold during 2015. Biggest destinations are Germany, US, and Turkey.

Sources: International Organization for Migration (2015) and UN High Commissioner for Refugees (2017a).

surpassing in scale even the massive displacement in Europe caused by World War II; this left an estimated 40–50 million refugees in its wake, and prompted the creation of the first international refugee and migration organizations. During 2015, the world saw the highest levels of forced displacement globally recorded since 1945, with the number of refugees almost doubling in less than four years, thanks mainly to the Syrian civil war. In addition to the nearly 66 million people in the world estimated by the UN to have been forcibly displaced by 2016 (up from 38 million in 2005) (see Table 10.3), about 10 million people were classified by the UN as being in a condition of **statelessness**. This left them with access to none of the services normally available to citizens, such as getting a job, going to school, or having access to health care.

In spite of the scale of the problem, defining a refugee is not easy. The 1951 Geneva refugee convention (see later in this chapter) says that a refugee is someone who is (1) outside their country of nationality or habitual residence; (2) has a well-founded fear of being persecuted because of their race, religion, nationality, membership of a particular social group or political opinion; and (3) is unable or unwilling to avail themselves of the protection of that country, or to return there, for fear of persecution. But this definition does not make allowance for **internally displaced persons** (IDP), assumes that refugees are prompted by fear of persecution rather than other pressures (such as natural disasters, for example), and assumes that refugees have no plans to return home.

There are also many misconceptions about the dimensions of the refugee problem, not least of which is the view promoted by many Northern politicians that refugees are mainly headed to Europe or North America; in fact, the South has a much bigger refugee problem, in large part because Southern countries are closer to those parts of the world suffering the most political and economic disruption. War, for example, almost always produces refugees, as illustrated by the cases of conflicts between India and Pakistan, the war in Vietnam, the violence targeted against Kurds, the US-led invasion of Afghanistan and Iraq, conflicts sparked by the Arab Spring in many North African and Middle Eastern states after 2011, and the ongoing civil

Statelessness: A condition under which a person does not have citizenship of a state, usually as a result of civil war.

Internally displaced person: Someone forced to leave their home as a result of disruption but who has not crossed international borders.

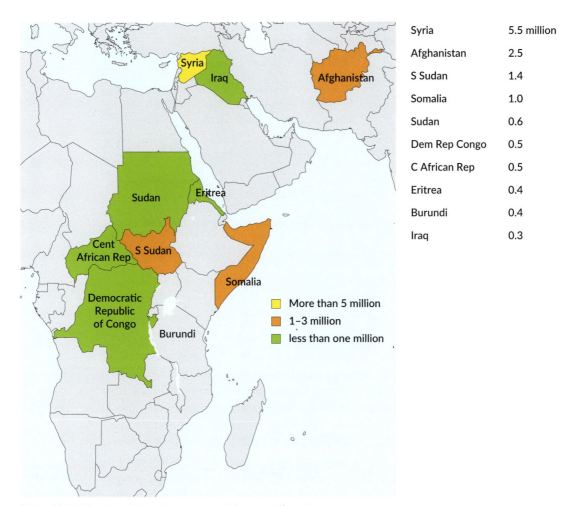

Syria	5.5 million
Afghanistan	2.5
S Sudan	1.4
Somalia	1.0
Sudan	0.6
Dem Rep Congo	0.5
C African Rep	0.5
Eritrea	0.4
Burundi	0.4
Iraq	0.3

Map 10.1: The ten biggest sources of the world's refugees
Source: Based on UN High Commissioner for Refugees (2017b).
Note: Data are for 2016.

wars in Libya and Syria that in 2018 remain the most drawn-out consequences of the Arab Spring.

The longest and most intractable refugee problem is that created by the conflict between Israel and Palestine, ongoing since the creation of Israel in 1948 thanks to the failure of all parties involved to agree the terms for the creation of a viable Palestinian state. As of 2015 there were more than five million Palestinian refugees, many of whom were born and have lived all their lives in some of the nearly 60 Palestinian refugee camps situated in Jordan, Lebanon, Syria, the Gaza Strip, and the West Bank.

To this has more recently been added the problem of Syria. When the pro-democracy movement known as the Arab Spring began in 2011, it spread throughout North Africa and parts of the Middle East, and sparked demands in Syria for the removal of the authoritarian regime of President Bashar al-Assad, in power since 2000. The Assad government responded with violent suppression, Syria became divided between government forces, anti-government forces, and the Islamic State, so far costing the lives of an estimated 200–500,000 Syrians. The conflict also

Source: Barcroft Media/Getty Images

Rohingya refugees make their way into Bangladesh from Myanmar, where a military crackdown on the Muslim minority in 2017 triggered an exodus and a major humanitarian crisis.

sparked a massive refugee crisis, with millions leaving for safer parts of the country or crossing into Iraq, Jordan, Lebanon, or Turkey.

Yet another refugee crisis has recently emerged in Myanmar, placing the spotlight on the Rohingya, a Muslim minority living in a predominantly Buddhist country. Although they have lived there for centuries, claiming to be the descendants of Arab traders, the government refuses them citizenship and even excludes them from the national census, regarding them instead as unauthorized immigrants from Bangladesh. Violence broke out against the Rohingya in 2017, with charges that thousands were killed, women and girls were raped by the Myanmar military, and villages were burned. In the face of the violence, many left Myanmar and moved to Bangladesh, where they were housed in makeshift refugee camps. The UN described the military campaign as a 'textbook example of ethnic cleansing'.

THE GLOBAL MIGRATION REGIME

In other chapters in the second half of this book, we have seen often-substantial regimes built around matters such as human rights, finance, and trade. Migration is clearly a topic that could benefit from international cooperation, given that every country in the world is either a source or a destination (or both) for migration. But states jealously guard their rights to control the flow of migrants, the result being that most policy is made at the national level, and the development of a global regime has focused mainly on the needs of refugees, and – to a lesser degree – migrant workers.

Prior to World War I, migration was an option only for those with the resources needed to move, or for those taking part in government-sponsored schemes such as those used by the British government – including land grants and bounties – to

COMPARING NORTH AND SOUTH 10

CONTRASTING PERSPECTIVES ON MIGRATION

Immigration is often thought of as a Northern phenomenon, the assumption being that poorer Southerners are drawn by the economic opportunities offered by wealthier Northern states. But the picture is not that simple, and globalization has helped make it more complex: not only are there substantial flows of North–North and South–South migration, but large numbers of people move within countries rather than across borders, and they should not be overlooked. Consider these numbers:

▶ Nearly 58 per cent of the world's migrants live in the North, but about 61 per cent of them originated somewhere else in the North.

▶ About 42 per cent of the world's migrants live in the South, but about 87 per cent of them originated somewhere else in the South (UN Population Division, 2015).

South–South flows of migration are growing faster than South–North flows, adding to the changing balance. In some cases, the push-pull factors are economic, as in the case of workers chasing jobs in the oil fields of Saudi Arabia or the gold fields of South Africa. But South–South flows are also encouraged by the sheer proximity of Southern states to regions of political conflict. This is why countries such as Pakistan, Lebanon, Iran and Jordan are among the major hosts of refugees.

For their part, most Northern countries are opposed to the idea of accepting large numbers of refugees, and would rather invest in providing humanitarian assistance that keeps refugees as close as possible to their countries of origin; hence, for example, the controversial agreement by the European Union in 2016 to provide Turkey with €6 billion ($7 billion) to fund services for refugees from the Syrian civil war, taking the pressure off the EU. Some countries – notably the United States – also engage in **humanitarian intervention** so as to remove the kinds of pressures that create refugee problems. They often fail – the occurrence of crises and atrocities in Rwanda, the Darfur region of Sudan, Syria, and the Democratic Republic of Congo point to its limitations.

As far as internal migration is concerned, the picture that most readily comes to mind in the South is of civil war or natural disasters forcing people off the land in a country such as South Sudan or Colombia, and moving elsewhere within their home countries. This certainly accounts for a large number of the 380 million people who were estimated by one study (Esipova et al., 2013) to have migrated internally between 2008 and 2013. But for many others, particularly in the North, the motivations are more typically economic, such as a change of job. The study found that the four most mobile countries in the world were New Zealand (where 26 per cent of adults had reported moving), the United States (24 per cent), Finland (23 per cent), and Norway (22 per cent). The study noted that in wealthier countries there were three groups of people who had particularly high levels of mobility:

▶ Those with a college education were twice as likely to move as those without.

▶ Those aged 15–29 were twice as likely to have moved as those aged 50 or older.

▶ First-generation immigrants were twice as likely to have moved as native-born residents.

encourage emigration to Australia in the 19th century. A programme of subsidized travel and settlement in the 1960s and 1970s, involving the payment by migrants of a token fee of £10 (about $25 at the time), led to the creation of the label 'ten pound poms' (based on the Australian nickname for people from Britain).

The rarity of migrants and foreign travellers meant that – as we saw in Chapter 5 – little was at first demanded in the way of documentation; passports were first introduced only during World War I. The new controls grew in tandem with migration, made more common thanks to the expansion of opportunities, the greater ease of travel, and the wider availability of the resources needed to travel. The design of passports was standardized by the League of Nations, and the passport books used today began to be introduced in the mid-1920s, although they were not always required. The technology involved has since changed as states have tried to improve their ability to track the movement of citizens; passports have become more difficult to forge, and security has tightened with the introduction of watermarked paper, digitized photographs, and a move towards including microchips and biometric data, such as fingerprints and iris patterns.

A passport is not always enough for travel, many countries also requiring incoming visitors to have a **visa**, allowing governments to keep better records and tighter controls on the movement of travellers, and to place limits on their numbers. The requirement varies from country to country, with the citizens of most Northern countries requiring visas to visit relatively few countries, while the citizens of countries such as Afghanistan can travel to few countries without a visa.

The legal and institutional arrangements for travel and migration have also tightened, as state laws have been joined by international treaties designed to clarify the definition and rights of migrant workers or refugees, and by international organizations working to monitor and address their problems. Refugees have been at the heart of most international agreements, beginning after World War I in the face of the refugee problem created by the war and by the Russian Revolution. These combined to spark the 1933 signature of the Convention Relating to the International Status of Refugees. This was the first such agreement to guarantee the right to 'non-refoulement', which forbids the forced removal of a refugee to a country where they run the risk of persecution (for more details, see Fitzmaurice, 2012). This has been a right in international refugee law ever since.

As the world moved towards war in the 1930s, there was little further progress on building an international regime for migrants and refugees, and only eight countries ratified the 1933 treaty. But the seeds of the idea had been sown, and when World War II created an even bigger refugee problem than World War I, governments were more receptive to the idea of taking action. Even before the second war had ended, and the United Nations had been created, the UN Relief and Rehabilitation Administration had been founded, and was given the job of overseeing refugee protection at the end of the war. It was closed down in 1947 and most of its functions transferred to a new International Refugee Organization, active between 1946 and 1952.

In 1947, the new UN Commission on Human Rights adopted a resolution requesting early action on the problem of displaced peoples in Europe. This led to the drafting of the Convention Relating to the Status of Refugees, which was signed in Geneva in 1951 and came into force in 1954; a 1967 protocol removed its focus

Humanitarian intervention: A military intervention prompted by human rights abuses, natural disasters, war crimes, or genocide, with a view to easing refugee-generating problems.

Visa: A document that authorizes a foreigner to enter a country, usually for a specified maximum period of time, and or a specified reason, such as business, education or tourism.

on post-war Europe. The treaty was designed to define a refugee and to outline the rights and obligations of refugees. For example, someone who has committed a crime against humanity outside their country of refuge cannot claim refugee status, and someone given the status of a refugee cannot be expelled from their country of refuge except under specifically defined conditions. As a refugee, they have the right to work and to have access to housing and an education, and obligations to follow the laws of their host country.

The office of the UN High Commissioner for Refugees (UNHCR) was created in 1950, while Europe was still wrestling with its post-war refugee crisis. Headquartered in Geneva, Switzerland, it inherited the work of the International Refugee Organization, and its focus on the European refugee problem soon expanded to other parts of the world, the challenges it faced growing to new levels with the extent of the problem of displacement. The UNHCR is funded almost entirely by voluntary contributions, most of which come from governments, and it has had to raise more to deal with the growing global refugee problem; its annual budget rose from $1 billion in the 1990s to $7.5 billion in 2016 (UN High Commissioner for Refugees, 2017a). Its task is to help provide emergency assistance, to protect rights of asylum and safe refuge, and to lobby governments in regard to policies on asylum and refuge. It is headed by a High Commissioner elected by the UN General Assembly for renewable five-year terms, and sponsors 20 June each year as World Refugee Day.

Another international organization with more focused interests is the UN Relief Works Agency for Palestinian Refugees in the Near East (UNRWA), which was set up in 1949 to provide assistance to these refugees. The lack of progress towards a resolution of the Israeli–Palestinian problem means that there is little sign that its presence will cease to be needed any time soon. Of the world's 21.3 million refugees in 2015, 5.2 million were Palestinian refugees registered by the UNRWA, the balance of 16.1 million coming under the mandate of the UNHCR.

Another body founded in the wake of World War II, and with a wider mandate than refugees, is the International Organization for Migration, founded in 1951 with a focus on the movement of migrants in Europe. Part of the UN, and also headquartered in Geneva, it has undergone several changes of name and purpose, beginning as a logistics agency and expanding to become the major international organization promoting an understanding of migration issues.

While refugees are the subject of the 1951 Geneva Convention, the closest equivalent treaty dealing with migrants was not agreed until 1990, and it met with much less political enthusiasm. It was not until 2003 that the International Convention on the Protection of the Rights of All Migrant Workers and Members of Their Families had won enough support to enter into force, only 49 states had signed and ratified by 2018, and an additional 15 have signed but not ratified. Most of the ratifying countries are those that are major sources of migrant workers, and who see the treaty as an important source of protection for their citizens, while almost none of the major destination countries of migrant workers – including all the members of the EU, as well as Australia, Canada, South Africa, the United States, and the Gulf states – have either signed or ratified.

The treaty defines a migrant worker as anyone 'who is to be engaged, is engaged or has been engaged in a remunerated activity in a State of which he or she is not a national', and does not include refugees or students. It lists many of the same rights as those found in the Universal Declaration of Human Rights (see Chapter 7), such as freedom of thought and expression, freedom of religion, freedom against forced or compulsory labour, the right to liberty and security of person, and protection from arbitrary arrest or detention.

Alongside the intergovernmental organizations and treaties – and often reflecting their limitations – is a thriving community of national and international NGOs dealing with migrants' rights and needs, and with the problems of refugees. They not only challenge the policies of states (or the lack of such policies), but also fill the gaps where states have failed to take action. National bodies typically focus on helping arriving migrants to settle in their new countries of residence, while international NGOs focus on alleviating problems for refugees, even if only as part of their broader concerns with poverty and health care. Among many organizations, the latter are noteworthy:

▸ The International Committee of the Red Cross is the oldest and best-known humanitarian organization, and was founded in Geneva in 1863 with the goal of improving the treatment of soldiers wounded on the battlefield. It adopted its current name in 1876, and has gone on – in its own words – to provide 'an impartial, neutral, and independent organization whose independently humanitarian mission is to protect the lives and dignity of victims of war and internal violence and to provide them with assistance'. It has offices in more than 80 countries, and has won the Nobel Peace Prize an unprecedented three times: in 1917, 1944, and 1963.

▸ The International Rescue Committee is a New York-based humanitarian aid organization that was founded in 1933 at the suggestion of Albert Einstein, and that responds to crises by providing health care and education, working to ensure access to clean water and sanitation, operating savings and loans associations, providing legal assistance and job training, and helping resettle refugees.

▸ Save the Children traces its roots back to efforts in Britain after World War I to work to end malnutrition among children impacted by war, while Refugees International is a Washington DC-based organization that was founded in 1979 to campaign on behalf of displaced and stateless people.

To describe this network of intergovernmental and non-governmental organizations as a regime is to give the impression of a more structured approach to migration than exists in reality. But even if migration is treated as a national matter, the connections among states make it impossible for them to work in isolation.

THE EFFECTS OF MIGRATION

Just as we need to understand push and pull factors when we look at migration, so we need to understand the effects on both the source countries and the destination countries. In doing so, there is a danger of allowing myths and biases to enter the equation, a problem that has been particularly evident in the recent and often emotional debate over migration in the European Union, India, South Africa, and the United States. For some, migrants are seen as a welcome addition to the local economy and culture; for others, they are seen as threats. There is a high degree of racism, **xenophobia**, and **nativism** in the debate, the dominant national cultures in the destination countries often looking askance at the growing social and cultural diversity that has followed in the wake of migration.

The major impact on source countries is the potential for a brain drain. This can be a problem when the brightest and most ambitious citizens find too few opportunities at home, or are driven out by low salaries, over-regulation, or barriers to career development, and take their skills to other countries with more amenable environments. The United States, for example, has become an attractive destination for medical doctors, engineers, and software engineers from India, while the British National Health Service relies heavily on foreign nationals, who make up more than a quarter of its doctors and 11 per cent of its staff overall (Siddique, 2014). The brain drain is not always necessarily a problem, however; the outflow of professionals may be welcome for those poorer countries that have a surfeit of qualified workers for whom there are enough jobs, emigrants can be valuable channels for ideas and business opportunities back to source countries, and **remittances** sent home to their families by emigrants can play an important role in the economic development of poorer countries. India and China were by far the biggest recipients of remittances in 2016, each attracting payments of more than $60 billion, followed by the Philippines, Mexico, Pakistan and Nigeria (World Bank, 2017).

The impacts of migration tend to have deeper and more lasting effects on receiving countries, mainly because they become the permanent new homes of migrants, who each impact – in their own individual ways – the political, economic and social life in their new homes. Opinion is divided between those who see immigrants as an opportunity and those who see them as a threat – see Table 10.4. The opportunities are provided mainly by the injection of new skills and ideas into receiving countries, while the threats are often a matter of perception rather than of objective analysis, although the ties between immigration and national security have recently moved further up the agenda (see Givens, 2010). The cases of the European Union and the United States illustrate some of the similarities and the differences in the causes and effects of migration.

European Union (EU). Europe has for centuries been the scene of active migration, whether as a result of war or persecution, or in the wake of changing economic opportunities. The movement of people within the region has combined with the redrawing of political borders to create a complex mosaic of states, nations, minorities, and religions. No European state is homogeneous, all of them have national minorities, and the loosening of internal borders within the EU since the 1970s has encouraged new flows of immigrants among its member states, with new migrants from outside Europe adding to the diversity. The resulting changes have led to what Parsons and Smeeding (2006) describe as an 'historic transformation'. Although many Europeans do not like what they see, and there has been a reaction in the form of support for anti-immigrant political parties, there are many others who welcome the new diversity, and yet others who take the pragmatic view that – as Europeans become older and population growth tails off – the region's best hope of maintaining its generous social security arrangements and replenishing its workforce is through immigration.

About ten per cent of the total population of the EU (54 million people) was foreign born in 2015, while the number of unauthorized immigrants probably ran

Table 10.4: The pros and cons of migration

Pros	Cons
Immigrants are highly motivated to succeed.	Not all immigrants bring welcome skills and ideas, or contribute to economic or social growth.
Immigrants often do lower-paid service jobs that long-term residents are unwilling to do.	Immigrants are often accused of taking jobs and depressing wages.
Immigrants often help their home countries through ideas, opportunities, and remittances.	Emigration denies those skills and ideas to the home countries of emigrants.
By retaining links with home, migrants help build stronger international ties and contribute to the social and economic development of their home countries.	Unless migrants can (or are allowed to) integrate, tensions can grow between immigrants and native populations.
A multicultural society is more interesting and dynamic than a homogeneous one.	Immigration can pose a threat to culture and national identity, generating the tensions and segregation arising from multiculturalism.
Migration sends a more positive global message about the host country.	Poorer immigrants might consume more resources in the form of welfare.
With populations becoming older in many wealthy countries, immigration adds younger workers and new taxpayers.	Immigration can add new pressures to countries with already large populations.

into the low millions. The wealthier western member states are – not surprisingly – the strongest magnets, while matters are different in Eastern Europe: it attracted few immigrants during the Cold War, then became an exporter rather than an importer of labour, and even now most states in the region have fewer than five per cent of their population foreign born. It is also important to remember that not everyone wants to come to the EU, and many have left for other parts of the world, as in the case of Spaniards and Portuguese moving to Latin America (Boudreaux and Prada, 2012).

The biggest political challenges have been raised by immigration from outside the EU, for which the EU as a whole has had to work to develop joint policies, the urgency for a resolution growing in the wake of war and instability in North Africa and the Middle East. There have been improvements in managing the EU's external borders, and in cooperation among police forces and border officials, but there is still no common EU immigration policy, thanks mainly to the extent to which immigration sparks public controversy, limiting the amount of political support for a harmonized EU policy that may be either more liberal or more restrictive than national policy (Givens and Luedtke, 2004). There is also widespread support for the view that the member states should have the right to decide how many immigrants they will accept, and a belief that the EU already has enough people, and that it should be tightening rather than loosening its borders.

GLOBAL AND LOCAL 10

GIVING MIGRATION A HUMAN FACE

Migration is a huge phenomenon, generating enormous numbers: 244 million migrants, 66 million forcibly displaced people, 380 million internal immigrants, and 3 million students studying outside their home countries. But global numbers are often cold and impersonal, and they are given more life when reflected in the individual stories of immigrants and their impact at the local level.

▶ A student graduates from a university in India, applies (and is accepted) to a Ph.D programme in political science in the United States, then applies for a tenure-track position at an American university. Her student visa is converted into a work visa, then into a legal residence permit, and she eventually finds herself applying for US citizenship and gradually loosening her ties with 'home'.

▶ A man born and brought up in a small village in Senegal is recruited by a Sufi Muslim movement known as the Mourides (Judah, 2011), which helps him find his way to Italy, where he makes a 'living' selling counterfeit handbags, purses, sunglasses, and even fake phone cards to tourists.

▶ A family from the city of Aleppo in Syria is forced to uproot itself in the face of fighting between government and opposition forces, and to make its way by whatever means possible to Greece, where it is housed in a refugee camp while the father – a successful businessman at home – applies for asylum. But one of the children in the family drowns during the sea crossing.

▶ At the age of 17, a South African named Elon Musk (pictured) moves to Canada, where he obtains citizenship through his mother. He moves to the United States as a student, founding a web software company that he sells when he is 28 for $307 million. He then helps develop the online payment company PayPal, founds the space exploration company SpaceX, and takes over leadership of the electric car company Tesla. By 2017, aged 46, he has a net worth of $15 billion.

Source: Anadolu Agency/Getty Images

▶ Facing insecurity and few job prospects at home, a Pakistani uproots himself from the city of Karachi and applies to become a temporary worker in the nearby United Arab Emirates. There he joins almost 8 million other immigrants who are needed to sustain growth and the high standard of living enjoyed by the oil-rich state.

The United States. The United States has a long history as a country of migrants, its population growing dramatically during the 19th and early 20th centuries with waves of immigrants arriving mainly from Europe. Britain was the earliest source, followed in the mid-19th century by northern Europe (Germans remain to this day

Table 10.5: Comparing migrant numbers in the US and the EU

Place	Population	Authorized immigrants	Unauthorized immigrants	Authorized immigrants as % of total population
European Union	505 million	54 million	Low millions	10
United States	320 million	43 million	11 million	14

Sources: Eurostat at http://ec.europa.eu/eurostat; Migration Policy Institute at http://www.migrationpolicy.org.

this biggest ethnic group in the United States), followed in the early 20th century by immigrants mainly from eastern Europe and Italy, and new waves since 1945 arriving mainly from Latin America and east/southeast Asia. The US also, of course, has the particular experience of the forced migration of several hundred thousand slaves, and has yet to effectively address the tensions and inequalities that have arisen from racism. Related discrimination was also on show in the late 1800s with resentment against the arrival of Irish immigrants, in the 1900s with the arrival of Jewish immigrants, and more recently with the rapidly growing Latino and Asian populations of the country.

The United States remains a major destination for immigration, being home in 2015 to just over 43 million legal residents who were foreign-born. Legal immigrants made up about 13 per cent of the total population, a significant increase since 1970, when they made up just under five per cent of the population. The biggest sources of immigration to the United States are Mexico, India, China, and the Philippines. Meanwhile, the number of unauthorized immigrants in the United States is estimated to be about 11 million, or three per cent of the total population. Emigration has helped make the United States an ethnically diverse country: as of 2015, 62 per cent of Americans were white, 18 per cent were Latino, 12 per cent were black, and 5 per cent were Asian (United States Census Bureau, 2017). Trends suggest that, by mid-century, the United States will no longer have a single racial or ethnic majority.

Unlike the European Union, the United States has a single immigration policy, but like the European Union it faces the same tensions that have arisen from the diversity of immigrants. Concerns about that diversity, combined with concerns about the number of unauthorized immigrants making their way to the country, fed into support for the presidential candidacy of Donald Trump in 2016, and his controversial promise of building a wall along the US–Mexican border, and limiting arrivals from several Muslim countries. White America and white Europe hears the same worried discussions about the changing racial and religious make-up of its homeland, although opinion polls on both sides of the Atlantic find that such concerns are expressed by only a minority of residents.

DISCUSSION QUESTIONS

1. Given the effects of globalization, economic change, and increased mobility, to what extent can migration realistically be limited?

2. What is a migrant?

3. What are the implications of the growing numbers of international university students?

4. Why has progress on the development of a global migration regime been so modest?

5. On balance, is migration a good thing or a bad thing?

6. What are the advantages and disadvantages of a brain drain for both source and destination countries?

KEY CONCEPTS

- Asylum-seeker
- Brain drain
- Brain gain
- Chain migration
- Emigration
- Humanitarian intervention

- Immigration
- Internally displaced person
- Migrant
- Migration
- Mobility
- Nativism

- Pull factors
- Push factors
- Refugee
- Remittances
- Statelessness
- Visa
- Xenophobia

USEFUL WEBSITES

Convention Relating to the Status of Refugees at http://www.unhcr.org/en-us/1951-refugee-convention.html

International Committee of the Red Cross at https://www.icrc.org

International Organization for Migration at https://www.iom.int

International Rescue Committee at https://www.rescue.org

UN High Commissioner for Refugees at http://www.unhcr.org

UN Relief Works Agency at https://www.unrwa.org

FURTHER READING

Collier, Paul (2013) *Exodus: How Migration is Changing our World* (Oxford University Press). An assessment of the motives behind migration, how migrants are perceived, and the effects on the destination countries and those left behind.

Fiddian-Qasmiyeh, Elena, Gil Loescher, Katy Long, and Nando Sigona (eds) (2014) *The Oxford Handbook of Refugee and Forced Migration Studies* (Oxford University Press). An edited collection of studies of the refugee problem, including chapters on its causes and dimensions, and on the legal responses.

Koser, Khalid (2016) *International Migration: A Very Short Introduction*, 2nd edn (Oxford University Press). A brief survey of migration, including chapters on the definition of migrants, unauthorized migration, refugees, and asylum-seekers.

Mavroudi, Elizabeth, and Caroline Nagel (2016) *Global Migration: Patterns, Processes, and Politics* (Routledge). A survey of the politics of migration, looking at its history and the dynamics of the political responses.

Opeskin, Brian, Richard Perruchoud, and Jillyanne Redpath-Cross (eds) (2012) *Foundations of International Migration Law* (Cambridge University Press). An edited collection dealing with aspects of international migration law, including chapters on human rights, patterns of migration, and international institutions.

Online Resources

Visit www.macmillanihe.com/McCormick-GS to access additional materials to support teaching and learning.

ENVIRONMENT

11

PREVIEW

This chapter looks at the environment as a global issue, beginning with an overview of environmental problems, of our changing understanding about their causes and effects, and of the meaning of ideas such as sustainable development. It goes on to look at the global environmental regime, and at the focus and effects of key pieces of international environmental law. The chapter finishes with two cases: the threats faced by biodiversity, followed by the ultimate global threat of climate change. It reviews the causes and effects of both problems, and discusses the political, economic and social arguments that have shaped the response.

HIGHLIGHTS

▸ Environmental problems have both broadened and deepened since the industrial revolution, thanks mainly to population growth, increased resource consumption, and our heavy reliance on pollutive fossil fuels.

▸ As understanding of the dynamics of environmental problems has improved, so there has been a paradigm shift towards the idea of sustainable development.

▸ Awareness of the causes and effects of environmental mismanagement has grown particularly since the 1960s, but the North and the South continue to approach the topic from different perspectives.

▸ A large body of environmental law has been agreed in the post-war era, but much of the pressure for change has come from citizen action rather than government initiative.

▸ The breadth and depth of human activity has made itself felt on biodiversity, with severe threats posed to species and ecosystems.

▸ Climate change stands as the ultimate global problem, having global effects and demanding a global response if it is to be effectively addressed.

Source: iStockphoto

UNDERSTANDING THE ENVIRONMENT

In the late 1980s, scientists studying the Pacific discovered an unusually high concentration of garbage floating over an extended area, carried on ocean currents known as gyres. Although it has since come to be known as the Great Pacific garbage patch, it cannot be seen by the naked eye or by satellites. Instead, it consists of higher concentrations than usual of plastics, chemical sludge, and other forms of waste, all of it suspended in ocean water. Occasionally, smaller patches of visible waste will be found floating in the ocean, or washed up on coasts, emphasizing the way in which humans have long used the oceans as a handy dump for whatever they no longer need. While out of sight may be out of mind, however, much of this waste does not go away, and may even work its way back up the food chain to be eaten by humans.

Ocean waste is just one instance of the damage incurred by human action on the **environment**, which consists of our physical surroundings, combining the natural environment with the built environment: the homes in which we live, the offices in which we work, the shops in which we purchase goods, the towns and cities we have built, and the transport networks we use. Humans (like all living things) have been shaping their environment for millennia, but the changes have accelerated since the industrial revolution. The cumulative effects have been so substantial that some suggest we are today living through a distinctive geological epoch known as the **Anthropocene**. This is a label that was proposed as early as the 1870s, and popularized more recently by the Nobel laureate Paul Crutzen (2002), illustrating the changes made by humans to the earth at least since the industrial era, but perhaps dating back to the agricultural revolution about 12,000 years ago. It is reflected in the growing size of the human population, the spread of human settlements to almost every corner of the world, widespread and often profound changes to landscapes and ecosystems, the rise in levels of airborne and waterborne pollutants, and the sharp increase in the number of species extinctions (Zalasiewicz et al., 2010).

Almost every activity in which humans participate has an environmental dimension, the causes and effects having political, economic, financial, social, and even ethical implications. The effects are felt most notably in the different arenas illustrated in Figure 11.1. Human-induced environmental change is nothing new, with numerous examples dating back thousands of years: they include the build-up of salt in the soils of the Fertile Crescent of the Middle East, the erosion that was implicated in the drought that contributed to the collapse of the Mayan civilization in the 8th and 9th centuries, and the introduction of invasive species and diseases as part of the Columbian Exchange between Europe and the Americas in the 15th and 16th centuries.

The depth and the breadth of the changes has accelerated since the industrial revolution: a combination of mechanization and urbanization, built on a foundation of the use of pollutive fossil fuels such as coal (and later oil and natural gas), and helped along by improvements in transport, social welfare, and medical science that have spurred population growth, demand for natural resources, and our ability to exploit, control and reshape our surroundings (see Josephson, 2012). Initially, the changes took place with little concern about their broader effects in either time or space, but advances in scientific understanding gave us new insights into the environmental costs of industry and urbanization. A turning point in attitudes came in the 1960s,

Environment: The physical surroundings in which an entity – whether a human, animal, plant, insect, bacterium, or an inanimate object – exists.

Anthropocene: The suggested name for a new geological epoch marked by widespread human change to geology and ecosystems.

Figure 11.1: Key environmental concerns

PROBLEM	FEATURES
AIR QUALITY	Threats posed by industrial and vehicle emissions, by coal-fired power stations, and by the burning of wood in cities in the South.
WATER QUALITY	Threats posed by urban and agricultural run-off, by the dumping of waste, and by accidental oil and chemical spills.
CHEMICALS	Their impact on ecosystems and living organisms.
WASTE	Including its production, shipment, and disposal, with distinctions being made between human, municipal, agricultural, industrial and radioactive waste.
NATURAL RESOURCES	Including the use and management of land, forests, fisheries, and crops.
ENERGY	Its production and use, including fossil fuels (coal, oil, and natural gas) and renewables (such as solar, wind, and hydropower).
BIODIVERSITY	Threats ranging from loss of habitat to the effects of invasive species, pollution, population growth, and over-exploitation.

when public opinion in the North became more attuned to the causes and effects of environmental change, and when environmentalists became more politically active, a change that led to the passage of new laws and the creation of the earliest national government departments dealing with the environment.

The new awareness of these problems has also sparked a review of human values, with hard questions being asked about the dominant economic **paradigm**: social welfare is maximized by the free market, there is an infinite supply of natural resources, and rivers, oceans and the air are convenient sinks into which to dump waste. As the effects of this approach have become clearer, **environmentalism** has emerged as a reaction based on pointing out the ways in which the environment – and human welfare – is threatened, arguing not just the political and economic case for change, but also suggesting that humans are ethically responsible for protecting the earth's ecological integrity. At first, the focus of environmentalism was on addressing the visible effects of human activity, including air and water pollution. But science has since taught us more about the nuances of human-induced environmental change, and about its less visible effects on ecosystems, sparking more strategic approaches to addressing those problems, and a search for new paradigms.

One alternative is **sustainable development**, which argues that unrestrained capitalism does not work, and that renewable resources should be more carefully managed so as to ensure their indefinite supply. In the words of a 1987 report

Paradigm: A model, pattern or framework based on the values, beliefs, and ideas that guide action.

Environmentalism: A philosophy, theory, or ideology that encourages deeper understanding of the environmental impact of human actions.

Sustainable development: Economic development that is planned and implemented in such a way as to meet short-term needs without compromising future needs.

Source: Getty Images/National Geographic RF

Few problems exemplify the failure of consumer society as clearly as waste. This Caribbean beach is polluted with waste thrown carelessly into the ocean without much thought for its long-term consequences.

from the UN-sponsored World Commission on Environment and Development, development is sustainable only when it 'meets the needs of the present without compromising the ability of future generations to meet their own needs' (Brundtland et al., 1987: 43). Governments and planners have increasingly adopted this idea, which has moved into the core of decision-making on how best to use resources. The idea has since been broadened with discussions about **green growth**, while the principles of **green politics** are reflected in the work of political parties supporting policies based on sustainability.

There has also been a globalization of awareness about the causes and effects of environmental problems. Initially, these problems – and their solutions – were approached from a local perspective, or from the view that out of sight was out of mind; if pollutants were blown away by the air or washed away into rivers and lakes, they ceased to be of concern. But science soon revealed that this was not the case, and that local problems often became international or global problems. One of the earliest concerns about the global environment was set off by radioactive fallout from atmospheric nuclear tests in the 1950s, which were brought to an end with the 1963 Partial Test Ban Treaty. Later, new concerns would be raised by acid pollution carried across borders by prevailing winds, by damage to the ozone layer caused by synthetic chemicals used in propellants and refrigerants, and by the ultimate global problem of climate change. It also became clear that the causes of environmental problems in wealthier industrialized countries were often different from those in poorer and more rural countries, as were the best responses – see Comparing North and South 11. States could no longer address these problems in isolation.

Another paradigm shift can be found in recent debates about **environmental justice**. This argues the need to make sure that environmental policy is made and

Green growth: Economic growth based on using natural resources and managing the environment in a sustainable manner.

Green politics: A political philosophy based on building a sustainable society rooted in environmental awareness, social justice, non-violence, and grassroots democracy.

Environmental justice: The view that all parties should be treated equally in the development and implementation of environmental planning and policy.

COMPARING NORTH AND SOUTH 11

CONTRASTING PERSPECTIVES ON THE ENVIRONMENT

When environmental consciousness was starting to emerge in the 1960s, it was focused mainly on the problems of industrialized countries, including air pollution, water pollution, the effects of chemicals on nature and on human health, and the problems of waste production and disposal. It was only later that attention was drawn to the often different problems faced by the emerging countries of the South, most of which were rooted in rapid population growth and the kind of poverty that encouraged people to make whatever use they could of resources, without thinking too much about long-term problems such as soil erosion and overfishing. If the North was witnessing the environmental effects of wealth, for the South it was the environmental effects of poverty. Northerners wanted Southerners to learn from their mistakes, but the kinds of changes they suggested were often seen in the South as a brake on their economic development plans.

Most Northerners assume that they will have uninterrupted supplies of food, energy, and the numerous consumer goods they often take for granted. They long paid little attention to the use of chemicals, the environmental effects of the burning of fossil fuels such as coal and oil, the impact of the expanding transport networks needed to carry goods from producer to consumer, or what happened to the waste food, paper, packaging, glass, and metals conveniently collected from their homes by local refuse services. Attitudes have since changed, and most people make more of an effort to consume more carefully, but it is still hard to avoid using electricity generated by coal-fired or nuclear power stations, or to live in homes or to drive road vehicles that are energy inefficient, or to avoid living off chemically based agriculture.

Meanwhile, the environmental effects of poverty in the South can be seen in the often under-regulated growth of cities, resulting in traffic congestion, the use of open fires for cooking and keeping warm, and the expansion of slums that lack clean water or sanitation. In the rural areas of the South, short-term needs might encourage people to cut down trees for fuelwood or to open access to land on which to grow crops, setting aside long-term concerns about the destruction of forest habitats, the worsening of soil erosion, or the siltation of rivers. When you are focused on making a living or feeding your family, the welfare of nature and natural resources will be low down your list of priorities. Many parts of the South are now experiencing the kinds of environmental problems witnessed in the North as a result of the industrial revolution, the difference being that many of those problems come as a result of striving to compete with the North, of supplying the North with cheap consumer goods, and of hosting pollutive industries moved from the North in the wake of a tightening of environmental regulations.

implemented with the involvement of everyone affected, regardless of race, wealth, religion, or any other political, social or economic category (see Walker, 2012). Justice is not served, for example, when used batteries dutifully turned in for recycling by American consumers are sent to Mexico, where the lead is extracted using methods that are illegal in the United States. Or when e-waste in the form of old computers and mobile phones are illegally shipped from Europe to dumps in West Africa. Or when jobs are moved from wealthy countries to poorer countries with weaker environmental laws. Critics of environmentalism have often accused it of being too concerned with the needs and interests of the wealthy, and so focused on making sure that the quality of life for the 'haves' is not compromised that they overlook the needs of the 'have nots' and the often different problems they face. Environmental injustices are often found within countries, but they have become a global problem as the mismatches between the habits and the powers of rich and poor countries have widened.

Not everyone is convinced about the seriousness of environmental problems, or that the laws and regulations adopted in response to those problems are helpful. Just as there has been a growth in support for environmentalism and green policies, so there has been an anti-environmental backlash in many parts of the world. Some have questioned the science behind environmental problems, while others have argued that environmental regulation is a brake on economic development, and continue to place their faith in established technologies and sources of energy, sometimes even suggesting that the claims of environmentalists are just part of an elaborate hoax. As we will see later in this chapter, the doubts and the resistance figure centrally in the debate over climate change, slowing down efforts to change policy.

THE GLOBAL ENVIRONMENTAL REGIME

Before World War II, there was little structured effort made to address environmental problems, in spite of air pollution in major cities and polluted water downstream from factories. The few early initiatives came mainly from non-governmental organizations set up to preserve nature locally or to provide city residents with amenities that would give them respite from polluted air. It was only in the 1960s that a confluence of better scientific understanding and heightened public and political awareness encouraged a more structured response. This began at the domestic level but soon became international as the trans-border qualities of environmental problems were better understood, and as governments began to cooperate on shaping policy. Even so, the environment still does not rank at the top of most national government agendas, and much of the initiative for change has continued to come from citizens and NGOs rather than from government.

Thanks to their efforts, the global environmental regime has grown: there is a substantial body of international environmental law, a large community of governmental and non-governmental organizations, and a better understanding that many environmental problems cannot be resolved by states working alone. Effective management of the Rhine means that the countries through which it flows (Switzerland, France, Germany, and the Netherlands) must work together; Japan must negotiate with China if it is to address air pollution blown on the winds from growing Chinese cities; African and European governments have had to work together to guard against the international dumping of toxic wastes; and – as we saw in Chapter 2 – many natural resources are global resources that need global management.

The body of international environmental law is deep and broad, one database (Mitchell 2016) identifying more than 3,600 international agreements on a wide range of environmental topics, ranging from the narrow and bilateral to the global and multilateral – see Table 11.1 for examples. Most of these agreements have come since 1945 as a result of increased international cooperation on the environment, improved scientific understanding, and expanded public support for action. Quantity

Table 11.1: International environmental treaties: Some examples

Year signed	Where signed	Topic
1946	Washington DC	Whaling
1954	London	Pollution of the sea by oil
1971	Ramsar	Wetlands
1972	London	Marine pollution by dumping of wastes
1973	Washington DC	International trade in endangered species
1979	Geneva	Long-range transboundary air pollution
1979	Bonn	Migratory species of wild animals
1980	Canberra	Antarctic marine living resources
1985	Vienna	Ozone layer
1989	Basel	Transboundary movements and disposal of hazardous wastes
1992	New York	Climate change
1992	Rio de Janeiro	Biological diversity
1994	Vienna	Nuclear safety
1994	Geneva	Tropical timber
2001	Stockholm	Persistent organic pollutants

does not necessarily translate into quality, however, and in spite of the large body of domestic and international law, many environmental trends remain negative, and progress in many areas remains slow. The positions taken by states on environmental problems depend on several key influences:

▸ The extent to which they are affected by environmental problems that cross borders, or to which they need to work with neighbouring states on the management of shared resources such as rivers, lakes, and fisheries. European states have had to work together on air pollution, for example, because they are relatively small and much of their pollution crosses shared borders.

▸ How much states stand to gain or lose in relations with other states. On the one hand, they do not want to bear more than their fair share of the costs involved in addressing a problem, but – on the other hand – they do not want to harm relations with their allies and trading partners. The most persistent challenge in addressing climate change, for example, has been deciding who has the greatest responsibility to reduce greenhouse gas production.

▸ The impact of domestic economic influences, such as the power of key industries, or the relative wealth of states. The major producers and exporters of oil and coal, for example, will take a different position on energy policy than importing states.

▸ The influence of domestic environmental movements and consumer awareness. Environmentalist thinking tends be more advanced, and consumers tend to be more demanding about the environmental impact of the products they buy, in the North as compared to the South.

▸ The place of states in the global economic and trading system. The biggest economic powers have louder voices and wider potential influence than their smaller counterparts, which have tended to be marginalized in the environmental debate.

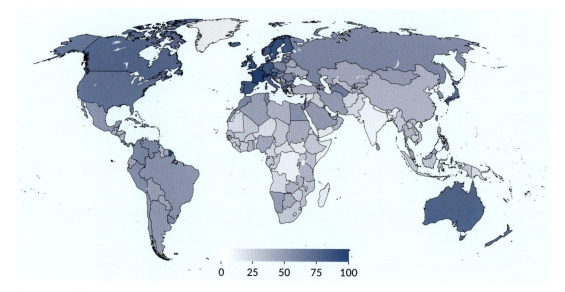

Map 11.1: Environmental Performance Index
Source: Environmental Performance Index 2018.

In addressing environmental problems, some countries have clearly been more active and progressive than others. One indicator of this is the Environmental Performance Index maintained by Yale and Columbia Universities in the United States. This ranks almost all of the countries of the world according to a variety of environmental indicators, giving each a score out of 100. It finds the best results in most European countries (Switzerland topped the list in 2018), along with Australia, Singapore, the United States, and Canada, while India, Bangladesh and several sub-Saharan Africa countries languish at the lower end of the scale – see Map 11.1. The tension between the most and the least active countries is described as the **leader–laggard dynamic**, and has long been at the heart of efforts to achieve positive change on dealing with environmental problems.

Looking at the bigger picture, and referring back to arguments made in Chapter 5, some see the role of states in making environmental policy declining in the wake of globalization, trade, technology transfer, and the key role played by multinational corporations in making the kinds of choices that have the most important impact on environmental policy (see later in this section). But the nature of environmental problems means that international cooperation remains key to making progress, cooperation encouraged by a significant network of international governmental and non-governmental organizations.

Leader–laggard dynamic: The tension between countries taking contrasting positions on environmental policy, often resulting in the need to compromise.

Source: MB Photography

Research sponsored by UNEP has helped give new scientific certainty to the effects of climate change, one of which is the melting of polar ice caps.

The main IGO with an environmental focus is the UN Environment Programme (UNEP), created in 1973 and headquartered in Nairobi, Kenya. Its formal mission is to 'provide leadership and encourage partnership in caring for the environment by inspiring, informing, and enabling nations and peoples to improve their quality of life without compromising that of future generations' (UN Environment Programme, 2017). It does this mainly through monitoring environmental trends, helping develop and sometimes manage international treaties, and promoting education and public information. It has a particular interest in climate change, working with the World Meteorological Organization to co-sponsor the Intergovernmental Panel on Climate Change, created in 1988 to produce assessments of the state of understanding of climate change science. UNEP also planned, organized, and promoted the signature of the 1992 UN Framework Convention on Climate Change.

UNEP faces most of the standard problems faced by IGOs, including a reliance on the voluntary cooperation of states, and few independent powers. It also has a few additional problems related to its specific mission, the biggest of which is structural: unlike specialized and autonomous agencies of the UN (such as the World Bank and the International Monetary Fund), it is a programme of the UN, which means that it lacks the status or independence of an agency, and – as a subsidiary of the UN General Assembly – relies for most of its income on voluntary rather than mandatory contributions from UN member states. It also finds itself at a disadvantage because it must coordinate the work of other UN agencies (which sometimes resent its demands), and must often base its actions on short-term opportunities rather than always working to a long-term plan. Opinion is divided on its performance, with some (such as Biermann and Bauer, 2005) suggesting that it would be better transformed into a new World Environment Organization with more autonomy, a budget based on mandatory contributions, and a stronger voice in UN environmental affairs.

Several other specialized UN agencies have remits that include environmental interests:

▸ The *Food and Agriculture Organization* (FAO) is interested in the effects of environmental problems on the management of land and natural resources.

▸ The *World Meteorological Organization* is deeply involved in generating data and monitoring development on climate change.

▸ The *UN Educational, Scientific and Cultural Organization* (UNESCO) is responsible for the designation of World Biosphere Reserves and World Heritage Sites.

▸ The *World Bank* has changed its lending policies so as to be more supportive of sustainable development.

Many other IGOs have more focused policy or geographical interests, ranging from the management of shared rivers (such as the Danube, the Mekong, and the Niger) to the management of forests, fisheries, and protected areas. As with all IGOs, their powers and results vary according to the amount of authority and support they are given, and the reach of their responsibilities.

One particularly controversial IGO, which deals with an emotional and focused issue, is the International Whaling Commission (IWC). Founded in 1946, its original goal was to ensure the sustainable exploitation of whales, but it has since been the focus of concerted efforts to end whaling altogether. A global moratorium on whaling went into force in 1985, while the Indian Ocean Whale Sanctuary was created in 1979 and the Southern Ocean Whale Sanctuary in 1994, providing areas within which all commercial whaling is prohibited (see Dorsey, 2013). The number of whales caught has fallen dramatically as a result, but Japan, Norway and Iceland have all resisted the pressure to end whaling. Japan continues to catch whales in the interests of what it describes as scientific research, while also arguing that eating whale meat is an important cultural tradition (even though few Japanese actually do so). It has recruited several non-coastal states to the board of the IWC, seeking their support in return for official development aid.

On the non-governmental front, there are numerous domestic NGOs with an interest in the environment, many of which have evolved into international NGOs using a wide range of political, economic and social tools. The oldest national groups date back to the 19th century, and include the Royal Society for the Protection of Birds (UK, founded 1889), Naturschutzbund Deutschland (Germany, 1899), the Norwegian Society for the Conservation of Nature (1914), and Nature Canada (1939). Since the growth of environmental awareness in the 1960s and 1970s, more groups have been founded that work internationally, including the following:

▸ The *World Wide Fund for Nature*, founded in Switzerland in 1961, raises money for the protection of biodiversity, and has national offices in nearly 70 countries.

▸ *Friends of the Earth*, founded in the United States in 1969, has interests in a wide range of environmental issues, with national and local groups in 75 countries.

▸ *Greenpeace*, founded in Canada in 1971, uses direct action and campaigning to draw public attention to problems such as whaling, nuclear power, and pollution.

▸ *Green Cross International*, founded in Switzerland in 1993 by former Soviet leader Mikhail Gorbachev, focuses on the links between the environment, poverty, and security.

▸ The *African Biodiversity Network*, founded in Kenya in 1996, provides coordination for national groups in 12 countries.

Since business plays a pivotal role in both creating and responding to environmental problems, it has been a key actor in shaping (and often blocking) efforts to improve policy. Companies working in the energy industry, agriculture, forestry, and fisheries have been particularly influential, nowhere more so than if they work across borders. Much of what we tend to hear about the environmental role of multinational corporations is controversial at best, and negative at worst. They are routinely charged with placing profits above environmental welfare, and with closing down operations in countries with higher environmental standards and moving them to those with lower standards, as well as cheaper labour. They are also implicated in efforts by poorer countries to exploit their natural resources at almost any cost, a case in point being the role of the big multinational energy companies in carelessly exploiting Nigerian oil. Shell Oil, in particular, has come under scrutiny for its connection with oil spills in Nigeria's south-east Delta region, and has been accused by Amnesty International of impinging on the rights and livelihoods of local people.

But the picture is not that simple. All businesses want to maximize profits, minimize costs, and keep shareholders happy, but they also want to keep their customers happy and to build positive corporate reputations. As consumers (at least those in the North) have demanded more environmental responsibility of themselves and of corporations, so business habits have changed, and many companies have made a virtue out of necessity by capitalizing on claims of their new environmental sensitivity and using it as a marketing tool (see Crane et al., 2009). The movement to encourage **corporate social responsibility** has been gaining ground since the early 1990s, with companies cutting costs by reducing energy inputs and waste, while building greener images that can help attract new customers and create new markets (Schmidheiny, 1992). Many have changed their approach only in response to political and public pressure, to be sure, but many have also self-regulated by going beyond the demands of public policy, and – as we saw with the example of fossil fuels in Chapter 2 – many have led the way in the development of new and greener technologies.

> **Corporate social responsibility**: The argument that corporations should place social and environmental issues at the core of their decision-making.

If businesses do not take the initiative, then consumers can encourage them by making different choices and demands: although one person acting alone will not be able to make much of a difference, if enough consumers change their demands, the cumulative effect can be substantial. Environmental and consumer movements have encouraged people to better understand the links between actions and effects, and to change their consumption habits. But while such change is happening, it remains unusual and unconventional (Shirani et al., 2015), and it is still mainly only a phenomenon among consumers in the North rather than among the growing middle classes of the South.

BIODIVERSITY

The Lord Howe stick insect is a black insect that is about 10 cm (four inches) long as an adult, and is native to a small island about 600 km (370 miles) off the east coast of Australia. Once common, its numbers fell after rats escaped from a ship that ran aground on the island, and it was declared extinct in the 1930s. But it was rediscovered in 2001, becoming what scientists like to call a Lazarus species (one that has come back from the dead), and efforts have since been made to eradicate rats from the island so as to allow the insect to recover.

There might not seem to be cause for concern in the welfare of an obscure species living on an island of which most people have never heard, but the plight of the Lord Howe stick insect exemplifies the way in which human activities have pushed species to the brink of extinction, or beyond. Since the health of the environment is intimately tied to the health of the millions of species that make up the diversity of life on earth, and since the welfare of humans is so intimately tied to the health of the environment, the story of individual species becomes a matter of concern to everyone.

The term **biodiversity** describes the variety of all the species of life that live on earth: their number, the populations of different species, their geographical spread, the genetic variety within species, and the variety of ecosystems and natural habitats (Hall, 2010). The breadth and depth of human activity mean that there are few species that have not been touched, altered, or affected in some way. There are, in turn, many reasons why we should be concerned: as well as the moral and ethical arguments about our responsibility to life on earth, there are practical considerations. The web of life on earth is a vast interconnected system that guarantees our food supplies, releases nutrients into the soil, sustains the water cycle, produces oxygen, ensures decomposition, supplies medicinal products, and helps with recovery from natural disasters. Without that system, life on earth would not be possible, a reality summarized in the warning by the American biologist E. O. Wilson (2007): 'If we were to wipe out insects alone … on this planet – which we are trying hard to do – the rest of life and humanity with it would mostly disappear from the land. And within a few months'.

In spite of what is at stake, we know remarkably little about the condition of biodiversity. We know there is a problem, but we have little real idea about the extent of the problem; we can only guess at the number of species that have ever existed, or that exist today, which means that we can only make educated guesses regarding how many have been threatened or driven to extinction by human action. Estimates of the number of species on earth range from a few million to tens of billions. Research by Locey and Lennon (2016) concludes that there could be as many as one trillion species of microbes alone, of which science had so far identified just 0.001 per cent.

As far as our knowledge of endangered species goes, the authoritative source is the Red List maintained by a Swiss-based INGO, the International Union for Conservation of Nature. But while its 2015 edition contained information on just over 77,000 species, and it has helped draw attention to the plight of so-called 'charismatic megafauna' such as tigers, African elephants, and pandas, it is anyone's guess how far the list is representative of the wider problem of endangered species. Many have almost certainly become extinct without our even knowing, and we have no idea how many more are endangered.

Biodiversity: A contraction of the term *biological diversity*, describing the variety and the populations of the many species of life on earth.

Source: Getty Images/iStockphoto

A bull elephant on the plains beneath Mount Kilimanjaro in Tanzania. The poaching of elephant for ivory exemplifies the problems faced by the world's charismatic megafauna.

While we know little about the variety of life on earth, we have a better idea about the kinds of threats it faces, which have been grouped by Wilson into five types, using the acronym HIPPO – see Figure 11.2. First, there is habitat destruction, stemming mainly from the clearance of forests and other natural vegetation for agriculture, and from urban development. This dates back centuries in those parts of the world that first underwent the agricultural and industrial revolutions, where little today remains in the way of natural habitat. The fastest changes are now coming to those parts of Latin America, Africa, and Asia witnessing the fastest expansion of cities, and the clearance of forests. Tourism also plays a critical role in the damage inflicted on habitats, which is ironic given how much it often relies upon the attractions of nature.

Figure 11.2: The five major threats to biodiversity

THREAT	EXAMPLES
HABITAT DESTRUCTION	Clearance of forests, changes to wetlands, and degradation of mangroves and coral reefs.
INVASIVE SPECIES	Introduction through shipping and trade, planting of crop plants and trees, spread of disease, accidental and deliberate releases.
POLLUTION	Urban run-off, agricultural run-off, extraction and transport of coal and oil, dumping of waste, climate change.
POPULATION	Spread of towns and cities, supporting infrastructure, expansion of demand for resources.
OVERHARVESTING	Unsustainable use of forests, fisheries, food crops.

Source: Based on Wilson (2003).

Second, nature is threatened by the introduction of non-native species to parts of the world that lie beyond their natural geographic range, posing a threat to native species, ecosystems and habitats. One of the more persistent effects of globalization, this happens as a result of the transfer of food and soil, the export of exotic pets, the carrying of diseases by humans, the escape of ornamental plants into the wild, the deliberate introduction of crop plants and trees into new environments, the cleaning out of ballast tanks by ships, and the introduction of insects in wood. Anyone who has travelled internationally will know that immigration checks often include questions about any agricultural products they may be carrying in their luggage. One infamous example of an invasive species was the release in 1859 of a few rabbits on a single farm in Australia for hunting and sport. They quickly multiplied and spread, going on to threaten many of the species of fauna and flora that are unique to Australia. Numerous efforts have been made to contain them, including the building of rabbit-proof fences and the introduction of myxomatosis (a disease that is lethal to rabbits), but nothing has worked.

Third, pollution has been a problem, with – for example – agricultural and urban run-off that harms rivers and lakes, oil drilling and transportation that threatens sensitive ecosystems, and the dumping of waste in such large quantities that enormous floating garbage patches have been found in the Pacific and the Caribbean. The problem has been exported as factories close down in the North and are moved to parts of the South with weaker environmental regulations, and as consumer demand in the North leads to more (and often unregulated) industrial growth in the South, and more coal mining and oil extraction. To all this is now added the problem of climate change – see later in this chapter.

Fourth, threats are posed by expanding human population and its growing needs and demands. Although this is perhaps the most ambiguous of the five major threats, it stems from the expansion of human settlements, the building of infrastructure to support those settlements, and the growing demand for resources such as food and fresh water. Although the populations of most Northern countries have stabilized and even begun to decline in some cases, Northern consumers have deep demands for energy and consumer products (many of which are imported). In the South, meanwhile, populations are often growing fast, with the same effects on biodiversity as the North saw during the industrial revolution.

Finally, overharvesting occurs when species or natural habitats are used unsustainably. We saw in Chapter 2 the implications for forests, oceans, and fisheries, where over-use and bad management not only threaten individual species of trees or fish or food crops on which we rely, but undermine the broader ecosystems in which each is found. So when tropical rain forests are cleared for timber, agriculture, or mining, along with them go rich natural habitats and the multitude of species found in those habitats, many of which have been thought to have gone extinct without ever having been recorded or identified.

The response to these five problems has been piecemeal at best. There are numerous international agreements focused on a type of habitat (such as wetlands, or the Antarctic), on species (such as migratory species in general, or polar bears in particular), or on a phenomenon (such as trade in endangered species such as pandas, tigers, and rhinos), but there is only one that takes the broad view: the 1992 Convention on Biological Diversity. Its initial goal was to encourage states to develop

Source: Getty Images

Tropical forests are home to an abundance of biodiversity, but also face pressing threats as they are cleared for timber, agriculture, and mining.

national biodiversity strategies, to which the overambitious goal was added in 2002 of 'significantly' reducing the rate of biodiversity loss by 2010. This was hard to do given how little certain information we have on the extent of the problem, and when the pressures behind HIPPO are so hard to address. In 2010, the additional goal of 'mainstreaming biodiversity across government and society' by 2020 (by, for example, making people more aware of the value of biodiversity) was introduced into the treaty.

One practical approach to protecting biodiversity has been to set aside protected natural areas, including national parks and nature reserves. The United States became a global leader in 1872 when it created the world's first national park at Yellowstone, since when almost every country has done the same; one estimate (International Union for Conservation of Nature, 2017 suggests that about 10 per cent of the earth's land surface – an area about the size of South America – is now protected in some way. Not only does this fall short of the 17 per cent target set for 2020 by the Convention on Biological Diversity, but the area protected varies dramatically from one country to another, as does the quality of protection.

Efforts have also been made to set up marine reserves, but protecting them has proved even more difficult than protecting reserves on land, particularly given that coral reefs and mangroves (for example) are threatened by broader problems such as climate change. Seventeen mainly tropical countries – including Australia, Brazil, China, Indonesia, Madagascar, Peru, and South Africa – have drawn focused attention because they have been classified as 'megadiverse' in recognition of the number and variety of species to which they are home. But many of them are either rapidly industrializing, have fast-growing populations, or are witnessing significant rates of environmental change thanks to deforestation, leaving them all particularly prone to the effects of HIPPO.

CLIMATE CHANGE

The Maldives is an island state in the Indian Ocean that rarely makes international news headlines; it has a population of about 325,000, and a small economy that relies mainly on tourism. It is also notable for the fact that its highest point is about two metres (6 feet) above sea level, making it particularly susceptible to the danger of storm surges and changes in sea level. Duly alarmed by the threat of rising seas in the wake of **climate change**, the government hit on the idea in October 2009 of holding a cabinet meeting under water, with ministers wearing scuba gear and communicating with white boards and hand signals. The meeting lasted only half an hour, but photographers and journalists wearing snorkelling gear were present, and the event produced an arresting series of images that were taken up worldwide.

Of all the problems and challenges discussed in this book, none is as truly global as climate change. Many of the other phenomena we have reviewed are global in the sense that they are found and experienced all over the world, and are central to our understanding of the global system, and of human society within that system. But they are often experienced differently, and to different degrees, in different places. As we saw in Chapter 10, for example, migration is more critical in those parts of the world witnessing the greatest numbers of emigrants and immigrants, and while human rights theoretically apply to every one of us, the record regarding their protection – as we saw in Chapter 7 – varies from country to country, and among different political, economic and social groups.

By contrast, climate change is global in the sense that none of us can escape its effects. It may be felt more immediately in those parts of the world experiencing the most visible effects (such as melting glaciers, drought, or extreme weather events, among others), but as the global climate changes, it will be hard not to notice. The problem can even be considered existential in the sense that it is grounded in human existence; perhaps not whether we will continue or not to exist as a species, but certainly in the sense that the quality of our existence will change. And while solutions can be explored and imposed at the local, state, or regional level, the response to climate change must be organized and implemented globally. Climate change is, in short, the quintessential global problem, and the ultimate example of the tragedy of the commons discussed in Chapter 2.

The problem stems from human action. The **greenhouse effect** is a natural phenomenon by which solar radiation is trapped within the earth's atmosphere by water vapour, carbon dioxide (CO_2) and methane, creating a climate with stable temperatures that helps makes life on earth possible. The atmosphere has periodically become warmer and colder, and the polar ice caps have contracted and expanded; we know of five ice ages in all, the last of which ended about 10,000 years ago. But what we are witnessing today is an enhanced greenhouse effect tied mainly to our habit of burning coal, oil, and natural gas, leading to higher atmospheric concentrations of carbon dioxide. Added to this, more intensive agriculture has resulted in higher methane emissions, and the removal of forests has reduced the amount of vegetation that acts as a natural sink for CO_2. As the concentrations of greenhouse gases (GHGs) have risen, so have average global temperatures (see Figure 11.3), with multiple consequences:

▸ Weather patterns have changed, with winters and summers in temperate regions becoming milder, and changes to crop-growing patterns.

Climate change: Changes to the global climate resulting from an enhanced greenhouse effect, caused – in turn – by rising concentrations of greenhouse gases such as carbon dioxide, produced mainly by the burning of fossil fuels.

Greenhouse effect: A natural phenomenon involving the trapping in the atmosphere of solar emissions, making possible life on earth as we know it.

▶ There have been more extreme weather events, such as hurricanes, tornadoes, heat waves, droughts, floods, and forest fires.

▶ Ice caps, glaciers, snow-packs and floating ice have melted, while oceans have become warmer, causing the volume of ocean water to expand and coastal water levels to rise.

▶ Multiple threats have been posed to biodiversity and ecosystems, including ecological changes in wetlands and mangrove swamps, and alterations in the routes taken by migratory species.

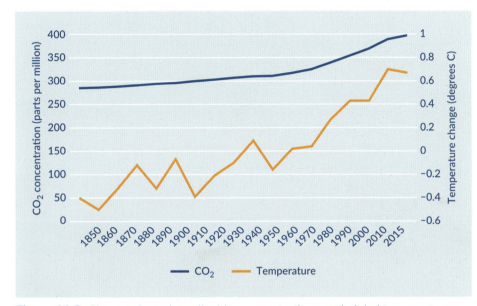

Figure 11.3: Changes in carbon dioxide concentrations and global temperatures
Source: Based on data from US National Oceanic and Atmospheric Administration (2017).

The science of climate change has been understood since the late 1800s, but the problem remained more theoretical than real until data gathered in the 1950s revealed a worrying rise in atmospheric CO_2 concentrations. The first warnings of the potential effects were issued in the 1980s, several international conferences were convened on the topic, and in 1988 the UN founded the Intergovernmental Panel on Climate Change (IPCC) to facilitate the exchange of scientific information on the problem. Negotiations were also held that led to the 1992 signature of the UN Framework Convention on Climate Change. Like most international treaties, it contained only broad principles, the harder commitments being negotiated at subsequent meetings of convention signatories.

Prime among those meetings was the one held in 1997 in Kyoto, Japan, which produced a protocol to the treaty setting targets for specific reductions of greenhouse gas emissions. But there was a difference of opinion about the targets, the time scale involved, and the relative contributions of older industrialized countries and newly industrializing countries. The Kyoto target – a 6–8 per cent reduction in GHG emissions in developed states by 2008–12 from 1990 levels, without any commitments being imposed on developing states – came and went with many countries failing to reach it, and most of the progress stemming either from regional agreements or from changes in energy consumption shaped by market forces.

GLOBAL AND LOCAL 11

CLIMATE CHANGE AND ENVIRONMENTAL MIGRANTS

We saw in Chapter 10 that migration is most often prompted either by economic motives or by war and instability. But another cause is environmental change, as in historical cases of human-induced drought, such as the Dust Bowl mentioned earlier in the chapter. To this list has – more recently – been added climate change and its many actual or potential consequences (see White, 2011); it may be a global problem, but its effects are felt locally as tropical storms and hurricanes become more intense, as droughts and forest fires become more common, and as rising waters soak coastal cities and communities. And while most of the pollutants that have caused climate change come from the major industrial centres of the world, the effects are felt everywhere, potentially creating a new class of **environmental migrants**.

Taking just the issue of potential rises in sea level, many of the biggest cities in the world lie on coasts, and many have already experienced flooding in the wake of more extreme hurricanes, typhoons, and tsunamis. Among the cities most at risk from rises in sea level are Dhaka, Jakarta, Lagos, London, Miami, Mumbai, New York, Sao Paulo, and Shanghai. Each will either have to make substantial investments in protecting itself from flooding, or will find its residents selling up and leaving for higher ground. It is hard to predict the size of this new wave of migration with any certainty, but it promises to be substantial.

Climate change is also predicted to change crop-growing patterns. The capacity to grow crops and support livestock depends on the right combination of soil quality, temperature, precipitation, and pasture for livestock, as well as the ability to fight off disease and pests. If temperatures become too warm, if water supply declines, and if pests and diseases proliferate – all of which are likely if climate changes – then crop yields will fall. The Food and Agriculture Organization of the UN (2017b) notes that the world currently produces more than enough food to meet human needs, but it also points out that 815 million people (11 per cent of the global population) regularly go hungry, that world hunger is on the rise, and that the food security situation has 'visibly worsened' in those parts of sub-Saharan Africa, south-eastern and western Asia most impacted by conflict and by 'climate-related shocks'.

Continued global changes of this kind will undermine the wealth of local agricultural communities, which will only be able to survive with investments in water supply and improved plant nutrition, or government subsidy. This may work for wealthier countries with advanced agricultural industries, but it will be much harder for poorer countries, particularly those in Africa facing the twin prospects of declining food production and growing population. Many already face serious refugee problems, which are likely only to worsen in the face of climate change.

Environmental migrants: People obliged to relocate as a result of environmental disruptions such as drought, soil erosion, desertification, and climate change.

▶ In the case of regional agreements, the European Union – which had already seen its CO_2 emissions fall slightly since 1990 – set its own ambitious goal in 2007 of a 20 per cent reduction in GHG emissions by 2020, from a 1990 base (see Delreux and Happaerts, 2016, Chapter 9). It set out to achieve this mainly with a market-based emissions trading scheme based on setting air quality standards in a given area, setting caps on emission levels, and allowing affected industries that are below the levels to trade the right to pollute with those that are above the levels. The results were positive: a 21 per cent cut in CO_2 emissions between 1990 and

2014 (Netherlands Environmental Assessment Agency, 2015), meeting its 2020 goal several years ahead of schedule. But at least part of the reduction has been the result – ironically – of warmer winters, and of outsourcing manufacturing to other countries, such as China.

▶ In the United States, meanwhile, market forces have been more important. It has cut its GHG emissions, but mainly because coal is expensive and dirty to extract and transport, because many American power companies have made the switch to cheaper and cleaner natural gas, and because many manufacturing jobs have gone overseas. American CO_2 emissions grew in the 1990s before levelling off and then falling by ten per cent between 2005 and 2014.

With the demise of the Kyoto protocol in 2012, new negotiations were launched, resulting in a new climate change accord in Paris in December 2015. This was acclaimed as a breakthrough, committing signatories to making efforts to hold the global average temperature to 'well below' 2°C (3.6°F) above pre-industrial levels, and to achieve a global peaking of GHG emissions 'as soon as possible'. In other words, it set a temperature ceiling rather than the kinds of emissions targets included in Kyoto, and left it up to signatories to develop their own plans, the emphasis being on the need to move away from fossil fuels and towards renewable sources of energy such as solar, wind and hydro power. So many countries rushed to ratify it that the accord came into force in 2016, four years ahead of schedule. The Obama administration in the United States supported the agreement, but the Trump administration moved quickly in 2017 to withdraw, leaving the United States as the only country in the world not to support the accord.

In order to understand the dynamics of the response to climate change, we must understand the contrasting positions of different groups of countries. The biggest producers of carbon dioxide (in absolute terms) are China, the United States, India, the European Union, and Russia (in that order), who among them account for 70 per cent of global production. At first glance, then, these would seem to be the parts of the world with the most responsibility for taking action. But while the EU has indeed taken action, the US position is influenced by the size and reach of its energy and automobile industries, and by anti-regulation sentiment on the political right. There are still many Americans who question the link between climate change and human activity, who want to protect the interests of the domestic coal industry, and who argue that the US should not have to take action without reciprocal action on the part of China and India, whose emissions grew – respectively – fourfold and sevenfold between 1990 and 2014 – see Figure 11.4. But the US produces far more carbon dioxide per person (16 tonnes) than China and India (8 tonnes and 4 tonnes, respectively), and thus might reasonably be expected to be held to higher targets.

Meanwhile, emerging economies have a point when they argue that they should not have their development plans undermined by emissions limits when the older industrialized countries have spent decades building their economies on the back of mainly uncontrolled air pollution; the North created the problem, runs the logic, and so should be taking the lead in fixing it. The so-called BASIC states (Brazil, South Africa, India and China) have played a particularly prominent role in the debate (Hochstetler and Milkoreit, 2015), committing to work together but also to walk away as a group should their demands not be met.

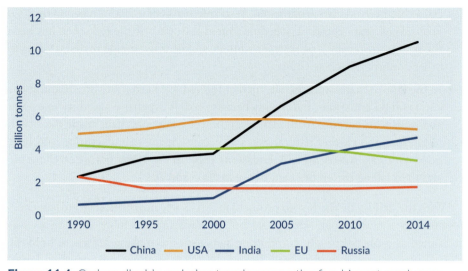

Figure 11.4: Carbon dioxide emission trends among the five biggest producers
Source: Based on data in Netherlands Environmental Assessment Agency (2015).

While the major oil-producing states worry about the economic impact of a switch to renewable sources of energy, many countries rich in tropical forests have lobbied for increased investments from the North in forests as carbon sinks, and a group of more than 40 small coastal and island states see themselves most immediately threatened by the impact of rising sea levels, but are also too small and relatively poor to have much political or economic leverage. Questions have also been asked about whether emission reductions should be based on overall output, per capita output, output per unit of GDP, current emission levels, or historic emission levels, how much credit should be given for past reductions, and how much credit should be given for efforts to plant forests.

The problem of climate change is enormous, cutting as it does to the heart of entire economic systems. Almost everywhere in the world, people depend on coal, oil and natural gas for energy (as well as fuelwood in many parts of the South), agriculture has become increasingly intensive, and forests (natural sinks for carbon dioxide) have been cleared more vigorously. To encourage changes in the kinds of activities that have sparked climate change, and to do so quickly enough to slow that change before the effects become irreversible, is a tall order. Progress to date has been mixed at best, the gains made in Europe and North America being more than offset by the growth of emissions in China and India.

DISCUSSION QUESTIONS

1. Is the dominant economic paradigm still dominant?

2. How can the contrasting environmental views of the North and the South be resolved?

3. Would the transformation of UNEP into a World Environment Organization help improve the international response to environmental problems?

4. Who is most culpable for creating environmental problems: businesses or consumers?

5. What kind of argument is likely to be most telling in addressing the difficulties faced by biodiversity: ethical, ecological, or practical?

6. Given free rein, how would you go about addressing the problem of climate change?

KEY CONCEPTS

- ▸ Anthropocene
- ▸ Biodiversity
- ▸ Climate change
- ▸ Corporate social responsibility
- ▸ Environment
- ▸ Environmental justice
- ▸ Environmental migrants
- ▸ Environmentalism
- ▸ Green growth
- ▸ Green politics
- ▸ Greenhouse effect
- ▸ Leader–laggard dynamic
- ▸ Paradigm
- ▸ Sustainable development

USEFUL WEBSITES

Environmental Performance Index at http://epi.yale.edu

Intergovernmental Panel on Climate Change at http://www.ipcc.ch

UN Environment Programme at https://www.unenvironment.org

FURTHER READING

Biermann, Frank, and Philipp H. Pattberg (eds) (2012) *Global Environmental Governance Reconsidered* (MIT Press). An edited collection that looks at recent developments in organizations active on environmental matters at the global level, the mechanisms they use, and the links among them.

Dinar, Shlomi (ed) (2011) *Beyond Resource Wars: Scarcity, Environmental Degradation, and International Cooperation* (MIT Press). An edited collection which argues that environmental scarcity and degradation can spark conflict, but that they can also provide an impetus for cooperation and negotiation between states.

Maslin, Mark (2014) *Climate Change: A Very Short Introduction*, 3rd edn (Oxford University Press). A short survey of the science, effects, responses, and solutions to climate change.

McCormick, John (2018) *Environmental Politics and Policy* (Palgrave). An overview of the nature of environmental problems and policy, contrasting national and global approaches, and including chapters on problems such as air and water pollution, waste, and climate change.

Wilson, Edward O. (2010) *The Diversity of Life* (Harvard University Press). A review (first published in 1992) of the scale of earth's biodiversity by the Pulitzer Prize-winning American biologist.

Online Resources

Visit www.macmillanihe.com/McCormick-GS to access additional materials to support teaching and learning.

WAR AND PEACE

12

PREVIEW

This chapter looks at the meaning of war and peace. It begins with a discussion of the different kinds and causes of war, noting the increased rarity of interstate wars. It then discusses the qualities of peace, noting the differences between the absence of war (negative peace) and efforts made to sustain a positive peace. It then looks at the structure and the personality of the global security regime, focusing on the kind of peacekeeping operations in which the United Nations participates. The chapter ends with a discussion of terrorism: its meaning and causes, and responses to the threats it poses.

HIGHLIGHTS

▸ War has been far more extensively studied than peace, meaning that we have a better understanding of the causes of war than of the conditions needed for peace.

▸ The definition of the terms *war* and *peace* is unclear, raising many problems about how we understand and discuss them.

▸ Peace is much more than the absence of war, although it is questionable whether true peace can be attained without the absence of the kinds of pressures that lead to war.

▸ We have made little progress in achieving Kant's conditions for the attainment of perpetual peace.

▸ The global security regime consists of a combination of diplomacy, negotiations through the United Nations, peacekeeping, and collective security agreements.

▸ For many people, terrorism is now a more serious threat than that of interstate war.

Source: Superstock

UNDERSTANDING WAR

At 9.02am on 27 August 1896, a small flotilla of British naval vessels opened fire on the palace of the Sultan of Zanzibar, an island off the eastern coast of Africa that is today part of Tanzania. The attack was sparked by a dispute over a succession in power, when a pro-British Sultan died and was succeeded by someone the British did not support. The new Sultan was given an ultimatum: step down, or face the consequences. He held his ground, and the bombardment began. It lasted about 38 minutes, leaving an estimated 500 killed or wounded, and resulting in the capitulation of the new Sultan, who was replaced with a leader more conducive to British interests. The event is often described as the shortest war in history, but was it really a war? And if not, why not?

Looking at more recent events, the United States has famously been involved in numerous conflicts since 1945, in Korea, Vietnam, Lebanon, Bosnia, Afghanistan, and Iraq, to name a few. Hundreds of thousands have died along the way, often massive physical damage has been left behind, and the confrontations have had all the features of the kind of large-scale and state-sponsored violence we associate with war. And yet the last time that the United States formally declared war on another country was in June 1942, when it made a declaration against Bulgaria, Hungary and Romania. Does this mean that it has not been at war since the end of World War II in 1945? And if not, what were those conflicts in Vietnam and Iraq?

It is ironic that while humans are fascinated by war, and have gone to war with one another with depressing frequency over the centuries, they have failed to develop a clear definition of the term. It is not for want of trying, because – as we will see later in this chapter – war has been studied in much greater depth than peace. And yet the term continues to overlap loosely with others such as *armed conflict*, *police action*, and *extended military engagement*. It is also used freely and even arbitrarily in multiple more marginal contexts, such as the 'war' on drugs, the 'war' on poverty, or the 'war' on hunger.

To further complicate matters, war is not only an act but can also be seen as a condition: states can be at war not only when their armed forces are actively engaged with one another, but also when they are in a state of disagreement that they plan to resolve by force, whether or not they have made a public declaration to that effect. For example, Britain and Germany were formally at war from 3 September 1939, but hostilities did not break out in a sustained manner for another eight months, ending the period which later became known as the 'phoney war'. And while fighting in the Korean War ended with an armistice signed in July 1953, no peace treaty was ever signed, meaning that the two Koreas are still technically at war with one another.

War is normally understood to mean sustained armed conflict between states, a view reflected in Common Article 2 of the Geneva Conventions, which defines interstate armed conflict as 'declared war or any other armed conflict which may arise' between two or more contracting parties of the conventions, even if the state of war is not recognized by one of them. There is no discussion of the length of the conflict or the number of casualties, or even the need for actual fighting. There is also no mention of anything other than fighting between states, and no mention of conflicts or wars within states. A Protocol to the Conventions was agreed in 1977 to the effect that international armed conflicts included those 'in which peoples are fighting against colonial domination and alien occupation and against racist regimes in the exercise of their right to self-determination'. This inclusion of non-state actors

War: A period of sustained, coordinated violence involving states, non-state actors, and/or groups within states.

was controversial, and discouraged countries such as the United States, India, Iraq and Israel from signing on to the protocol.

One effort to define war, by the US-based Correlates of War Project (2017), settled on the arbitrary idea that a war was a conflict involving at least 1,000 battlefield deaths. Using this definition, the 1969 'Football War' between El Salvador and Honduras (when tensions between the two countries spilled over into violence during a round of qualifying matches for the 1970 football World Cup) was a war because it resulted in about 2,000 deaths, even though it lasted barely 100 hours. Meanwhile, the Falklands War (a large-scale military operation by Britain to expel Argentinian invaders from the Falkland Islands in the South Atlantic in 1982) was technically not a war, because there were only 907 deaths (Gvosdev and Stigler, 2011).

The need for a definition is important because states at war with one another are subject to particular legal rights and humanitarian obligations that may not exist outside wartime conditions. For example, the Geneva Conventions on the treatment of wounded military personnel, prisoners of war, and civilians apply only during times of significant armed conflict. The need for a definition became particularly obvious after the September 2001 terrorist attacks in the United States, when the Bush administration declared a 'global war on terror', giving itself the right to belligerent privileges normally applicable only during a time of armed conflict: it, for example, could keep detainees incarcerated indefinitely at the Guantanamo Bay prison in Cuba, and it could – without warning and with full immunity – launch drone strikes against what it defined as legitimate targets.

Prompted by this anomaly, the International Law Association launched in 2005 a five-year study of the meaning of war, pointing out that while the effort to develop legal controls on war had resulted in 'an impressive collection of institutions, rules, norms, and principles', there was still no clear definition of war in international law (O'Connell, 2012). Part of the explanation, noted the report, was that war was often 'obvious': when there was major fighting between the armed forces of states or well-organized fighting forces within states, war was clearly under way. The report went on to point out that the term *armed conflict* was being used more often than *war* by the international community, that armed conflict existed only when there was an 'intense exchange of fighting by organized armed groups', and that not every engagement of armed forces could be considered an armed conflict, least of all where no damage or deaths occurred. It concluded by defining armed conflict as intense armed fighting between organized groups.

For present purposes, we will use the definition developed by Levy and Thompson (2010), who suggest that war is a condition involving 'sustained, coordinated violence between political organizations'. They go on to specify that war is violent (distinguishing it from conflicts of interest, rivalries, and threats of force), that it must involve at least two reciprocating actors, and that it must involve organizations (which can be states, groups within states, or non-state actors such as terrorist organizations) rather than individuals, that it must have a purpose, and that it must go beyond short-term skirmishes and clashes. We should also note that there are several different kinds of war:

▶ *Civil war* involves parties and citizens within the same state. Many of today's wars are civil, often based – at least in Africa – on disputes sparked by disagreements over territory, resources, or control of governments. Afghanistan, Iraq, Libya,

> **Civil war**: A conflict between parties and citizens within the same state, nation or community.

GLOBAL AND LOCAL 12

WARS BETWEEN AND WITHIN STATES

Although war is conventionally regarded as involving conflict between or among states, interstate wars are becoming increasingly rare. Slaughter (2011) suggests that the era of large-scale multi-year conflicts might be over, and that future conflicts are more likely to be fought on the digital frontier, using special forces, or targeting individuals rather than states. Aside from the US-led invasions of Afghanistan and Iraq, the most damaging and disruptive conflicts of recent decades have been civil wars, including those in Colombia, Libya, Somalia, Sudan, Syria, and Yemen.

There are several possible explanations for these trends, including the improved use of diplomatic tools to resolve disagreements before they break down in violence, the ability of ordinary people to use social media and other means to mobilize and turn their disapproval of war into political action, and the role played by globalization in strengthening the economic links among countries, making them less inclined to go to war – see the discussion about democratic peace theory in Comparing North and South 12. The global element of this box, then, is less about the global or international scale of war than about the impact of deepened global connections on pushing states away from war.

The local element enters into the equation through the persistence of civil wars in many Southern states, particularly those in Africa. In many African states, at least one of the root causes of civil war is the heritage of colonialism (see Comparing North and South 12), but in other parts of the world they stem from a variety of mainly localized reasons that are often hard to summarize. In the case of the Colombian civil war (under way since the early 1960s), a dispute over land ownership dating back to the 1920s spilled over into US-led efforts to undermine communist influence in the country during the Cold War, which spilled over into violence associated with drug trafficking. In the case of the Syrian civil war (under way since 2011), pre-existing discontent with the authoritarian regime of President Bashar al-Assad fed into the democracy movement sparked by the Arab Spring to encourage opposition groups to attempt a violent overthrow of the regime, which was met with extreme violence by the national military. Matters were made worse in 2013 when ISIS become involved in the conflict.

Syria, and Yemen have all recently been the sites of civil wars, most of which are ongoing.

▶ *Guerrilla war* involves insurgents fighting governments with small arms, using a combination of sabotage and hit-and-run tactics. One of the most notable examples was the insurgency that brought Fidel Castro to power in Cuba in 1959.

▶ A *cold war* is characterized by a contest involving ideas rather than direct military engagement, but might include – as in the case of the Cold War between the US and the Soviets from the late 1940s to 1990 – military conflict through surrogates, known as proxy wars. Cold War proxy wars included those in Korea and Vietnam.

▶ *Total war* describes an unrestricted conflict in which all resources are mobilized, war is given priority over all else, and military and civilian targets are included. The two world wars stand as prime examples.

▶ *World war* involves many different states in different parts of the world. Only World War I (1914–18) and World War II (1939–45) have been labelled as such, but the Seven Years' War (1754–63) was arguably a global conflict, because it involved most of Europe as well as Russia and the Americas.

Source: AFP/Getty Images

Smoke billows following Syrian government bombardments against rebels on the outskirts of the capital of Damascus. The Syrian civil war has been one of the deadliest in recent history, taking hundreds of thousands of lives.

As for the wars currently under way in the world (see Table 12.1), there is no definitive list, a reflection of the difficulties in defining war and of the on-again/off-again nature of many conflicts. In the latter case, the dispute between India and Pakistan over Kashmir that began in 1947 has never really gone away, and has resulted in 47,000 fatalities during periods ranging between unrest and outright war.

Table 12.1: Wars currently under way

Location	Start of conflict	Estimated fatalities to date
Afghanistan	1978 (USSR 1979–89)	1.25–2 million
Democratic Republic of Congo	1994	1–6 million
Iraq	2003 (US-led invasion)	250,000–1 million
West Africa – Boko Haram insurgency	2009	40,000–50,000
Syria	2011	300,000–500,000
Yemen	2015	10,000

The same applies to the conflict in the Democratic Republic of the Congo, at its peak between 1994 and 2003, but which has never entirely gone away. Despite the violence and disruption, notes *The Economist* (2018), 'scarcely any outsider has a clue what the fighting was about or who was killing whom'. The longest sustained periods of fighting and accumulations of fatalities have occurred in a combination of civil wars, insurgencies, and invasions in Afghanistan, Iraq, West Africa, Mexico, and Syria. The risks to security – whether domestic or global – are better reflected not in the number of wars under way, but in different levels of political stability. As we saw in Chapter 5, one such ranking is the Fragile States Index based on such indicators as economic development, human rights, demographic pressures, group grievances, and external intervention. Map 12.1 shows the overlap between instability and conflict, the prospects for war being greatest in Africa and parts of the Middle East.

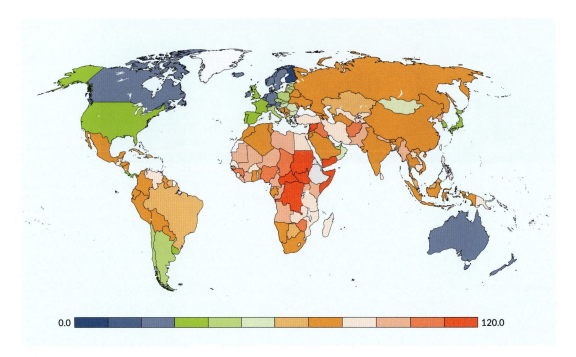

Map 12.1: Fragile States Index
Source: Based on Fund for Peace (2017). Scale runs from most stable (blue) to least stable (red).

THE CAUSES OF WAR

Although war and peace are often seen as two sides of the same coin, war has been far more extensively studied than peace. 'For every thousand pages published on the causes of wars', argues Blainey (1988), 'there is less than one page directly on the causes of peace'. One explanation for this, he argues, is the widespread (and inaccurate) assumption that peace is the normal state of affairs, and hence is less interesting as an object of study than war. Another is that research archives have numerous historical documents on the causes of war, simply because war is more newsworthy than peace. There is just as much documentation on peace he notes, but it is less obvious and attracts less attention.

At least part of the persistent human interest in war stems from its drama, encapsulated in the myth about war described by Fox (2014): 'the history of humankind is equivalent to the story of great deeds done by famous rulers and leaders (mostly men) and the wars they have prepared for and fought. Peace, viewed from this standpoint, consists of the dull, uneventful periods between wars that are unworthy of examination'. Expanding on this idea, military strength has often been associated closely with national identity, the regional or global reach of states being defined by their capacity (or lack of capacity) to wage war.

In spite of the many studies of war, and the development of many theories regarding how they start, there is no such thing as a universal explanation for the cause of war. Instead, it is clear that the disagreements that lead to war differ by time, place, and by the capabilities and attitudes of the combatants. Many subsidiary questions come to bear:

▶ What makes war possible?

▶ Why do wars occur when they do?

▶ Why are some states more often engaged in war than others?

▶ Are wars simply accidents waiting to happen?

▶ What are the historical and cultural contexts that lead to war?

▶ Are there common themes, or is every war different?

▶ How do we explain the origins of particular wars?

Much of the debate revolves around the competing views of **realism** and **liberalism** in the study of international relations (as well as the study of the global economy). On the one hand, realists argue that wars happen because of the anarchic nature of the global system, which leaves the world without the kind of international authority needed to help address the tensions that arise from the rational self-interest of states. States are motivated to use conflict and cooperation to ensure their security and to protect their interests in an anarchic global system. On the other hand, liberals argue that international cooperation is both possible and desirable, and that war is not inevitable. Although many efforts have been made over the centuries to set up mechanisms by which states can resolve their disputes without resorting to violence – the League of Nations and the United Nations being the most recent – war is not illegal, and there is no higher authority above the level of states with the capacity to prevent war or to stop it once it has started.

The clearest cause of war is the perception by one party that it is threatened by another. If one attacks the other, or poses a real and immediate security threat, war is likely to follow. But threats are sometimes imagined or contrived rather than real, the tensions that lead to war instead stemming from deep ideological or religious differences, from fear, from a desire by a state to assert itself, or from an effort by a leader to distract the citizenry from domestic political problems. In some instances, the case can be made for **just war**, but the problem with morality is that it is a subjective concept, since humans have different moral compasses. But if a war is to be considered just, it must include all of the following features: there must be

Realism: The theory that we live in an anarchic global system (one without rules or an authority above the level of the state), and that international relations are driven by a struggle for power among self-interested states.

Liberalism: The theory that international cooperation is possible and desirable, that war is not inevitable, and that international organizations and international law are important in understanding and driving international relations.

Just war: War that is morally defensible.

a reasonable cause, war must be used only as a last resort, it must be waged by a legitimate authority, it can only be fought to redress a wrong suffered, it must have a reasonable chance of success, the end must be proportional to the means used, it must focus on legitimate targets (excluding civilians), and its end goal must be to re-establish peace (see Walzer, 2015).

The justice of war is usually relatively clear when a state uses violence in self-defence. The problem, though, is that self-defence is an easy concept to abuse, particularly when pre-emptive invasions are launched or threatened, and it might be difficult to determine if the supposed threat was real. There was a strong moral argument in favour of Britain and France declaring war on Germany on 3 September 1939. The spark was the German invasion of Poland, to which Britain and France had given defence guarantees several months before, but the broader motivation was the need to stop Nazi expansionism; it was a war in which the forces of good and bad, of right and wrong, were relatively easy to identify.

But many other wars have had questionable causes, as in the case of two launched by the United States. The first was the Vietnam War (known to the Vietnamese as the American War), the escalation of which was based on the questionable domino theory that if one Southeast Asian state fell to communism, the others would follow. There was no clear threat to US security, the steady escalation of the conflict soon became controversial, and the war ended in American defeat in 1975.

The second war with questionable merit was the US-led invasion of Iraq, which was portrayed by some in the Bush administration as a response to the terrorist attacks of September 2001, even though the latter were carried out by 19 Saudi Arabian nationals on the instructions of al-Qaeda. An invasion of Afghanistan was launched less than a month after the 9/11 attacks on the basis that al-Qaeda was being harboured by the Taliban in Afghanistan, but the link between Iraq and the 9/11 attacks was never established. Instead, the US and its British allies claimed that the regime of Saddam Hussein in Iraq either possessed or had plans to develop biological and chemical weapons of mass destruction. While Saddam had used chemical weapons against Iraqi Kurds in the 1980s, no such weapons were found after the US-led invasion, and it was later established that Iraq had ceased their production and stockpiling.

Some insight into the causes of war can be gleaned by looking at the types of wars that have been fought over time, including the following:

▶ *Religious war* is based on religious differences, as in the case of many fought in Europe prior to the 19th century, the more recent wars between Hindu India and Muslim Pakistan, and the current conflict between the West and Islamic militants.

▶ *Wars of conquest*, as in the case of many invasions launched during the imperial era by the Spanish, the French, and the British. Such wars are no longer common, one of the few more recent examples being the invasion of Kuwait by Saddam Hussein in 1990.

▶ *Wars of independence*, where movements have fought for self-determination from a colonial power. Recent examples include the wars of independence fought in the former Yugoslavia in the early 1990s, resulting in the establishment of Slovenia, Croatia, Bosnia, and Kosovo, and those resulting in the creation of Eritrea and South Sudan.

▶ *Territorial wars*, sparked by disputes over borders or attempted secessions. The unresolved dispute between India and Pakistan over Kashmir is a prime example, as is the dispute over territory between Israel and the Palestinians that has been under way since 1948, and has several times spilled over into all-out conflict.

The causes of war, then, are many and varied, and we must be careful to make a distinction between their apparent causes and their actual causes. There is rarely a straightforward explanation when it comes to determining why one state goes to war with another. And, as we will now see, there is rarely a straightforward explanation when it comes to deciding how to achieve and maintain peace, whether within or among states.

UNDERSTANDING PEACE

As we have seen, **peace** has been studied far less thoroughly then war, in spite of the fact that it has been much more common (and desirable) than war. To some extent it suffers from the problem mentioned by Blainey (1988), that it is considered the normal state of affairs, or the default position. Hence being at peace is not considered to be unusual, while war and conflict – inspired by their dramatic qualities – are more unusual and interesting, and hence more deeply studied. But it could also be argued that while it has been relatively easy to establish the different types of conditions that lead to war, greater rewards are promised for establishing the conditions that lead to peace.

The simplest (and most simplistic) definition of peace is the absence of war, a condition described by the German philosopher Johan Galtung as **negative peace**. But can there truly be peace without the absence also of the kinds of pressures that lead to war? As Albert Einstein argued, 'You cannot simultaneously prevent and prepare for war' (quoted in Nathan and Norden, 1960). If states have the capacity to wage war, and continue to prepare for war by maintaining militaries, then the best that can be said is that they are in a temporary or conditional state of peace. Most of the Cold War period between the late 1940s and 1991 was peaceful (other than wars fought through surrogates of the Americans and the Soviets), but overall peace was maintained only because the nuclear powers had the capacity to launch wars on a global scale; this idea of mutually assured destruction (MAD) could hardly be described as a desirable form of peace. True peace exists only when there is no likelihood of the outbreak of war, when states and other parties have the capacity to disagree without resorting (or even threatening to resort) to violence, and when no preparations are being made for war.

Is true peace possible, then, given that most states maintain militaries? If so, then only about two dozen states (see later in this section) are in a true state of peace, because they have no standing armies, or maintain only limited defence forces. Perhaps we could broaden the definition to include states that maintain militaries only for self-defence, such as Japan. And perhaps we could broaden it further by including states that maintain militaries but pursue a policy of **neutrality** in world affairs, such as Austria, Finland, Ireland, Sweden, and Switzerland. Or perhaps it does not matter whether militaries are present or absent, so long as active efforts are made to avoid conflict through diplomacy, justice, and human rights for all, creating a condition of **positive peace**.

Peace: A condition in which different parties are able to disagree without resorting to violence.

Negative peace: A peace defined by the absence of violence, as opposed to the efforts to maintain a sustained peace found in the case of positive peace.

Neutrality: A policy based on avoiding wars and on not taking sides in conflicts involving other states.

Positive peace: A peace sustained by positive efforts to avoid conflict through the building of systems and networks promoting the constructive resolution of disagreements, and ensuring equal access to opportunities and resources for all.

We should also ask ourselves whether peace should only be defined in relation to war and the maintenance of militaries, because the kinds of violence that disrupt peaceful coexistence do not stop with the capacity to wage war. Terrorism, for example, is incompatible with peace, and violence is not just about efforts to kill and wound; the maintenance of discriminatory institutions and practices can harm people psychologically, socially, and economically, preventing them from having access to basic needs and opportunities in a phenomenon known as **structural violence**. While this is not necessarily based on the maintenance and use of militaries, it can result in similar levels of suffering. But unlike physical violence or war, which can be brought to an end through peace agreements, structural violence is more difficult to address because it is built into the structure of society. The kind of structural violence implicated in the creation of poverty, for example, is not only sometimes hard to identify, but also hard to stop.

The Holy Grail is the kind of **perpetual peace** described by the British philosopher Jeremy Bentham in his 1789 *Plan for an Universal and Perpetual Peace*, and made more famous six years later by the German philosopher Immanuel Kant (1724–1804) in his essay *Perpetual Peace: A Philosophical Essay* (Kant, [1795] 2009). Arguing that the natural state of humans living side by side was one of war (by which he meant open hostilities or the threat of war), Kant wrote that, to be meaningful, a state of peace had to be established, rather than simply relying on an absence of hostilities (see discussion in Bohman and Lutz-Bachmann, 1997). He then listed the conditions that he thought were required, including the following:

> **Structural violence**: The maintenance of processes and conditions that trap people through discrimination, degradation, and abuse.

> **Perpetual peace**: A peace that is permanent and sustainable, and made possible by the absence of the conditions that can lead to war.

▸ No peace treaties should be signed that held out prospects for future war (otherwise they would be no more than truces).

▸ No states should come under the dominion of other states.

▸ Standing armies should be abolished.

▸ States should not permit acts of hostility during war that would undermine confidence in the subsequent peace.

▸ States should live under a league of peace (seeking to end all wars forever) as distinct from a treaty of peace (seeking to end only one war).

▸ Peaceful strangers should not be treated as enemies.

Few of these conditions have been met by most states, so we can reasonably conclude that we live in a global system that is some way from achieving a condition of perpetual peace. But this begs the obvious question of why this should be so. Many point the finger of blame at states, which have been the major protagonists in wars, and even create the pressures that lead to civil wars. Perhaps, then, if we could do away with states, take a more global approach to the relations among humans and to the management of resources, and cease defining ourselves by the ideologies and religions that are so closely associated with states, we might move further along the road to perpetual peace. Or is this hopelessly idealistic?

One of Kant's conditions on which there has been little progress is the abolition of standing armies. Only a handful of mainly smaller states have adopted this idea (see Table 12.2), but for different reasons: European microstates feel no need to have militaries because they are not subject to invasion, several Pacific states left

Table 12.2: States without standing armies

Europe	Americas and Indian Ocean	Pacific
Andorra	Costa Rica	Kiribati
Iceland	Dominica	Marshall Islands
Liechtenstein	Grenada	Micronesia
Monaco	Haiti	Nauru
San Marino	Panama	Palau
Vatican City	St Lucia	Samoa
	St Vincent and the Grenadines	Solomon Islands
	Mauritius	Tuvalu
		Vanuatu

Source: Based on Stearns (2013).

the US responsible for their defence after achieving independence, the Costa Rican army was abolished in 1948 by a new leader fearful of losing power through a possible military coup, and the Haitian military was disbanded in 1995 after years of involvement in coups and attempted coups; rather than protecting Haiti against (non-existent) foreign invaders, the military had come to pose a threat to internal political development.

Why do so many other countries – particularly those that are neutral – maintain standing armies? Some might feel the need to be able to defend themselves, even if they pursue a policy of **non-intervention** in the affairs of other states. But there are few states in the world that face real threats, and few that have extensive interests outside their borders that might need defending. Even then, interests can be protected through legal and reciprocal economic means, and through international cooperation. Most countries also realize that military power can be expensive in human and financial terms, has little value in the resolution of problems such as terrorism and poverty, does not always prevail, and can create tensions where none might otherwise exist; if one state maintains a large military, other states might feel threatened and might feel the need to maintain their own large militaries to order to ensure their ability to defend themselves.

An alternative to violence is **passive resistance**, associated most famously with leaders such as Mahatma Gandhi in India and Martin Luther King Jr. in the United States, with the suffragette movement in Britain and the United States, with the silent protests of women seeking information on their missing loved ones during the 'Dirty War' in Argentina between 1976 and 1983, and with efforts by the Solidarity workers union to challenge the communist government in Poland during the late 1980s. The underlying principle here is that violence begets violence, and that the most effective way to bring about change in an oppressive regime is to take the moral high ground and eschew violence (see Kurlansky, 2006). It does not always work, but if war is tied to justice or morality, then it is hard for a state to take the moral high ground when its forces are killing or wounding peaceful protestors.

Non-intervention: A policy based on avoiding all wars (except those fought in self-defence) and alliances, and keeping out of the internal affairs of other states.

Passive resistance: Efforts to bring about change through the use of non-violent means such as an unwillingness to cooperate, or breaking the law.

Table 12.3: Winners of the Nobel Peace Prize: Some examples

Year	Winner	Achievement
2016	Juan Manuel Santos (Colombia)	Efforts to end Colombian civil war.
2014	Malala Yousafzai (Pakistan)	Campaigning for education for children.
2012	European Union	Advancing peace in Europe.
2009	Barack Obama (United States)	Promotion of international diplomacy.
2001	United Nations and Secretary-General Kofi Annan	Encouraging world peace.
1999	Doctors Without Borders	Humanitarian work.
1997	International Campaign to Ban Landmines	Efforts to ban and clear anti-personnel landmines.
1993	Nelson Mandela and F W de Klerk (South Africa)	Encouraging peace in South Africa.
1988	UN Peacekeeping Forces	Encouraging and monitoring peace.
1979	Mother Teresa (Albania)	Humanitarian work among the poor of India.
1977	Amnesty International	Promotion of the rights of prisoners of conscience.
1964	Martin Luther King Jr.	Promotion of non-violent change.

To some extent, insights into how peace is understood and defined are offered by looking at the list of the winners of the Nobel Peace Prize – see Table 12.3. In his will, Alfred Nobel (who was, ironically, the inventor of dynamite and one-time owner of the Swedish arms company Bofors) specified that one of the prizes he created should be awarded annually to 'the person who shall have done the most or the best work for fraternity between nations, the abolition or reduction of standing armies and for the holding and promotion of peace congresses'. Winners have ranged between the popular and the controversial, and awards have often been made less as a reward than as a symbolic gesture or as an effort to encourage winners to pursue peace.

THE CONDITIONS NEEDED FOR PEACE

In much the same way as peace is often defined as the absence of war, so the conditions needed for peace might be defined as the absence of the causes of war. In this spirit, Blainey (1988) argued that war and peace are simply alternating phases of the relationship between rival states or communities, that the reasons behind war ending and peace starting are a reversal of the reasons behind a peace ending and a war starting, and that if we can understand the causes of war, we can also understand the causes of peace. But this is too simplistic, because one is not necessarily the opposite of the other, and while we talk about the causes of war, it is more helpful to talk about the conditions needed for peace. At a minimum, they include the following:

▶ People must be able to freely take part in government. If they feel that their voice is not being heard, they are more likely to feel resentment towards government, and more likely to resist its work. If they are desperate enough, and feel that there are enough others who feel the same way, they might resort to violence.

▶ People must have the assets and opportunities that they need in order to fulfil their ambitions. This means they need jobs with reasonable pay, homes in which they feel secure, and access to basic services such as education, health care, energy supply, clean water, and sanitation.

▶ People must have no fear of physical or psychological threats, must believe that society is treating them equally and fairly, must be assured that agents of the security system (such as the police) are working with and for them, and must believe that they have access to a fair and efficient system of justice based on equality before the law.

▶ People must feel confident that they face no threats of violence from other states. This means clear recognition of the sanctity of national borders, no concerns about asymmetric military capabilities, and clear recognition of the freedom to have different political, ideological, economic, social or religious values and goals.

These are mainly the kind of conditions that need to be achieved within states, the logic being that if we remove the causes of domestic conflict, we are more likely to remove the conditions that lead to international or global conflict. There are few people who seek or enjoy war, and most will resort to violence either out

Source: AFP/Getty Images

UN peacekeepers from Brazil patrol the streets of Port-au-Prince, the capital of Haiti, a country that has recently suffered a devastating combination of political instability, natural disasters, and economic decline.

COMPARING NORTH AND SOUTH 12

CONTRASTING VIEWS ABOUT WAR AND PEACE

The North – particularly its European states – was once the scene of the most serious and sustained wars in human history. If Europeans were not fighting each other, they were often launching wars of conquest in other parts of the world. But much has changed since the end of World War II, and most of the world's most serious conflicts now occur in the South. These mainly take the form either of civil wars or of invasions by Northern states, as often as not involving the United States.

As to why Northern states no longer face much risk of fighting each other, **democratic peace theory** suggests that it is because they are democracies, and have built domestic institutions that constrain their inclination to go to war with one another (one factor being public opinion and its resistance to casualties), and instead rely on the peaceful resolution of disagreements (see Doyle, 2011, for example).

There is a powerful economic element involved as well, since democracies have deep connections through trade, investments, and technology, giving them less incentive to engage in military conflicts with one another; hence it might be just as appropriate to talk about capitalist peace theory. This was famously expressed by Friedman (2000) in his suggestion that no two countries with a branch of McDonald's had ever gone to war with one another. Not everyone agrees with the arguments of democratic peace theory, citing historical examples of wars between democracies (World War I happened in spite of the network of commercial links that tied most of its protagonists), or suggesting that the argument only holds at certain times and under certain conditions.

As to why Southern states – particularly those in Africa and the Middle East – so often experience civil wars, part of the explanation lies in the legacy of colonialism. This resulted in the creation of states whose populations had little in common and that brought together different groups of peoples with different histories and interests. In trying to build workable new states, they often found themselves at odds over the distribution of political power and economic resources, the tensions spilling over into war.

Conflict in Southern states in recent decades has also come as a result of invasions from Northern states, often in the form of coalitions led by the United States, which has developed something of a reputation as a belligerent military power. Since 1945 it has built the world's largest military, has intervened in conflicts in many parts of the world (including Afghanistan, Iraq, Lebanon, and Vietnam), and currently spends nearly as much on defence each year as the next nine countries combined (see Figure 12.1). Why does the United States go to war so often and maintain such a large military? Have the threats grown? Does it have more interests to protect? Is it something inherent in the American national psyche? Has the power and reach of the US defence industry ensured increased spending even in the absence of real threats? There are many questions and few hard answers.

Democratic peace theory: The theory that democracies rarely or never go to war with one another.

of frustration or for self-defence. Removing the causes of those frustrations and threats will be the most likely path to encouraging peace. But we also need to look at international relations and at the kinds of pressures that lead to conflict, and therefore at how best to address them in order to avoid conflict – see Comparing North and South 12.

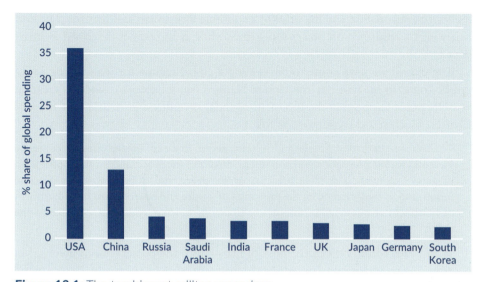

Figure 12.1: The ten biggest military spenders

Source: Based on data in Stockholm International Peace Research Institute (2017).

Note: Figures are for 2016.

THE GLOBAL SECURITY REGIME

As we saw in Chapter 6, we live in an anarchic world, meaning that there is no global system of government, and states are left to define their own interests and the threats to those interests, as well as to decide how to promote and protect their interests. Ideally, they do this peacefully and through a process of negotiation, using **diplomacy**. As Winston Churchill once memorably quipped, 'To jaw-jaw is always better than to war-war'. In spite of the frequency of war, history reveals that states mainly handle their disputes peacefully and without much fanfare; war, in this sense, is the noisy and bloody failure of diplomacy. During periods of peace, states interact with one another according to known and accepted standards of behaviour.

> **Diplomacy**: The art and practice of managing relations between states through negotiation and compromise.

Occasionally, states might not be able to agree, and might express their displeasure with other states through such means as the imposition of economic sanctions, the occasional show of force involving the movement of a state's military into the neighbourhood of another state as an implied threat, or the eviction of other states from international organizations. An example of the latter was Russia's suspension in 2014 – in the wake of its annexation of the Crimea – from the G8 Group of the world's major economies, which then reverted to its earlier title of the G7.

While power is the capacity to achieve intended objectives, it comes in different forms that can be employed in different circumstances to send different messages. Military power is usually clear, visible, loud, and dramatic. By contrast, civilian power focuses on efforts by states to achieve their objectives using non-military means, including diplomacy. Overlaying the distinction between military and civilian power is the distinction between **hard power** and **soft power**, or between sticks and carrots (see Knorr, 1973; Nye, 2004; and Lukes, 2005). The former involves efforts to exert influence and achieve objectives through the use of threats, coercion, sanctions, and – in the most extreme case – military force. The latter is an attempt to exert influence and achieve objectives through the use of encouragement and incentives, such as

> **Hard power**: The exertion of influence through the use of threats and coercion.

> **Soft power**: The exertion of influence through the use of encouragement and incentives.

diplomacy, negotiation and the offer of economic investment and rewards. The deft balancing of hard and soft power tools, meanwhile, is sometimes described as smart power.

The closest we have come to developing a global regime for maintaining peace can be found in the work of the United Nations (see Chapter 6). Since its creation in 1945, peace has been at the top of its agenda, as outlined in Article 1 of the UN Charter, which stated its purpose as follows:

> To maintain international peace and security, and to that end: to take effective collective measures for the prevention and removal of threats to the peace, and for the suppression of acts of aggression or other breaches of the peace, and to bring about by peaceful means, and in conformity with the principles of justice and international law, adjustment or settlement of international disputes or situations which might lead to a breach of the peace.

Peacekeeping:
Efforts to keep peace through the insertion of impartial and external military, police or civilian personnel into troubled regions following the agreement of a peace accord or a ceasefire.

Preventive diplomacy:
Diplomatic efforts to prevent or reduce the chance of the outbreak of conflict.

Collective security:
The idea that all states in a security alliance agree that the security of one is the concern of them all.

With peace front and centre, the UN has – from the outset – been involved in coordinating **peacekeeping** operations in different parts of the world. Based on the idea of **preventive diplomacy**, UN peacekeeping involves brokering agreements among the parties involved in actual or potential conflicts, and then committing multinational military forces as a buffer. These forces wear the distinctive blue helmets or berets of UN peacekeepers, are usually unarmed or lightly armed, and operate under strict conditions that usually allow them to use force only in self-defence. The first UN peacekeeping force was the UN Truce Supervision Organization that was deployed in May 1948 to monitor ceasefires and supervise armistice agreements in the Middle East. Since then, UN peacekeepers have been active in India, Pakistan, Lebanon, Cyprus, El Salvador, Haiti, Cambodia, Somalia, Rwanda, the Balkans, and Angola, to name a few. While their presence has not always been welcomed, their cumulative work led to UN Peacekeeping Forces being awarded the Nobel Peace Prize for 1988.

A more threat-based form of keeping the peace (and one of which Kant would not have approved) is the principle of **collective security**. This happens when two or more countries form a defensive alliance, and accept that the security of one of them is the concern of all of them, and hence if one is threatened or attacked, they all help out. There have been numerous such alliances throughout history, most have been either bilateral or regional, and most have been based on treaties and have not resulted in the creation of a new supervisory body. One of the exceptions is the North Atlantic Treaty Organization (NATO), founded among Western states in 1949 in order to send a signal to the Soviet Union that it should not invade Western Europe. This is most clearly reflected in Article 5 of the founding North Atlantic Treaty:

> The Parties agree that an armed attack against one or more of them in Europe or North America shall be considered an attack against them all and consequently they agree that, if such an armed attack occurs, each of them, in exercise of the right of individual or collective self-defence recognised by Article 51 of the Charter of the United Nations, will assist the Party or Parties so attacked by taking forthwith, individually and in concert with the other Parties, such action as it deems necessary, including the use of armed force, to restore and maintain the security of the North Atlantic area.

Source: Anadolu Agency/Getty Images

A meeting of defence ministers at the NATO headquarters in Brussels, Belgium. NATO is a Western defensive alliance whose mission has undergone a change of focus since the end of the Cold War.

In 1955, the Soviets responded with the creation of the Warsaw Pact (formally the Treaty of Friendship, Co-operation, and Mutual Assistance), designed to send a similar message about the consequences of a NATO attack, and confirming the Cold War military division of Europe. With the end of the Cold War, the Warsaw Pact was dissolved and the original goal of NATO became largely moot; it has since evolved into an organization under which its members not only continue to promote collective security, but also to launch military operations outside the NATO area, including those in the Balkans, Iraq, Afghanistan, and counter-piracy operations off the Horn of Africa.

TERRORISM

In 15 January 2018, rush hour was under way as usual in the Iraqi capital of Baghdad. In the downtown al-Tayaran Square, people were on their way to work, and dozens of labourers were gathered as usual, hoping to find part-time work. Amid the bustle, no-one noticed two people winding their way through the crowds, and suddenly obliterating themselves by setting off suicide bombs. Many around them died instantly, and many more were seriously wounded. Emergency calls brought ambulances and security forces to the scene, which was sprinkled with bodies and limbs, lying amid pools of blood and of debris scattered by the bombs. At least 38 people were dead and more than 100 were injured, the jihadist group ISIS later claiming responsibility.

This is just one isolated example in a litany of terrorist incidents that have regrettably become an almost routine part of life in many parts of the world, particularly the Middle East. Baghdad had been relatively free of terrorist incidents for several months, but suicide bombs and car bombs were far from unknown there, as they were in other Iraqi cities, and in many other countries around the world; few have escaped the scourge, making almost everyone feel insecure to one degree or another.

For many in Europe, North America, the Middle East, and Africa, **terrorism** has become more real – whether as a threat or an actual event – than war, prompting changes in the way life is lived: security procedures in airports have been tightened, those attending large public events must often go through screening, barriers have been built around government buildings, and anyone finding themselves surrounded by large crowds could be forgiven for wondering about the possibility of being attacked by suicide bombers, or by individuals wielding guns or knives, or driving cars or trucks. More broadly, terrorism has resulted in changes to the goals of foreign policy, to the definition of the threats faced by states, and to the technology of security.

We have already seen plenty of examples in this book of terms whose meaning is contested, so it probably comes as no surprise to find that the same problem applies to terrorism. It might once have been understood as 'the deliberate killing of innocent people at random, in order to spread fear through a whole population and force the hand of its political leaders' (Walzer, 2004). But this definition does not account either for state terrorism (where a government tries to spread fear among its citizens and members of the opposition), or for state-sponsored terrorism (when a government supports the activities of terrorist groups in other countries). It is a term that has also been used increasingly loosely to describe almost any kind of violent attack that goes beyond the simply criminal and that might involve a political, social, or religious motivation. Whatever the source, the method or the motivation, terrorism is intentional (rather than incidental), is designed to be random and unpredictable, is psychologically driven, is designed to instil fear, and is intended to indiscriminately target non-combatants (see Lutz and Lutz, 2013: Chapter 1).

Terrorism is nothing new, and even though the use of terms such as *terrorist* and *terrorism* has grown exponentially since the 1970s. There have been numerous incidents throughout history where groups or individuals have used violence against the innocent for political ends. Examples include the killing by Jewish activists of collaborators with Roman rule in Judaea in the 1st century CE, the 11th-century activities in Persia of the Hashshashin (from which derives the word *assassin*), and the Reign of Terror in France in 1793–94, which spawned the first use of the term *terrorism*. While terrorism is widely condemned, the line between terrorists and freedom fighters is often vague, and yesterday's terrorists have often become today's heroes. The achievements of rebels in the American War of Independence, for example, are today widely lauded, and yet their methods included mob attacks, looting, kangaroo courts, tarring and feathering, public humiliation, and the confiscation of property. Similarly, Israel rightly condemns terrorist attacks against its people and land, and yet the creation of Israel in 1948 was achieved in part by the activities of groups such as the Lehi and the Irgun, the latter involved in a 1946 explosion at the King David Hotel in Jerusalem that killed 91 people.

The causes behind terrorism have been many and varied, including the struggle for political independence, efforts to spread a religious or political philosophy, or

Terrorism: The threatened or actual use of violence against property or civilian targets so as to generate fear and to intimidate governments into making political or social change.

Source: Getty Images News/Getty Images

Armed police patrol the streets of New York. The threat of terrorism has meant a tightening of security in many parts of the world, and an extension of state powers in the interests of public safety.

attempts to change economic or social behaviour, as in the case of the activities of groups trying to end the exploitation of natural resources or experimentation on animals. Examples of terrorism at work include the activities of anarchists in Germany and Italy, Irish nationalists struggling to reunify Ireland, Basque separatists seeking independence from Spain, Palestinian groups working for the creation of an independent Palestine, and insurgents trying to undermine the governments of Afghanistan and Iraq. The use of terrorism is usually a sign of frustration, and often grows out of poverty, the failure of government to address grievances, the rejection of economic or social norms, the lack of democracy, foreign occupation, or resistance to the influence of foreign powers. It is no coincidence that many of the motives in this list are missing from the list of conditions for peace outlined earlier in this chapter.

The number of incidents of terrorism worldwide has grown dramatically in recent years – see Figure 12.2 – thanks mainly to the intensification of the problem in countries such as Afghanistan, Iraq, Nigeria, Pakistan, and Syria. We have also seen a rise in the number of communities impacted, the number of fatalities, and the impact of global terrorism, which has left few societies unchanged. Where once it might have involved a single person attacking another with whatever weapon was most readily available, the means used have widened to include automatic weapons, suicide bombings, car bombs, trucks and cars driven into crowds, and planes flown into buildings. The rise of global terrorism has taken the threats far beyond the domestic, and has meant rising concerns – and changes of policy – for a wide range of countries. The list of countries that have experienced major terrorist events just since 2000 is considerable, including Afghanistan, Algeria, Belgium, Britain,

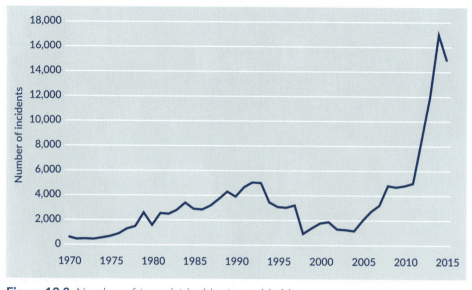

Figure 12.2: Number of terrorist incidents worldwide
Source: Based on data in Global Terrorism Database (2018).

Colombia, France, India, Indonesia, Iraq, Kenya, Nigeria, Pakistan, Peru, the Philippines, Russia, Spain, Sri Lanka, Turkey, the United States, and Yemen.

Global terrorism today is most readily associated with the activities of militant Islamist groups such as al-Qaeda, ISIS, the Taliban, Boko Haram, and numerous affiliated bodies, all focused on a combination of resistance against the inroads of the West (mainly the United States and its European allies) into their countries, and the spread of a socially conservative form of Islam. While most of their violence has been directed domestically, as in the Middle East and – in the case of Boko Haram – Nigeria, it has also reached an international scale through attacks or planned attacks by sympathizers. Even the threat of terrorism has come to be an efficient weapon in the arsenal of such groups. All of this raises the question of the extent to which terrorism and globalization have become intertwined. Today's networks of terror are often inspired by their fears of globalization (or by their exclusion from its benefits), the targets chosen by terrorists are international, and globalization itself might be threatened by efforts to tighten security across borders (see Khan and Estrada, 2017).

DISCUSSION QUESTIONS

1. Why do humans so often go to war with one another?

2. Do you agree that the era of large-scale multi-year conflicts is probably over?

3. What do we need to do to better understand the conditions needed for peace?

4. Which, if any, of Kant's conditions for perpetual peace have been met?

5. What needs to be done to improve the global security regime?

6. What is the most effective response to terrorism?

KEY CONCEPTS

▸ Civil war

▸ Collective security

▸ Democratic peace theory

▸ Diplomacy

▸ Hard power

▸ Just war

▸ Liberalism

▸ Negative peace

▸ Neutrality

▸ Non-intervention

▸ Passive resistance

▸ Peace

▸ Peacekeeping

▸ Perpetual peace

▸ Positive peace

▸ Preventive diplomacy

▸ Realism

▸ Soft power

▸ Structural violence

▸ Terrorism

▸ War

USEFUL WEBSITES

Correlates of War Project at http://www.correlatesofwar.org

Global Terrorism Database at https://www.start.umd.edu/gtd

Nobel Peace Prize at https://www.nobelprize.org/nobel_prizes/peace

North Atlantic Treaty Organization at http://www.nato.int

UN Peacekeeping at http://www.un.org/en/peacekeeping

FURTHER READING

Barash, David (ed.) (2014) *Approaches to Peace: A Reader in Peace Studies*, 3rd edn (Oxford University Press). A collection of articles on the meaning of war, negative peace, terrorism, positive peace, and non-violence.

Fox, Michael Allen (2014) *Understanding Peace: A Comprehensive Introduction* (Routledge). A study of the qualities, nature and conditions of peace, reviewing how peace is possible and desirable.

Levy, Jack S., and William R. Thompson (2010) *Causes of War* (John Wiley). An assessment of war and the different theories regarding its causes, at both the interstate and the domestic level.

Martin, Gus (2016) *Understanding Terrorism: Challenges, Perspectives, and Issues*, 5th edn (Sage). A textbook survey of the definition, causes, and types of terrorism, including discussion of its international dimensions.

Walzer, Michael (2015) *Just and Unjust Wars: A Moral Argument with Historical Illustrations*, 5th edn (Basic Books). A classic philosophical treatise on the moral issues surrounding the causes and conduct of war.

Online Resources

Visit www.macmillanihe.com/McCormick-GS to access additional materials to support teaching and learning.

CONCLUSIONS: FUTURE DIRECTIONS IN GLOBAL STUDIES

At about the time I was putting the finishing touches to this book, I made my first trip to Hong Kong. I had been told that it was a good point of entry to the new Asia, and calculated that visiting one of the world's leading global cities would inspire me as I wrapped up this book on global studies. Based on everything I had ever learned about the city, I was expecting to see a fusion of cultures, as well as strong evidence of globalization, global trade, and the new role of China. In the event, I found all of this and more, along with a few problems as well.

Visitors arrive at the new international airport (built on reclaimed land) and are greeted by the sight of planes bearing the livery of Chinese airlines that are poised to become key new players in the international airline industry. Passengers are guided efficiently through customs and immigration, after which they can catch taxis that take them across new highways and suspension bridges to Kowloon, or can take airport express trains that pass within view of a massive container port as they travel to downtown stations.

Hong Kong Island and Kowloon are a visual feast, with skyscrapers bearing the names of companies ranging from the Bank of China to the Bank of America, Citibank, HSBC, Standard Chartered Bank, Hyatt Regency, and Marriott, sharing space with the International Finance Centre and the International Commerce Centre. Overhead walkways carry streams of workers – most of them young – to and from their offices, through indoor malls filled with luxury outlets. Alongside all the international brands and the sense of globalization at work, Chinese culture seems to thrive, and within view of the high-rises are neighbourhoods in which almost everyone is Chinese, and local people shop in outdoor markets. People are friendly, prices are reasonable, and – above all – everything seems to work.

To be sure, all is not perfect in Hong Kong. The air was hazy from pollution, housing is so expensive as to push it far past the reach of most workers to buy, the luxury outlets in the malls are disconcertingly quiet, local culture is being pushed aside, economic growth has been sluggish, and in spite of China's guarantees to honour a 'one country, two systems' political framework since Hong Kong's return from British administration in 1997, limits have been imposed on freedom of speech and political choice. My visit also coincided with an announcement that rules had been changed so as to allow China's leader, Xi Jinping, a lifetime appointment.

Even so, it was impossible to miss the effects of globalization, and to see – even in a small corner of China – the prospects of an Asian century. A visit to a global city such as Hong Kong emphasizes how many changes are taking place in the world as culture, science, technology, politics, government, human rights, finance, trade, migration, the environment, and security all cease to be defined exclusively by the local and the national and have become subject to the pressures of the global.

To be sure, globalization is controversial. While it has helped create new wealth and opportunities, it has also exacerbated poverty and inequality. It is not always a force for good, and many people have yet to benefit from the possibilities of global connections. But this is less a reason to reject it than to better understand its shortcomings and to address them. In some cases, this is happening: governments, corporations, civil society groups, and consumers are often rethinking the way they approach global connections, and are working on ways of making them more equitable.

At the same time, though, there are many who feel threatened by these global connections, and are responding with a reassertion of nativism and nationalism. Instead of seeing the world as a global system, and learning about its actual and potential benefits, many fear what they see and are reacting by building literal or metaphorical walls that are designed to keep out the new and the exotic. They worry about the growing diversity of the societies in which they live, they baulk at new competition from countries with which they are often unfamiliar, they believe news headlines designed to paint a threatening picture of the world, and they seek to protect themselves by trying to recreate the 'good old days'.

Actually, those old days were rarely all that good. To be alive today is, for most people, to know a time when the quality of life is better than it has ever been before: we live longer, we are better educated, we travel more safely, our environment is cleaner, we face less danger of war, we understand more about the world around us, and we are subjected less to the kinds of unpredictable threats that often faced our ancestors. We also better understand the causes of the conflicts, poverty, social pressures, and exploitation that endanger the lives of those in more trying circumstances, even if we have often failed to turn that knowledge into tangible progress.

At the same time, to be alive today is also to witness a degree of change that is broader, faster, and deeper than it has probably ever been before at any time in human history. The sardonic observation that nothing is certain in life except death and taxes is not quite right. Death is indeed certain, but many people are too poor to pay taxes, and the observation fails to emphasize a third and fundamental certainty of life, which is change. Nothing remains static, whether we are talking about physical and biological forces – such as weather, evolution, aging, or the passage of time – or about systemic forces, such as the way in which societies, institutions, and cultures change.

Taking a global view helps us better appreciate the positive nature of many of the changes we face, helps us better appreciate the extent of the inequalities within human society, and helps us learn from one another as we try to understand the causes and effects of change. We can look at the world from the limited perspective of our own community, ethnicity, religion, culture, ideology, or state, but this will only tell us part of the story. It is better to take a more inclusive view, to try and see things from the perspective of others, and – by doing so – to build a more complete set of understandings about the world in which we live. Global studies can help us do this. It has already made much progress, but – as noted in the Introduction – it is a relatively new field of study, and continues to offer many unmet possibilities. We can see this more clearly by speculating about where we might go from here.

▶ Globalization is nothing new, and the forces of free markets, technological change, and political cooperation suggest that it will continue to evolve indefinitely. Governments might build walls and try to control the movement of people and ideas, but where there is a will there is a way, and the long-term will to build connections and to seek new opportunities will outweigh short-term efforts to protect narrow interests.

▶ Population will grow for the foreseeable future, in some places faster than in others. The expanding and broadening needs of humans will still place pressure on food production and natural resources, for which we must continue to seek solutions. Meanwhile, the harm caused by pollutive fossil fuels will push us towards a future based on renewable sources of energy. The long-term effects of human action on the environment will continue to be felt as climate change worsens and biodiversity faces ever greater pressures; how we respond to these problems will define the quality of life for future generations.

▶ Identity and culture will continue to be redefined as people mingle more with others from different parts of the world, and learn more about what makes them similar and different. The vast majority of people still define themselves as citizens of one country or another, as members of one ethnicity or another, or as members of one religion or another, but the idea of global citizenship is growing.

▶ The boundaries of science and technology are continually expanded, the changes now happening so quickly that we barely have time to adapt to new developments before they are surpassed. Medical science is constantly improving, but the threats to human health also evolve, with infectious diseases moving more rapidly across borders. We are going through a digital revolution whose possibilities are remarkable, while information and communication systems extend their global reach, and international travel continues to become more accessible to more people.

▶ States are undergoing a metamorphosis in the wake of globalization and international cooperation, and the way they relate to one another will doubtless continue to change. As they interact, so new attention continues to be drawn to the definition and the state of human rights globally, and new concerns will be expressed about the state of democracy, now in retreat in several parts of the world. Interstate war seems to be a thing of the past, but civil wars continue to bloom, terrorism poses deeper threats, and perpetual peace remains hard to achieve.

▶ The ties that bind economies will continue to become more complex, such that we will come to be impacted more than ever by global developments, by trade, by the rise of multinationals, and by the changing relationship between the biggest economies and the major suppliers of raw materials. Economic inequality will unfortunately remain a problem indefinitely, the gap between the very rich and the poor growing ever larger, and the push and pull factors behind migration exerting continued pressure on people and communities.

Change can be good and it can be bad. It can be promising and it can be threatening. It can be obvious and it can be subtle. Whatever form it takes, though, it is inevitable, and we can either acknowledge it and work to shape it in a positive fashion, or we can resist it and allow ourselves to fear its consequences. Understanding change at those levels that are closest to our daily live – the communities, localities and states in which we live – is difficult enough, but it is much more challenging when we look at the global level. This is where global studies makes its contribution: by better understanding the connections among us at a global level, the diversity of world in which we live, and the manner in which global change impacts local change (and vice versa), we can better understand and perhaps prepare for the changes yet to come.

GLOSSARY

This glossary contains all the marginal definitions in the book.

Anarchy	A condition in which organized government is absent. Anarchists argue that governments are unnecessary and harmful, and favour self-governed societies based on voluntary associations.
Anthropocene	The suggested name for a new geological epoch marked by widespread human change to geology and ecosystems.
Asylum-seeker	Someone who seeks permanent residence in another country out of fear for their personal safety if obliged to return home.
Authoritarian system	One in which power is concentrated in the hands of a ruling elite, which manipulates society in order to remain in power.
Authority	The acknowledged right of a state to act or to rule.
Biodiversity	A contraction of the term *biological diversity*, describing the variety and the populations of the many species of life on earth.
Brain drain	The emigration of trained and talented individuals from one country to another, resulting in a loss of skills resources in the former. The obverse is a **brain gain** or the addition of skills resources in target countries.
Bretton Woods system	The international economic system designed to encourage post-war peace and prosperity through free trade and exchange rate stability.
BRIC	A collective acronym for Brazil, Russia, India, and China, reflecting their newly influential global roles.
Capitalism	An economic philosophy based on leaving as many decisions as possible on production, distribution, and prices to the free market.
Central bank	A national bank responsible for maintaining the value of a state's currency, limiting the amount of money in circulation, setting interest rates, and guarding against inflation.
Chain migration	The long-term process by which immigrants linked by social networks follow pioneer immigrants from the same community or family.
Citizenship	The idea of legally 'belonging' to a given state as a result of birth or being given citizenship, and having related rights and responsibilities.
Civil liberties	The rights and freedoms that humans have relative to their governments.
Civil rights	The rights that protect humans from discrimination based on who they are.
Civil society	The arena within which citizens engage with one another to address problems of shared concern, reflected at the global level in the features of **global civil society**.
Civil war	A conflict between parties and citizens within the same state, nation or community.

Civilization

An advanced stage of human development, marked by features such as political and social organization. A synonym for *culture*, but with a broader and more collective application.

Climate change

Changes to the global climate resulting from an enhanced greenhouse effect, caused – in turn – by rising concentrations of greenhouse gases such as carbon dioxide, produced mainly by the burning of fossil fuels.

Cold War

The war of words and ideas that took place between the late 1940s and the late 1980s involving the United States, the Soviet Union, and their respective allies or client states.

Collective security

The idea that all states in a security alliance agree that the security of one is the concern of them all.

Colonialism

Efforts by the governments or citizens of one region to occupy and control foreign territories with a view to settlement, economic exploitation, or strategic advantage.

Common pool resources

Resources (such as the atmosphere and the oceans) whose size or extent makes it difficult or impossible to prevent individuals from making use of them.

Comparative advantage

The theory that if countries specialize in producing goods and services in which they have advantages (such as bigger endowments, or cheaper labour), and if they trade freely with one another, then everyone will benefit.

Corporate social responsibility

The argument that corporations should place social and environmental issues at the core of their decision-making.

Cosmopolitanism

Association with the world, with universal ideas, and with the belief that all humans belong to a single community that transcends state boundaries and national identities.

Cultural imperialism

The promotion and imposition of one culture on another, by a dominant power or state over one that is less powerful.

Culture

The values, beliefs, habits, attitudes, and/or norms to which a society subscribes and responds, often unconsciously and even in the face of individual differences.

Culture shock

The discomfort that people might feel when moving to or experiencing a culture other than the one with which they are most familiar.

Democracy

A political system in which government is based on a fair and open mandate from all qualified citizens of a state, and is based on the rule of law.

Democratic peace theory

The theory that democracies rarely or never go to war with one another.

Democratization

The process by which states build the institutions and processes needed to become stable democracies.

Demographic transition

A model used to explain how population numbers change in concert with changes in economic and social patterns, and improved health care.

Demography

The study of statistics and trends relating to population, such as birth and death rates, income, disease, age, and education.

Development

The improvement of the economic and social well-being of peoples, communities, or states. Often used only in the context of poorer states.

Development aid

Assistance provided by wealthier countries to poorer countries, in the form mainly of technical aid targeted at the long-term alleviation of poverty.

Diaspora	The scattering or movement of a population beyond its geographical or native homeland, or the population that lives over an extended area outside its homeland.
Digital citizenship	Using information technology in order to engage with politics, government, society, and community.
Digital divide	Differences in levels of access to information and communication technology, whether between individuals, communities, geographic areas, or countries.
Digital revolution	The revolution in the generation, storage, and sharing of digital information.
Diplomacy	The art and practice of managing relations between states through negotiation and compromise.
Doha round	The most recent (and failed) set of negotiations aimed at further developing the global trading system.
Dumping	Exporting a product and selling it in large volumes at a price that is lower than the price charged in the originating market.
Echo chamber	A metaphor describing the manner in which ideas circulate within a closed system, and are amplified and reinforced by repetition.
E-commerce	The buying or selling of goods and services online.
Economic union	The existence of a single market among participating countries, with free movement of people, capital, goods and services, and a common external trade policy.
Economics	The study of the production, distribution, and consumption of goods and services, including such matters as money, markets, supply, demand, costs, competition and efficiency.
Emigration	See *migration*.
End of history	The idea that a political economic or social system will evolve to the point where it would reach its conclusive end-state.
Environment	The physical surroundings in which an entity – whether a human, animal, plant, insect, bacterium, or an inanimate object – exists.
Environmental justice	The view that all parties should be treated equally in the development and implementation of environmental planning and policy.
Environmental migrants	People obliged to relocate as a result of environmental disruptions such as drought, soil erosion, desertification, and climate change.
Environmentalism	A philosophy, theory, or ideology that encourages deeper understanding of the environmental impact of human actions.
Ethnic cleansing	The systematic and usually forced removal of an ethnic minority from the territory of another ethnic group with a view to achieving ethnic homogenization.
Ethnicity	A group of people who identify with one another based on a shared ancestral, social, and cultural background, often determined by a common language.
Ethnocentrism	Viewing or judging other cultures from the perspective of the values and norms of one's own.
Exchange rate	The value of one currency relative to another.
Failing state	A state with deep structural problems, often major internal divisions, weak governing institutions, and failed or failing economies.
Fair trade	A social movement designed to give producers in poorer countries a bigger share of the profits from the sale of their commodities.

Food security	A condition in which people have access to sufficient, safe and nutritious food.
Fordism	A term inspired by the Ford Motor Company, describing mass production of standardized goods on an assembly line, using specialized and semi-skilled labour.
Foreign direct investment	Any large-scale investment made in a business by foreign governments, businesses, or individuals.
Fossil fuels	Fuels formed from the decay of organic matter over millions of years, including coal, oil, and natural gas.
Free trade	The condition under which all barriers to trade are removed, creating an open and competitive marketplace, either between two countries, or among three or more.
Free trade agreement	One that reduces or removes mutual barriers to trade among participating countries, while retaining barriers to the movement of people and capital.
Genocide	Intentional efforts to wholly or partially destroy a group of people because of their ethnicity, race or religion.
Gini coefficient	A measure of income inequality, used to show the distribution of wealth in a given population.
Global city	A city whose size and political/economic reach is such that it has come to exert an influence beyond the state in which it is located.
Global civil society	See *civil society*.
Global culture	Those aspects of culture (deriving mostly from the West) that have taken on global dimensions.
Global financial crisis	The crisis sparked in 2007 by financial deregulation and speculation in the United States, which spread quickly to Europe.
Global governance	The accumulation of institutions, processes, agreements, procedures, norms and actions that help us address transboundary needs and problems.
Global studies	The systematic study of the global system and of its related features, qualities, trends, institutions, processes, and problems.
Global system	The collected elements and components – including people, institutions, principles, procedures, norms and habits – whose interactions make up the global whole.
Global village	A metaphor conveying the idea that electronic media have reduced the size of the world by tightening the connections among humans.
Globalism	A philosophy, ideology or policy based on taking a global view of politics, economics, society, security and the environment.
Globalization	The process by which the political, economic, social, and cultural links between people, corporations, and governments in different states become integrated through cooperation, trade, travel, communications, media, investment, market forces, and technology.
Glocalization	The idea that changes can occur at the global level and at the local level simultaneously, and that both levels are connected, one driving the other.
Gold standard	An arrangement by which countries fixed the value of their currencies to gold. Abandoned by Britain and the United States in the 1930s, and no longer used.
Governance	The sum of the many ways in which collective decisions are made and implemented, with or without the input of formal institutions.

Government	The system of institutions, processes and laws responsible for addressing the needs of the residents of a state.
Great power	A state with a large military and continental or global interests.
Green growth	Economic growth based on using natural resources and managing the environment in a sustainable manner.
Green politics	A political philosophy based on building a sustainable society rooted in environmental awareness, social justice, non-violence, and grassroots democracy.
Green revolution	The post-war growth in global food production resulting from changes in agricultural science, including the use of chemicals, improved water supply, and the development of high-yield crops.
Greenhouse effect	A natural phenomenon involving the trapping in the atmosphere of solar emissions, making possible life on earth as we know it.
Gross domestic product	The core measure of the size of economies, calculated by giving a dollar value to all goods and services produced by a country in a given year.
Hard power	The exertion of influence through the use of threats and coercion.
Human rights	The natural, universal and inalienable rights to which all humans are entitled.
Humanitarian intervention	A military intervention prompted by human rights abuses, natural disasters, war crimes, or genocide, with a view to easing refugee-generating problems.
Humanitarianism	A general concern for the welfare of humans.
Identity	A concept of self based on attributes that range from age and gender to ethnicity, culture, place of birth, job, and language.
Immigration	See *migration*.
Imperialism	A policy – usually by a government or a state – to extend power and influence through diplomacy or military conquest.
Infectious disease	One caused as a result of contamination by microorganisms capable of hosting and transferring the disease, such as bacteria, viruses, and parasites.
Institution	An informal or formal set of rules and procedures that define practices, assign roles, and guide interactions.
Intellectual property	Inventions and creations of the mind, including designs, copyrights, trademarks, and patents.
Intergovernmental organization	A body that promotes or facilitates cooperation among states, and consists of state members.
Intergovernmentalism	A theory/model based on the idea that key cooperative decisions among states are made as a result of negotiations among representatives of those states.
Internally displaced person	Someone forced to leave their home as a result of disruption but who has not crossed international borders.
International law	The set of rules governing relations among states, and consisting of a combination of customs and formal agreements.
International non-governmental organization	A body that works to encourage international cooperation through the work of non-state members such as individuals or private associations.
International organization	A body set up to promote cooperation between or among states, with either governments or non-governmental actors as members.
International relations	The study of (mainly) political and economic interactions between or among states, with a focus on diplomacy and policy.

International studies	The study of interactions, comparisons and commonalities involving two or more states.
Just war	War that is morally defensible.
Leader–laggard dynamic	The tension between countries taking contrasting positions on environmental policy, often resulting in the need to compromise.
Legitimacy	Recognition that a state has the right to wield authority within its borders.
Liberalism (trade)	The view that open markets and fewer trade controls are in the broader interest of everyone.
Liberalism (international relations)	The theory that international cooperation is possible and desirable, that war is not inevitable, and that international organizations and international law are important in understanding and driving international relations.
Malnutrition	A mismatch between supply and demand in nutrition, which may mean having too little food or consuming too much.
Mass media	Channels of communication – such as television, radio, and websites – that reach a large number of people.
Megacity	A city with a population of at least ten million people. The list has been growing, and is today topped by Tokyo, Delhi, Shanghai, Mexico City, and Sao Paulo.
Microfinance	Lending and investing at a small scale to help small businesses in developing countries.
Migrant	Someone who has moved from one region of a country to another, or from one country to another.
Migration	The movement of people from one place to another, including outward movement (**emigration**) and inward movement (**immigration**).
Mobility	The capacity to move, whether from one location to another, one job to another, or even one social class to another.
Modern	Literally the present or contemporary times, and a term most often used in connection with history, technology, social norms, culture, and the arts.
Monetary union	The existence of a single currency among participating countries, with a joint policy on controlling money supply and interest rates.
Most-favoured nation status	An agreement under the terms of membership of the WTO by which all members agree to treat each other equally.
Multiculturalism	A belief in a society made up of multiple cultures, and recognition of those cultures.
Multinational corporation	A private enterprise that has facilities and income-generating assets in two or more countries, managing its global activities from its home state.
Multinational state	A state consisting of multiple different national groups living under a single government.
Nation	A group of people who identify with one another on the basis of a shared history, culture, language, and myths.
National debt	The amount that a government owes as a result of running a budget deficit and/or a trade deficit, much of it often owed to foreign investors.
National identity	Identification with a state or nation, as determined by a combination of language, place of birth, and citizenship.
Nation-state	A state whose citizens share a common national identity.

Nationalism	The belief that nations have the right to determine their own destiny, to govern themselves, to have their own states, to place their interests above those of other nations, and to control movements across their borders.
Nativism	See *xenophobia*.
Natural law	The view that certain rights are derived from nature rather than the rules of government or society.
Natural resources	Materials or commodities found naturally on earth that have value to humans and other living organisms, including land, food, water, plants, animals, soil, minerals, fuels, and timber.
Natural rights	Rights that exist as a result of the universal law of nature, and that cannot be given or taken away by government.
Negative peace	A peace defined by the absence of violence, as opposed to the efforts to maintain a sustained peace found in the case of positive peace.
Neo-imperialism	Efforts by powerful actors to extend their influence by demanding changes or concessions from less powerful actors.
Neo-liberalism	An economic philosophy based on economic liberalization that has been adopted by many Northern countries since the 1980s.
Neutrality	A policy based on avoiding wars and on not taking sides in conflicts involving other states.
Non-intervention	A policy based on avoiding all wars (except those fought in self-defence) and alliances, and keeping out of the internal affairs of other states.
Non-state actor	Institutions that are not part of the structure of states (although they may have state members) but that influence policy, whether at the local, national, international or global level.
North and **South**	Short-hand terms for 'advanced' and 'developing' economies, most of which are found – respectively – in the northern and southern halves of the world. Often prefaced by the adjective *global*.
Outsourcing	The process by which a company uses an external vendor to provide a service that the company might normally have provided for itself. This happens on a global scale as companies outsource to countries with cheaper labour and weaker regulations.
Pandemic	An outbreak of an infectious disease over a large region, spilling over borders and perhaps spreading globally.
Paradigm	A model, pattern or framework based on the values, beliefs, and ideas that guide action.
Passive resistance	Efforts to bring about change through the use of non-violent means such as an unwillingness to cooperate, or breaking the law.
Patriotism	Love of country, identification with country, or devotion to country, as reflected in a pride in the history, symbols and myths of that country.
Peace	A condition in which different parties are able to disagree without resorting to violence.
Peacekeeping	Efforts to keep peace through the insertion of impartial and external military, police or civilian personnel into troubled regions following the agreement of a peace accord or a ceasefire.
Perpetual peace	A peace that is permanent and sustainable, and made possible by the absence of the conditions that can lead to war.
Political prisoner	A person who is imprisoned because their actions or beliefs run counter to those of the government of the day.

Political system	The interactions and organizations (including government) through which a society reaches and enforces collective decisions.
Positive peace	A peace sustained by positive efforts to avoid conflict through the building of systems and networks promoting the constructive resolution of disagreements, and ensuring equal access to opportunities and resources for all.
Poverty	A scarcity of money, material possessions, opportunity, and basic needs, which can be measured in both quantity and quality.
Preferential trade agreement	One giving preferential access for specified products from members of a trading bloc by reducing but not eliminating tariffs.
Preventive diplomacy	Diplomatic efforts to prevent or reduce the chance of the outbreak of conflict.
Primary health care	Health care that is basic, personal, and general, and geared towards initial treatment rather than dealing with specialized or advanced problems.
Prisoner of conscience	A person who is physically prevented from expressing or holding opinions by a government or a state.
Protectionism	The view that domestic markets should be protected from the kind of competition often posed by international trade.
Push factors	Problems and pressures that encourage people to leave their home region or state. The opposite of **pull factors**, or opportunities that draw people to a new region or state.
Race	A grouping or classification of humans based on their heritable physical differences, such as skin colour and facial features.
Realism	The theory that we live in an anarchic global system (one without rules or an authority above the level of the state), and that international relations are driven by a struggle for power among self-interested states.
Refugee	Someone who is forced to move from their home as a result of local political, economic, social or environmental disruption.
Regime	A set of rules, norms, institutions and agreements surrounding a given issue and around which the expectations of interested actors converge.
Regional development bank	A bank set up and run within a given region, pooling contributions from its shareholders to offer low-interest loans to countries in the region.
Regional integration	The promotion of cooperation and collective action among a group of neighbouring states based on the identification of shared interests and goals, and the development of common policies and collective laws.
Relativism	The view that human rights are culturally relative, and that there is no one-size-fits-all set of rights.
Religion	Belief in – and worship of – a superhuman controlling power, usually in the form of a deity or deities, and driven by a combination of beliefs, myths and rituals.
Remittances	Payments sent home to their families by people working outside their home states or regions.
Renewable energy	Energy generated by sources that are potentially or actually infinite in supply, such as solar, wind, and hydro power.
Reproductive rights	The right of an individual to decide whether or not to reproduce, and to have access to appropriate information and health care.
Reserve currency	A foreign currency that is held by governments, and is used to help them pay off debts or to reduce exchange rate risks.

Resource curse	A situation in which the value of a single profitable resource can create economic problems for a country.
Science	The systematic study of the physical, natural and social world with the goal of establishing core truths and developing general laws.
Secularism	A belief in the separation of religion and the state.
Security state	A state that follows the activities of its citizens through closed-circuit television, the monitoring of phone calls and internet use, and other means.
Slavery	An arrangement by which humans are defined as property, and individuals can be owned, bought and sold.
Small and medium enterprises	Independent companies with small numbers of employees and small turnovers, making them distinct from larger (and often multinational) corporations.
Social science	The study of human society and of the interactions among people within society. Distinct from the natural sciences, such as physics and biology.
Socialism	An economic philosophy based on redistributing opportunity and wealth through greater government involvement in the marketplace.
Soft power	The exertion of influence through the use of encouragement and incentives.
South	See *North* and *South*.
Sovereignty	The principle that a state answers to no higher political or legal authority.
Special Drawing Right	An artificial currency created and maintained by the IMF, supplementing standard reserve currencies.
State	A territory with a population and a government whose existence and independence are recognized under international law.
Statelessness	A condition under which a person does not have citizenship of a state, usually as a result of civil war.
Structural violence	The maintenance of processes and conditions that trap people through discrimination, degradation, and abuse.
Superpower	A state with the capacity and willingness to be active globally, particularly in a military sense.
Supranationalism	A theory/model based on promoting the joint interests of cooperating states, with a transfer of authority to those IGOs.
Sustainable development	Economic development that is planned and implemented in such a way as to meet short-term needs without compromising future needs.
Technology	The techniques, skills, methods, and processes used to solve problems, produce goods and services, improve the quality of life, and extend life.
Technology transfer	The transfer of technology from a creator to a secondary user, for example through licensing.
Terrorism	The threatened or actual use of violence against property or civilian targets so as to generate fear and to intimidate governments into making political or social change.
Third World	An informal grouping of developing Asian, African, Middle Eastern and Latin American states that were not immediately part of the US-led capitalist bloc or the Soviet-led communist bloc.
Tourism	Short-term travel for business or pleasure.

Trade	The exchange of goods and services among producers and consumers, whether through barter or using a medium of exchange such as currency.
Tragedy of the commons	An economic theory which argues that individual self-interest encourages the over-use of common pool resources, personal gain prevailing over the well-being of society.
Treaty	An agreement between or among states that holds them responsible for upholding specified principles or meeting specified goals and deadlines.
Treaty secretariat	A body charged with monitoring the application of an international treaty, and with encouraging negotiations among signatory states.
Universal Declaration of Human Right	The definitive outline of human rights, adopted by the UN General Assembly in 1948.
Universal health care	Health care made available to everyone at little or no direct cost, regardless of pre-existing conditions or ability to pay.
Universalism	The view that all humans possess an equal sets of rights, regardless of who they are, where they live, or where they come from.
Visa	A document that authorizes a foreigner to enter a country, usually for a specified maximum period of time, and or a specified reason, such as business, education or tourism.
War	A period of sustained, coordinated violence involving states, non-state actors, and/or groups within states.
Wealth	An abundance of money, material possessions, and opportunity, which can be measured in both quantity and quality.
West	A political, economic and cultural concept associated with Europe and with communities that grew out of European settlement and invasion. Distinguished from Eastern ideas associated with Asia, notably China, Japan and India.
Western	Ideas and values associated with 'the West', which originally meant Europe but has since broadened to include all societies created and shaped by European colonization.
Westphalian system	The modern state system that emerged out of the 1648 Peace of Westphalia, based on the sovereignty of states and political self-determination.
World war	Military conflict involving many states in different parts of the world.
Worldview	The manner in which each of us – as individuals or as members of like-minded groups – perceives the world.
Xenophobia	The fear, rejection or exclusion of those defined as foreigners in a community or a state, closely related to racism. The obverse is **nativism**, or the view that the interests of natives should be favoured over those of immigrants.
Zero population growth	A rate at which fertility and mortality balance each other out so that population neither increases nor decreases.

BIBLIOGRAPHY

Abusharaf, Rogaia Mustafa (ed.) (2006) *Female Circumcision: Multicultural Perspectives* (Philadelphia: University of Pennsylvania Press).

Anderson, Benedict (1983) *Imagined Communities: Reflections on the Origins and Spread of Nationalism* (London: Verso).

Anderson, M. S. (1998) *The Origins of the Modern European State System, 1494–1618* (Abingdon: Routledge).

Aslan, Reza (2009) *How to Win a Cosmic War: God, Globalization, and the End of the War on Terror* (New York: Random House).

Baldwin, Richard (2016) *The Great Convergence: Information Technology and the New Globalization* (Cambridge, MA: Belknap Press).

Barber, Benjamin R. (1995) *Jihad vs. McWorld: Terrorism's Challenge to Democracy* (New York: Ballantine Books).

Barnett, Michael N., and Kathryn Sikkink (2011) 'From International Relations to Global Society', in Robert E. Goodin (ed.) *The Oxford Handbook of Political Science* (Oxford: Oxford University Press).

Beauchamp, Zack (2014) 'Where People Really Love Their Countries   and Where They Kinda Don't' in *Vox*, 18 May, at https://www.vox.com (retrieved May 2018).

Beck, Ulrich (2006) *The Cosmopolitan Vision* (Cambridge: Polity Press).

Bellamy, Richard (2008) *Citizenship: A Very Short Introduction* (Oxford: Oxford University Press).

Benenson, Peter (1961) 'The Forgotten Prisoners', in *The Observer*, 28 May.

Bernstein, William J. (2008) *A Splendid Exchange: How Trade Shaped the World* (New York: Atlantic Monthly).

Bhagwati, Jagdish (2007) *In Defense of Globalization: With a New Afterword* (Oxford and New York: Oxford University Press).

Bhagwati, Jagdish N., Pravin Krishna, and Arvind Panagariya (eds) (2016) 'The World Trade System Today' in Bhagwati et al. (eds) *The World Trade System: Trends and Challenges* (Cambridge, MA: MIT Press).

Bhardwa, Seeta (2017) 'International Student Table 2017: Top 200 Universities', in *Times Higher Education*, 26 April.

Biermann, Frank, and Steffen Bauer (eds) (2005) *A World Environment Organization: Solution or Threat for Effective International Environmental Governance?* (Aldershot: Ashgate).

Black, Jeremy (2002) *Europe and the World, 1650–1830* (Abingdon: Routledge).

Blainey, Geoffrey (1988) *The Causes of War*, 3rd edn (New York: Free Press).

Blair, Dennis C., and Keith Alexander (2017) 'China's Intellectual Property Theft Must Stop', in *New York Times*, 15 August.

Bohman, James, and Matthias Lutz-Bachmann (eds) (1997) *Perpetual Peace: Essays on Kant's Cosmopolitan Ideal* (Boston, MA: MIT Press).

Boudreaux, Richard, and Paulo Prada (2012) 'Exodus of Workers from Continent Reverses Old Patterns', in *Wall Street Journal*, 14 January.

Bourguignon, Francois (2015) *The Globalization of Inequality* (Princeton, NJ: Princeton University Press).

Boyle, Godfrey (ed.) (2012) *Renewable Energy: Power for a Sustainable Future*, 3rd edn (Oxford: Oxford University Press).

Breitmeier, Helmut, Arild Underdal, Oran R. Young, and Michael Zürn (2006) *Analyzing International Environmental Regimes: From Case Study to Database* (Cambridge, MA, MIT Press).

Brook, Daniel (2013) *A History of Future Cities* (New York: W. W. Norton).

Brown, Keith R. (2013) *Buying into Fair Trade: Culture, Morality, and Consumption* (New York: New York University Press).

Brown, Wendy (2010) *Walled States, Waning Sovereignty* (Brooklyn, NY: Zone Books).

Browne, Waldo R. (ed.) (1946) *Leviathan in Crisis: An International Symposium on the State, its Past, Present, and Future* (New York: Viking).

Brundtland, Gro Harlem, et al. (1987) *Our Common Future: World Commission on Environment and Development* (Oxford: Oxford University Press).

Caspersen, Nina (2011) *Unrecognised States: The Struggle for Sovereignty in the Modern International System* (Cambridge: Polity Press).

Chandler, Alfred D., and Bruce Mazlish (eds) (2005) *Leviathans: Multinational Corporations and the New Global History* (Cambridge: Cambridge University Press).

Chandy, Laurence, and Brina Seidel (2016) 'Is Globalization's Second Wave about to Break?'. Brookings Institution, *Global Views* No. 4, October.

Chin, Rita (2017) *The Crisis of Multiculturalism in Europe: A History* (Princeton, NJ: Princeton University Press).

Chiras, Daniel D., and John P. Reganold (2009) *Natural Resource Conservation: Management for a Sustainable Future*, 10th edn (London: Pearson).

CIA World Factbook (2017) 'Distribution of Family Income: Gini Index', at https://www.cia.gov/library (retrieved July 2017). Data for 2008–15.

Clark, Barry (2016) *The Evolution of Economic Systems: Varieties of Capitalism in the Global Economy* (Oxford: Oxford University Press).

Clark, Christopher (2012) *The Sleepwalkers: How Europe Went to War in 1914* (New York: HarperCollins).

Cohen, Daniel (2007) *Globalization and Its Enemies* (Cambridge, MA: MIT Press).

Collier, Paul (2007) *The Bottom Billion: Why the Poorest Countries are Failing and What Can Be Done About It* (New York: Oxford University Press).

Conway, Ed (2014) *The Summit: Bretton Woods, 1944 – J. M. Keynes and the Reshaping of the Global Economy* (New York: Pegasus).

Correlates of War Project (2017) Website at http://www.correlatesofwar.org (retrieved December 2017).

Cosgrove, Serena, and Benjamin Curtis (2018) *Understanding Global Poverty: Causes, Capabilities and Human Development* (Abingdon: Routledge).

Craig, Iona (2017) '"Only God Can Save Us": Yemeni Children Starve as Aid is Held at Border' in *The Guardian*, 12 November.

Crane, Andrew, Dirk Matten, Abagail McWilliams, Jeremy Moon, and Donald Siegel (eds) (2009) *The Oxford Handbook of Corporate Social Responsibility* (Oxford: Oxford University Press).

Crawford, James (2007) *The Creation of States in International Law*, 2nd edn (Oxford: Oxford University Press).

Crisp, Nigel (2010) *Turning the World Upside Down: The Search for Global Health in the 21st Century* (London: Royal Society of Medicine Press).

Crutzen, Paul J. (2002) 'Geology of Mankind', in *Nature* 415:6867, 3 January, p. 23.

De Keersmaeker, Goedele (2017) *Polarity, Balance of Power, and International Relations Theory* (London: Palgrave Macmillan).

Delreux, Tom, and Sander Happaerts (2016) *Environmental Policy and Politics in the European Union* (London: Palgrave).

Desai, Raj M., and James Raymond Freeland (2014) 'What the New Bank of BRICS is all About', in *The Washington Post*, 17 July.

Diamond, Larry, Marc F. Plattner, and Christopher Walker (eds) (2016) *Authoritarianism Goes Global: The Challenge to Democracy* (Baltimore, MD: Johns Hopkins University Press).

Dimitrov, Radoslav S. (2006) *Science and International Environmental Policy: Regimes and Nonregimes in Global Governance* (Lanham, MD: Rowman & Littlefield).

Donnelly, Jack (2013) *International Human Rights*, 4th edn (Boulder, CO: Westview Press).

Dorsey, Kurkpatrick (2013) *Whales and Nations: Environmental Diplomacy on the High Seas* (Seattle: University of Washington Press).

Doyle, Michael W. (2011) *Liberal Peace: Selected Essays* (Abingdon: Routledge).

Dyson, Tim (2010) *Population and Development: The Demographic Transition* (London: Zed Books).

Economist, The (2018) 'Africa's Broken Heart: Congo is Sliding Back to Bloodshed', 15 February.

Economist Intelligence Unit (2016) *Democracy Index 2016*, at https://www.eiu.com (retrieved May 2018).

Ehrlich, Paul (1968) *The Population Bomb* (New York: Ballantine Books).

Elsea, Jennifer (2002) 'US Policy Regarding the International Criminal Court', Congressional Research Service/US Library of Congress, 3 September.

Environmental Performance Index 2018, at https://epi.envirocenter.yale.edu/2018-epi-report (retrieved January 2018).

Esipova, Neli, Anita Pugliese, and Julie Ray (2013) 'The Demographics of Global Internal Migration', in *Migration Policy Practice* 3:2, April–May, pp. 3–5.

European Court of Human Rights (2017) at http://www.echr.coe.int (retrieved April 2017).

Favell, Adrian (2008) *Eurostars and Eurocities: Free Movement and Mobility in an Integrating Europe* (Oxford: Blackwell).

Fenton, Steve (2010) *Ethnicity*, 2nd edn (Cambridge: Polity Press).

Fink, Carole K. (2017) *Cold War: An International History*, 2nd edn (Boulder, CO: Westview Press).

Fioramonti, Lorenzo (2013) *Gross Domestic Problem: The Politics behind the World's Most Powerful Number* (London: Zed Books).

Fitzmaurice, Peter (2012) 'Between the Wars – The Refugee Convention of 1933: A Contemporary Analysis', in David Keane and Yvonne McDermott (eds) *The Challenge of Human Rights: Past, Present and Future* (Cheltenham, UK: Edward Elgar).

Foltz, Richard (2010) *Religions of the Silk Road: Premodern Patterns of Globalization*, 2nd edn (New York: Palgrave Macmillan).

Food and Agriculture Organization of the United Nations (2015) *Global Forest Resources Assessment 2015* (Rome: FAO).

Food and Agriculture Organization of the United Nations (2016a) *The State of Food and Agriculture 2016: Climate Change, Agriculture and Food Security* (Rome: FAO).

Food and Agriculture Organization of the United Nations (2016b) *The State of World Fisheries and Aquaculture 2016* (Rome: FAO).

Food and Agriculture Organization of the United Nations (2017a) *The State of Food Security and Nutrition in the World 2017* (Rome: FAO).

Food and Agriculture Organization of the United Nations (2017b) 'The State of Food Security and Nutrition in the World', at http://www.fao.org/state-of-food-security-nutrition/en (retrieved December 2017).

Fortune Global 500 (2018) at http://fortune.com/global500 (retrieved March 2018).

Fox, Michael Allen (2014) *Understanding Peace: A Comprehensive Introduction* (Abingdon: Routledge).

Fox, W. T. R. (1944) *The Super-Powers: The United States, Britain, and the Soviet Union – Their Responsibility for Peace* (New York: Harcourt Brace).

Fraser Institute (2016) Economic Freedom Index, at https://www.fraserinstitute.org (retrieved July 2017).

Freed, Dan (2016) 'JP Morgan's Dimon rolls eyes up at gloom and Davos billionaires'. Reported by Reuters, 23 February, at https://www.reuters.com (retrieved May 2018).

Freedom House (2017) *Freedom in the World 2017* (New York: Freedom House).

Friedman, Thomas L. (2000) *The Lexus And The Olive Tree: Understanding Globalization* (New York: Anchor/ Random House).

Friedman, Thomas L. (2007) *The World is Flat: A Brief History of the Twenty-First Century* (New York: Picador).

Friedman, Thomas L. (2016) *Thank You for Being Late: An Optimist's Guide to Thriving in the Age of Accelerations* (New York: Picador).

Fukuyama, Francis (1989) 'The End of History?', in *The National Interest*, Summer.

Fund for Peace (2017) Fragile States Index 2017, at http://fundforpeace.org/fsi (retrieved January 2018).

Gardner, Brian (2013) *Global Food Futures: Feeding the World in 2050* (London: Bloomsbury).

Garner, Steve (2017) *Racisms: An Introduction*, 2nd edn (London: Sage).

Gilley, Bruce (2009) *The Right to Rule: How States Win and Lose Legitimacy* (New York: Columbia University Press).

Givens, Terri (2010) 'Immigration and National Security: Comparing the US and Europe', in *Whitehead Journal of Diplomacy and International Relations* 11:1, Winter/Spring, pp. 79–88.

Givens, Terri, and Adam Luedtke (2004) 'The Politics of European Union Immigration Policy: Institutions, Salience, and Harmonization', in *Policy Studies Journal* 32:1, February, pp. 145–65.

Glaeser, Edward (2012) *Triumph of the City: How Urban Spaces Make us Human* (London: Pan).

Glendon, Mary Ann (2002) *A World Made New: Eleanor Roosevelt and the Universal Declaration of Human Rights* (New York: Random House).

Global Slavery Index (2016) at https://www.globalslaveryindex.org/index (retrieved June 2017).

Global Terrorism Database (2018) at https://www.start.umd.edu/gtd (retrieved January 2018).

Goklany, Indur M. (2007) *The Improving State of the World: Why We're Living Longer, Healthier, More Comfortable Lives on a Cleaner Planet* (Washington DC: Cato Institute).

Goldsmith, Jack, and Tim Wu (2008) *Who Controls the Internet? Illusions of a Borderless World* (Oxford: Oxford University Press).

Gören, Erkan, (2013) 'Economic Effects of Domestic and Neighbouring Countries' Cultural Diversity' in *ZenTra Working Paper in Transnational Studies* 16/2013, 23 April. At https://ssrn.com/abstract=2255492 (retrieved November 2017).

Griffith-Jones, Stephany, David Griffith-Jones, and Dagmar Hertova (2008) 'Enhancing the Role of Regional Development Banks'. G-24 Discussion Paper 50, July (New York: United Nations).

Grugel, Jean, and Matthew Louis Bishop (2014) *Democratization: A Critical Introduction*, 2nd edn (Basingstoke: Palgrave Macmillan).

Gubler, Duane J. (2007) 'The Continuing Spread of West Nile Virus in the Western Hemisphere' in *Clinical Infectious Diseases* 45:8, 15 October, pp. 1039–46.

Guillen, Mauro F. (2016) *The Architecture of Collapse: The Global System in the 21st Century* (Oxford: Oxford University Press).

Gustavsson, Jenny, Christel Cederberg, Ulf Sonesson, Robert van Otterdijk, and Alexandre Meybeck (2012) *Global Food Losses and Food Waste* (Rome: FAO).

Gvosdev, Nikolas, and Andrew Stigler (2011) 'Defining War in an Ill-Defined World', in *The New York Times*, 28 June.

Gwartney, James, Robert Lawson, and Joshua Hall (2016) *Economic Freedom of the World: 2016 Annual Report* (Vancouver: Fraser Institute).

Haass, Richard (2017) *A World in Disarray: American Foreign Policy and the Crisis of the Old Order* (New York: Penguin).

Hall, C. Michael (2010) 'Tourism and Biodiversity: More Significant than Climate Change?', in *Journal of Heritage Tourism* 5:4, November, pp. 253–66.

Hardin, Garrett (1968) 'The Tragedy of the Commons', in *Science* 162:3859, 13 December, pp. 1243–48.

Harper, Sarah (2016) *How Population Change Will Transform Our World* (Oxford: Oxford University Press).

Harper, Sarah (2018) *Demography: A Very Short Introduction* (Oxford: Oxford University Press).

Henrich, Joseph, Steven J. Heine, and Ara Norenzayan (2010) 'The Weirdest People in the World?', in *Behavioral and Brain Sciences* 33:2–3, pp. 61–83.

Higgott, Richard, Geoffrey Underhill and Andreas Bieler (eds) (2011) *Non-State Actors and Authority in the Global System* (Abingdon: Routledge).

Hochstetler, Kathryn, and Manjana Milkoreit (2015) 'Responsibilities in Transition: Emerging Powers in the Climate Change Negotiations', in *Global Governance* 21:2, April–June, pp. 205–26.

Hoekman, Bernard M., and Petros C. Mavroidis (2016) *The World Trade Organization*, 2nd edn (Abingdon: Routledge).

Hoornweg, Daniel, and Kevin Pope (2014) 'Socioeconomic Pathways and Regional Distribution of the World's 101 Largest Cities'. Working Paper No. 04, January; Global Cities Institute, University of Toronto, Canada.

Hsiang, Solomon M., Marshall Burke, and Edward Miguel (2013) 'Quantifying the Influence of Climate on Human Conflict', in *Science* 341:6151, 13 September.

Huemer, Michael (2013) *The Problem of Political Authority: An Examination of the Right to Coerce and the Duty to Obey* (Basingstoke: Palgrave Macmillan).

Human Rights Watch (2017) *World Report 2017* (New York: Human Rights Watch).

Hunt, Lynn (2007) *Inventing Human Rights: A History* (New York: W. W. Norton).

Huntington, Samuel P. (1996) *The Clash of Civilizations and the Making of World Order* (New York: Simon & Schuster).

Ikenberry, G. John (2000) 'Don't Panic: How Secure Is Globalization's Future?', in *Foreign Affairs* 79:2, May/June, pp. 145–51.

International Air Transport Association (2018) 'Facts & Figures', at http://www.iata.org/pressroom/facts_figures/Pages/index.aspx (retrieved March 2018).

Independent Commission on International Development Issues (1980) *North/South: A Programme for Survival* (London: Pan).

International Energy Agency (2016) *Key World Energy Statistics*, at http://www.iea.org/publications/freepublications/publication/KeyWorld2016.pdf.

International Organization for Migration (2015) *Global Migration Trends Factsheet*, at http://gmdac.iom.int/global-migration-trends-factsheet (retrieved June 2017).

International Organization for Migration (2017) 'Who is a Migrant?', at https://www.iom.int/who-is-a-migrant (retrieved June 2017).

International Telecommunications Union (2017) *ICT Facts and Figures 2017*, at http://www.itu.int/en/ITU-D/Statistics/Pages/facts/default.aspx.

International Union for Conservation of Nature (2017) Website at https://www.iucn.org (retrieved October 2017).

Jackson, Robert (2007) *Sovereignty* (Cambridge: Polity Press).

Jacob, Margaret C. (2006) *Strangers Nowhere in the World: The Rise of Cosmopolitanism in Early Modern Europe* (Philadelphia: University of Pennsylvania Press).

Jessop, Bob (2016) *The State: Past, Present, Future* (Cambridge: Polity Press).

Jones, Adam (2017) *Genocide: A Comprehensive Introduction*, 3rd edn (Abingdon: Routledge).

Jones, Reece (2017) *Violent Borders: Refugees and the Right to Move* (London: Verso).

Josephson, Paul (2012) 'Technology and the Environment', in J. R. McNeill and Erin Stewart Mauldin (eds) *A Companion to Global Environmental History* (Chichester: John Wiley).

Judah, Tim (2011) 'Senegal's Mourides: Islam's Mystical Entrepreneurs' at BBC Online, 4 August.

Juergensmeyer, Mark (2017) *Terror in the Mind of God: The Global Rise of Religious Violence*, 4th edn (Oakland, CA: University of California Press).

Kagan, Robert (2008) *The Return of History and the End of Dreams* (New York: Knopf).

Kant, Immanuel ([1795] 2009) *Perpetual Peace: A Philosophical Essay* (London: Penguin).

Karns, Margaret P., Karen A. Mingst, and Kendall W. Stiles (2015) *International Organizations: The Politics and Processes of Global Governance*, 3rd edn (Boulder, CO: Lynne Rienner).

Kassam, Ashifa, Rosie Scammell, Kate Connolly, Richard Orange, Kim Willsher, and Rebecca Ratcliffe (2015) 'Europe Needs Many More Babies to Avert a Population Disaster', in *The Guardian*, 22 August.

Keating, Christine, and Cynthia Burack (2016) 'Sexual Orientation, Gender Identity and Human Rights', in Michael Goodhart (ed.) *Human Rights: Politics and Practice*, 3rd edn (Oxford University Press).

Khan, Alam, and Mario Arturo Ruiz Estrada (2017) 'Globalization and Terrorism: An Overview', in *Quality and Quantity* 51:4, July, pp. 1811–19.

Khanna, Parag (2016) 'These 25 Companies Are More Powerful Than Many Countries' in *Foreign Policy*, 15 May.

King, Stephen D. (2017) *Grave New World: The End of Globalization, the Return of History* (New Haven, CT: Yale University Press).

Kivisto, Peter, and Paul R. Croll (2012) *Race and Ethnicity: The Basics* (Abingdon: Routledge).

Knorr, Klaus (1973) *Power and Wealth: The Political Economy of International Power* (New York: Basic Books).

Kotkin, Joel (2014) 'The World's Most Influential Cities', in *Forbes*, 14 August.

Kovarik, Bill (2016) *Revolutions in Communication: Media History from Gutenberg to the Digital Age*, 2nd edn (London: Bloomsbury).

Krasner, Stephen D. (ed.) (1983) *International Regimes* (Ithaca, NY: Cornell University Press).

Kurlansky, Mark (2006) *Nonviolence: The History of a Dangerous Idea* (New York: Modern Library).

La Rue, Frank (2011) 'Report of the Special Rapporteur on the Promotion and Protection of the Right to Freedom of Opinion and Expression'. UN Human Rights Council, Seventeenth Session, 16 May.

Langlois, Anthony J. (2016) 'Normative and Theoretical Foundations of Human Rights', in Michael Goodhart (ed.) *Human Rights: Politics and Practice*, 3rd edn (Oxford University Press).

Levy, Jack S. (1983) *War in the Modern Great Power System, 1495–1975* (Lexington, KY: University Press of Kentucky).

Levy, Jack S., and William R. Thompson (2010) *Causes of War* (Chichester: John Wiley & Sons).

Locey, Kenneth J., and Jay T. Lennon (2016) 'Scaling Laws Predict Global Microbial Diversity', in *Proceedings of the National Academy of Sciences* 113:21, 24 May, pp. 5970–75.

Lomborg, Bjørn (ed.) (2012) *RethinkHIV: Smarter Ways to Invest in Ending HIV in Sub-Saharan Africa* (Cambridge: Cambridge University Press).

Lukes, Steven (2005) *Power: A Radical View*, 2nd edn (Basingstoke: Palgrave Macmillan).

Lutz, James M., and Brenda J. Lutz (2013) *Global Terrorism*, 3rd edn (Abingdon: Routledge).

Lyon, Sarah, and E. Christian Wells (2012) *Global Tourism: Cultural Heritage and Economic Encounters* (Lanham, MD: AltaMira Press).

McBride, James (2015) 'Building the New Silk Road'. Backgrounder published by Council on Foreign Relations, 22 May, at https://www.cfr.org/backgrounder/building-new-silk-road (retrieved May 2018).

McCormick, John (2015) *European Union Politics*, 2nd edn (London: Palgrave).

McCormick, John (2017a) *Environmental Politics and Policy* (London: Palgrave).

McCormick, John (2017b) *Understanding the European Union*, 7th edn (London: Palgrave).

McCrone, David, and Frank Bechhofer (2015) *Understanding National Identity* (Cambridge: Cambridge University Press).

Mackenzie, Ruth, Cesare Romano, and Yuval Shany (2010) *The Manual on International Courts and Tribunals*, 2nd edn (Oxford: Oxford University Press).

Macmillan, Margaret (2014) *The War That Ended Peace: The Road to 1914* (New York: Random House).

McLellan, James E., and Harold Dorn (2015) *Science and Technology in World History: An Introduction*, 3rd edn (Baltimore, MD: Johns Hopkins University Press).

McLuhan, Marshall (1964) *Understanding Media: The Extensions of Man* (New York: McGraw Hill).

Malthus, Thomas (1798) *An Essay on the Principle of Population* (London: J. Johnson).

Manik, Julfikar Ali, and Jim Yardley (2013) 'Building Collapse in Bangladesh Leaves Scores Dead', in *New York Times*, 24 April.

Marmot, Michael (2016) *The Health Gap: The Challenge of an Unequal World* (London: Bloomsbury).

Martelle, Scott (2014) 'The Slow-spreading News of American Independence', in *Los Angeles Times*, 4 July.

Martin, Claude (2015) *On the Edge: The State and Fate of the World's Tropical Rainforests* (Vancouver: Greystone Books).

Martin, Eric (2012) 'Goldman Sachs's MIST Topping BRICs as Smaller Markets Outperform', on Bloomberg website at https://www.bloomberg.com (retrieved May 2018).

Mathews, Jessica Tuchman (1997) 'Power Shift', in *Foreign Affairs* 76:1, January/February, pp. 287–93.

Mattli, Walter (1999) *The Logic of Regional Integration: Europe and Beyond* (Cambridge: Cambridge University Press).

Minahan, James B. (2000) *One Europe, Many Nations: A Historical Dictionary of European National Groups* (Westport, CT: Greenwood).

Mitchell, Ronald B. (2016) *International Environmental Agreements Database Project*, at http://iea.uoregon.edu/page.php?query=home-contents.php (retrieved August 2017).

Moore, Gordon E. (1965) 'Cramming more Components onto Integrated Circuits', in *Electronics* 38:8, 19 April.

Moyo, Dambisa (2009) *Dead Aid: Why Aid is Not Working and How There is a Better Way for Africa* (New York: Farrar, Straus & Giroux).

Murtin, Fabrice, and Marco Mira d'Ercole (2012) 'Household wealth inequality across OECD countries: New OECD evidence'. *OECD Statistics Brief* 21, June.

Nathan, Otto, and Heinz Norden (eds) (1960) *Einstein on Peace* (New York: Simon & Schuster).

Nederveen Pieterse, Jan (2013) 'What is Global Studies?' in *Globalizations* 10:4, pp. 499–514.

Nederveen Pieterse, Jan (2015) *Globalization and Culture: Global Mélange*, 3rd edn (Lanham, MD: Rowman & Littlefield).

Netherlands Environmental Assessment Agency (2015) *Trends in Global CO2 Emissions: 2015 Report* (The Hague: Netherlands Environmental Assessment Agency).

Nielsen, Sara Trab (2010) 'Coastal Livelihoods and Climate Change', in Dorte Verner (ed.) *Reducing Poverty, Protecting Livelihoods, and Building Assets in a Changing Climate: Social Implications of Climate Change for Latin America and the Caribbean* (Washington DC: World Bank).

Nongbri, Brent (2013) *Before Religion: A History of a Modern Concept* (New Haven, CT: Yale University Press).

Nye, Joseph S. (1970) 'Comparing Common Markets: A Revised Neofunctionalist Model', *International Organization*, 24:4, Autumn, pp. 796–835.

Nye, Joseph S. (2004) *Soft Power: The Means to Success in World Politics* (New York: Public Affairs).

Nye, Joseph S. (2015) *Is the American Century Over?* (Cambridge: Polity Press).

O'Connell, Mary Ellen (ed.) (2012) *What is War? An Investigation in the Wake of 9/11* (Leiden: Martinus Nijhoff Publishers).

O'Neill, Jim (2001) 'Building Better Global Economic BRICs'. Global Economics Paper No. 66, Goldman Sachs, 30 November.

Organization for Economic Cooperation and Development (2015) *OECD Reviews of Health Care Quality: Japan 2015. Raising Standards* (Paris: OECD).

Organization for Economic Cooperation and Development (2017) *International Migration Outlook 2017* (Paris: OECD).

Ostrom, Elinor (1990) *Governing the Commons: The Evolution of Institutions for Collective Action* (Cambridge: Cambridge University Press).

Overy, Richard (2017) *The Origins of the Second World War*, 4th edn (Abingdon: Routledge).

Oxfam International (2018) *Reward Work, Not Wealth* (Oxford: Oxfam).

Pan, Christoph, and Beate Sibylle Pfeil (2004) *National Minorities in Europe* (West Lafayette, IN: Purdue University Press).

Parsons, Craig, and Timothy M. Smeeding (2006), 'What's Unique about Immigration in Europe?', in Craig Parsons and Timothy M. Smeeding (eds), *Immigration and the Transformation of Europe* (Cambridge: Cambridge University Press).

Passel, Jeffrey S., and D'Vera Cohn (2015) 'Unauthorized Immigrant Population Stable for Half a Decade' (Washington, DC: Pew Hispanic Center).

Pedersen, Susan (2015) *The Guardians: The League of Nations and the Crisis of Empire* (Oxford: Oxford University Press).

Pew Research Center (2012) 'The Global Religious Landscape', at http://www.pewforum.org/2012/12/18/global-religious-landscape-exec (retrieved May 2018).

Pew Research Center (2013) 'The Global Divide on Homosexuality', at http://www.pewglobal.org (retrieved October 2017).

Pew Research Center (2015a) Global Attitudes survey, Spring, at http://www.pewresearch.org (retrieved May 2018).

Pew Research Center (2015b) 'The Future of World Religions: Population Growth Projections, 2010–2050', 2 April, at http://www.pewforum.org (retrieved May 2018).

Pew Research Centre (2017) 'The Changing Global Religious Landscape', 5 April, at http://www.pewforum.org (retrieved May 2018).

Prendergast, Mark (1993) *For God, Country and Coca-Cola* (New York: Scribner's).

Primoratz, Igor, and Aleksandar Pavković (eds) (2007) *Patriotism: Philosophical and Political Perspectives* (Aldershot: Ashgate).

Reimann, Kim D. (2006) 'A View from the Top: International Politics, Norms and the Worldwide Growth of NGOs', in *International Studies Quarterly* 50:1, March, pp. 45–67.

Robertson, Roland (1992) *Globalization: Social Theory and Global Culture* (London: Sage).

Robins, Nick (2012) *The Corporation That Changed the World: How the East India Company Shaped the Modern Multinational*, 2nd edn (London: Pluto Press).

Rosenboim, Or (2017) 'Globalism and Nationalism: Why Interconnectedness Does Not Threaten Sovereignty', in *Foreign Affairs*, 10 July.

Safran, William (1991) 'Diasporas in Modem Societies: Myths of Homeland and Return', in *Diaspora: A Journal of Transnational Studies* 1:1, Spring, pp. 83–99.

Said, Edward (2001) 'The Clash of Ignorance' in *The Nation*, 4 October.

Sands, Roger (ed.) (2013) *Forestry in a Global Context*, 2nd edn (Wallingford: CAB International).

Sassen, Saskia (2005) 'The Global City: Introducing a Concept' in *Brown Journal of World Affairs* 11:2, Winter/Spring, pp. 27–43.

Schmidheiny, Stephan (1992) *Changing Course: A Global Business Perspective on Development and the Environment* (Cambridge, MA: MIT Press).

Schwab, Klaus (2016) *The Fourth Industrial Revolution* (New York: Crown).

Selin, Henrik (2014) 'Global Environmental Law and Treaty-Making on Hazardous Substances: The Minamata Convention and Mercury Abatement', in *Global Environmental Politics* 14:1, February, pp. 1–19.

Shamshad, Rizwana (2017) *Bangladeshi Migrants in India: Foreigners, Refugees, or Infiltrators?* (New Delhi: Oxford University Press).

Sharpe, Eric J. (1983) *Understanding Religion* (New York: St Martin's).

Shaw, Malcolm N. (2014) *International Law*, 7th edn (Cambridge: Cambridge University Press).

Shirani, Fiona, Catherine Butler, Karen Henwood, Karen Parkhill and Nick Pidgeon (2015) '"I'm Not a Tree Hugger, I'm Just Like You". Changing Perceptions of Sustainable Lifestyles', in *Environmental Politics* 24:1, pp. 57–74.

Siddique, Haroon (2016) 'Figures Show Extent of NHS Reliance on Foreign Nationals', in *The Guardian*, 26 January.

Simons, Gary F. and Charles D. Fennig (eds.) (2017) *Ethnologue: Languages of the World*, 20th edn (Dallas, TX: SIL International).

Skovgaard-Smith, Irene (2017) 'The Complex World of the Global Citizen', on BBC Capital at http://www. bbc.com/capital, 10 November (retrieved May 2018).

Slaughter, Anne-Marie (2011) 'War and Law in the 21st Century: Adapting to the Changing Face of Conflict', in *Europe's World* 19, Autumn, pp. 32–37.

Spinney, Laura (2017) *Pale Rider: The Spanish Flu of 1918 and How it Changed the World* (London: Jonathan Cape).

Srinivasan, Ramesh (2017) *Whose Global Village? Rethinking how Technology Shapes our World* (New York: New York University Press).

Stearns, Peter N. (ed.) (2013) *Demilitarization in the Contemporary World* (Urbana, IL: University of Illinois Press).

Sterri, Aksel Braanen (ed.) (2014) *Global Citizen: Challenges and Responsibility in an Interconnected World* (Rotterdam: Sense).

Stevens, Harry (2017) 'Let's Talk about Racism – India is Open to Foreigners if They are White', in *Hindustan Times*, 24 May.

Stockholm International Peace Research Institute (2017). Military Expenditure Database, at https://www. sipri.org (retrieved May 2017).

Stokes, Bruce (2017) 'What it Truly Takes to be "One of Us"'. Pew Research Center poll, 1 February.

Sultana, Farhana, and Alex Loftus (eds) (2012) *The Right to Water: Politics, Governance and Social Struggles* (Abingdon: Earthscan).

Sussman, Robert Wald (2014) *The Myth of Race: The Troubling Persistence of an Unscientific Idea* (Harvard, MA: Harvard University Press).

Thompson, Janna (2009) *Intergenerational Justice: Rights and Responsibilities in an Intergenerational Polity* (Abingdon: Routledge).

Todaro, Michael P., and Stephen C. Smith (2016) *Economic Development*, 12th edn (Boston, MA: Pearson).

Tomlinson, B. R. (2003) 'What was the Third World?', in *Journal of Contemporary History* 38:2, April, pp. 307–21.

Treves, Tullio (2015) 'Historical Development of the Law of the Sea', in Donald Rothwell, Alex Oude Elferink, Karen Scott, and Tim Stephens (eds) *The Oxford Handbook of the Law of the Sea* (Oxford: Oxford University Press).

Triandafyllidou, Anna (2009) 'Clandestino Project: Undocumented Migration: Counting the Uncountable. Data and Trends Across Europe'. Final Report, 23 November 2009. Prepared for the European Commission, at http://clandestino.eliamep.gr (retrieved May 2018).

UN Conference on Trade and Development (various years) *World Investment Report* (Geneva: UNCTAD).

UN Development Programme (2017) Human Development Index 2016, at http://hdr.undp.org/en/ content/human-development-index-hdi (retrieved May 2018).

UN Educational Scientific and Cultural Organization (1969) 'Four Statements on the Race Question' (Paris: UNESCO).

UN Educational Scientific and Cultural Organization (2017) Institute for Statistics, at http://uis.unesco.org (retrieved June 2017).

UN Environment Programme (2017) Website at http://web.unep.org/about (retrieved August 2017).

UN High Commissioner for Refugees (2017a) Website at http://www.unhcr.org (retrieved June 2017).

UN High Commissioner for Refugees (2017b) *Global Trends: Forced Displacement in 2016*, at http://www.unhcr.org (retrieved June 2017).

UN Population Division (2014) *World Urbanization Prospects: The 2014 Revision, Highlights*, at https://esa.un.org/unpd/wup/publications (retrieved May 2018).

UN Population Division (2015) *Trends in International Migrant Stock: The 2015 Revision* (New York: UN Department of Economic and Social Affairs, Population Division).

UN Population Division (2017) *World Population Prospects 2017*, at https://esa.un.org/unpd/wpp (retrieved May 2018).

Union of International Associations (various years) *Yearbook of International Organizations*, at UIA website at https://www.uia.org (retrieved December 2017).

US Census Bureau (2017) Website at https://www.census.gov (retrieved November 2017).

US National Oceanic and Atmospheric Administration (2017) Website at http://www.noaa.gov (retrieved October 2017).

Van den Bossche, Peter, and Denise Prévost (2016) *Essentials of WTO Law* (Cambridge: Cambridge University Press).

Vermeulen, Sonja J., Bruce M. Campbell, and John S. I. Ingram (2012) 'Climate Change and Food Systems', in *Annual Review of Environment and Resources* 37, pp. 195–222.

Walker, Gordon (2012) *Environmental Justice: Concepts, Evidence and Politics* (Abingdon: Routledge).

Walzer, Michael (2004) 'After 9/11: Five Questions about Terrorism', in *Arguing About War* (New Haven, CT: Yale University Press).

Walzer, Michael (2015) *Just and Unjust Wars: A Moral Argument with Historical Illustrations*, 5th edn (New York: Basic Books).

Webster, Paul, and Jason Burke (2012) 'How the Rise of the Megacity is Changing the Way we Live', in *The Observer*, 21 January.

Weiss, Thomas (2013) *Global Governance: Why? What? Whither?* (Cambridge: Polity Press).

White, Gregory (2011) *Climate Change and Migration: Security and Borders in a Warming World* (New York: Oxford University Press).

Wiesner-Hanks, Merry E. (2013) *Early Modern Europe, 1450–1789* (Cambridge: Cambridge University Press).

Williams, Glyn, Paula Meth, and Katie Willis (2014) *Geographies of Developing Areas: The Global South in a Changing World* (Abingdon: Routledge).

Wilson, E.O. (2003) *The Future of Life* (New York: Vintage).

Wilson, E.O. (2007) 'My Wish: Build the Encyclopaedia of Life'. Speech at acceptance of TED Prize, March, at https://www.ted.com/talks/e_o_wilson_on_saving_life_on_earth/transcript?language=en (retrieved May 2018).

Woodward, Kath (2014) *Social Sciences: The Big Issues*, 2nd edn (Abingdon: Routledge).

Woodward, Richard (2009) *The Organisation for Economic Co-operation and Development* (Abingdon: Routledge).

World Bank (2017) 'Migration and Remittances: Recent Developments and Outlook'. Migration and Development Brief 27, at http://pubdocs.worldbank.org (retrieved June 2017).

World Bank Economic Indicators (2018) at https://data.worldbank.org/indicator (retrieved March 2018).

World Economic Forum (2017) *The Global Gender Gap Report 2016* (Geneva: World Economic Forum).

World Health Organization (2014) '7 Million Premature Deaths Annually Linked to Air Pollution'. News release, 25 March, at http://www.who.int/mediacentre/news/releases/2014/air-pollution/en (retrieved May 2018).

World Health Organization (2016) Drinking-Water Fact Sheet, at http://www.who.int/mediacentre/factsheets/fs391/en (retrieved November 2017).

World Health Organization (2017) Obesity and Overweight Fact Sheet, updated October, at http://www.who.int/mediacentre/factsheets/fs311/en (retrieved May 2018).

World Health Organization (2018a) Website at http://www.who.int (retrieved February 2018).

World Health Organization (2018b) Fact Sheets on Infectious Diseases, at http://www.who.int/topics/infectious_diseases/factsheets/en (retrieved February 2018).

World Health Organization (2018c) Ebola Virus Disease Factsheet, at http://www.who.int/mediacentre/factsheets/fs103/en. Updated January 2018 (retrieved February 2018).

World Tourism Organization (2017) *Tourism Highlights: 2017 Edition* (Madrid: WTO).

World Tourism Organization (2018) Website at http://www2.unwto.org (retrieved February 2018).

World Trade Organization (2017a) *World Trade Statistical Review 2017*, at https://www.wto.org/english/res_e/statis_e/wts2017_e/wts2017_e.pdf (retrieved May 2018).

World Trade Organization (2017b) Website at https://www.wto.org (retrieved September 2017).

Wydick, Bruce (2016) 'Ten Reasons Fair-Trade Coffee Doesn't Work'. Blog at *Huffington Post*, http://www.huffingtonpost.com, 7 August (retrieved May 2018).

Yardley, Jim (2013) 'Report on Deadly Factory Collapse in Bangladesh Finds Widespread Blame', in *New York Times*, 22 May.

Young, Oran R. (2002) *The Institutional Dimensions of Environmental Change: Fit, Interplay, and Scale* (Cambridge, MA: MIT Press).

Yunus, Muhammad (2007) *Banker to the Poor: Micro-lending and the Battle Against World Poverty* (New York: Perseus).

Zalasiewicz, Jan, Mark Williams, Will Steffen, and Paul Crutzen (2010) 'The New World of the Anthropocene', in *Environmental Science and Technology* 44:7, 1 April, pp. 2228–31.

Zartman, I. William, Paul Meertz, and Mordechai Melamud (eds) (2014) *Banning the Bang or the Bomb? Negotiating the Nuclear Test Ban Regime* (Cambridge: Cambridge University Press).

INDEX

Boldface numbers indicate key references and definitions